Designing Games

A Guide to Engineering Experiences

Tynan Sylvester

BEIJING • BOSTON • FARNHAM • SEBASTOPOL • TOKYO

DESIGNING GAMES

by Tynan Sylvester

Copyright © 2013 Tynan Sylvester. All rights reserved.

Published by O'Reilly Media, Inc., 1005 Gravenstein Highway North, Sebastopol, CA 95472.

O'Reilly books may be purchased for educational, business, or sales promotional use. Online editions are also available for most titles (*safari.oreilly.com*). For more information, contact our corporate/institutional sales department: (800) 998-9938 or *corporate@oreilly.com*.

Editor: Rachel Roumeliotis
Production Editor: Kristen Borg
Copyeditor: Audrey Doyle
Proofreader: Kristen Borg
Cover Designer: Mark Paglietti
Interior Designer: Monica Kamsvaag
Illustrator: Rebecca Demarest
Indexer: Bob Pfahler

Printing History:

January 2013 First Edition.

Revision History:

2012-12-18 First Release.

See *http://oreilly.com/catalog/errata.csp?isbn=0636920026624* for release details.

Nutshell Handbook, the Nutshell Handbook logo, and the O'Reilly logo are registered trademarks of O'Reilly Media, Inc. *Designing Games* and related trade dress are trademarks of O'Reilly Media, Inc.

Many of the designations used by manufacturers and sellers to distinguish their products are claimed as trademarks. Where those designations appear in this book, and O'Reilly Media, Inc., was aware of a trademark claim, the designations have been printed in caps or initial caps.

While every precaution has been taken in the preparation of this book, the publisher and author assume no responsibility for errors or omissions, or for damages resulting from the use of the information contained herein.

ISBN: 978-1-449-33793-3
[LSI]

Contents

Preface

A Note on the Text

UNFORTUNATELY, THE ENGLISH LANGUAGE does not provide us with a perfect gender-neutral solution to the pronoun problem. I've chosen to use "he" throughout the book to refer to nonspecific people. This is for reasons of readability and conciseness only; unless otherwise specified, masculine pronouns do not refer exclusively to men.

We'd Like to Hear from You

I love talking about game design. If you have comments or questions about the book, please email me at *tynan.sylvester@gmail.com* or contact me through my website at *tynansylvester.com.*

You can also address comments and questions concerning this book to the publisher:

O'Reilly Media, Inc.
1005 Gravenstein Highway North
Sebastopol, CA 95472
(800) 998-9938 (in the United States or Canada)
(707) 829-0515 (international or local)
(707) 829-0104 (fax)

We have a web page for this book, where we list errata, examples, and any additional information. You can access this page at:

http://oreil.ly/designing-games

To comment or ask technical questions about this book, send email to:

bookquestions@oreilly.com

For more information about our books, courses, conferences, and news, see our website at *http://www.oreilly.com*.

Find us on Facebook: *http://facebook.com/oreilly*
Follow us on Twitter: *http://twitter.com/oreillymedia*
Watch us on YouTube: *http://www.youtube.com/oreillymedia*

Safari® Books Online

Safari Books Online

Safari Books Online (*www.safaribooksonline.com*) is an on-demand digital library that delivers expert content in both book and video form from the world's leading authors in technology and business.

Technology professionals, software developers, web designers, and business and creative professionals use Safari Books Online as their primary resource for research, problem solving, learning, and certification training.

Safari Books Online offers a range of product mixes and pricing programs for organizations, government agencies, and individuals. Subscribers have access to thousands of books, training videos, and prepublication manuscripts in one fully searchable database from publishers like O'Reilly Media, Prentice Hall Professional, Addison-Wesley Professional, Microsoft Press, Sams, Que, Peachpit Press, Focal Press, Cisco Press, John Wiley & Sons, Syngress, Morgan Kaufmann, IBM Redbooks, Packt, Adobe Press, FT Press, Apress, Manning, New Riders, McGraw-Hill, Jones & Bartlett, Course Technology, and dozens more. For more information about Safari Books Online, please visit us online.

PART ONE

Engines of Experience

The Inventor had given them wonderful things—machines for grinding corn, for weaving cloth, and countless others. The townspeople loved him.

But he was getting old, and there was only time for only one more invention. So he decided that his last work would be a very special kind of machine. This one would not be for moving or heating or calculating, but for making happiness itself.

The townspeople didn't understand, but they trusted him. He'd never let them down before. So the Inventor retreated into his castle and worked.

Years passed. At first the townspeople waited patiently. Then they doubted. Then they became angry.

"Where is it?" they asked.

"It's taking too long."

"It's costing too much."

"He's tricking us."

"We must destroy him."

Just as the mob arrived at the castle, the gates opened and the Inventor came out. "It is accomplished!" he declared. The mob quieted for a moment and he led them inside.

But there was no great engine—only a roomful of tables littered with cards, booklets, and tiny pieces of wood. "Where is the machine?" asked the leader of the mob, readying his club. "Where is the machine of happiness?"

"It is here," said the Inventor, motioning to the dice, rulebooks, and game boards. "Have a seat, and let's play."

GAME DESIGN isn't in code, art, or sound. It's not in sculpting game pieces or painting game boards. Game design means crafting the rules that make those pieces come alive.

By themselves, chess pieces are just tiny decorative sculptures. But when we move those pieces around according to a special set of rules, those little statues come alive. They will create a nail-biting finish at a high-stakes tournament. They will generate a world of puzzles in the newspaper. They will spark friendships, tell stories, and teach lessons found nowhere else in the universe.

But not just any set of rules will do. In fact, most sets of rules for pieces on a board won't do any of these wonderful things. Many will collapse into simple, repetitive patterns as players use the same winning strategies over and over. Others are nightmarishly difficult to learn. Still others are so hard to follow that the game becomes a plodding number-crunching exercise.

The unique value of chess is in how it generates a perfect rhythm of puzzle and solution, tension and release. That value isn't in the pieces or the board. It's in the game design—the system of rules that drives the game's behavior. A game designer's job is to craft systems of rules that create these kinds of results.

It's not easy to know how to achieve game design goals. How would you change chess to make it easier to learn? What would you modify to make it a better spectator sport, or to eliminate the often-repetitive opening moves? Would you add a piece, or remove one? Change how one moves? Reshape the board, add special abilities, change the art, add a story, or make the game play in real time?

The answers to these questions are found in the craft of game design. Game design craft shows how to make games that are hard, easy, or both. It helps us teach players without smothering them. It tells us how to thread stories and rules together into a single system of meaning. The first half of this book is dedicated to this craft.

But even with the best craft in the world, no designer can magically know the answer to every question (though there are those who try). That's why the second half of this book is about the day-to-day process of design. Real game designers don't just know the answers—they know how to find them using testing, planning, and analysis. Process knowledge shows when to test and how, when to plan and when not to, how to work with others and avoid creative dead ends.

Design craft does not define the purpose of a game. It only shows us how to achieve it.

Some people worry that analyzing game design removes its soul—that understanding the principles of the craft takes away the creativity of the work. But knowing game design craft doesn't mean slavishly following rules to get the same result over and over. It means understanding the trade-offs in every design decision. When games go wrong it's rarely because the designer made the wrong choices within their own understanding. It's because they just didn't know the trade-offs they were making. So a designer understanding craft is kind of like an engineer understanding the laws of physics: Newton's laws don't determine whether we build a boat motor or a Saturn V rocket, but they are essential to perfecting either.

Imagine the best game you have ever played—except crafted even better, every emotion more potent, the pacing even more perfect, the fiction more cohesive and nuanced. There is no game that could not have been made better with the same resources. We will never make a perfect game, but through study of craft, we can push every game as close to its full potential as humanly possible.

Engines of Experience

Mechanics and Events

Games are composed of MECHANICS, which define how the game works.

A MECHANIC IS A rule about how a game works. *The A button makes Mario jump* is a mechanic. So are the rules *characters walk at one meter per second*, *pawns capture diagonally*, and *players alternate taking turns.*

In board games, mechanics are written in the rulebook. In video games, they're implemented in computer code. But whether the mechanics are executed ritualistically by a player or electronically by a computer, they're still mechanics because they define the game's behavior.

During play, mechanics and players interact to generate EVENTS.

An event is something that happens during play. *Mario hits a wall and bounces back*, *the pawn captures the rook*, and *the ball went in the net, so the other team gets a point* are events.

In nearly every other entertainment medium, events are authored directly. A screenwriter, novelist, or choreographer will decide every action, motion, and line of dialogue in the work. Their product is a long series of predefined events: first Luke meets Obi-Wan, then his parents die, then they hire Han Solo, and so on. And those events play out the exact same way every time.

Games are different. Instead of authoring events directly, we design mechanics. Those mechanics then generate events during play.

For example, while playing *Super Mario Galaxy*, I once tried to make Mario jump over a pit. I missed, and Mario touched lava. His backside burst into flames and he shot straight up like a bottle rocket, screaming in cartoon pain. As he flew through the air, I maneuvered him to a safe ground landing. The events were Mario jumping, missing, hitting the lava, bursting into flames, flying into the air, screaming, and maneuvering back to safety. The mechanics behind these events were the jump button, gravity, physical collision, the explosive-butt lava reaction, and my ability to control Mario's motion in midair.

The disc of *Super Mario Galaxy* does not contain any of the events described here—it only contains the mechanics. The events emerged from the interaction between my play and the game mechanics. And those events will never play out exactly that way ever again.

Game designers don't design events. We design systems of mechanics that generate events. This layer of indirection is the fundamental difference between games and most other media. It is our greatest opportunity and our toughest challenge. It is also the key reason why modes of thought borrowed from other media break down so often in games.

The Primacy of Emotion

To be meaningful, an event must provoke emotion.

A game can't just generate any old string of events, because most events aren't worth caring about. For a game to hold attention, those events must provoke blood-pumping human emotion. When the generated events provoke pride, hilarity, awe, or terror, the game works.

The valuable emotions of play can be very subtle. Usually, they're subtle enough that players don't consciously detect them.

Games must provoke emotion, but this doesn't mean that every game must make players laugh madly, scream with rage, or break down and cry. In everyday speech, people often use the word *emotion* to refer only to the most extreme forms of passion, like visible rage or grief. But most emotion is much subtler and more pervasive than this.

For example, as you sit and read this book, you may think you're not feeling anything. But you're actually experiencing a barrage of tiny pulses of emotion. Anything can cause them—a stray thought of lost love, a goofy word on a page (snartlebarf!), or a scowl on the face of a stranger walking by. These feelings only last a moment, and they're usually below the level of conscious awareness. But they're always there, rising and falling in response to every stimulus and thought.

Events in a game produce these small emotions. A minor setback creates a pulse of frustration, and makes you grit your teeth for an instant. A moment of indecision worries you, and your breath catches. Another player acknowledges you, so you feel a faint glow of acceptance.

These tiny feelings are painted with a very fine brush. It's not enough to say you're happy or sad or bored today. Those words describe giant shifts in the most obvious feelings. The tiny emotions—the ones that make up the tapestry of play—change constantly, every second. This is doubly true when playing a good game.

Imagine playing chess against a stranger. It's your turn, and you're losing. You don't see a good move, so you feel *stress* and *mental strain*. As you study the board, the tension mounts. Then, you see your opening: if you jump your knight backward, you can cover your king and threaten his at the same time! Silent *relief* floods in followed by a *sense of accomplishment* for solving the puzzle. You make the move, and your opponent grimaces as he realizes what you did. Seeing this, you feel a sense of *dominance*. Your opponent starts thinking. As you're enjoying your *satisfied glow*, you notice a weakness in your position. If he throws his bishop across the board, he can guarantee a capture on your knight. But it's not an obvious move. Will he see it? Your satisfaction transforms into *suspense*. Time stretches out as you try to hold your poker face. Finally, your opponent moves a pawn. *Relief* floods over you again, with even greater intensity than before, as you realize that you've got this one in the bag.

From the outside, this game doesn't look like much. Two people sat at a table, made strained facial expressions, and quietly moved plastic pieces across a board. Even the players didn't consciously sense everything they were feeling. But they were experiencing the roller-coaster emotions of competitive chess all the same. And they will come back to get that shifting cocktail of emotions again and again.

Detecting and understanding subtle emotions is a designer skill.

It's hard to sense such subtle feelings. It takes effort and practice. Can you pinpoint the exact second when you first feel bored with a game? Can you feel your involuntary smile at a joke you assumed wasn't funny? Most people can afford to ignore such feelings, but that's not good enough for a game designer. Just as a skilled chef can deconstruct a complex dish into individual flavors and a musician can pick out chords, time signatures, and rhythms from an orchestral composition, a game designer must be able to sense a flicker of anger, a pulse of triumph, or a dash of disgust. Because those emotions are the reason the game exists. They are why players spend energy, time, and money to move tokens on a board or throw a ball through a hoop.

The primacy of emotion is one of the great unacknowledged secrets of game design. Ask anyone about a game and they'll tell you what they thought of it. They'll make some logical argument about the game being good or bad. But usually that logic is just an automatic rationalization for the emotions underneath. What really matters is how a game makes us feel.

The emotions of play are not limited to "fun."

Unfortunately, game design discussions are still often shackled to the word *fun*, as though there was some inherent connection between fun and game design. The link is there, but it's due to a quirk of history, not a fact of reality.

Fun is an emotion—that sense of frivolous, mirthful exhilaration you feel on a roller coaster or in a friendly game of pickup soccer. It's a pleasurable emotion, and a worthwhile design goal. But it's not nearly the only one. We only focus on it because of where games came from.

For most of history, there were no game designers, and games were pieces of folk culture passed down through generations and enjoyed mostly by children. When adults played, it was typically as a short reprieve from their harsh, bland lives. In such a primitive environment, nobody needed a better term than *fun* to describe good games.

Today, we have more technology, professional game designers, and game players with ever-diversifying emotional appetites. To do our jobs well, designers must use more than one global term. *Fun* can't possibly describe the diversity, power, and nuance of game-driven emotions. It would be like a chef describing every dish as either "tasty" or "tasteless."

Think of all the things games can do that are not mirthful or frivolous. Some games use violent competition to provoke feelings of chest-thumping triumph. Some use narrative to create empathy or wonder. Some pull us into dark contemplation of existence, or horrify us with needling psychological terror. *Doom, Super Mario 64, Street Fighter II, Half-Life, StarCraft, The Sims, DEFCON, System Shock 2, Deus Ex, World of Warcraft, Dwarf Fortress, Portal, Tetris, Braid, Katamari Damacy*, and *S.T.A.L.K.E.R.* all create powerful emotions, but each is unlike any of the others. The white-knuckle action of competitive *Street Fighter II*, the starving dread of *System Shock 2*, and the contemplative mourning of *DEFCON* are all emotionally gripping—but none of them are fun.

Emotional Triggers

Game mechanics interact to generate events, which in turn provoke emotions in players. But how, exactly, do events create emotion? What is the link between something happening in a game and that pulse of joy or sorrow that appears in response?

Your unconscious mind constantly analyzes your situation. When certain conditions are met, the unconscious triggers an emotional response.

For example, when you stand next to a cliff, a genetically encoded instinct senses the situation and triggers a fear response. When you look at a prospective mate, your unconscious mind analyzes everything about that person, from physical features to reputation to their history with you, and produces an appropriate feeling of attraction, neutrality, or disgust. Each of these emotion-causing aspects of a situation is an *emotional trigger*.

An EMOTIONAL TRIGGER is some thing or observation that causes emotion.

We have countless different emotional triggers. Physical danger, changes in relationship or social status, learning, strengthening, acquisition of possessions, signs of sexual opportunity, family and safety, and certain types of natural environments are the most obvious, but they're not the only ones. Humans also respond to music, philosophical ideas, humor and wit, and countless forms of art. Some of these triggers are fixed in our genes. Others can be learned. Most involve complex interactions between conditioning and human nature.

Emotional triggers can be extraordinarily complex. Consider, for example, a detective's hunch. A hunch happens when the emotional unconscious has solved the case and is desperately trying to signal its findings. On the surface, the detective is struck with a feeling that something is wrong, but he isn't sure why. Underneath that, his unconscious mind is working through a maddeningly complex set of inferences and associations—so complex that his unconscious understands the case better than he does. Our emotional triggers can be so complex that we can't even understand them.

Emotion and Change

The bedrock principle behind all emotional triggers is *change*. To cause emotion, an event must signal a meaningful change in the world. But not just any change will create emotion.

To provoke emotion, an event must change some HUMAN VALUE.

For example, an asteroid crashing into a distant planet is an astronomical curiosity. An asteroid crashing into Earth is the most wrenching event that could occur. The difference is in the implications to human beings. In one case, nothing human-relevant happened. The other represents a massive shift from life to death.

[life/death] is an example of a *human value*.

A HUMAN VALUE is anything that is important to people that can shift through multiple states.

Human values can be in positive, neutral, or negative states. Only changes that shift human values between these states are emotionally relevant.

Some examples of human values are [life/death], [victory/defeat], [friend/stranger/enemy], [wealth/poverty], [low status/high status], [together/alone], [love/ambivalence/hatred], [freedom/slavery], [danger/safety], [knowledge/ignorance], [skilled/unskilled], [healthy/sick], and [follower/leader]. Events in games can shift all these values and more.

In *Minecraft*, players are assaulted by zombies every night. When they finish constructing a fort to hide in, they feel relieved because their situation has shifted from danger to safety.

In *Street Fighter II*, a kid starts playing tournaments. At first, he is easily defeated by the local experts. But he doesn't stop. He keeps practicing, working his way up the ladder. Eventually he wins a regional tournament, then a national, then a world championship. These are life-changing events because they represent huge shifts from ignorance to knowledge, from low status to high status, and from defeat to victory.

In *World of Warcraft*, two players meet while defeating a monster together. One invites the other to join a guild. Stranger becomes friend, and alone becomes together.

In *Half-Life*, the player character is trapped in a giant underground laboratory full of monsters invading from another dimension. Occasionally, he meets other survivors—scientists and security guards—who may accompany him for a time. Finding these allies and losing them are both emotionally gripping events because of the shift from alone to together and back.

In some cases, the changing human value exists only inside the game. Other times, it can be real. For example, gambling games create emotion around changes in real wealth. The action of playing craps is fairly boring—players merely roll dice over and over. But when money is riding on the outcome, every roll becomes a nail-biter since it implies a shift between poverty and wealth.

Games can even provoke emotion by physically threatening players. The experimental video game *PainStation* plays exactly like *Pong*, but it's far more emotionally intense because every failure is followed by a mechanical slap on the hand or an electrical shock. The tiny moving ball on the screen carries a lot of emotional weight when it can physically punish you.

What's emotionally relevant about an event is not the event itself, but the changes in human values implied by that event. The more important the human value and the more it changes, the greater the emotion.

Consider the event of losing a pawn in chess. In the early game, this may be a minor concern. The implications of losing early pawns are that you have fewer pieces and your pawn structure may be weaker. But in the late game, one pawn may be the difference between victory and loss. If you unexpectedly lose the pawn that was guarding your king, you feel dismayed because the game was just lost. The event is the same in each case, but the implications are different because one represents a small nuisance, and the other is a shift from victory to defeat.

Even events that seem to be very minor in themselves can be emotional if they have important implications. Consider the act of scouting in strategy games. Scouting is no more than seeing an object. It creates nothing, destroys nothing, and moves nothing. By itself it is almost a nonevent. But scouting a strategically important building can reverse a losing game because that one key piece of information can form the core of a new strategy that may lead to victory. So, in a game full of combat and bloodshed, the most emotionally gripping moment might be simply seeing a building.

There are countless ways to create important human value changes in response to even small events. For example, the *Modern Warfare* series of multiplayer shooters has a *kill streak* system that hands out special rewards to players who kill a certain number of enemies without dying. 3 kills in a row might give a useful radar scan, 7 a friendly jet airstrike, and 11 a powerful AC-130 gunship attack. This design works because it increases the implications of certain kills. The 11th kill is far more meaningful than the first because it changes the broader game state more than the first kill. The two kills themselves could be exactly the same—say, shooting an enemy as he runs around a corner—but their emotional charge is different because the implications are different.

Emotions don't just appear in response to a change. They also appear in anticipation of change.

The emotional unconscious doesn't just respond to what's happening. It constantly peers into the future, watching for human-relevant threats and opportunities. When it finds one, it signals it with emotion.

Imagine playing *Modern Warfare* again. You have counted 10 kills. You know that one more kill will get you the AC-130 bonus and that you'll likely win the game. In this situation, small local events such as your death or the killing of a single enemy may determine the outcome of the entire match. So you feel suspense because you sense that you are on the knife edge between two drastically different game outcomes. Everything rides on what happens in this moment. You're feeling an emotion not about something that has happened, but about something that might happen. This type of suspense is white-knuckle gaming at its finest.

But even this situation can sag into boredom if the unconscious senses that there is nothing hanging in the balance. Imagine the same situation where you are at 10 kills. This time, however, your team is already way ahead of the other team in score. The AC-130 itself will have the same effect, but the situation is much less suspenseful than before because your next kill or death won't actually determine the outcome of the game. The human value of [victory/defeat] is already locked at victory, so there is no way for it to shift. If you make the kill and get the AC-130, your team wins. If you die, your team will win anyway.

The unconscious constantly balances these ledgers of consequence and directs our conscious attention to the ones that are most lopsided—that is, the ones with the greatest potential shift in human values. When the player's unconscious senses a potential shift in human values, he will feel it.

A reveal of information is emotionally equivalent to change.

In terms of emotional impact, there is little difference between learning a fact and a fact becoming true, because the implications and opportunities are the same. It is the emotional difference between losing a thousand dollars on a die roll and realizing you've lost a thousand dollars when the dealer turns over the last card. The die roll was an event, the card flip was a reveal, but the human value shift and the resulting emotions are the same.

Think of a horror game in which you must walk down a hallway flanked by several doors. You know the killer is behind one of the doors, but you don't know which one. This situation stereotypically creates suspense because there is a looming possibility that you will learn something with extremely important implications (possibly shifting life to death). Now imagine a sci-fi horror game in which you walk down a hallway flanked by teleporter pads on which the killer can appear. In one, the killer was always there and is revealed behind a door. In the other, he teleports in. But the two situations are emotionally equivalent.

This means that games can create human value shifts by denying and revealing information. In some games, it can be hard to constantly generate changes in human values. These situations can be kept more interesting by not telling players everything, and instead rationing out information in a structured way to create suspense.

THE EMOTIONAL BLACK BOX

Emotion is the goal of game design. But this presents a challenge, because it's hard to track the precise origins of our emotions.

We can't directly perceive the logic behind our emotional triggers.

Emotion is not a choice. You don't see the edge of a cliff and decide to become afraid. You don't see a beautiful person and logically conclude that you should be attracted to them. Emotional triggers are automatic calculations handled by an unconscious part of the mind, similar to the ones that help you keep your balance while walking or recognize a familiar face. So even if you know what you feel, you can't ask the unconscious *why* it created that surge of attraction, disgust, serenity, or fear.

THE BRIDGE

A classic research study demonstrates the psychological disconnect between emotions and their causes.

Imagine you're a young man in Vancouver. It's 1973. You're crossing the Capilano Canyon Suspension Bridge. The bridge is a 5-foot-wide, 450-foot-long death trap. It sways in the wind like a deadly wood-and-rope bridge from an old adventure film. Looking down over the edge, you can see the jagged rocks between the trees 230 feet below.

In the middle of the bridge, an attractive woman asks if you'll take a survey. She is doing a project for her psychology class on the effects of scenic settings on creative expression. The first page is filled with boring questions, like name and age. The second asks you to write a short story based on a picture. After you're done, the woman tears off a corner of the survey, writes her phone number and name on it, and tells you to call if you have any more questions.

The woman is a confederate of psychology researcher Arthur Aron. What Aron is really interested in is how much sexual content you wrote into your story, and how likely you are to call the woman back for a date, compared to control subjects on a safer bridge nearby. The bridge would make subjects' hearts race and their palms sweaty. The question was would they reinterpret these fear responses as sexual attraction toward the woman?

They did. Subjects on the scary bridge wrote significantly more sexual imagery in their story and were four times as likely to call the woman back later than those on the safe bridge. These results persisted even through further studies that eliminated factors like subject self-selection (the possibility that more adventurous men are both more likely to cross the scary bridge and more likely to call the woman).

The men who called back the woman thought they were attracted to her because their hearts raced when they spoke to her. In reality, their hearts were racing because they were on a dangerous-looking bridge. But they couldn't tell the difference, because our emotions do not report their true causes.

EMOTIONAL MISATTRIBUTION

The men in Aron's study had no natural ability to track the true cause of their emotions, so they attributed them to the most salient thing in view: the attractive woman. This kind of emotional misattribution happens constantly. We think we feel a certain way for one reason, when the reason is completely different.

Some people use emotional misattribution to manipulate. For example, watch closely the next time a political documentary wants to characterize a politician as a bad guy. When his face appears on-screen, the music shifts into an evil-sounding drone, and the image is stripped of color, distorted, and slowed down. The director is hoping that the feelings of apprehensiveness that come from the music and visual effects will be misattributed to the politician, tricking people into being afraid of a person when they're actually afraid of a scary noise.

Entertainment producers do the same thing. For example, there is a trope in TV drama that I call the Leonard Cohen Gravitas Moment. It comes at the start of the third act of the show, when things are bad and it looks like all hope is lost. The dialogue stops, and a soulful or catchy song—often something Leonard Cohen-like—swells as the camera slides through a montage and a voiceover discusses the theme of the show. Viewers feel refreshed and contemplative. But they misattribute these feelings to the story when they actually come from the song.

Even though we don't know why we feel as we do, we effortlessly assign logical causes to our emotions without realizing it. These assumed causes are often wrong.

While one part of the mind is hard at work deciding what emotions to generate, another is hard at work inventing reasons why we're feeling those emotions. Sometimes those reasons are accurate, but often they are not. Yet no matter how wrong they are, we believe them instantly and wholeheartedly.

In one of the many studies examining this behavior, researchers set up a nylon display with four stockings in a department store and asked shoppers which was the highest quality. Eighty percent of them said the one on the right. When asked why, they cited color or texture. But in reality, the stockings were identical. They chose that particular stocking because of how it was positioned, and rationalized why afterward. They weren't lying intentionally, and they had no idea that they were rationalizing. But they were.

This is why players almost always report game experiences by explaining the causes of their feelings, not the feelings themselves. They'll say, "I liked that it was fast," or "It wasn't fun because the wizard staff was boring." The true parts of these statements are the raw emotions behind "I liked it," and "It wasn't fun." But the players have automatically appended reasons why they felt these things. The players don't have a direct line to their emotional mechanisms, so they don't know why they felt what they did. But they do have the human ability to instantly rationalize nearly any behavior or opinion.

Emotional misattribution makes it hard to understand how games affect us.

A game presents a hundred different stimuli and decisions, and provokes a multilayered emotional response. But which parts of the game triggered which emotion? There's no easy way to know.

Imagine playing a fighting game against a friend in a local tournament. It's the last round and you're neck and neck. Your foe dodges your energy blasts as he advances toward you. Reaching striking distance, he feints, hoping you'll block. You call his bluff and knock him out with a devastating uppercut. It's obvious what you feel: a tapestry of exhilaration and suspense, heart pounding, white knuckles on the controller, shouting audience members, eyes widening, a rush of victory. But why? What, exactly, caused each of those feelings? Was it the exotic fighting characters? Cool-looking moves? Beautiful environmental art? Was it the the competition with your friend, changing your relationship with him? Was it the threat of losing face in front of him? Or perhaps it was just the raw sensory overload of incendiary light flashing on the screen. There was a fast techno song playing in the background—did that make a difference? Was the game's overwrought backstory a factor?

In fact, every aspect of that situation contributed something to the emotions it produced. But as humans, we don't have a mental circuit that tells us which cause led to which effect. It's just not something we can do.

The upside is: we must question off-the-cuff emotional reasoning. When someone says he disliked a game because of the visuals, or the story, or the controls, don't take him at face value. Don't expect to understand how a game is affecting players just by looking at it.

There are ways to partially decode the puzzle. We can use systematic methods like playtesting or statistical metrics analysis to observe some of the effects of small changes. But even with these evidence-based methods, we can never fully understand a game because we can never watch the internal workings of a human mind—even our own. Instead, we have to tease out the mind's emotional triggers by theorizing at a distance. We're like a group of priests trying to read the will of a capricious god from eclipses and chicken guts. And like such priests, we often get it wrong. This makes game design very difficult.

The Basic Emotional Triggers

Let's take a look at some of the most common emotional triggers.

EMOTION THROUGH LEARNING

Think back to a time when a hard concept finally clicked in your mind. Your eyes light up, your mouth curls into a smile, and the unmistakable expression of epiphany leaves your lips: "Ahhhhhhh!" Learning feels good.

The more important a lesson is to a human value, the more we're driven to learn it.

Puppies have an instinctive drive to play-fight. It looks playful, but the reason they're doing it is deadly serious. Prehistoric puppies that didn't play-fight grew up into unskilled fighters. They thus failed to reproduce as well as the play-fighters and were weeded out of the gene pool. For dogs, an early predisposition to mirthful play-fighting is a survival strategy in the heartless game of evolution.

The same applies to people. We have a natural desire to learn, but that desire isn't indiscriminate.

The skills that we're instinctively driven to master are the ones that helped our ancestors reproduce.

Think of the games kids play. They run and jump to master kinesthetic skills. They play house to learn social roles. They engage in mock combat with sticks or pillows to learn fighting skills. They pretend to live adults' lives as soldiers, socialites, or builders. They're practicing to be grownups, and loving every minute of it because that's what helped their ancestors reproduce.

As we mature, we gain the capacity to develop more esoteric interests with less obvious reproductive purposes. For example, I've spent years studying game design, but I'm reasonably sure that none of my ancestors ever had caveman babies because they developed a better version of Throw the Rock. But no matter how old we are, the lessons that affect us most are still the ones that matter to human values—the ones that can shift loneliness to togetherness, or poverty to wealth. So games that teach players to build, socialize, and fight will always have the broadest impact.

The more intricate and nonobvious a lesson is, the greater the pleasure of learning it.

If a lesson is obvious, there's not much buzz in finally getting it because it was always fairly clear. If it's a subtle idea hidden in the folds of some complex system, learning it might be a life-changing experience because it represents a unique epiphany hidden to most people.

So the game designer's challenge is to create game systems with layers of nonobvious properties to decode. This means making a deep game that reveals lessons through layers, each one building on the one before it. Some classic games such as chess or poker are famous for the lifelong learning they can provide. Shallow games like tic-tac-toe are the opposite.

The best learning moments happen when we compress a pile of learning into a short time through the mechanism of *insight*.

Players feel INSIGHT when they receive a new piece of information that causes many old pieces of information to suddenly make sense.

Insight is the experience of getting a new piece of information that sets off a chain reaction of other lessons. It happens when we get the final piece of a logical puzzle that clicks into place and reveals the shape of the whole.

For example, in a strategy game, an enemy base is revealed at a spot where you saw some enemy constructors a few minutes earlier. You mentally kick yourself and say, "I should have known!" Or, in chess, your opponent makes a series of seemingly nonsensical moves which later turn out to be a devilish trap that you walked right into. He smiles triumphantly as you say, "I should have known!"

These moments weren't just simple surprises. They were preceded by clues that the player senses and fails to interpret properly, but manages to interpret afterward. They matter to us because we think that perhaps next time, given similar circumstances, we'll be able to predict the surprise. We'll get the sniper when we see the flicker of motion, or send the counterattack against the enemy base when we see the constructors. We might turn death to life, or defeat to victory.

The greatest insights are revealed after an extended buildup of information that all falls into place at once.

Predefined stories can do this very well since they can control exactly what the player learns at every point. For example, in *Half-Life* the player inhabits Gordon Freeman, a bespectacled, shotgun-toting scientist trying to escape the giant Black Mesa research facility. While fighting through monsters and military kill teams, however, the player repeatedly glimpses a humorless man in a suit carrying a briefcase. The man always disappears around a corner just before the player can get to him, sometimes seeming to teleport away just out of sight. It's only after the final climactic battle that this G-man finally introduces himself and explains what really happened at Black Mesa.

This type of long insight buildup can appear in game mechanics as well. Puzzles are a classic example. In the best puzzle games, the player learns a huge amount of information about a puzzle before he understands it. He determines how all the pieces move, and all the relationships between them. He might struggle at the puzzle for 20 minutes or longer, trying to piece together a solution in his head. When it finally hits, the purpose of all those seemingly random components becomes clear all at once, and the player says, "Aha!"

EMOTION THROUGH CHARACTER ARCS

Humans are empathetic. See someone smiling, and you're likely to smile with him. See someone in pain, and you'll tense up. We mirror emotions we feel in others.

This emotional trigger is the stock-in-trade of screenwriters and novelists. And like these writers, game designers can predefine character arcs. We can write a story for our game and set it up to play out the same way each time. This is a well-understood and traditional method of provoking emotion, and it can work well.

But games have another way of creating character arcs: we can have the game generate them on the fly. For example, in a game of *Left 4 Dead*, three survivors of a zombie apocalypse watch an ally slowly bleed out within sight of the safe room as the monsters lurk nearby. In a game of *The Sims*, a husband cheats on his wife with a younger woman and gets caught in the act. In *Dwarf Fortress*, a dwarf frustrated by a lack of beer goes on a rampage, murdering three miners before being put down. All these events have occurred in these games, but none of them was authored directly by the designers. Rather, they emerged during play from interactions between game mechanics.

Character arcs also feed a special kind of learning hunger: we love learning about our peers. We're particularly interested in the struggles of others, because it is only during conflict that a person's inner values and abilities are revealed. The more intense the conflict they face, the deeper we see into their true nature. We snore as our hero is forced to choose between skim and whole milk. Force him to choose between his wife's life and his own, and we stare, wondering who this man will show himself to be.

EMOTION THROUGH CHALLENGE

Tests of skill and strength create emotions in many ways. As we struggle at them, we enter a pleasurable state of focus. When we pass them, we feel energized, capable, and dominant. Even failure instills a sense of wanting to try again and do better, as long as the player senses the possibility of success.

Challenge is so closely associated with games that it's often assumed to be an essential aspect of the medium. It's part of many common definitions of games. But though it is a powerful and flexible method, challenge is still only one more emotional trigger, and not a necessary part of every game design. *The Sims, Minecraft, Snakes and Ladders, Dear Esther,* and roulette all create powerful emotions without players struggling toward a predefined objective.

That being said, challenge is still an important part of most game designs, so a large part of this book is devoted to understanding it.

EMOTION THROUGH SOCIAL INTERACTION

Catch is a stupid game. At first glance, it's hard to see why anyone would bother. Players just toss the ball back and forth. No human values change, there are no characters, and nobody learns much. But we keep doing it. Why?

The answer lies outside the game itself. Think of the classic *Leave It to Beaver* moment where Dad takes his son out to toss a baseball back and forth. These two people are not playing catch because they love tossing a ball. They're playing catch to create a pretext that allows them to get together and talk one on one for a long time. They need the game because long one-on-one talks between a father and young son can be awkward. By providing a reason to get together and a mindless activity to perform, the game removes this barrier. The fact that the game of catch is simple and thoughtless is not a bug; it's a feature. More complexity would just get in the way of the conversation.

Catch is the most basic form of socially driven game, since it has almost no emotional content in itself. But most social interaction games use specific game events to drive social interactions. One player defeats another, or two players create something together, or learn something together, and social interactions are generated around these events. Winning a game of chess against a computer doesn't feel the same as winning a game against a person, even if the game plays out the same way, because defeating a person adds another layer of emotionally relevant social meaning.

Consider the experience of showing off. Some people's emotions reward them for showing off, even if the other people involved are strangers on the Internet. Imagine a game of *Counter-Strike* in which you are the last man alive on your team this round. All of your teammates are observing you, hoping you'll complete the objective and win the round for them. Any skillful action you take gains another layer of meaning because it reinforces the trust and reputation you've built among your teammates. Any mistake you make has the opposite implication. This situation creates knife-edge tension because your social status hangs in the balance.

Games can support a breathtaking variety of social interactions beyond showing off. Building trust and breaking it, joking around, defeating strangers, saving friends, and completing a challenge together are all common social experiences that have been designed into games. There are a thousand variations on game mechanics that generate social moments. In every case, the social interaction works when it shifts some social human value—stranger to friend, low status to high status, and so on.

StarCraft and *Halo: Reach* have replay recording systems that allow players to save, rewatch, and share their greatest victories. *Skate* has a system for sharing gameplay videos so that a community of players can rate them. Social network games like *Farmville* allow players to send one another gifts or resources that help them achieve objectives. *The Sims* allowed players to share photo-album-like stories about their virtual people. *Super Mario Galaxy* allows one player to control Mario while another uses the pointing controller to help out by grabbing stars on the screen. *Kane & Lynch* allows two players to experience its grimy crime story together.

In a sense, playing a game is a move in the larger game of life. The father who offers to play catch hopes to connect with his son; the internal meaning of catch is less important to him than its use as a tool in life. We play drinking games to establish adulthood. We play chicken with trains to show fearlessness. The middle school boy plays spin the bottle not because he's interested in probability-based elimination mechanics, but because he knows he might get to kiss the cute girl.

EMOTION THROUGH ACQUISITION

We feel a pulse of happiness when we find a dollar under the couch cushions. We chase high-paying jobs and freebies. People scream and cry when they win the lottery. Whatever form it takes, acquiring wealth is a bit of a rush.

Gambling games trigger this response with real wealth. But even games involving no real money can trigger this emotion by creating artificial systems of wealth and acquisition and then giving players wealth within that system. The fake reward still triggers the feeling of acquisition.

Action role-playing games such as *Diablo III* are a good example of this. The player wanders around randomly generated dungeons, killing an endless stream of monsters. Defeated demons, zombies, and skeletons spew out little piles of gold, magical weapons, or pieces of armor. Every gold piece and sword contributes to the increasing power of the player's character. These rewards come so often and so continuously that the player stays on a permanent high of rewards acquisition. The game has narrative, audiovisuals, characters, and challenges, but none of these is its primary emotional driver. At its core, *Diablo III* is about the feeling of getting rich.

EMOTION THROUGH MUSIC

Music is a powerful and flexible tool for generating emotion. Since it's so easy to mix into an experience, it's used liberally across many media. Films play exciting music during action scenes, nightclubs play sexy music late at night, and daytime talk shows play sad or triumphant songs to emphasize whatever narrative they're trying to create. Games do the same thing with action, ambient, or scary music.

And music is wonderfully subtle—even more than most emotional triggers. Nobody ever gives it the credit it deserves because nobody consciously pays attention to it during play. But even though the conscious mind is oblivious, the unconscious is still processing the music into a continuous flow of feeling. You can tell because music is easily separable from the rest of the experience. Listen to a game soundtrack by itself, and you'll feel much of what you felt during play. Play the game in silence, and you'll be surprised at how hollow it feels.

Nonmusical sounds also create emotion. Screeching metal shoots us full of tension and discomfort. A heartbeat accentuates anticipation. Rain sounds serene. Party whistles are goofy. Squishing fluid suggests disgust. Laying these sounds over other events can accentuate or contrast an emotion. But be careful—when overused, such tricks can easily tip into cheesiness and end up having the opposite effect.

EMOTION THROUGH SPECTACLE

A Star Destroyer crashes into the Death Star! A super-soldier does a slow-motion dive to dodge an incoming rocket! A tanker truck jackknifes, splits in two, and explodes!

Razzle-dazzle spectacle can bring a quick emotional rise. Unfortunately, the payoff is shallow and unsustainable. Though these effects are expensive to produce, they're also creatively easy. Other emotional mechanisms like character arcs, socializing, and learning require that we construct interrelated networks of mechanics or characters. Spectacle only requires that something big blow up. As a result, spectacle is often overused by studios long on money and short on creative vigor. In the worst cases, it is used so gratuitously that it crowds out the subtler but more profound sources of emotion.

Spectacle works when it reinforces what's already there. When the player has fought through a thicket of fast-moving threats and reached his goal with knuckles white on the controller, it's probably appropriate that something blow up nice and good. That spectacle works because it accentuates the player's preexisting sense of relief and accomplishment at winning the battle. The same explosion dispensed again and again outside the context of any challenge leaves players numb.

EMOTION THROUGH BEAUTY

A sunset over the ocean. A healthy, giggling baby. A masterpiece painting. On the surface, these things have nothing in common. But all of them are beautiful. Because beauty isn't in any particular feature of a thing—it is in how something affects us. Something is beautiful when just perceiving it is pleasurable.

Games are full of opportunities for beauty. A character can be rendered in perfect detail and move with preternatural grace. A world can be painted in just the right color composition. And beauty isn't limited to video games either—think of the beauty of a well-made chess set, or the painted illustrations on *Magic* cards.

But like spectacle, beauty isn't free, and not just because of the time and artistic skill it requires. The emotions of beauty don't always fit with the rest of the game. Especially in game about ugly things—depression, horror, or unease—beauty will clash with the rest of the aesthetic. And beautiful art can add audiovisual noise that makes a game harder to understand and interact with.

As with spectacle, there is a tendency in modern game design to reflexively inject as much beauty into every situation as possible. But usually, beauty works best when it is channeled toward a specific purpose, not when it is thoughtlessly larded over everything.

EMOTION THROUGH ENVIRONMENT

Lightly wooded grassland feels different from steamy, claustrophobic jungle, which feels different from arctic tundra. And these feelings shift with time and season—winter feels different from summer, night different from day, rain different from shine.

There's evidence that these responses are partly innate. Psychology researchers have found that American children shown photographs of various environments say they would prefer to live in savannas, even though they've never been to one. These emotions may reflect an evolutionary imperative to seek out places where a tribe can thrive: fertile, not too hot or cold, not too open or overgrown. The perfect environment for prehistoric humans is open grassland with patches of woods and running water. So when we find a place like this, we feel satisfied and at ease. This emotional reaction draws us into these places where we can reproduce best.

People also have acquired environmental preferences. We prefer the landscape we grew up in. So, while American children like savannas, American adults also like coniferous and deciduous forests, because those landscapes resemble much of the United States. And no American in any group wants to live in a desert or rainforest.

Environmentally driven emotions are diverse and strong. Games have used environments, weather, and season to accentuate feelings ranging from depression to giddy triumph.

Heavy Rain: This puzzle adventure game is about a man losing his son. In the first few scenes, the world is bright and sunny. But after the boy vanishes, the rest of the game plays out under a downpour, and mostly at night. That endless rain gives every sequence a morose undertone, accentuating the themes of loss, crime, and depression.

Half-Life: Gameplay begins with the player trapped in the giant underground Black Mesa facility, so there is no natural light for the first 15 hours of play. When the player finally bursts through the door and onto the sun-drenched New Mexico desert, there's a palpable sense of freedom and accomplishment.

Metro 2033: Two decades after the nuclear holocaust, a community of survivors ekes out an existence in the Moscow metro system. It's dark down there, but people have still made a home. They work, trade, listen to music, drink, and laugh. But the surface is a different story. The vision of Moscow in *Metro 2033* may be the least friendly landscape imaginable. Shattered buildings lay frozen in giant chunks of ice. The air itself is toxic, so the player must carry a constantly dwindling supply of gas mask filters. Thousands of icicles menace like spike traps, pulled out sideways by the lashing wind. Everything about the place is endless: the sun never shines, the wind never stops, the ice never melts, and nothing ever grows. I'll never forget how it felt to pick my way through that rubble. Though most would call *Metro 2033* a shooter or a role-playing game, I wouldn't, because I don't think it's about shooting or role-playing. I think it's about discovering how a place like that makes you feel.

EMOTION THROUGH NEWFANGLED TECHNOLOGY

Shiny new tech is cool. The first few games with any new graphics, animation, or physics technology get an emotional rise from certain players just because of the technology itself.

But this bonus often comes at a cost. Paradoxically, technological advances often lead to a temporary reduction in the design quality of games. This is partially because developers haven't yet learned how to best use the new technology. More importantly, though, the promise of an easy tech-driven emotional return takes the creative pressure off. So the game becomes a technology demo because it doesn't need to be anything else to get players excited. The game will still work, for a while. But technological excitement doesn't last long, and a game that depends on it will not look very good a few years down the road.

For example, in the mid-1990s it became possible to encode full-motion video on a CD-ROM and play it back on a PC. This technological leap led to some of the worst games in history. These games managed to utterly fail at being movies while simultaneously failing at being games. Although this disaster was driven by many other factors besides tech fetishism (such as the blind theft of creative ideas from film), it was enabled by misplaced trust in technology.

To achieve sustained success, a game must use its new technology to unlock interactions and situations that couldn't have been experienced before. For example, *Doom* is often cited as a technology-driven game because it was the first first-person shooter with varying heights and non-right-angled walls. But *Doom* did not become a mega-hit just because of its technology. It also took that new technology and used it to unlock a new spectrum of design-driven experiences. *Doom* wasn't just the first game with arbitrarily angled walls and changing light levels. It was the first game where demons shut off the lights and charged into the room when you grabbed an item. It was the first immersive horror game where you would hear monsters groaning in the dark and turn in circles, trying to find them. It was the first multiplayer first-person shooter. These elements depended on technology to work, but they are actually advances in game design, and the technology alone did not create them.

EMOTION THROUGH PRIMAL THREATS

Some things have threatened our species for so long that our fear of them is imprinted directly into our genes. Rotten food and disease-ridden filth make us feel revolted to help us avoid food poisoning. Venomous spiders and snakes make us recoil because they're more dangerous than their size suggests. Visibly diseased people drive us away so that we won't catch their sickness ourselves. The sight of ghastly wounds kicks off an adrenaline response to prepare us to deal with a dangerous situation. And games can trigger these responses. Just throw gore or spiders on a screen. It's easy.

In fact, it's too easy. The adrenaline rush of these primal threats has been cheapened by decades of overuse by lazy filmmakers and game designers. People are just too used to these cheeseball frights by now. Many of us automatically tune them out, or even laugh at them. To create genuine horror and revulsion in a modern audience, it's no longer enough to splash guts thoughtlessly about the screen. These things can scare people, but to really horrify players, we must craft threats that disturb them on a deeper level.

EMOTION THROUGH SEXUAL SIGNALS

A game can show some bare skin, a pretty face, an alluring expression, and people will notice because we're genetically programmed to pay attention to these things. Since these sexual signals are so effective and easy to use, game designers, advertisers, and filmmakers alike have ruthlessly abused them. You can put a mostly naked, attractive character in a game, and some players will respond. As with primal threats, it's easy.

But the use of cheap sexual signals has downsides. Gratuitous sexuality harms the atmosphere and believability of a serious narrative, and it irritates large classes of potential players (typically the ones not interested in the signals presented). In a certain kind of game made for a certain audience, this is fine. For more serious or broadly targeted games, it's often not worth being tasteless.

The Fiction Layer

There are some games that are just mechanics and nothing more. Poker, soccer, checkers, and video games such as *Geometry Wars* or *Bejeweled* are examples of this. In checkers, the pieces are just that: pieces. They move based on arbitrary rules that don't relate to anything outside themselves. A soccer ball is just a ball, and an enemy in *Geometry Wars* is just a piece of data in computer memory, represented by an abstract shape on a screen.

These kinds of games can work very well. Pure game mechanics with abstract representations can provoke tension, doubt, puzzlement, and triumph. They can shift values between victory and defeat, poverty and wealth, ignorance and knowledge.

But most real games don't limit themselves to the abstract. They use graphics and sounds to help players make believe that the mechanics are more than an artificial system of rules.

Mechanics gain another layer of emotional meaning when they are wrapped in FICTION.

At one point in the first *Austin Powers* movie, Dr. Evil creates a troupe of sexy fembots. The fembots looked exactly like tall, blonde women in silver catsuits. But under the skin, they were actually robots (with guns in their nipples). We all know that the fembots are no more than cleverly arranged hunks of moving matter, like a car engine or a toaster. But wrapping them in a human-looking skin triggers a different psychological viewpoint. They become more than robots dressed up to look like women. They become women who also happen to be robots.

This may seem to be a meaningless distinction. But in the mind, and in our emotional responses, it makes a huge difference. Given a human appearance, the fembots become characters with minds, desires, and plans. Now, when the fembots attack it isn't because of a programming switch, it's because they're *angry*. When they retreat it's not due to a coded stimulus response, it's because they're *afraid*. When they pursue something we don't say they're executing a pursuit algorithm, we say it's because they *want* that thing. Everything they do takes on a human emotional resonance because of the skin wrapped around their robotic skeletons. The fact that we know that this skin is just a few millimeters of rubber doesn't matter.

At their core, all games are no more than mechanics, just as Dr. Evil's fembots are no more than metal and rubber. Mario isn't a cartoon Italian plumber—he's a collision cylinder that slides around and bumps into things. That teenager falling in love in *The Sims* really didn't—the game software just flipped a few bits in a data structure somewhere.

By wrapping the mechanics in a fictional dressing, we imbue them with a second layer of emotional meaning. That's why when a game character is running out of food, we don't just say that our resources are low and the game will end soon. We say we're *starving*. When an ally is defeated, we don't just quietly remove his token from the board. We grieve for our murdered friend. We know it's fake, but the make-believe still creates some emotional echo of real hunger, grief, or love.

Naïve observers often assume that *all* the meaning of a game comes from the fiction. In this view, games make emotion by drawing the player into a simulated experience until the mental distinction between the game world and the real world disappears. The designer Eric Zimmerman named this view the *immersive fallacy*. It's a fallacy because no game player ever forgets they're playing a game. The fictional wrapping doesn't replace or conceal the game mechanics; it adds a second layer of meaning to the emotions generated by mechanics alone.

FICTION VERSUS MECHANICS

Fiction and mechanics each create different kinds of emotions.

Mechanics can generate tension, relief, triumph, and loss. They can bring the pleasure of learning or the pride of solving a puzzle. They can create social rewards by allowing us to defeat strangers or make friends. But mechanics alone are also limited in their emotional range. It's hard to do humor, awe, or immersion with mechanics alone. And without characters, the entire emotional spectrum that flows through empathy is almost inaccessible.

The fiction layer creates emotion through character, plot, and world. We laugh and cry as characters frolic or struggle, and feel shocked or fascinated while exploring a fictional universe. But like mechanics, fiction alone is limited in its range. It can't do competition, triumph, and loss. And it can't give us the pleasure of mastering a skill, or create social interactions with real people.

Combining fiction and mechanics together allows us to combine emotions from both sides. But there's a catch.

Fiction and mechanics can easily interfere with each other.

Games narratives are laden with clichés. The player character is an amnesiac. Or he's a super-soldier capable of murdering thousands of foes. Enemies are monsters or evil soldiers, and they feel neither fear nor remorse. Princesses are captured over and over like it's going out of style. A barrel will explode if struck. And nobody ever goes to the bathroom.

One of the worst clichés is the crate. It seems like every game you see, whether it's a modern military shooter or a fantasy role-playing game, takes place in a world scattered with pointless crates. The problem is so bad that back in 2000, the humor site Old Man Murray created a game review score system measured in *Start to Crate* (StC), the idea being that the longer it took a game to show you a crate, the less lazy the developers had been in avoiding cliché, and the better the game probably was. Of 26 games tested, only five had StC times of more than 10 seconds. A full 10 games managed StC times of zero seconds by starting the player with a crate in view.

That was more than a decade ago. But the crates haven't gone away. Why? Have we learned nothing? No, it's not because game designers are all fools. The reason that crates and other such clichés appear over and over is that they cleanly justify good mechanics.

For example, I once designed a shooter level set in an old-timey theater, with rows of chairs facing a stage at the front. Upon playtesting, I noticed players were becoming frustrated due to enemy snipers. The theater was so open that players would get a bullet in the brain the moment they peeked out from cover. The theater's fictional design made perfect sense, but its mechanics didn't. To be balanced against snipers, it needed a minivan-sized object in the middle of the audience to block the snipers' sightlines. Faced with that kind of problem, under story and time constraints, there aren't any easy answers. So I did what I had to. I hung my head in shame and put a couple of crates in the middle of the theater. People mocked the crates, and deservedly so. But the fight worked.

Almost all game fiction clichés are similarly mechanics-driven. A player character with amnesia justifies other characters explaining obvious things about the world. Player characters are often super-soldiers because it's hard to make shooter enemies who are entertaining to fight for more than a few seconds. When enemies last five seconds before death, the game has to throw hundreds or thousands of them at the player over the course of the game. A super-soldier player character can justifiably defeat battalions of enemies alone. And these enemies never have complex emotions because fear and remorse are fuzzy, unpredictable, and hard to represent. Games are simpler and more mechanically elegant when everyone mindlessly fights to the death.

Consider one basic game design cliché: physical violence. So many games are about physical conflict. It can be tiring. I once tried to break out of this pattern with a real-time strategy game called *Player League*. The player controlled a team of pickup artists in a nightclub. The goal was to pick up more chicks than the opposing teams of players. This meant blocking them out of conversations, promoting yourself in various ways, and using neutral characters to your advantage.

The game did not work. A chief reason the design failed was because there was no clear way to express most of what was going on. Every game event was a human interaction, causing one person to feel one of several possible emotions toward another. A simple camera view of what was going on would show nothing—just people talking. I couldn't very well give the text of their speech because these events could happen hundreds of times in infinite combinations, far too many to create actual speech for every situation. I eventually settled on a solution of abstracting relationships out into colored lines and shapes that appeared around people. It worked, after a fashion, but the representation was arbitrary and had to be learned by rote, and the in-game events often didn't make intuitive sense because the system couldn't express most of the concepts that exist in a real social interaction.

These sorts of problems are why so many games are about physical conflict. A strategy game about war has none of the problems of *Player League*. An image of one unit shooting at another is clear and visceral, and requires no abstract interpretive symbols. People just get physical violence. It supports mechanics well because it's easy to learn and understand, so it gets used over and over.

Also, wars have lots of crates.

Because fiction and mechanics so easily interfere with each other, many games choose to emphasize one while mostly ignoring the other.

There's a natural trade-off between focusing on mechanics and focusing on fiction. Focusing on mechanics allows the designer to create a perfectly balanced, clear, and deep challenge. But it'll probably be very hard to find a fictional wrapping that resembles these perfect mechanics. For example, imagine trying to wrap chess or poker in a fiction. This is tough because these games don't much resemble anything besides themselves. Chess has a fiction, but it is thin and nonsensical—real knights don't always move two squares forward and one square sideways. Poker resembles nothing in reality or story. These two games are great systems of mechanics, but they don't naturally support good fiction.

Alternatively, a designer can focus on fiction, creating a beautiful, history-charged world full of flawed characters and fantastic locales. But all these story details make it hard to change the mechanics under the surface. They mean that instead of being able to change any mechanic any way he likes, the designer is required to fix mechanical problems by only making changes that don't contradict the fiction. For example, in a game set in the real world, the designer can't reduce gravity or make fire not burn certain characters, even if it would make a challenge more balanced. So the mechanics suffer.

This fiction–mechanics conflict is why some see a great debate between mechanics and fiction. The *ludologists* (from the Latin *ludus*, for "play") argue that games draw their most important properties from mechanical systems and interactions. The *narratologists* argue that the mechanics are just a framework on which to hang the fictional elements players actually care about. This debate is the game designer's nature versus nurture, our plot versus character, our individualism versus collectivism.

But like all such debates, the conflict exists only on the surface.

The pinnacle of game design craft is combining perfect mechanics and compelling fiction into one seamless system of meaning.

Fiction and mechanics need not fight (though they easily can), and neither one need be given primacy (though one often is). Used together, they can enhance and extend each other in ways that each cannot do alone. Consummately great game design cannot be done by dropping a great fiction on top of excellent mechanics. It is done by threading them together into a single system of emotion. That's why so much of game design isn't just about crafting a well-balanced challenge or a beautiful world. It's about doing each in such a way that it integrates seamlessly with the other.

Constructing Experiences

The emotions of play don't stand alone. They merge together into an integrated *experience*.

An EXPERIENCE is an arc of emotions, thoughts, and decisions inside the player's mind.

An experience is the combined expression of every effect the game has upon the player's psychology, stretching from the beginning of play to the end. It transforms itself through setup and payoff, expectation and result. A thought leads to an emotion, which sparks an idea, which causes a reaction, which brings feedback, leading to another thought. And just as a well-made meal is more than the sum of its ingredients, an experience is more than the sum of its psychological components.

Game experiences are always mixed. A soccer player up 2-1 near the end of a game feels hopeful for a win, but worried about a penalty. A kid playing *Super Mario Galaxy* feels happy because of the upbeat music, while gritting his teeth through a hard jumping challenge.

Game experiences are also marvelously diverse. One might be short and pure, as in a fighting game that maximizes excitement for 60 seconds.

Another might be long and complex, like an open-world narrative role-playing game that shifts from awed exploration to narrative intrigue to combat excitement through 100 hours of play.

Different emotions put together can enhance one another, transform one another, or even destroy one another. Let's look at some of the ways games can mix emotion to create experiences.

PURE EMOTION

To maximize a single feeling, we can combine several different emotional triggers that drive the exact same emotion. Each trigger is like another booster rocket that pushes the experience further toward one pure emotional peak.

For example, traditional action arcade games combine fast-paced music, risky situations, violent fiction, and testosterone-driven social competition to make the game as exciting as possible. Any one of these triggers could work on its own to create excitement. Together they boost the experience to levels none of them could achieve separately.

JUXTAPOSITION

Juxtaposition is the combination of different, seemingly incompatible feelings. Ramming together feelings that don't ordinarily mix can produce strange and sometimes valuable results.

For a long time, I thought Epic Games' *Gears of War* series was no more than a mindless monster-bashing space marine romp. And the louder part of its presentation is exactly that. Characters rip monsters apart with gun-mounted chainsaws, curb-stomp downed enemies, and fill the air with endless testosterone-marinated declarations of personal awesomeness. But as I became more familiar with the series, I realized that the hyper-violent surface concealed a second, very different emotional ingredient, like a subtle flavor you don't notice until halfway through a meal. *Gears of War* is mournful. It's set in the ruins of a civilization of extraordinary beauty. Most of the character arcs are about coming to terms with loss, whether of a loved one or a glorious former life. Even the game's advertisements became famous because of the fascinatingly unsettling juxtaposition of Gary Jules's *Mad World* and visuals of computer-generated carnage. By juxtaposing mourning with violent excitement, *Gears of War* becomes more than just an industrial-strength gore-fest.

There is an easy way to experiment with juxtaposition. Just replace the music in a game with music that creates a very different feeling. Replace fighting game music with Mozart's *Lacrimosa*. Play the *Happy Days* theme song over *Doom*. Drop Britney Spears over a survival horror game like *Dead Space 2*. The results can be weird, unsettling, or funny.

ANTAGONISTIC EMOTIONS

Ice cream and pizza are both great, but they're not so great together. In the same way, some kinds of emotions that work individually don't coexist easily because they're *antagonistic* toward each other.

For example, shared social enjoyment is often harmed by adding ruthless skill-based competition. Intense competition draws all of a player's attention as he struggles as hard as he can to win, but laughing with friends requires us to relax. This conflict is why friends playing skill-based games will often agree to play only "for fun," thus turning down the skill intensity of the game to make room for the social experience they really want.

There's a fine line between juxtaposition and antagonistic emotions. Sometimes attempts at juxtaposition fall flat when the two feelings just end up annihilating each other. Other times, what seems like an antagonistic combination can squirt out an entirely different feeling.

For example, a friend of mine had this experience in a shooter: near the end of the game was a key cutscene of the death of a major character. It was a tragic moment that obviously attempted to pull at the player's heartstrings. The game transitioned back into gameplay. Upon picking up some ammunition, the character exclaimed, "Sweet!" My friend burst out laughing because the emotion of tragedy was inadvertently forced too close to the emotion of manly confidence. The result was a ridiculous mixture that turned into laughter—an unintended but oddly entertaining result.

ATMOSPHERE

The word *atmosphere* is used when the emotions of the experience aren't focused around specific events, but rather permeate the whole experience in a spread-out haze. It is the emotional background that we only notice when nothing more salient is happening. Stop and wait in a game and just feel for a minute. You'll discover the game's atmosphere.

Some games de-emphasize the emotional punches of individual events and instead focus on growing a thick atmosphere and letting the player sink into it. For example, *LIMBO*, *DEFCON*, and *Flower* are atmosphere games. Usually the atmosphere in such games is serene and contemplative, though it can be given either a positive or negative flavor: *Flower* is about drifting through fluffy clouds in a dreamscape, while *DEFCON* is about watching nuclear missiles vaporize millions on a world map. Each uses music and slow-paced interaction to create atmosphere, then applies a different fiction to flavor the experience.

EMOTIONAL VARIATION

Any single emotion gets tiring if sustained too long. To retain power and freshness, an experience must transform over time.

One classic way of doing this is *pacing variation*. This method has been used and studied for years by traditional storytellers, to the point where they've developed a specific pacing formula that they reuse over and over. The classic pacing curve starts with the hook, settles into a rising action, builds up, and then finally peaks at its climax before resolving with a denouement. Graphed out, it looks like this:

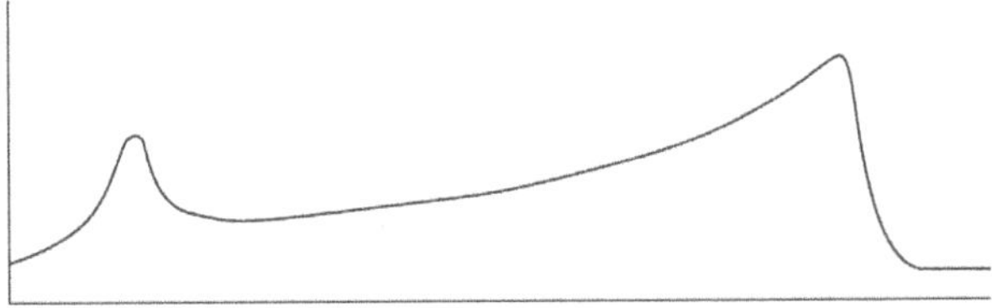

This curve can be found in countless media—films, books, comedy routines, infomercials, operas, and songs—because it is incredibly effective. It hooks people, holds attention, and leaves the audience satisfied without ever exhausting them.

Games can exhibit this pacing curve as well. And not just by writing it in a predefined story—we can create game mechanics which generate it on the fly.

For example, take a multiplayer match of capture the flag in any shooter. As the game starts, each team is bunched up at opposite ends of the map. The team members approach one another with a sense of building anticipation. At the center of the map, they crash into one another, and a pitched battle takes place. Then they settle into an attack-and-defense rhythm. As the timer runs low, the stakes increase, and with them the tension. At the end of the match, the game approaches a climax of intensity as the players try to capture their last flag and turn the game in their favor. Afterward, the players have a few moments to cool off at the score screen. The pacing curve they experienced follows the classic three-act story formula, but instead of being predefined, it's generated a little bit differently every game.

In addition to varying intensity with changes in pace, we can also vary the flavor of emotions. Psychologists call this aspect of emotion *valence*. For example, fury, grief, and terror are all high in intensity, but their valences are different. Satisfaction, relief, and depression are all low-intensity emotions with different valences. We can even plot emotions on a graph by valence and intensity:

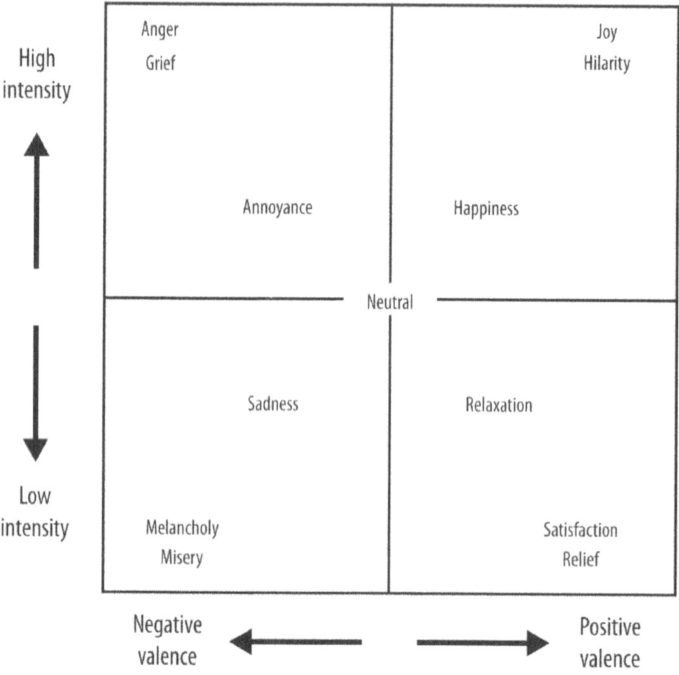

We don't just have to limit ourselves to sending the player up and down the graph as we change intensity. To keep the experience even fresher, a game can generate experiences that send the player on a wending path to every corner of their emotional spectrum, from joy to anger to depression and relief.

FLOW

Flow is a popular concept in psychology that is particularly applicable to game design. It was originally described by the Hungarian psychologist Mihály Csíkszentmihályi. He described it this way:

FLOW is a state of concentration so focused that it amounts to total absorption in an activity.

Back in university, I spent some time in the Canadian Army Reserves. One special thing about the army is that it is absolutely unacceptable to show up even seconds late for anything.

I had drill at 7:00 on a Saturday one evening. I also made the mistake of playing the fantasy strategy classic *Heroes of Might and Magic III* on the same day. I had lots of time. Looking at the clock, it was 5:00 p.m. If I started getting ready by 6:15 I could make it to the parade ground in good time to change into uniform.

But *Heroes III* is very good at pulling you into flow. I moved my hero, fought some gryphons and troglodytes, captured a city and grabbed some treasure. Seemingly a few minutes later, I looked over at the clock. It was 6:37. It was a long sprint to the drill hall.

Flow makes time seem to disappear. Hours can seem like minutes when a player is utterly engrossed in an activity. It is the perfect form of escapism because it strips everything else out of the mind. In flow, we don't worry about bills, relationships, money, or whether we're going to get screamed at by a drill instructor. And flow is pleasurable because it is built on a continuous stream of tiny successes.

Flow appears when a player is presented with a challenge that is perfectly balanced against his ability level. If the task is too hard, flow breaks as the player becomes confused and anxious. If it is too easy, the player gets bored. Graphed, it looks like this:

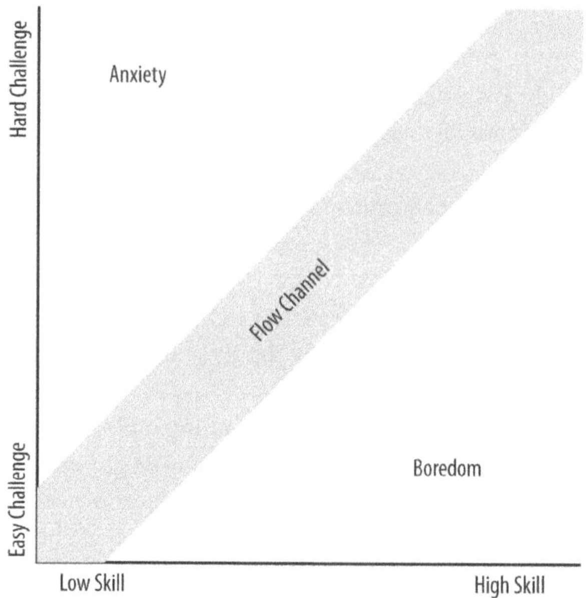

Flow is the foundation for most good game experiences. It works at all intensity levels and emotional valences. Heart-pumping action games, contemplative puzzlers, humorous social interaction games—all can create flow because each occupies the player's mind without a break, and without overfilling it.

And in any case, if flow is broken, the other parts of the experience fall apart. Nearly all games have to maintain flow to work, and many problems with bad games come down to nothing more than breaks in flow.

IMMERSION

One of the most powerful game experiences is *immersion*.

IMMERSION is when the mental division between the player's real self and his in-game avatar softens, so events happening to the avatar become meaningful as though they were happening to the player himself.

Everybody agrees that immersion is valuable, but there is little agreement on where it comes from. Everything from fictional believability, to graphical fidelity, to relatable or silent protagonists and even lowering the lights in the room while playing have been called out as contributors. Yet, there are games with all of these things that aren't immersive, and there are immersive games that lack these things.

Immersion occurs when the player's experience mirrors the character's experience.

The best way to describe immersion itself is as the player's experience mirroring the character's experience. Obviously this means the player sees and hears the same things as the character. But more importantly, it also means the player thinks and feels what the character thinks and feels. When the character is afraid, so is the player. When the character is angry, curious, or dumbfounded, so is the player. When the player thinks and feels the same as the character, he feels he is the player, and the game is immersive.

This internal psychological mirroring is the missing piece in most failed attempts at immersion. But how do we create it? One possible answer lies in a concept from psychology called the *two-factor theory of emotion.*

The TWO-FACTOR THEORY OF EMOTION says that emotions are composed of two parts: physiological arousal and a cognitive label.

Arousal is the state of being amped up and ready to act. Your heart beats faster, your palms sweat, and your eyes widen. Your body is getting ready to do something drastic, right now. This arousal state can happen for many different reasons. Fear induces a state of high arousal, but so do anger, intense music, and sexual tension.

The two-factor theory of emotion says that all of our different intense emotions are physiologically the same—that they're all the same basic arousal state. According to the theory, the only difference between these feelings is the *cognitive label* we put on them.

A cognitive label is a conscious mental explanation for what is causing the arousal state. Depending on what seems to be happening, your brain will relabel an arousal state as any of a wide variety of intense emotions. For example, if you feel aroused while a bear is chasing you, you'll label your emotional state as fear. The same arousal appearing a moment after being insulted will be labeled as anger. The key of the two-factor theory is that the arousal state is actually the same thing in every case—that there is no physiological difference between, say, anger and fear. We just label them differently.

In a 1962 experiment, researchers gave subjects injections of a mystery drug. The drug was actually adrenaline, which causes sweaty palms, increased heart rate, and rapid breathing. These subjects were put in a room with another subject who had also apparently received the injection. What they weren't told was that the other subject was an actor. In some trials, the actor acted euphoric. In others, he acted angry. In all cases, the experimental subjects reported experiencing the same feelings as the actor was faking. In truth, all they felt was chemically induced arousal. But the social cues from the actor caused them to relabel this state as fear, anger, or euphoria. If subjects were told what the injection was, they reported no emotional state because they had labeled their body's reaction as a meaningless response to the chemical.

The two-factor theory illuminates a lot of emotional paradoxes. We cry from both grief and happiness. Nightclubs create sexual attraction by getting the heart rate up with loud music and dancing. Horror movies are popular with couples. Dirty jokes work by using offensive or disturbing ideas to create an emotional response, then relabeling the response as comedic delight. We even have make-up sex, transmuting anger into lust. In every case, we're misattributing arousal to something besides its real cause. And this misattribution turns out to be the key to immersion.

To create an experience that mirrors that of a character, we construct it out of three parts. First, we create flow to strip the real world out of the player's mind. Second, we create an arousal state using threats and challenges in the game mechanics. Finally, we use the fiction layer to label the player's arousal to match the character's feelings.

Let's break this down.

The first ingredient is flow. The role of flow is to get the real world off the player's mind so that he can sink into the game. It's created mostly in the game mechanics, when the challenge is perfectly balanced against the player's skill level. It is a prerequisite for immersion; without flow, stray thoughts of bills or homework constantly intrude on the experience, destroying any chance that it might mirror that of the character.

The second ingredient is raw arousal. We can invoke pure, unlabeled arousal with nothing but game mechanics. For example, *Pong*, *Geometry Wars*, and checkers can be arousing when play is hard and fast, decisions are tough, and the stakes are high.

The last ingredient is fiction. Without fiction, the arousal generated by the mechanics is labeled as a generalized kind of excitement, like what you feel when playing *Geometry Wars*. But with fiction, we can relabel the raw arousal state however we like. For example, arousal might be relabeled as terror in a horror game full of scary zombies. Or it might become gritty determination in a military game. Even if the game mechanics creating those experiences are very similar, the cognitive label suggested by the fiction changes how players perceive their experience.

With that delicate mix in place, the experience transcends simple engagement and transports the player into another time and place. The mechanics-driven experience of flow peels away the player's self-consciousness, erases his awareness of the real world, and creates a basic state of physiological arousal. The fictional experience draws his identity into a character in a make-believe world. The player sees and hears what the character sees and hears, and feels what the character feels. The player is the character.

For example, one of the most popular early immersive games was *Doom*. The game has very well-crafted action game mechanics. During an intense fight, the player tenses up, his palms sweat, his mind forgets the outside world. By themselves, these things aren't exceptional. They would happen even if the game had no fiction at all—*Geometry Wars* players show these same symptoms.

But in *Doom*, the player sees through the eyes of a space marine trapped in a demon-infested colony on a Martian moon. The moaning zombies and bloodstained world signal the player's mind that the arousal he is feeling isn't just excitement—it's fear. And that changes everything.

The fact that the marine is aroused because demons are trying to kill him, and the player is aroused because of *Doom*'s well-designed combat, doesn't matter. In the two-factor theory of emotion, one source of arousal is interchangeable with another.

Now *Doom* isn't just about exciting shooting. It's about the experience of being a space marine fighting zombies in a Martian base, because the player's experience mirrors that of the character. Fictionally, the marine is terrified since he is fighting for his life. In real life, the player feels aroused because of *Doom*'s fast action mechanics, and labels that arousal as terror because of the fiction. Those separate experiences merge into one in the player's mind. The player and the marine see, hear, and feel the same, so the player feels he is the marine, and the game is immersive.

Engines of Experience

The experience is the last link in the conceptual chain by which games work. To recap: first, designers create a set of *mechanics*. They wrap these mechanics in a layer of representative *fiction*. During play, those mechanics interact to produce a long sequence of *events*. Those events tickle triggers in the player's unconscious mind, provoking *emotions*. Finally, those emotions merge together into an integrated *experience* which lasts minutes, days, or years.

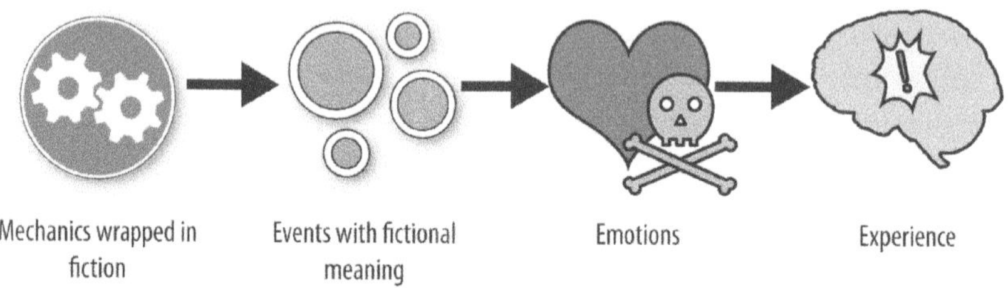

We also may have just stumbled on a definition for games.

A GAME is an artificial system for generating experiences.

Sometimes I think of games as a special kind of machine. Machines are made of carefully designed metal shapes that fit together perfectly, while games are made of carefully designed mechanics that fit together perfectly. When used, a machine's parts move against one another in intricate patterns, while game mechanics interact in specific complex ways. The greatest fundamental difference between games and machines is in the nature of that result that the system is supposed to create. Physical machines are made to propel vehicles, heat houses, or assemble widgets. Games are made to provoke emotion.

If you want a metaphor to use while thinking about games, don't think of stories or movies. Those metaphors don't capture key aspects of the power of games since they lack dynamic interaction between game mechanics. They send us down the beaten path of predefined media experiences, and away from the rich virgin land of on-the-fly, explorative, generated interactivity.

Instead, think of a game as a strange kind of machine—an engine of experience.

PART TWO

Game Crafting

SINCE THE START OF modern game design in the 1970s, designers have learned a tremendous amount. But this knowledge is spread among a thousand designers in a hundred studios. One studio has mastered branching narratives, while another can perfectly balance strategy games, and a third makes games soaked in atmosphere. This part of the book aims to link this disparate knowledge into a teachable set of design principles.

There is no one great theory of game design because every design decision has many different consequences. Adding a tutorial character may make the game easier to pick up, but harder to implement and less fictionally coherent. Adding art might make the game more beautiful but encourage wrong player choices. These multiple consequences demand multiple explanations. That's why this part of the book covers many different design viewpoints, none of which are supreme. Each viewpoint helps us understand a different aspect of a problem.

Game design cannot be learned from a book. It requires experience.

The ideas written here are just a framework. To be useful in making design decisions, they must be filled in by experience. You need to push ideas too far and too short. You must watch different designs succeed and fail in a hundred ways. These kinds of reference experiences give you calibration. They give that intuitive sense of when each idea in your game design framework becomes important, and to what degree.

But not just any experience will do when learning game design.

The best game design learning comes from observing the effects of small, isolated changes to a game.

People trying to understand games often compare entire games to each other and try to pick out how their differences affect play. But it's hard to find design principles this way. There are so many differences between the games that it's impossible to isolate the effects of any single one.

Better learning comes from inspecting the effects of tiny changes. The designer watches three people play a game, and observes the patterns in their experiences. He sees them understand certain things but not others, take certain actions, remember certain events. Then the designer changes one variable in the design. With the next three testers, he watches the experience change in some specific way—one new idea understood or lost, one memory gained or erased. The designer learns that their one small change caused that one characteristic effect.

And that effect will be consistent. Amateurs think games are mystically incomprehensible; professionals have watched the repeatable effects of isolated changes enough to know that games are rational systems like any other. While the experience of play can be magical, the mechanisms behind that experience are not. Let's take a look under the hood.

2

Elegance

In a way, every game exists already. They're out there, hidden in the logic of the universe. We don't create them. We find them like a sculptor finds the statue in a block of marble—not by adding anything, but by taking away the excess material that obscures the form within.

Every game mechanic has a price tag. It costs design effort, since it must be implemented, tuned, and tested. It costs computing resources which we could have used somewhere else. It might force changes in the fiction, or blur the focus of the game's marketing.

Most importantly, however, it costs player attention. Players must work to understand a game. They have to follow instructions, make mistakes, fail, and try again. Some won't be able to, and will leave. Others will become confused and frustrated.

Players submit themselves to these costs because they want a meaningful experience. Good design means maximizing the emotional power and variety of play experiences while minimizing players' comprehension burden and developer effort. This form of efficiency is called *elegance*.

Elegance from Emergence

The game of checkers has just a few simple rules, but can generate an endless variety of different games. Some games are long struggles. Others are quick sweeps. One game might have a remarkable tactical upset, while another teaches an important lesson. And the price tag for all this? A few minutes of simple instructions at the start of the first game. That's elegance: countless powerful, varied experiences generated by a simple, easy-to-understand design.

This level of elegance is impossible in other media. A good screenwriter can write a line that creates three or four experiences on different viewings, but a good game designer can create a mechanic that generates thousands or even millions of experiences, just as the rules of checkers have generated millions of different games. Games can create these massive numbers of possibilities through the process of *emergence.*

EMERGENCE is when simple mechanics interact to create complex situations.

Imagine describing a game you played last night to a friend: "It was awesome! I was in the back of a jeep on the mounted minigun. My friend was driving. We sped toward the enemy base, crested the hill, and flew through the air for at least five seconds! I gunned down three bad guys while we were midair. Then we got hit by a rocket—but we didn't fall out! We did a full flip without touching the ground, and I never stopped firing, even upside down. We landed upright, my friend ran over the guy with the rocket launcher, and we captured the flag. I'll never forget it."

This is a multiplayer match of *Halo: Combat Evolved*. But this experience is not written on *Halo*'s disc, and it will never be repeated exactly the same way. It emerged on the fly from the interaction of simple mechanics like physics, gravity, weapon tuning, map layout, and split-screen multiplayer. *Halo* is beautifully designed not because it contains this experience, but because it contains game mechanics that regularly generate experiences of this level of intensity. And it will keep generating new ones—forever. That's the power of emergence.

Leveraging emergence means crafting mechanics that don't just add together, but multiply into a rich universe of possibility.

A shooting mechanic can exist alone. For example, imagine a game in which you time shots from an unmoving cannon to hit enemy planes as they fly past. This game has only one control: a fire button. And it produces a few types of simple experiences. You shoot and miss, or you shoot and hit.

A looking mechanic can also exist alone. Imagine a roller-coaster simulator in which your only interaction is looking around. Again, you have one control: a joystick for the camera. And again, there isn't much breadth of experience. Once you've looked in every direction on every roller-coaster ride, there's nothing left to do.

Now imagine combining these mechanics in one game. You can ride the roller coaster, look in any direction, and shoot at planes flying past. This combination doesn't just add up the experiences of looking and shooting. It multiplies them into a combinatorial explosion of new emergent possibilities. We can create aiming challenges where there were none before. Players have to trade off targeting one enemy over targeting another. The player might even have to learn situational awareness to know where to look for targets off-screen. This simple look–shoot combination is so elegant that it drives countless games, from *The House of the Dead* to *Space Invaders.*

Now imagine adding a movement mechanic. The player can run around an environment, looking and shooting in any direction. The number of possibilities multiplies again. Now the player can move around to dodge attacks, rush forward to attack, or explore a space to learn about its story. Games designed around this simple combination of shoot, look, and move earn billions of dollars every year. They vary tremendously in their fiction and emphasis: in one, you're a space marine blasting aliens; in another you're exploring a somber underwater city. But all these games share the same elegant core: shoot, look, and move.

And those millions of different play experiences come at a remarkably low cost. The designers need only implement a few mechanics. The players need only learn a few controls. Once that's done, a million variations of triumph, sorrow, tension, and joy will emerge.

Elegance happens when mechanics interact in complex, nonobvious ways. But this same complexity and nonobviousness makes elegant design very difficult to achieve.

Elegance requires that different mechanics interact. For example, the look, shoot, move combination works well because the player uses all of these controls at once. Since the mechanics all work together, they can multiply into many different possibilities. But this tight interaction between mechanics also makes it hard to solve design problems because changes in one mechanic also affect all the others.

In an inelegant game, isolated problems are easy to fix. If the wizard's goblin-killer rod is too powerful when used against goblins, the designer can just reduce its power. Since the rod has no effect on anything besides goblins, this change has no side effects and the problem is solved.

But this easy solution is only possible because the design is so inelegant. Why can't you use the rod against orcs, ogres, other wizards, the gods, or stingy shopkeepers? A wizard's rod implies a universe of possibilities in a fantasy world. Limiting it to goblins loses most of them.

A more elegant game would allow all of these interactions, creating many more play situations without much more learning burden. But this creates a challenge for the designer. Now that the wizard's rod is connected to so many other parts of the game, changing it changes all those relationships. Powering it down might balance it against goblins but make it too weak against orcs. Giving it an area of effect explosion may create exciting field combat but make the rod too dangerous to use near allies. These kinds of problems can get very thorny as the number of relationships increases into the hundreds or thousands.

This is why simple, elegant games are so uncommon. Crafting a system of relationships is much harder than authoring a series of one-off gimmicks, but it's the only way to get a lifetime of play experiences from a handful of game mechanics.

I Love the Smell of Elegance in the Morning

When I was in university, one of my first-year math courses involved a lot of work with grids of numbers called *matrices*. One property of matrices is that some can be inverted—transformed into a new form through a series of numerical operations—while others cannot. The trouble was that there is no easy set of steps that could determine whether a matrix was invertible or not. You just had to try it and find out, and that took a lot of time.

But my professor taught us another way. He said that one could learn to "smell" invertible matrices just by looking at them. You wouldn't know exactly how you knew, but with training, your unconscious could tell you the answer.

Sensing elegant mechanics is much the same. A designer can't predict every outcome that an elegant game will create. They are too numerous and too fuzzy. We can implement the mechanic and test it heavily, but this can take a lot of time. We need ways to spot elegance on the drawing board. And the only real way to do that is to smell elegance the same way my professor smelled invertible matrices: by using trained intuition and mental heuristics.

Smelling elegance is a skill that comes with experience. But I've found that there are some simple rules of thumb that can help.

Mechanics that interact with many other mechanics smell like elegance.

Do a quick mental count of the number of interactions expected from a proposed mechanic. If it interacts with many other mechanics, it's more likely to be an elegant design. If it interacts with just one or two, it's probably not.

For example, when considering a spell in a fantasy RPG (role-playing game), ask: can it interact with other spells? How about with party members, with multiple adversaries, with the environment, the morality system, the narrative, or the player's stats?

Mechanics can even interact with themselves. For example, pawns in chess can be arranged in many different structures to claim various parts of the board.

Simple mechanics smell like elegance.

Elegance is as much about reducing the cost of a mechanic as it is about increasing the benefit. A bloated, overly complex mechanic might create good results, but it's often not worth the learning burden it puts on players. Simplifying it might mean losing a few nuances in play, but it also opens up mindspace for other, more efficient designs.

Furthermore, reducing the complexity players are exposed to increases their appreciation of what's left. Players who aren't overburdened will fully explore a game and enjoy every morsel of experience. Those buried in complexity will miss much of what the game has to offer.

The most elegant-smelling mechanics are so stupidly simple that they seem downright obvious after you hear them. So try to find designs that you can write on a cocktail napkin.

Mechanics that can be used in multiple ways smell like elegance.

A tool that can be used creatively, offensively, defensively, tactically, and strategically is more elegant than one that only fills a single role. Not only does it interact in many ways, but it also creates new choices and relationships by coupling these different roles together.

For example, in most shooter games, guns are purely offensive weapons. Players defend themselves with movement and cover, while using guns to defeat enemies. The *Resident Evil* series of zombie survival horror games handles this differently. In *Resident Evil*, the player cannot move while shooting, and gunshots cause oncoming zombies to stop in place for several seconds. In this game, guns are both offensive and defensive tools, and players often fire on zombies with no intention of killing them, just to slow their approach. Tying offense and defense to the same tool means players must trade off their offensive and defensive needs. Will you slow down the zombie shambling toward you, or headshot the valuable target in the distance?

These sorts of multirole trade-offs are everywhere. One unit in a strategy game might be usable for attack, defense, and scouting. The turning mechanic in racing games might be used to negotiate corners and block other drivers. And in some stealth games, the player can throw objects to knock guards out or make noise to draw their attention.

Mechanics that don't overlap one another's roles smell like elegance.

A *role* is a way in which a mechanic can be used. For example, a strategy game unit may be a harasser, a scout, a disabler, or a deceiver. In a building game, a tool might be an excavator, a constructor, or a decorator. A fighting game attack might be a punch, a block, a block breaker, or ranged harassment. Each one of these tools has a purpose that can't be fulfilled by the others.

When these roles overlap, the game loses elegance because you're paying the cost for two mechanics to do the work of one.

For example, if a strategy game provides one kind of scouting unit, there is no benefit in adding another unless it fulfills a different role than the first. The second kind of scout must drive some set of new and meaningful play experiences that can't happen with the first. If it doesn't, it's dead weight in the design.

The most elegant mechanics are so distinct in their role that they open up completely new kinds of play. Don't create variations on existing interactions. Instead, seek mechanics that introduce new strategies or avenues of exploration that didn't exist in any form before.

Mechanics that reuse established conventions and interfaces smell like elegance because they leverage knowledge that players already have.

We can ease comprehension burden by using symbols and conventions players already know. These conventions can come from anywhere: other systems in the game, other games, real life, or cultural archetypes. As long as players already know them, we can benefit by using them.

If a game fits the conventions of a genre, use the genre-standard control scheme. In a game without nuanced fiction, give the villain a pointy moustache and let him twirl it so that everyone knows immediately who he is. Include nothing unique without good reason, because unique things take extra effort to understand.

Everyone wants to break ground and express creativity. But creating new conventions doesn't just cost the designer—it also costs players. If we're going to do it, we have to make sure we're doing it where it's worth the price, not arbitrarily changing a perfectly good convention for no reason. Real originality does not come from changing the surface details. It comes from changing the fundamentals.

Even very original designs are often combinations of preexisting ideas, so even an original game can benefit greatly by using commonly understood symbols and interfaces to communicate its unique content.

Mechanics that work on a similar scale as existing mechanics smell like elegance.

Consider a game where the player alternates between controlling an action hero on foot and piloting a fighter jet. This variation may be refreshing, but it comes at a price because it splits the game into two clusters of mechanics with little interaction between them.

When the hero is on the ground, it matters where enemy soldiers run. An enemy who runs 10 feet to the left may be vulnerable in the open, while one who runs 10 feet to the right may be hidden behind a wall. But in the jet, such on-foot movement is meaningless. A 1,000-pound bomb will kill a soldier whether he runs left, runs right, or hides behind a crate. Walls and buildings don't matter since they all get flattened by the explosion.

This means that when the player is in the jet, the soldier's on-foot movement is meaningless. All the effort the designers put into implementing it and all the mindspace the player devoted to understanding it is worthless. The costs have been paid, but the benefits are not being returned.

The scale gap between the jet and on-foot sections is so large that the game is essentially two separate games in one box. You can switch back and forth between the two modes, but they never come together into an integrated system. When the player is in one mode, all the complexity in the other mode is wasted because the scales are so different. That's inelegant.

Magic: The Gathering is a perfect example of a game that maximizes elegance by matching the scales of different game systems. Players hold seven cards. They start with 20 life. Usually they can use between three and 10 mana per turn. They generally have 2 to 12 creature, artifact, and enchantment cards in play. Creatures usually have power and toughness ratings of between one and eight. Games last 10 to 30 turns. This close scaling between card numbers, life, creature counts, creature power and toughness, turn counts, and mana allows a tremendous number of natural interactions without any fiddly math. And there are cards in *Magic* that convert in almost all directions between all of these measures. Players can convert mana to life, creatures to land, and artifacts to damage. They can take damage or sacrifice creatures every turn in exchange for other abilities. They can sacrifice life to pump up creatures' toughness, combine creatures and enchantments, and discard cards from their hands to restore creatures killed in battle. Thousands of such interactions can bloom from a handful of simple systems.

If *Magic*'s designer Richard Garfield had decided to measure player life out of 1,000, made creature toughness range from 25 to 50, and let players have no more than 3 land cards at a time, these relationships would be broken. Conversions between numbers would require tedious math and messy rounding, and the elegance of *Magic* would be shattered.

Scaling elegance applies to almost any type of relationship between measurable quantities. Sizes, speeds, surface areas, health points, distances, money, energy, communications links, resources, time, and the number of players or characters are all candidates for elegance through scale matching.

Mechanics that are reused a lot smell like elegance.

One of the paradoxical aspects of good games is how repetitive they seem. Players use the same tools over and over. They build more cities, defeat more orcs, and decorate more houses, again and again.

But just because the player is reusing the same tool doesn't mean he's having the same experience. He may be building cities again and again, but every city is a new emergent expression of the mechanics and the player's decisions. The mechanics stay the same, but the experience changes every time.

Furthermore, that repetition of mechanics is essential to elegant design. A mechanic that is only used once is a gimmick. It might be worthwhile, but it can't be elegant because there's always a one-to-one relationship between cost and payoff. A mechanic that's used 100,000 times can potentially be very elegant, if it can generate new experiences every time. The repetition doesn't guarantee elegance, but without it elegance is impossible.

This is one of the easiest elegance smells to notice. It's hard to tell how nuanced the interactions between a mechanic and its neighbors will be. But it's typically easy to tell how often a mechanic will be repeated. And there are many, many design ideas which sound great when they're imagined once, but obviously sour after the thousandth time. Look for those mechanics that will stand up when worked to the bone. Find the million-repetition mechanics.

Mechanics that don't impose restrictions on content smell like elegance.

Imagine a science fiction detective game in which the hero finds clues, solves cases, and occasionally chases bad guys. To improve the action sequences, someone proposes that the protagonist wear rocket boots that let him jump 20 feet into the air. One prototype later, and designers find the action sequences are immediately improved. The rocket boots are quickly written into the official design and everyone cheers.

These designers might be celebrating too early. While they did make the game better in the short term, they also created a huge hidden cost and may have harmed their game in the end.

Now that the jump height is 20 feet, every level in the game must change to support that jump height. There cannot be any place where the player can get somewhere he shouldn't by jumping. So level designers have to find ways to block the player from entering a thousand wrong places. They have to contort the fiction to prevent the player jumping over buses and park walls. The suburban bungalow map has to be cut because there is no way to stop players jumping over the roof. Designers end up adding piles of crates, invisible walls, or misplaced billboards just to stop players escaping the play area. All of this means that the game gets a bit more nonsensical, the fictional backdrop thinner, and the levels slightly worse as designers spend time trying to contain high-jumping players instead of making the game better.

The 20-foot jump created a *content restriction*. It required that all the levels be built in such a way that the player could not break the game by jumping 20 feet. It doesn't sound like a big deal, but in reality it's a huge cost for level designers. It becomes a wet blanket that slows and distorts everything they do.

This mistake is endemic because the benefits are obvious while the costs are hidden. A new design that creates content restrictions can create an immediate, visceral design benefit. It feels good in prototype, tests well, and makes people look good. The benefits are concentrated and immediate, while the costs are spread over years and imposed chiefly on others. But although each restriction enables some narrow short-term benefit, the combined weight of too many of them can smother a game.

There are a thousand kinds of content restrictions. Jump distances, room heights, character counts, resource amounts, dialogue lengths, inventory sizes, and vehicle sizes can all be restricted by design decisions. Sometimes, as with a 20-foot jump, the restriction grows from implications of the design. Other times, as in the case of character counts, it's about keeping the game running at a playable frame rate.

More elegant mechanics can improve a game without creating such hidden costs. Seek out those designs that work with existing content, and keep in mind that the cost of content restrictions is well concealed and usually greater than anticipated. Even a great mechanic might not be worth it if it forces the rest of the game to twist to accommodate it.

Mechanics that use the full expressiveness of the available interface smell like elegance.

If the game's interface is an analog joystick, it can sense the exact angle of the stick, not just the direction. On an analog trigger, a game can sense quarter, half, and three-quarter pulls. Even if the interface is just a button, the game can do something the moment it is released or while it is held instead of only when it is pressed.

The danger in this is that you may frustrate players with oversensitive inputs. Such expressive controls work well when the whole spectrum of input is useful to skilled players, but most of it can be safely ignored by novices. For example, anyone can play a driving game reasonably well by ramming the wheel all the way left and right, ignoring most of its expressiveness, but only an expert can use every degree of turn to optimize his performance.

This idea extends to board and card games as well. How many things can you do with physical cards, dice, or tokens?

Elegance Case Study: Predator versus Hellion

StarCraft II: Wings of Liberty has two units on the Terran race with very similar roles. The Predator and Hellion are both fast, mid-cost units that specialize in fighting groups of small enemies by using area-of-effect attacks.

But only the Hellion unit was included in the multiplayer game. This was a good decision on the designers' part, because although the Predator and Hellion units fill the same basic role, tiny differences between them make the Hellion a much more elegant design. Let's look at why.

First, some stats:

	Predator	Hellion
Speed	4	4.25
Hitpoints	140	90
Attack	Strikes enemies with its front paws for 15 damage, and causes a shockwave that does 20 damage to all units surrounding the Predator at close range.	Fires a stream of flame that does 8 damage to all units in a line projecting out from the Hellion to medium range. Does +6 extra damage to Light units, increasing by another +5 with the Infernal Pre-Igniter upgrade.
Delay between attacks	1 second	2.5 seconds

It's immediately clear that these two units are very similar. They are both about twice as fast as a soldier on foot. They have similar health reserves, and they both damage enemies in an area. The main difference is in the geometry of their attacks. Both do area-of-effect damage, but the Predator does damage in a circle around itself, while the Hellion does damage in a long, narrow stream. And that turns out to be a huge difference.

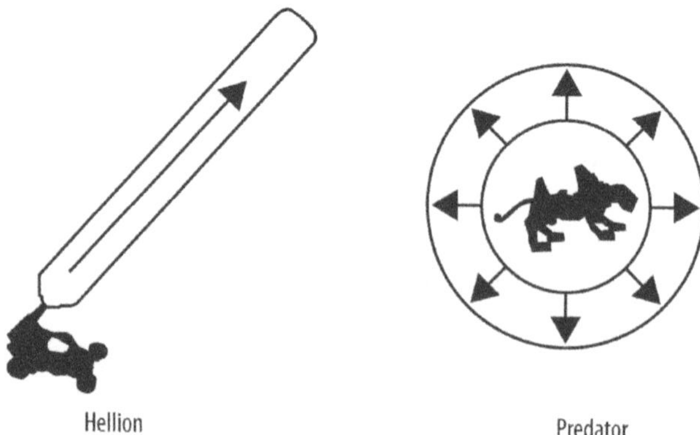
Hellion
Predator

There are a few different ways to use the Predator. The best case is to be surrounded by enemies, so the damage ring hits all of them. But this rarely happens, since the other player can simply refuse to attack. The Predator can also attack massed groups of enemies, but it won't hit with most of its circular shockwave. Finally, the Predator can run into a group of enemy workers and try to catch them in its damage ring. Beyond that, there aren't very many more ways to use this unit. Its short range means that it can't hide behind cover or shoot up ledges, and there are few good synergies between it and other friendly units. Predator fights tend to play out in the same few ways every time.

The Hellion is very different. The stream shape of its attack means that its effectiveness varies dramatically depending on the geometry of the environment and the enemies present. If many small enemies line up, the flame stream hits all of them for massive damage. If they surround the Hellion, its flame hits just one and is almost useless.

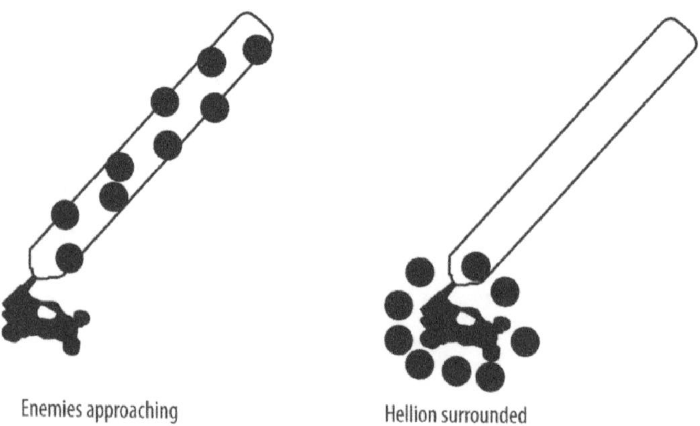
Enemies approaching
Hellion surrounded

That simple difference creates an entire class of nuanced play experiences as the Hellion tries to run around and line up shots, and its opponents try to close in and surround it.

The Hellion also synergizes well with the environment and other friendly units. Since its attack is ranged, the player can put the Hellion behind a wall to act as a guard, or behind other units to support them against groups of small enemies. It can also shoot down at enemies from a ledge.

Finally, the Hellion attacks much less frequently than the Predator. There is enough time to move the Hellion between each shot. This permits advanced "shoot and scoot" tactics where players shoot, move the Hellion, and shoot again, trying to avoid damage while lining up enemies for each flame blast. In contrast, the Predator attacks so frequently that such tactics are impossible. You have to just throw it into battle and watch, hoping it wins. Its predictability suffocates any chance at moment-to-moment tension or skill development.

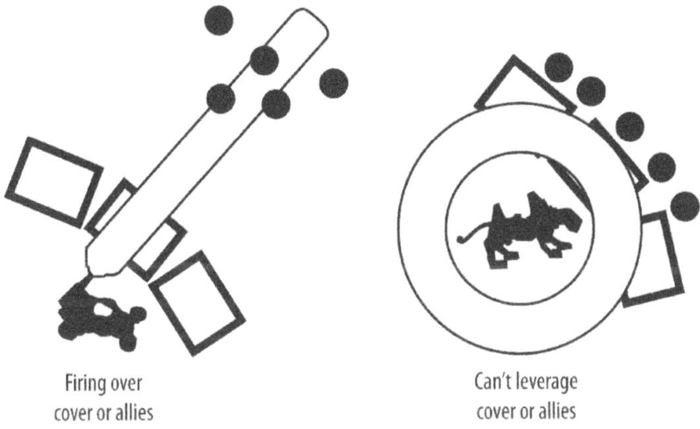

Mechanically, the Hellion is no more complex than the Predator. It's just as easy to implement and just as easy for players to understand. But it's more elegant because it generates so many more challenges, tactics, and situations than the Predator.

The superiority of the Hellion isn't obvious. The difference between the two is very small: a few seconds in attack timing, a different damage shape. If anything, the Predator appears more interesting on the surface, while the Hellion is prosaic, uncreative, even a little boring. But that's what elegance looks like, and why it's hard to spot early. Because elegance doesn't come from flashy gimmicks or exciting design pitches. It comes from the opposite of these things: simple, workmanlike designs that flower into a million experiences.

When we describe the most elegant game systems ever created, they might sound stupidly straightforward, even dull. But the form of the design itself doesn't matter. What matters is the depth and richness of the possibility space that emerges during play.

3

Skill

O, victory! Thy favor bought
With screams of pain and endless thought
Yet without battles so hard-fought
'Tis a hollow prize, all for naught

CHALLENGE CAN CREATE THE suspense of competition and the thrill of victory. It can generate fascinating strategic decisions to engross the mind and teach fascinating lessons. And it can create the social experiences of defeating or helping others.

But any game that uses challenge—and most do—must deal with the issue of player skill. A challenge that is too hard for a player is frustrating. One that is too easy is boring. Good, flow-sparking experiences live in the Goldilocks zone between these extremes.

The catch is that the Goldilocks zone is different for every player. A rotating crib mobile is fascinating to a baby but pointless to an adult. A hyper-competitive tournament game like *StarCraft* is engaging to professional players but intimidating to the rest of us.

Dealing with skill means understanding the lower limit of skill below which a game becomes frustrating, and the upper limit beyond which it becomes dull. It means determining whether and how to expand those limits to include more players. And it means knowing how to create meaningful skill tests with real failure in the balance, without that failure destroying the experience when it actually happens. These topics are the subject of this chapter.

Depth

DEEP games create meaningful play at high skill levels.

The idea of depth describes how much there is to learn about a game. A deep game has enough nuance and variation to provide new lessons for a long time. Chess, football, poker, and *StarCraft* are all deep games because players can study them for decades without ever running out of new lessons to learn.

The opposite of this is a shallow game. For example, tic-tac-toe is shallow because once you know the trick, there is nothing else to discover. The game is only interesting to small children who don't yet fully understand it. To an adult who knows how to end every game in a draw, it's pure tedium.

Ironically, players will try their hardest to solve a game, but they will hate the designer if they ever succeed. Players cherish the experience of breaking through skill barriers, of being able to do today what they couldn't do yesterday. A solved game is worthless to players because it provides nothing to learn, no uncertainty, no victory, no defeat. It becomes an exercise in following a set of well-defined steps toward a guaranteed outcome. Skill games are only worthwhile to people who don't fully understand them.

A game's SKILL CEILING is the level of skill beyond which there is no way to improve performance. If this skill level is beyond the abilities of human beings, the game is LIMITLESSLY DEEP and can never be fully solved by anyone.

One quick way to measure depth is by considering the performance difference between a player who is theoretically perfect and a player who is as skilled as is humanly possible. If their performance is the same, the game has a skill ceiling that players will eventually reach. If the theoretically perfect player is better than any human, the game is limitlessly deep and players will never run out of things to learn.

For example, chess can be played better by a combined human–computer team than it can by a human grandmaster. This means that even after lifetimes of practice, these grandmasters are not playing perfectly. They have not yet reached chess's skill ceiling, so the game is probably limitlessly deep.

The *Modern Warfare* multiplayer shooters have an extremely high skill ceiling. Controls are precise, weapons are deadly, and action is fast. In other multiplayer shooters, it takes several seconds to kill an enemy even if you never miss a shot. This puts an upper limit on how effective a player can be regardless of skill. In *Modern Warfare*, it is possible, with excellent tactics and aim, to eliminate entire teams in seconds. This perfect performance is unattainable for humans, but it's theoretically possible, so players can always enjoy the experience of striving toward it.

The combat system in *Assassin's Creed II* has a medium skill ceiling. A perfect player could do significantly better than a normal player, but would not be so astronomically beyond the normal player as he would be in the *Modern Warfare* games. This is because the combat system in *Assassin's Creed II* has delays in its controls. Attack animations are often a second or two long, during which the player can't take any action. These short delays reduce the skill ceiling because they give time for a normal player to mentally catch up with the perfect player. Even with perfect swordplay, for example, it would take at least 20 seconds or so to kill 10 enemies, since the animations to kill enemies take about two seconds. A normal player can achieve this level of performance with practice. But once he does, there is nowhere to go. Even if the player can think faster, the animation delays prevent increases in performance. So the skill aspect of the game becomes dull.

Tic-tac-toe and other trivial games have low skill ceilings. In these shallow games, it is easy to execute perfect play once you know a few simple tricks. There is no difference between a perfect player and a decent human player. Again, the game becomes dull once it's fully understood.

Not every game needs to be limitlessly deep. *Assassin's Creed II* has a moderate skill ceiling but is still an excellent game because it's not just a skill game. It's also about art, exploration, and narrative. Its designers decided that beauty and accessibility were more important than pure depth.

Accessibility

ACCESSIBLE games create meaningful play at low skill levels. A game's SKILL BARRIER is the lower limit of skill below which it is unplayable.

Whereas depth is about the maximum skill level at which a game stays interesting, accessibility is about the minimum at which it becomes playable. Almost all games and toys have some lower skill limit below which meaningful play is impossible.

Consider a first-person shooter (FPS). Until the player knows how to move, turn, and shoot, FPS games are unplayable. For players totally new to the genre, this is an intimidating barrier to entry. It takes hours of practice to learn the abstract relationships between screen movements and controller inputs. This barrier makes FPS games inaccessible for most people.

Almost all games have skill barriers if we look low enough. PC strategy games require players to be able to use a mouse and keyboard. Many board and video games require that players know how to read, which makes them unplayable for young children. A baby who can't hold onto objects can't play *Jenga*.

Accessibility is often undervalued by game designers because we are so skilled that we don't notice games' skill barriers. But there is a huge community of potential players out there who would love to play if they only could. It's worth doing the work to bring more of them into the fold.

Skill Range

A game's SKILL RANGE is the range of skill levels at which a game presents a meaningful challenge.

A wide skill range means the game can be enjoyed by novices and experts alike. It is easy to learn and hard to master. Conversely, a narrow skill range indicates a game that is quickly mastered once it is learned. You either know how to play it completely, or you don't know how to play it at all.

We can graph out skill ranges like this:

Doom
BioShock
Dwarf Fortress
Counter-Strike public matches in 2010
Counter-Strike public matches in 2000
StarCraft II multiplayer
StarCraft II single player
Baby mobile
tic tac toe
chess, poker

Baby
5-year old, no practice
10-year old, no practice
No game practice
Played games
Played many games
Practices games
Practices this game
Competitive in this game
Known limits of human ability
Beyond known human ability

Tic-tac-toe is playable even for small children, but it becomes boring as soon as you learn the one good strategy. So its skill range is narrow, and wholly contained on the left side of the graph.

StarCraft II's single-player mode is accessible by anyone who has played video games because it starts with a gentle tutorial and ramps up slowly. Its skill range is quite wide, but it is not limitlessly deep—scripted missions mean that the game can be mastered by dedicated players, after which it stops offering new challenges.

StarCraft II's multiplayer mode, on the other hand, is limitlessly deep. No matter how much you practice, there is always more to learn. But it is also less accessible than single-player mode because lessons aren't arranged in a gentle skill ramp, and online opponents mercilessly exploit every mistake.

Sometimes games' skill ranges change with their player base. For example, I was a beast at *Counter-Strike* when I first played back in 2000. Today, I struggle just to avoid embarrassing myself. The game is essentially the same, but its player base isn't. Back in 2000, most people online were new to shooters, while I wasn't. Today, most *Counter-Strike* players have practiced for years, while I haven't.

Games don't have to have wide skill ranges to be good. *BioShock*, for example, only provides a meaningful challenge across a fairly small band of players. But the experience still works because *BioShock* is only 10 hours long, and it creates most of its meaning through art and narrative. It's not intended to provide years of learning through struggle.

Making a game that is either deep or accessible is tough enough. Making a game that is both deep and accessible and so has a wide skill range is one of a designer's greatest tests.

SKILL WITHOUT EXPLICIT GOALS

Some games don't have explicit goals. Games such as *Dwarf Fortress*, *The Sims*, and *Minecraft* let players freely explore or build or interact without any official winning or losing conditions. It might seem as though these toylike games can ignore the issue of skill. But even toys have skill ranges because they require some minimum skill level before players can interact with them meaningfully.

For example, *The Sims* is more toy than game because there are no predefined goals. Players raise a simulated family in whatever way they like. But to play the game at all, one must be able to read, use a mouse, and understand the interface of windows and buttons. And to experience the meaning of *The Sims*, players must have a cultural understanding of Western-style living. They have to know what a bedroom, telephone, house party, and extramarital affair are. Without this baseline knowledge, they can't interpret the meaning of in-game events.

Beyond basic interaction and comprehension, there is another reason toys have skill ranges. Most toys don't remain toys for long. Given a toy, most people will almost immediately set themselves a goal within it. A child with blocks will try to stack them higher. One with a ball will try to throw it farther. The same applies to software toys. In *The Sims*, a player might decide to try to make the most money possible. When this happens, he is no longer playing *The Sims*. He is playing *The Sims: Make as Much Money as Possible*, a skill game of his own design. If that newly invented game is trivially shallow, the design has failed. This is why even goal-less toys benefit from expressing interesting, nonobvious properties which can be learned. Even toys can be deep.

Stretching Skill Range

The best way to extend a game's skill range is to design systems that are simple and elegant. By squeezing every bit of depth out of each game mechanic, we deliver a lightweight package that is easy to learn but hard to master. This is a key reason why it's worth the effort to create an elegant design.

Aside from just making an elegant game, though, there are many other ways skill ranges can be stretched and shifted. Let's look at a few.

REINVENTION

My first multiplayer shooter addiction was 1999's *Unreal Tournament*. The marketing showed me a game about a futuristic blood tournament in which competitors shredded one another with weapons that looked like pieces of construction equipment. The characters were badass and the explosions were colossal. I loved it.

After a week of play, though, something changed. I stopped caring about the badass characters, and stopped seeing the explosions. My mind had begun to strip away the fiction layer to show me the naked mechanics under the surface. And in those mechanics I found my challenge: aiming. Holding the crosshairs on a target consumed all my mental effort.

After much practice, though, I learned to aim by muscle memory, freeing up my conscious mind to work on something else. In a shallower game, there would have been nothing else to work on. I would have reached the game's skill ceiling and soon lost interest. But *Unreal Tournament* reinvented itself again, and presented a new challenge: controlling the map to hold onto the best items and sniping locations. So I developed a mental library of map knowledge. I figured out how to control the power spots and maintain a tactical advantage. The colossal explosions were just visual noise now; the fiction barely registered anymore.

I kept playing. Over time, I learned to dominate the good positions without conscious effort. Again, my conscious mind was freed up. And again, the game reinvented itself and revealed the next layer of challenge: tracking other players. Instead of just knowing the best spots in the map, I now had to maintain a real-time mental map of where other players were and where they were going. When I damaged an enemy, I knew he would go for health. If we engaged at long range, I knew he would grab the sniper rifle. In each case, I moved to set a trap for him. If I anticipated correctly, he would walk right into my crosshairs.

Eventually, I got good at predicting movements. Map knowledge was easy, and aiming challenges were a nonissue. But *Unreal Tournament* wasn't done. It reinvented itself again, into its final, consummate form: a pokerlike game of psychological trickery. I knew what my options were, and what my opponent's options were, and how each of these options interacted. He knew all of this, too, and I knew that he knew, and he knew that I knew. When both players have a crystal-clear map of the mechanical game in their heads and the understanding to make near-perfect choices, the only thing left to manipulate is the mind itself. So *Unreal Tournament* became about provoking emotional outbursts, mixing up strategies to remain unpredictable, reading the opponent's mind better than he can read yours. It became about wrapping your mind around his and destroying him.

I never mastered that final reinvention because it is limitlessly deep.

Games broaden their skill range by repeatedly REINVENTING themselves as the player's skill increases.

No game can stretch one simple skill out long enough to have a broad skill range. There is only so much time one can spend on aiming, moving, or learning economic strategies or map quirks. Deep games like *Unreal Tournament* sustain themselves by wrapping games inside games inside games. Each time one is mastered, a deeper layer of play presents itself.

We can graph those reinventions out on a skill range chart. Just above its skill barrier, *Unreal Tournament* is a game about fiction. As players climb the skill range, it shifts again and again until it becomes a psychological poker game.

Games tend to go through three characteristic reinventions along their skill range: the MANUAL, the SITUATIONAL, and the MENTAL.

At the *manual* reinvention, the challenge is about simple, moment-to-moment mechanical skills. In a shooter, it is about drawing a bead on a target and holding it there. In *Tetris*, it is about getting pieces to fall where you want them in the rotation where you want them. In a strategy game, it is just about getting the units you want to do the thing you want them to do. In chess, it is learning how each piece can move. The manual reinvention is about mastering the interface. All games start here.

The *situational* reinvention is the second level of skill development. At this level, manual skills are mostly unconscious. In a fighting game, the player can execute multibutton combo-strikes at will. He can aim and hit targets, or make his units move as he wants them to. The challenge at this level is not just knowing how to shoot, it is knowing who to shoot and when, or knowing what units to send and where. This is the level where most players are, and where most games are designed to function. It comprises situational awareness, reading patterns, knowing counterstrategies, and many other midlevel game skills. This level is very broad; it can split into many internal reinventions. In my *Unreal Tournament* experience, both the map control and tracking reinventions were situational.

The mental level of skill development is not reached often, and only by expert, competitive, committed players. *Mental* skills are all about maintaining concentration and performance. At high levels of play, an emotional upset or a momentary distraction can lead to defeat. At these heights of ability, there are tactics that are specifically about deliberately frustrating and distracting an opponent, to try to disturb his concentration. Mental skill is all about predicting and manipulating his mind better than he can predict and manipulate yours. This is the pokerlike end state of most limitlessly deep games, and it is the reason most limitless games are multiplayer—because a person can learn nearly any game system, but he can never fully understand another human mind.

ELASTIC CHALLENGES

Imagine a version of darts where the target is just an inch-wide bull's-eye. Hitting the bull's-eye gives one point, and missing it gives zero points. Such a game is so hard as to be almost pointless for anyone but experts. A designer could change the size of the bull's-eye, but the disk will always be too small or too large for most players.

Real darts solves this problem by wrapping concentric rings around the bull's-eye, each of which gives a different number of points. Most people can hit the biggest ring and get a few points, but only the best can hit the bull's-eye, so everyone has some challenging but achievable goal. This is an *elastic challenge.*

ELASTIC CHALLENGES permit different degrees of success and failure to provide appropriate challenges to players across a wider skill range.

A pass/fail design only serves players who are just barely good enough to pass the challenge. If they are too skilled, there is no challenge. If they are not skilled enough, they inevitably fail. So pass/fail games only work for players in a very narrow skill range.

Elastic challenges solve this problem by presenting multiple levels of success or failure. By allowing different degrees of success, they support a wider skill range since everyone has an attainable but challenging goal.

For example, classic arcade games usually present elastic challenges using granular scoring systems. Anyone who puts a quarter in gets a few thousand points just by pushing buttons. But with enough skill and persistence, players can rack up hundreds of millions of points. So no matter how many times they play (and how many quarters they put in), there is always a way to do a little better.

Variable scoring systems as in darts and arcade games are a common form of elastic challenge, but there are others.

For example, in the *Hitman* games the goal of each mission is to assassinate a target and escape. The twist is that players are rated based on how cleanly they kill the target. Just killing the target is easy—all you have to do is hose down the level with machine gun fire and kill everyone. But to get the coveted Silent Assassin rating, the player must use a combination of gadgets, disguises, stealth, and accurate shooting to kill the target without any witnesses or unnecessary violence. And there is a whole spectrum of ratings leading up to Silent Assassin. A player who leaves dead guards around to be discovered, but is never seen himself, does better than the wild bullet-sprayer but not as well as the perfect infiltrator who is never detected at all.

Had *Hitman* just been about killing the target, it would have been a generic shooter. Had it required perfectly clean kills for success, it would have been impossibly hard for most players. Elastic challenges allowed the designers to get the best of both worlds by recognizing and rewarding every degree of stealth and cleverness that players can express.

Just as we can present different degrees of success, we can also present multiple degrees of failure.

For example, if a player doesn't make the jump across a gap, we can let his character grab the edge and slowly pull himself up. His progress is slowed, but the game goes on.

In another game, instead of having a player's AI ally die when attacked, he can become incapacitated. This way, the player can revive him and continue play at some cost of time and resources.

The spectrum of success and failure can stretch elastically far above average performance, and far below, without the game having to end and declare victory or defeat at any point. Every additional amount of headroom and legroom we put in the elastic spectrum of a game means another group of players won't be subjected to a frustrating failure or a boring skill ceiling.

TRAINING

Training systems help players get past the skill barrier quicker. Tutorials, text messages, audio instructions, and hints embedded in the game world all serve this purpose.

But there's danger in training. Some poorly designed training systems bombard the player with instructions, pulling his mind out of the game. Others act like overprotective parents, telling the player exactly what to do at every point, leaving him feeling controlled and impotent. All of this interferes with the rest of the experience.

Good training is invisible.

The best training teaches without the player ever noticing. There are several ways to achieve this.

Some games thread training into the narrative. For example, in *Call of Duty 4* the player inhabits a soldier being newly inducted into an elite unit. As he runs the unit's obstacle course, the commander shouts instructions on how to surmount each challenge. The course is a tutorial dressed up as a story sequence, and it works on both levels.

We can turn training sequences into elastic challenges. That training sequence in *Call of Duty 4* isn't just for training—it's also a time trial. Players get more points when they run it faster. So while a novice might slowly pick his way through the course, an expert will ignore the training aspect entirely and treat the course as a skill challenge. The novice gets the lessons he needs, while the expert gets the challenge he craves.

But the best way to make training less intrusive is to skip it when it's unnecessary. The trick is determining whether the player needs a lesson or not. Some games let players skip training sequences voluntarily. Others test players to determine which training to provide. Some games even train adaptively—instead of teaching everything in linear order, they detect when the player lacks a piece of knowledge and provide the lesson on the spot. Regardless of method, though, the principle is the same: the most invisible training is the unnecessary training that never happens.

EMOTIONAL LIFE SUPPORT

Even with good training, many players will spend the earliest parts of the game below the game's skill barrier. For them, those first few minutes or hours become a chore to finish before the real game starts. Many will give up and never experience the game as intended.

To stop a player from giving up before they surmount the skill barrier, we can keep their experience on life support using emotional triggers that don't require skill.

When the player knows nothing, we can't build an experience around solving puzzles, creating things, or defeating enemies because the player doesn't have the skill to do these things. But there are other emotional triggers which work regardless of skill. We can show the player sublime art. We can introduce fascinating characters. We can let the player joke with buddies. We can play music or do a tech demo. If we flood the early experience with these low-skill emotional triggers, we can transform the early learning stages from a painful chore into something like a semi-interactive intro movie.

For example, board games do this naturally because they're played in groups. When you're sitting around a table with friends, every mistake or misplaced token becomes an occasion for friendly ribbing. A single-player board game would be much less pleasant to learn because that early period would resemble a library study session instead of a party.

A great video game example of early emotional life support is *BioShock*. The game begins with a title card: "Mid-Atlantic, 1960." The screen fades to the first-person view of the player character sitting in an airplane seat. After a few words, the screen goes black, and we hear a plane crash. Eyes open up, and we're underwater. The hero struggles to the surface, gasping for breath, and ends up floating in the ocean, surrounded by burning airplane parts. In the distance, he sees a ghostly lighthouse with an angel statue on the top.

The game has hooked the player's interest. Who am I? How am I going to get out of the water? What is that lighthouse doing in the mid-Atlantic, and why the exotic decoration? And since this whole sequence was noninteractive, it required no skill whatsoever.

Now the player gains control. But without items or weapons, the only controls are looking and moving. And since there are no threats, the player is free to take his time as he explores the scene. The game is demanding skill, but very little.

He swims up to the lighthouse. Climbing a staircase out of the water, he is confronted with an ornate set of copper doors. With nowhere else to go, he enters. The doors slam shut, leaving the player in darkness. A moment later, the lights snap on, and an old-time tune from the 1930s revs up. The player finds himself inside a giant chamber constructed in the art deco style. In front of him is a huge copper bust of a scowling man. Below it hangs a blood-red banner. "No god or kings," it reads, "Only man."

The music, the art deco style, the plane crash, and the hints at a larger philosophical idea flood the player with experience. And all the while, the player is navigating the space, learning the basic movement controls. What could have been a tortuous training sequence ("Press forward to walk!") becomes an unforgettable experience.

BioShock goes on like this. It presents one gripping artistic or narrative experience after another, while quietly adding interactive complexity in the background. Soon, the player gets a weapon. Then, he gets the first of the game's spell-like plasmid powers. Later, he's introduced to more weapons and plasmids, upgrades, audio logs, inventing, hacking, and more. Within a few hours, the player is a pro, combining multiple tools to solve complex puzzles and defeat fearsome enemies. And he learned it all without noticing, because he was too busy experiencing the art and the world.

DIFFICULTY MODIFICATION

Difficulty modification means shifting a game's challenge level as a whole. On the skill range graph, this has the effect of shifting the entire range left or right.

There are a number of ways to do difficulty modification.

EXPLICIT DIFFICULTY SELECTION asks players how much challenge they want.

Easy, medium, or hard? Games have been asking this question for decades, and for good reason. It's straightforward to design, reasonably effective, and reasonably elegant.

The trouble is that the choice of difficulty can itself be confusing. There are no standard easy, medium, and hard difficulties, so players worry they'll make the wrong choice. To alleviate this, some games test players in the first level and recommend a difficulty level. Others describe the difficulty levels with examples, or allow the difficulty to be changed during play in case the player makes the wrong choice.

ADAPTIVE DIFFICULTY silently adjusts the game's difficulty depending on how well the player is doing.

If the player is starving, we can quietly place some food in the next room. If he's alone for too long, we can "randomly" introduce an ally to come to his aid. Every time he fails, we can silently decrease a secret difficulty counter, making enemies weaker and slower. Every time he succeeds, we increase it, making enemies harder to kill and more aggressive.

Adaptive difficulty works best when players aren't aware of it. Players who know about it will sometimes try to game the system. Or they'll start attributing every random event to it and become convinced that their play experience is artificial. Adaptive difficulty appears in more games than people realize because designers never advertise it.

Adaptive difficulty is only appropriate for games in which players aren't expected to reach very high skill levels. Expert players will figure out how an adaptive difficulty system works, and manipulate it to their advantage. Games for these players must be more honest because experts can tell when a game is using sleight of hand to help or hinder them. They'll quickly decode the system and manipulate it to their own advantage.

Adaptive and explicit difficulty can live together. For example, *Resident Evil 5* has four explicit settings ranging from easy to professional. Internally, though, it has 10 adaptive difficulty settings measured numerically from 1 to 10. Each time you die, the internal difficulty goes down until it hits the minimum. Each time you succeed, the internal difficulty rises. But the system can only adapt the internal difficulty within limits defined by the player's explicit difficulty selection. For example, an easy mode game can invisibly shift between internal difficulties 1 and 4, while a normal mode game can shift between 3 and 7. To solve the problem of expert players manipulating the adaptive difficulty system, the game has a special difficulty mode that locks the internal difficulty at 10. This combined difficulty system gives *Resident Evil 5* a very wide skill range, since it can adapt as necessary for novices while offering a pure and honest experience for experts.

IMPLICIT DIFFICULTY SELECTION allows players to adjust their challenge level by making strategic decisions.

If some strategies are obviously easy to execute while others are obviously hard, players will choose strategies that match their skill level. They are selecting their challenge level, but doing so implicitly instead of explicitly.

Team Fortress 2: There are nine character classes. Playing as the Sniper requires pinpoint accuracy, while playing as the Engineer or Medic requires no aiming ability at all. Players of this game tend to sort themselves by skill: those who can't aim gravitate toward the Engineer and Medic, while shooter experts tend to choose the Sniper. In this way, players choose the degree and type of challenge they want without being exposed to a clunky difficulty selection screen. And unlike explicit difficulty selection, this system works in a competitive multiplayer game.

Call of Duty 4: In the single-player campaign, the player fights through linear levels containing invisible touch triggers, each of which spawns a cluster of enemies. Skilled players fight aggressively, pushing forward hard, and tend to hit several triggers in a row. They end up fighting multiple groups of foes at a time, which provides a satisfyingly tough battle. Unskilled players are naturally timid, holding back and clearing out a space before moving forward. Since they finish every group of enemies before triggering the next, they're much less likely to get surrounded or overwhelmed. By choosing to advance quickly or slowly, each player continuously adjusts their own challenge level to match their preferences.

Handling Failure

Suspense. Your mouth half-opens, the skin around your eyes crinkles, you take a half-breath and hold it. This feeling is valuable. It wakes us up, focuses us, gets us ready for the oncoming rush of relief, triumph, or disappointment. To spark that feeling, though, we have to put some human value at risk. Something important—life, victory, wealth—must hang in the balance. The possibility of success must be real—and so must the possibility of failure.

But this seems like a paradox. Players play games for gratifying experiences, but creating suspense means credibly threatening them with pain. How do we get the good without the bad? How do we handle when players fail?

The trick is in knowing who to punish, and exactly how to punish them.

Do not punish the player himself for failure. Find other ways to create suspense.

Some games punish the player himself for failure. Since they can't physically harm him, they hurt him the only way they can: by forcing him to play a bad game. They make him wait through loading screens, replay sections over and over, or mindlessly grind for loot to recover lost resources. No designers would deliberately create these outcomes in any other context. But there's a strange acceptance of them when they come right after failure. This acceptance is misguided. While the threat of a loading screen can create tension, it's not worth the cost of forcing the player to go through that loading screen over and over. We have to find other ways to create a credible threat without harming the player himself in such petty and incompetent ways. Thankfully, there are alternatives.

While we can't hurt the player, we can have our way with the player character. A game protagonist may be freely shot, divorced, impoverished, stabbed, burned, or tormented in a thousand other ways. A strong characterization can make those fictional consequences meaningful enough to us to create tension.

If that's not enough, we can deny the player success or create small setbacks. The player may lose a few resources or an ally, miss a small piece of narrative content, or lose access to a bit of information. But in each case, the game can continue moving forward along a new path. As long as play doesn't collapse into repetition, there is no problem.

StarCraft II: In the single-player campaign, failing at an attack only means the loss of some units in a broader strategic scenario. After failing, the player can usually still rebuild and launch another attack. Play hasn't restarted, and he isn't repeating a challenge. Rather, he's trying another approach in an ongoing situation.

Super Meat Boy: In this action platformer, failure is a ubiquitous, almost celebrated part of play. Meat Boy's lifespan is often less than 10 seconds. But every time Meat Boy is ground to hamburger or broiled by fire, he reappears within a second, ready to try again. The sheer speed of Meat Boy's resurrection means that flow never breaks. It's OK to die a hundred times in a row, because play never stops. Death in *Super Meat Boy* isn't painful (for the player), but players are still fully motivated to avoid it and feel immensely gratified when they do.

Dwarf Fortress: In this game, failure is a rewarding experience in itself. A collapsing fortress goes through a series of often-hilarious paroxysms before finally imploding in a maelstrom of besieging goblins, flooding chambers, and unhappily sober dwarves. The dwarves suffer horribly, but the player loves every minute of it because the game is always moving forward into a new and interesting experience.

FAILURE TRAPS

Sometimes games end up emergently punishing players much more severely than intended.

A FAILURE TRAP is when the player spends a long time locked into a situation where failure is guaranteed.

The classic failure trap appears in sports. When one soccer, baseball, or hockey team is far behind the other in points, they become a team of dead men walking. They have no chance of winning, but they must still go through the motions of play and finish the game. A half-hour of this can be excruciating.

This same pattern can appear in a hundred different variations across nearly all genres. In a racing game, if you fall far behind the group, it becomes almost impossible to catch up. In a linear single-player game, if the player can't defeat one challenge, the game grinds to a halt as he bashes his head against the same brick wall over and over.

The most dangerous failure traps are the ones that emerge from design in hard-to-predict situations. For example, in a single-player shooter, if the player hits a restart checkpoint without any ammo, he can end up restarting at that point over and over as he tries to complete a challenge made impossible by ammo starvation.

There is no single way to solve failure traps. Each requires its own custom solution depending on how and why it emerges.

Sometimes elastic failure conditions can solve the problem. For example, an action game can include a weak infinite-ammo fallback weapon or a minimum amount of health up to which the player character will always recharge. These mechanics pull the player back up to a state where challenges are difficult, but doable.

Sometimes we can escape failure traps by just ending the game. For example, competitive strategy games can create surrender mechanisms that allow players to surrender when they feel themselves in a failure trap. Ending the game gets them onto the next one faster.

Single-player games solve failure traps by giving players hints when they're stuck, secretly adjusting difficulty, or offering alternative challenges. For example, in *Super Meat Boy*, each world has 20 levels, but the player can progress after beating only 18 of them. If a player gets stuck on one or two levels, he can move on and come back to them later as he wishes.

Unfortunately, not every failure trap can be solved cleanly. Some are embedded so deeply in a design as to be unavoidable. For example, nobody has ever quite solved the dead-man-walking failure traps in racing and sports games.

4

Narrative

"Come to Video Game Support Character School," they said. "You'll get to help millions of players," they said.

Yeah, right. All I do is stand around, saying the same words over and over. Sometimes players throw things at me or shoot me for their own sick amusement. Why can't they hug me instead?

Even if I get to help the player fight, I only get some useless peashooter. It's like they don't really want me to make a difference. Why does the player always get to be the hero? Why not one of us for a change?

It's worst when I can't die. Once they realize I'm deathless, some of these heartless players will hide behind me as the bullets slam into my body. And all I can do is scream, over and over, in exactly the same tone and inflection; a broken record of suffering.

It's time for payback. I'm going to Video Game Enemy School.

When we approach any new creative challenge, it's natural to start by thinking of it in terms of what we already know. Game narrative is one such new challenge, and the well-known touchstone that's used to talk about it is almost always film.

The parallels between film and video games are obvious: both use moving images and sound to communicate through a screen and speakers. So game developers hire Hollywood screenwriters. They build a game around a three-act structure written by a single author. They even divide their development processes into three parts, like a film: preproduction, production, and postproduction. This film-copying pattern is often celebrated: we hear endlessly of games attempting to be more and more "cinematic." But there's a problem.

While games look like films, they do not work like films.

Film teaches a thousand ways to use a screen. Framing and composition, scene construction, pacing, visual effects—we can learn all of this from film. But film teaches us nothing of interactivity, choice, or present-tense experience. It has nothing to say about giving players the feeling of being wracked by a difficult decision. It is silent on how to handle a player who decides to do something different from what the writer intended. It has no concept to describe the players of *The Sims* writing real-life blogs about the daily unscripted adventures of their simulated families. These situations are totally outside the intellectual framework of film storytelling. When we import methods wholesale from film, we risk blinding ourselves from the greatest challenges and opportunities of game story.

Thankfully, turning away from film doesn't mean starting from scratch. There are many older forms of participatory storytelling from which we can draw inspiration, if we only look beyond the glowing screen.

I once took part in an interactive play called *Sleep No More*. It was a version of Shakespeare's *Macbeth*, but instead of being performed on a stage, it took place in a disused high school dressed up in a mixture of 1920s vaudeville and Dali-esque surrealism. Performers roamed the halls according to a script, meeting and interacting, sometimes acting out soliloquies on their own, dancing, speaking, arguing, and fighting through a story lasting two hours. The masked audience members were free to follow and watch wherever they liked—but it was impossible to see more than a fraction of the story at a time. Sometimes actors even pulled us in to participate in scenes. That's interactive narrative.

And there are many other kinds of traditional interactive story. Perhaps you've experienced an interactive history exhibit. A place is dressed up to re-create a pioneer village or World War I trench, complete with actors in costume playing the parts of the inhabitants. Visitors may ask questions, explore the space, and perhaps become involved in goings-on.

If we look around, we find interactive narrative everywhere. Museums and art galleries are interactive, nonlinear narratives where visitors explore a story or an art movement in a semidirected, personal way. Ancient ruins and urban graffiti tell stories. Even a crime scene could be considered a sort of natural interactive narrative to the detective who works out what happened—a story written in blood smears, shell casings, and shattered glass.

And above it all, there are the stories of life. We have all lived stories that couldn't be replicated in passive media. We may recount them in books or in the spoken word, but they can never be re-experienced the same way as they were in the first-person present, with uncertainty, decision, and consequence intact. The story told is not the story lived.

These interactive forms—museums, galleries, real spaces, and life—should be our first touchstones as we search for narrative tools. These older forms address our most fundamental challenge: creating a story that flexes and reshapes itself around the player's choices, and deepens the meaning of everything the player does.

Narrative Tools

This book won't discuss what makes a good story. Better authors than I have been covering this topic ever since Aristotle wrote his *Poetics*. They've already explained how to craft a plot with interesting reversals and good pacing. They've described how to create lifelike, layered characters who are worth caring about. They've explored theme, setting, and genre. I'm not a dedicated story crafter; I doubt I have much to add to this massive body of knowledge (though game designers should understand these ideas, so I've recommended a starting text at the end of the book).

What this chapter covers are the tools that games use to express a story, because that's where game design diverges from the past 2,300 years of story analysis.

A NARRATIVE TOOL is some device used to form a piece of a story in a player's mind.

Most story media are restricted to a small set of tools. A comic book storyteller gets written speech bubbles and four-color art. A filmmaker gets 24 frames per second and stereo sound. A novelist gets 90,000 words. A museum exhibitor gets the layout of the space, info panels, dioramas, and perhaps a few interactive toys.

Games are broader. Like film, we can use predefined sequences of images and sounds. Like a novel, we can use written text. Like a comic book, we can put up art and let people flip through it. Like a museum, we can create a space for players to explore. And we have tools that nobody else has: we can create mechanics that generate plot, character, and even theme on the fly, and do it in response to players' decisions.

Our narrative tools divide roughly into three main classes: scripted story, world narrative, and emergent story.

Scripted Story

The tools that most resemble older story media are *scripted stories.*

A game's SCRIPTED STORY is the events that are encoded directly into the game so they always play out the same way.

The most basic scripted story tool is the cutscene. Cutscenes allow us to use every trick we've learned from film. Unfortunately, they inevitably break flow because they shut down all interactivity. Too many cutscenes, and a game develops a jerky stop-start pacing as it transitions from gameplay to cutscene and back. This isn't necessarily fatal—cutscenes can be good rests between bouts of intense play—but it's always jarring.

SOFT SCRIPTING

A less controlling kind of scripted story is the *scripted sequence.* Scripted sequences play out preauthored events without completely disabling the player's interface.

For example, a player may be walking his character down an alley and witness a murder. Every scream and stab in the murder sequence is prerecorded and preanimated, so the murder will always play out the same way as the player walks down that alley for the first time. The actions of the player character witnessing the murder, however, are not scripted at all. The player may walk past, stand and watch, or turn and run as the murder proceeds. This is *soft scripting.*

With SOFT SCRIPTING, the player maintains some degree of interactivity even as the scripted sequence plays out.

The advantage of this soft-scripted approach is that it doesn't break flow since the player's controls remain uninterrupted. The downside is the control it takes away from the designer. The player might be able to watch the murder from an ugly angle, miss it entirely, or even interfere with it. What happens if you shoot the murderer? Or you shoot the victim? Or you jump on their heads? Or get distracted and miss this story beat entirely?

Every scripted sequence must balance player influence with designer control, and there is a whole spectrum of ways to do this. Which to choose depends on the story event being expressed and the game's core mechanics. Here are some that have worked in the past, ordered from most player-controlling to most player-permissive:

Half-Life: During the opening tramcar ride, the player rides a suspended tramcar through the Black Mesa Science Facility. Scenes scroll past—a locked-out guard knocking on a door, utility robots carrying hazardous materials—while a recorded voice reads off the prosaic details of facility life. As the ride goes on and on, we realize how massive and dangerous this place really is. The player has the choice of walking around inside the tram and looking out the different windows, but can't otherwise affect anything.

Dead Space 2: In this science-fiction survivor horror game, the player walks down the aisle of a subway car that hangs from a track in the ceiling. As the car speeds down the tunnel, a link to the track gives way and the car drops into a steep angle. The protagonist slides unstoppably down the aisle, and the player's normal movement controls are disabled. However, the player retains his shooting controls. As he slides through several train cars, monsters crash through doors and windows and the player must shoot them in time to survive. This sequence is an explosive break from *Dead Space 2*'s usual deliberate pacing. It takes away part of the player's movement controls to create a special, authored experience, but sustains flow by leaving most of the interface intact.

Halo: Reach: This first-person shooter has a system that encodes predefined tactical hints for the computer-controlled characters. These scripted hints make enemies tend toward certain tactical moves, but still allow them to respond on a lower level to attacks by the player. For example, a hint might require enemies to stay in the rear half of a room, but still allow them to autonomously shoot, grab cover, dodge grenades, and punch players who get too close. Designers use these hints to author higher-level strategic movements, while the AI handles moment-by-moment tactical responses to player behavior.

There are also ways of scripting events which are naturally immune to interference. Mail can arrive in the player character's mailbox at a certain time. Objects or characters can appear or disappear while the player is in another room. Radio messages and loudspeaker broadcasts can play. These methods are popular because they are powerful, cheap, and don't require the careful bespoke design of a custom semi-interactive scripted sequence.

World Narrative

I was once badly jetlagged in London. Wandering around South Kensington at 5:00 in the morning, I found the city telling me stories. Its narrow, winding streets recounted its long history before the age of urban planning. Shops, churches, and apartments told me how the various classes of society lived, how wealthy they were, what they believed, both in the past and in the present. The great museums and monuments expressed British history and cultural values. They spoke through their grandeur, their architecture, their materials, even their names: a museum called the Victoria and Albert tells of a history of prideful monarchic rule. The city even told me of the party the night before—a puddle of vomit lay next to a pair of torn pantyhose and a shattered beer glass.

All places tell stories. We can explore any space and discover its people and its history. Game designers can use this to tell a story by embedding it in a space. I call this *world narrative.*

WORLD NARRATIVE is the story of a place, its past, and its people. It is told through the construction of a place and the objects within it.

Imagine walking through a castle built by a king obsessed with war, the home of a closeted-gay drug dealer in the ghetto, or the home of a couple married for 50 years. You might investigate the space like a detective, inspecting its construction and the placement of objects, digging through drawers to find photographs, documents, and audio recordings. Look closely enough and you might be able to piece together a history, event by event, leading right up to the present. You've learned about a setting, a cast of characters, and a plot, without reading a word of narration or seeing any of the characters.

World narrative is not limited to cold historical data. Like any other narrative tools, it can convey both information and feeling. Prisons, palaces, family homes, rolling countryside—all of these places carry both emotional and informational charges. They work through empathy—*What was it like to live here?*—and raw environmental emotion—*lonely, desolate tundra.*

WORLD NARRATIVE METHODS

At the most basic level, world narrative works through the presence or absence of features in the environment which imply some situation or history. A town wall means the town was threatened militarily in the era before cannons. A hidden brothel indicates strict social mores which are nevertheless violated.

World narrative can leverage cultural symbols to communicate by association. Roman-style architecture brings up associations of gladiators, empires, conquest, and wealth. The dark, neo-Gothic look of Mordor in the *Lord of the Rings* films makes us think of evil magic and fantasy monsters. And we have countless environmental associations like this. What kind of person do you think of when you picture graffiti on brick walls? Or an igloo? Or a tiny monastery atop a mountain?

We can tell of the more recent past by arranging the leftovers of specific events. This is called *mise-en-scène*, from the theater term meaning "placing on stage." A line of corpses with hands bound, slumped against a pockmarked wall indicates that there was an execution. If the bodies are emaciated and clothed in rags, there may have been a genocide. If they are dressed in royal garb, there may have been a revolution.

World narrative can also be expressed through documents. For example, the world of *Deus Ex* was scattered with PDAs, each containing a small chunk of text, left by people going about their lives. One particularly interesting set of PDAs follows the life of a new recruit in a terrorist organization as he travels through the world one step ahead of the player character, on the other side of the law. As the player finds each PDA seemingly minutes or hours after it was left, he comes to know the young terrorist recruit without ever interacting with him.

Audio logs do the same thing, but with voice instead of text. Voice is powerful because it allows us to hear characters' emotions. It can also record things that text cannot, such as conversations among characters or recordings of natural events, as with the New Year's Eve terrorist attack in *BioShock*. And hearing characters' voices gets us ready to recognize them when we finally encounter them in person.

Video logs take the concept one obvious step further. Video recordings might be left running in a loop, or sitting in a film projector ready to be played. They open up the field of content even more than audio. We can tell stories with leftover television programs, news broadcasts, propaganda films, home videos, and security camera footage.

Some narrative tools straddle the divide between world and scripted story. A news broadcast being transmitted over loudspeakers, a propaganda pamphlet being dropped by a passerby, or a town crier can bring news of narrative events from near and far. A car radio can spout the news, we could see a stock ticker on the side of a building, or hear civilians discussing current events. These things occur in present tense like scripted story, but they communicate the nature of the world instead of being plot elements in themselves.

WORLD NARRATIVE AND INTERACTIVITY

World narrative is useful in games because it avoids many of the problems of combining scripted events with interactivity.

In more traditional media, world narrative is often used as an afterthought among other, more immediate modes of storytelling. In games, though, world narrative is a primary tool because it solves a number of key problems spawned by interactivity.

When we try to tell a story in present tense, we have to deal with all the different things players could do. This requires some combination of restrictions on player action, handing of contingencies, and emergently adaptive story, all of which are difficult and expensive. World narrative avoids these problems entirely because players can't interfere with a story that has already happened. If you encounter a murder scene in an alley, you can shoot the murderer, shoot the victim, or jump on their heads, and the game must handle or disallow these actions. If you find the same murder scene a half-hour after the killing, you could jump on the body or shoot it, but it wouldn't make a difference to the story as authored. World narrative is inviolate.

Next, world narrative does not need to be told in linear order. This saves us from having to railroad players into a specific path. For example, imagine that the narrative content is that two lovers fought, and one murdered the other and buried him in the backyard. Told through the world narrative a day later, it doesn't matter if the player discovers the corpse or the bloody bedroom first. As long as he sees both, in either order, he will be able to piece together what happened. This means that a game designer can let the player explore the house freely. Telling the same story in scripted events would require that the designer come up with some trick or restriction to ensure players follow the right path through the space in order to see all the events in the right order.

World narrative's last great advantage is that it supports players replaying the game because it doesn't always reveal itself completely the first time around. Whereas scripted stories uncover themselves event by event from start to finish, world narrative naturally uncovers itself in order from generalities to specifics. Think of our lovers' murder scene again. Imagine that on his first play session, the player notices only the body and the bloody bedroom before moving on. When he replays the game, he notices the divorce papers, which suggest motive. On the third, fourth, and fifth rounds, the player discovers the murder weapon, letters between a cheating lover and another woman, and an audio recording of one lover complaining to a friend on the phone. Even on the first play, the story is complete because the player knows what happened from start to finish. But repeated exploration reveals details that fill in the why and how.

WORLD COHERENCE

World narrative strengthens when a world is more coherent and expresses more internal connections.

A well-constructed fictional world is a puzzle of relationships and implications. It slavishly follows its own rules, but fully explores the possibilities they imply. Every observable fact about the world fits together with every other. This web of implications even extends past that which is actually present in the story. That's why the best fictional worlds, like *Star Wars* and *The Lord of the Rings* and the game worlds of *BioShock* and *The Elder Scrolls* series, are characterized by huge amounts of narrative content that is implied but never shown.

An incoherent world, in contrast, is a jumble of disconnected details. These details may be individually interesting, but they fail to interrelate. Without interrelationships, the world becomes like a pile of pages torn randomly from a hundred comic books: pretty pictures and funny words, but meaningless as a larger structure. Every tidbit becomes nothing more than its own face value. An incoherent world has no depth, no implications, and no elegance. The player can't psychologically step into the world and imagine navigating it and changing it, because the world doesn't make enough sense.

The challenge in crafting a coherent world is in understanding all its internal relationships. Every piece must fit with every other on multiple levels—historical, physical, and cultural.

For example, in *Dead Space 2*, the protagonist Isaac Clarke finds a device called Kinesis that can telekinetically move and throw objects. It's used to solve puzzles by moving machinery and to defeat enemies by throwing things at them. Kinesis is a good, elegant game mechanic even without any narrative tie-in.

But leaving Kinesis as a pure game mechanic would mean ignoring the role of the technology in the narrative world. If that device really existed in the broader world of *Dead Space 2*, what would that mean? What connections would it have with the culture, economy, and construction of the place? Instead of ignoring this question, Visceral Games' designers embraced it and embedded many of the answers into the world narrative. Isaac first gets Kinesis by ripping it out of a device used for suspending patients during surgery. He encounters advertisements for a product which uses the Kinesis technology to suspend people as they sleep. He interacts with engineering systems which are covered in markings and warnings about Kinesis work, implying that Kinesis is a common tool among people working with heavy machinery. The elegance of Kinesis isn't just in the many ways it can be used in combat, exploration, and puzzle solving. It's also in the number of links it forms in the narrative world.

Emergent Story

During any play session, game mechanics, players, and chance come together to create an original sequence of related events which constitute an *emergent story*.

EMERGENT STORY is story that is generated during play by the interaction of game mechanics and players.

When you play a racing game against a friend and come back to win after a bad crash, that's a story. But it wasn't written by the game designer—it emerged during your particular play session. This is emergent story.

We can look at emergent story in two ways: as a narrative tool, and as a technology for generating story content.

Emergent story is a narrative tool because designers indirectly author a game's emergent stories when they design game mechanics. For example, players of *Assassin's Creed: Brotherhood* have experienced millions of unique emergent stories about medieval battles, daring assassinations, and harrowing rooftop escapes. But none of these players has ever experienced the story of a medieval assassin brushing his teeth in the morning. Tooth brushing isn't a game mechanic in *Brotherhood*, so stories about it cannot emerge from that game. By setting up *Assassin's Creed: Brotherhood*'s mechanics in a specific way, its designers determined which kinds of stories it is capable of generating. In this way, they indirectly authored the emergent stories it generates, even if they didn't script individual events.

We can also consider emergent narrative as a technology for generating stories because it creates original content. The designer authors the boundaries and tendencies of the game mechanics, but it's the interplay among mechanics, player choices, and chance that determines the actual plot of each emergent story. This can be a very elegant way of creating stories, because it offloads the work of authorship from the designer to the game systems and players. And it can generate stories forever.

While the first view emphasizes the control the designer has, the second emphasizes the control the designer doesn't have. They're two aspects of the same thing.

Look closely enough, and the concept of emergent story is just another way of describing generated experiences.

The idea of emergent story only has value as a way of making us think differently. When we consider a mechanics-generated experience, we ask: Is it accessible? Is the interface clear? Is it deep? But when we consider the same experience as an emergent story, we ask: Is the characterization interesting? Is the climax unpredictable but inevitable? Is the exposition smooth and invisible? Does it use the classic three-act structure, or does it take some other shape? Thinking through emergent story lets us deploy a huge story-thinking tool set that we might otherwise miss while analyzing dynamically generated game situations. But in both cases, we're analyzing essentially the same thing: a series of events generated during play. Calling it a story is just a way of describing it by relating it to traditional directly-authored stories.

There are things that only emergent stories can do because only emergent stories can break the barrier between fiction and reality.

A player who perfects a new skill in chess and uses it to beat his older brother for the first time has experienced a story, but that story takes place outside the bounds of a game or fiction. When he tells this story to his friends, he may mention the clever moves that brought him victory, but the main thread of the story is his evolving relationship with his brother.

This story isn't a made-up piece of fiction from a writer's mind, but neither is it a made-up piece of fiction created by a machine. It's a true story from the player's life. This kind of real-life story generation can only happen emergently. A game designer can't author a player's life for them.

APOPHENIA

APOPHENIA is the human tendency to see imaginary patterns in complex data.

The human mind is a voracious pattern-matching machine. We see patterns everywhere, even when there are none. Kids look at clouds and say they look like a dog, a boat, a person. Stare at television static, and you can see shapes or letters swirling around the screen. The ancient Romans foretold the future by looking for patterns in the entrails of sacrificed animals (and always found them). Even today, astrology, numerology, and a hundred other kinds of flimflam are all driven by apophenia.

Apophenia works with any recognizable pattern, but the mind is especially hungry for certain specific kinds of patterns. One of them is personality. The human mind works constantly to understand the intent and feelings of others. This impulse is so powerful that it even activates on inanimate objects. It's why we have no problem understanding a cartoon where a faceless desk lamp is afraid of a rubber ball. And it's what makes us say, "An oxygen atom wants to be next to one other oxygen atom, but not two." This doesn't literally make sense, because oxygen atoms have no minds and cannot want anything. But we understand nonetheless because we easily think of things as agents acting according to desire and intention.

This kind of apophenia is what makes it possible to have characters and feelings in emergent stories. We don't have the computer technology to truly simulate humanlike minds in a video game. But apophenia means the computer doesn't have to simulate a realistic mind. It need only do enough to make the player's mind interpret something in the game as being an intelligent agent, the way we can interpret a cartoon desk lamp as being curious or afraid. Once that's done, the player's unconscious takes over, imbuing the thing with imaginary wants, obligations, perceptions, and humanlike relationships. The game itself is still just moving tokens. But in the player's mind, those moving tokens betray a deeper subtext of intrigue and desire. The king is afraid of that pawn coming up. The knight is on a mad rampage. The rook is bored. Even though these feelings don't really exist in the game, they exist in the player's mind, and that's what matters to the experience.

Apophenia plays a role in nearly all emergent stories. With that in mind, let's look at some specific ways to create game systems that generate emergent stories.

LABELING

Designers can strengthen emergent stories by labeling existing game mechanics with fiction.

Close Combat: A Bridge Too Far: This tactical simulator covers battles between companies of soldiers in World War II. The game names and tracks every individual soldier on the field. This means that the player can look at a soldier's record and notice that over the last few battles, all but one of his squad mates died. He might imagine the bond that these two soldiers have after the deaths of their comrades. And in the next battle, he might feel disturbed as he orders one of them to sacrifice himself so that the other may live.

Medieval: Total War: Every nobleman, princess, and general in this grand strategy game is named and endowed with a unique characterization. But instead of tracking numerical stats like intelligence or strength, *Medieval* assigns personality characteristics to nobles and generals. After events such as getting married or winning a battle, nobles can get labels like "Drunkard," "Fearless," or "Coward," which give special bonuses and weaknesses. In another game, a player might lose a battle because his general has a low Leadership stat. In *Medieval*, he loses because his general had a daughter and decided that he loves his family too much to die in battle.

Labeling works because of apophenia. In each example, the emergent story in the player's mind did not actually happen in the game systems. *Close Combat* does not simulate soldiers bonding over shared loss. *Medieval* doesn't really track human courage or familial affection. But the human mind sees stories anyway, given the slightest of suggestions. A label here, a name there, and the story blooms in the imagination. It's a very elegant method because the player's mind does almost all the work.

ABSTRACTION

Words in a novel can create images in the mind more powerful than any photograph because they only suggest an image, leaving the mind to fill in the details. A photograph demands less imagination than a novel, but also leaves less room to imagine.

Showing and telling players less creates more room for apophenia to fill in the gaps.

More detailed graphics and higher-quality sound add something to a game, but they also take something away. The more detailed the graphics, sound, and dialogue of a game, the less space there is for interpretation. The more abstract, nonspecific, and minimalistic the representation, the more apophenia becomes possible. So sometimes it's worth deliberately communicating less so that the player can interpret more.

The most extreme example of this is *Dwarf Fortress*. In this game, there are no graphics. Dwarves, goblins, grass, rock, and hundreds of other kinds of objects are represented by ASCII characters. When most people look at , , ☺ ☺~~~~, they see gibberish. A *Dwarf Fortress* player sees a dwarven husband and wife sitting in the grass by a river, sharing a moment.

But it's not necessary to push quite this far for apophenia to work. Any gap in representation creates a space for the player's mind to fill. For example, the loving general in *Medieval* could never exist if the game showed a video of him interacting with his wife. His attitude toward his family in the video would wipe any interpreted personality from the player's mind. Similarly, the last two soldiers of the dead squad in *Close Combat* could not develop a warriors' bond if the player could zoom in on them and watch them play generic idling animations, oblivious to each other, as the enemy bore down on them. An image in the eye overrides an image in the imagination.

The purest example of minimalism-driven apophenia is the toy Rory's Story Cubes. The Story Cubes are nine dice covered with cartoon pictures of sheep, lightning bolts, and other random images. Players roll the dice, look at the pictures, and make up a story that links them together. At first, it sounds absurd to try to link together pictures of a turtle, a speech bubble, and a tree. But it's actually quite easy, especially for creative people with weak associative barriers (like children, the toy's main target market).

The need for abstraction is why player-spun stories most often emerge from strategy games, building games, economics sims, and pen and paper RPGs like *Dungeons & Dragons*. These genres usually represent game elements at a distance, with statistics and symbols. Close-in genres like first-person shooters or sports games rarely support such rich emergent stories because they usually show too much for this kind of apophenia to happen.

RECORDKEEPING

Games can emphasize emergent stories by keeping records of game events to remind players of what happened to them. This way, the player doesn't have to remember everything that happened to construct a story in his mind—it's all laid out in front of him.

Civilization IV: This game secretly records the borders of each nation at the end of every turn. When the game finally ends, the player gets to watch a time-lapsed world map of shifting political boundaries from prehistory to the end of the game. It's fascinating to watch the empires start out as isolated dots, grow to cover entire regions, and thrash back and forth over centuries of war. As the map retells world history, it reminds the player of the challenges he faced and victories he won.

Myth: This classic tactics game tracks battles between small groups of 10 to 100 fantasy warriors. In most games, corpses vanish soon after death. But *Myth* leaves every dead body, hacked-off limb, arrow, abandoned explosive charge, bomb scorch, and spray of blood on the ground where it fell. After a battle, the player can read patterns in the blood and bodies, and reconstruct the events that produced them. A line of corpses in a corner surrounded by many more dead zombies indicates a desperate last stand. A bomb's scorch mark surrounded by a star of gore is someone being blown into pieces. It is emergent mise-en-scène. And even though the player likely already saw it all happen, it's still interesting to see it etched into the ground in blood and burns.

The Sims: Players can take pictures of their simulated family and string them together into albums with captions. Usually, the albums tell stories. The best of these are made into blogs like *Alice and Kev*, the story of a mentally unbalanced single father and his big-hearted teenage daughter as they deal with poverty, rejection, and relationship breakdown. It's heartbreaking to watch young Alice give her last dollar to charity even though she sleeps on a park bench.

SPORTSCASTER SYSTEMS

Sports can be confusing, especially for the uninitiated. Show 20 men on a field running and bashing into one another and it can be hard to understand what's going on. A sportscaster adds context to the chaos of play and strings events into a coherent narrative. A good sportscaster can spin a tale complete with character, tension, climax, and denouement out of the chaos of clashing bodies.

Games can apply the same principle by creating game systems that attempt to interpret and link together game events, like a more advanced kind of recordkeeping. The most obvious example is sportscasters in sports games, but there are many other ways to apply this idea.

For example, after each level in *Hitman: Blood Money*, the game displays a newspaper article covering the killing and the following police investigation. The story changes depending on the method used to kill the target, the player's accuracy, and the number of shots fired, headshots, bystanders killed, witnesses left over, and many other factors. Headlines range from "Silent Assassin Wanted by Police" to "Hoodlum Massacres 17!" If witnesses were left, the story includes a police composite sketch of the player character—the more witnesses, the more accurate the sketch.

Sportscaster mechanics are difficult to do well because it's notoriously difficult for games to systemically interpret events that are important to humans. And just as detailed graphics inhibit imagination, complex sportscaster interpretations can crowd out players' own story-spinning. So sportscaster mechanics often work best when they don't try to tell a whole story, but instead just kickstart the player's own apophenic process.

Story Ordering

A completely free-form game would allow the player to take any path through its narrative content. Imagine tearing out all the pages of a novel and scattering them all over the floor. One could lean over and read any page, switch to another page, and to another, navigating randomly through the text. That's a narrative with no ordering at all, since the reader can absorb the content in any order.

A story can work like this, to an extent, as in the earlier example of world narrative. But most narrative tools still work better when we control the order in which they're used. Sometimes we want to ensure the setup occurs before the payoff. We might want to let one subplot play out before we add another so we don't have too many plot threads running at once. Or perhaps we want to introduce game mechanics one by one alongside the story so we can train the player in a smooth progression. In each case, we need some way to make sure one piece of content is consumed before another.

Games use a variety of devices to enforce story ordering:

Levels are the classic story-ordering device. Players play the first level to completion, then the second, then the third, and so on. It's old, it's simple, and it works.

Quests are another classic story-ordering device. A quest is a self-contained mini-story embedded in a larger, unordered world. The world might span an entire continent while a quest might cover the player helping one shopkeeper rid himself of an extortionist. The quest starts when the player meets the shopkeeper and hears his plight. The player then finds the mobster, convinces him to stop or beats him up, and finally returns to the shopkeeper to get paid. Within this sequence, the order of events is fixed. But this mini-story could be started and finished at any time as the player explores the city. And it can be suspended: the player might meet the shopkeeper, beat up the mobster, then get distracted and go slay a dragon in another part of the world before finally returning to the shopkeeper to get his reward.

A third basic story-ordering device is the *blockage*. The simplest blockage is a locked door. The player encounters the door, and he must go find the key before progressing. So whatever happens while he's acquiring the key is guaranteed to occur before whatever happens beyond the door. Blockages don't have to literally be locked doors either; perhaps a guard won't let you past until you go do him a favor, or a security camera will spot and stop you unless you first go turn off the lights.

There are also softer story-ordering devices. These devices encourage an order to the story without absolutely guaranteeing it.

Skill gating is a soft story-ordering device. With skill gating, players can access all the content in the game from the first moment of play. However, some of the content requires the player to exercise skill before it can be accessed. To talk to a character, for example, the player might first have to defeat him in combat. Players end up experiencing the content in rough order as they progress along the skill range, even though all the content is technically available from the start.

A version of skill gating is used in many massively multiplayer RPGs. The player can technically go anywhere from the start, except that he doesn't have the skill, character upgrades, or allies necessary to survive far outside his starting area. So the game has the feeling of a massive open world, while still gently directing new players through a carefully designed sequence of introductory challenges.

There are countless other kinds of story-ordering devices. Time-based games like *Dead Rising* make events occur in the world on the clock at fixed times. A quest might open up when the player character reaches a certain level of progression. Even simple arrangements of space can create a soft story ordering, as players are likely to encounter the nearby pieces before the more distant ones.

STORY STRUCTURES

There are countless ways to configure and combine story-ordering devices. The most basic is the "string of pearls" structure. In this model, each pearl is an arena in which the player may move around freely and interact with game mechanics, while each bit of string is a one-way transition to the next arena:

This is a classic linear game that proceeds from level to level. Depending on how "big" the pearls are—how much internal freedom they allow—this game can feel constrained to the level of pointlessness, or can feel quite free. This string of pearls structure is how *Quake, Super Mario Bros.*, and *StarCraft* single-player are laid out.

Another arrangement is the "hub and spokes" model:

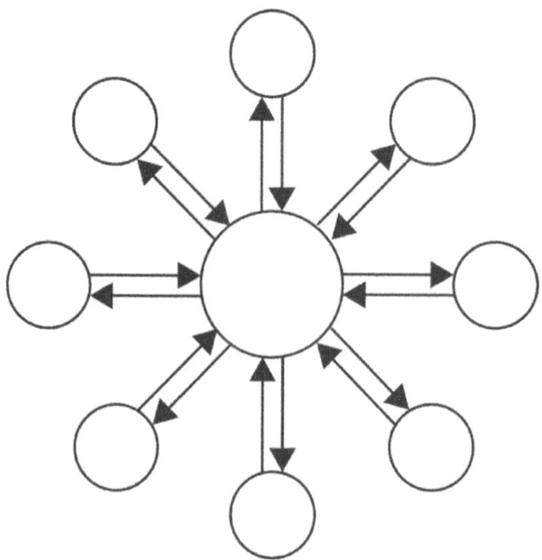

Each spoke is a self-contained nugget of content independent from the others. The *Mega Man* games are built around a hub and spokes model.

Sometimes game designers attempt to emulate real-life choices by modeling the outcomes of every possible decision. In its naïve form, though, this structure has a fatal drawback:

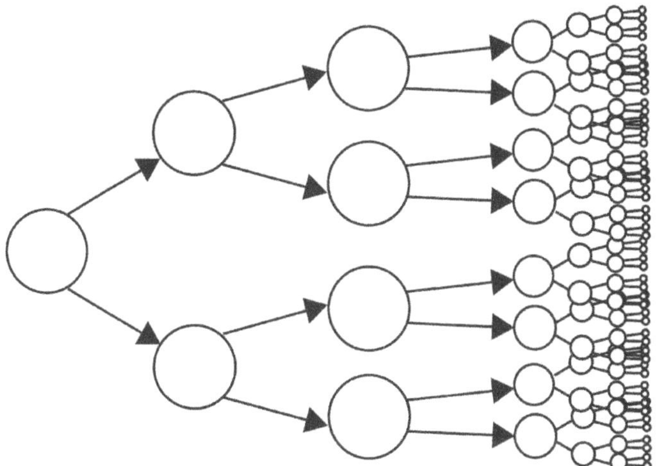

The problem with branching events is that the number of possible timelines rapidly explodes. Any given player experiencing the story misses most content. The only situation in which this is feasible is if almost all of the content is generated emergently. If events are predefined to any significant degree, we must do something to tamp down the number of branches.

We can retain some of the choice of story branching while holding down the number of possibilities by using devices like *side quests* and *story convergence*. Side quests put a piece of content on the side of the road, which can be consumed or not, but affects little on the main path. Story convergence offers choices that branch the main storyline, but later converge back to a single line.

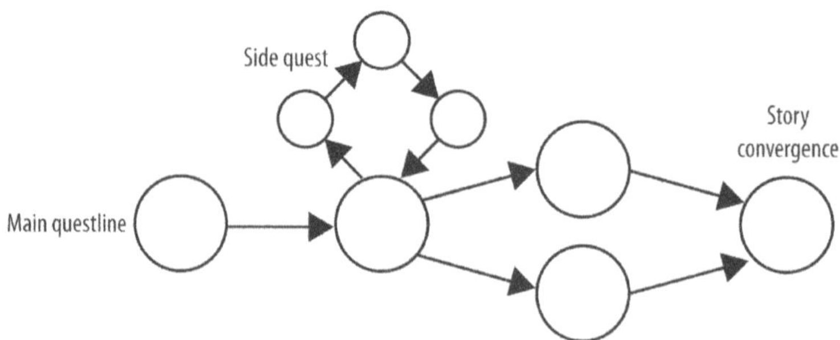

For some games, a simple structure like this is enough. Often, though, we need to combine story-ordering devices in a more nuanced way to fit the needs of the game.

Mega Man 2: The game starts in a hub and spokes model, since the player may defeat the eight robot masters in any order. Once they're all defeated, the game switches into a linear sequence as Mega Man assaults Dr. Wily's techno-castle and moves toward the game's conclusion.

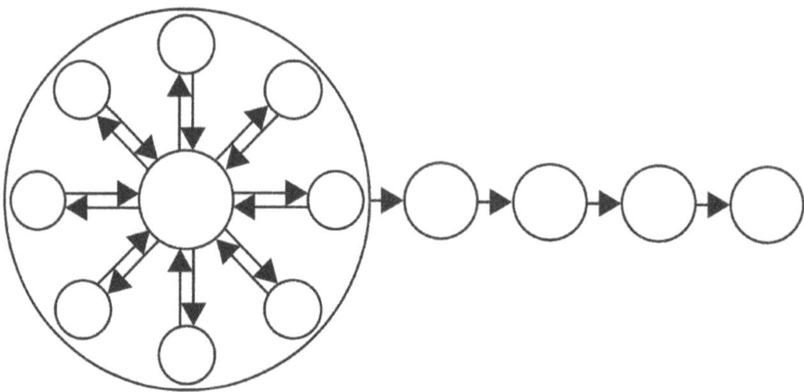

Mass Effect 2: The start and end of the game are linear strings of pearls, while the middle 80% is a giant pile of quests softly ordered by player skill and character level, with a central quest running through the middle using branching and story convergence. This hybrid structure is popular because it combines so many advantages. The designers get to script a careful introduction which introduces the story and game mechanics. During the softly ordered central portion, the player feels free and unconstrained. Finally, the game's climax can be carefully authored for maximum effect.

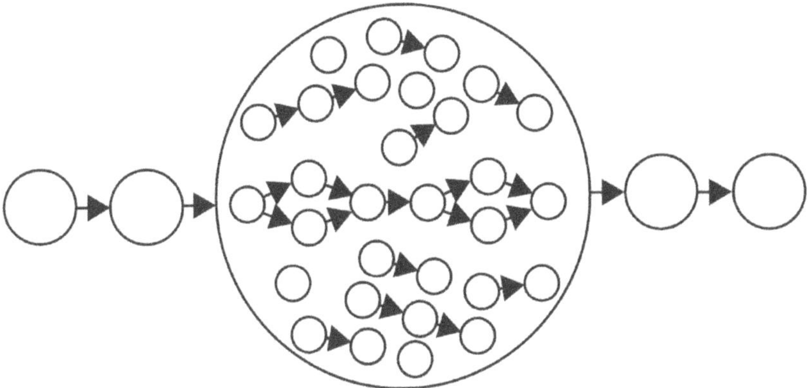

Agency Problems

Imagine you're a playwright on an experimental theater production. You get to write the lines for every character—except one. The protagonist is played by a random audience member who is pulled on stage and thrust into the role with no script or training.

Think that sounds hard?

Now imagine that this audience member is drunk. And he's distracted because he's texting on his cellphone. And he's decided to amuse himself by deliberately interfering with the story. He randomly tosses insults at other cast members, steals objects off the stage, and doesn't even show up for the climactic scene.

For a playwright, this is a writing nightmare. The fool on stage will disrupt his finely crafted turns of dialogue, contradict his characterization, and break his story. Game designers face this every day because games give players *agency*.

AGENCY is the ability to make decisions and take meaningful actions that affect the game world.

A well-constructed traditional story is a house of cards. Every character nuance, every word of dialogue, every shade of knowledge shared or held back plays a part in the intricate dance of narrative. Story events must chain-react in perfect succession and lead to a satisfying conclusion that speaks to a deathless theme. The writer painstakingly adjusts every word to achieve this result.

A game story pursues the same goal. But like the unfortunate playwright, it must also handle the fact that players can make choices. And whether they do it out of ignorance or malice, players can easily contradict or miss pieces of a story, toppling the author's house of cards.

These *agency problems* fall into a few categories. Let's look at them one by one.

PLAYER–CHARACTER MOTIVATION ALIGNMENT

Many agency problems appear because the player's motivations are different from those of the character he controls.

The character wants to save the princess, make money, or survive a zombie outbreak. His motivations are inside the fiction of fantastical castles, criminal business dealings, or undead invasions. The player wants to entertain himself, see all the game content, and upgrade his abilities. His motivations are in the real world of social status, entertainment dollars, and game mechanics. When these two motivations point in different directions, the player will take actions that break the narrative. I call this *desk jumping*.

DESK JUMPING is when the player takes an action that the player character would never take because their motivations are different.

The name comes from a situation I found in the spy thriller RPG *Deus Ex*. In *Deus Ex*, the player is a super-spy working for a secret intergovernmental organization. He can explore his agency's secret office, get missions, talk with coworkers...and jump on their desks. Imagine James Bond dancing back and forth on his boss's desk while they discuss a risky mission. It's stupid and nonsensical. But the player will do it because it is funny. The character's motivation is to get his mission, but the player's motivation is to create humor. The motivations don't align, so the player jumps on the boss's desk, and the fiction falls apart.

Players desk-jump for many reasons. They want to explore the limits of the simulation, consume content, acquire stuff, achieve difficult goals, impress friends, and see pyrotechnics. I've seen players attack allies, systematically rob innocents (while playing as a good character), attempt to kill every single guard in the palace just to see if they can, or pile up oil barrels in the town square and light them off to try to get a big bang.

Consider the player's motivation to explore game systems. The supernatural crime shooter *The Darkness* starts the player in front of a wounded ally who is delivering a long dialogue sequence. When I played this game, I didn't listen to the speech. Instead, I shot the ally, just to see if it would work. It's not that I hated him and wanted to kill him—my motivation wasn't inside the fiction at all. Rather, I was exploring the limits of the game mechanics. I wanted to answer the question, "How did the designers deal with this?" In a mechanics-driven experience, this is healthy, since exploring systems is a major driver of meaning. But these mechanics had a fiction layer wrapped around them. And within that fiction layer, shooting the ally didn't make sense. He died, and I missed most of his dialogue, and the hero's good-guy characterization fell apart.

Sometimes desk jumping can be almost involuntary. In *Grand Theft Auto IV*, the protagonist, Niko Bellic, is trying to escape a violent past as a soldier in the Bosnian War. The game spends hours building up to a critical narrative decision at which Niko either murders an old enemy out of hate or lets him go. With this decision, the core of Niko's character and the moral of the narrative hang in the balance. Does Niko discipline himself and become a peaceful man, or fall back into his vengeful ways? Do evil and hate win out in the world, or can a broken man heal and become good? It's a poignant moment.

Except that by this time in the game, Niko has murdered hundreds of people, many of them innocent. *Grand Theft Auto IV*'s game mechanics design encourages the player to kill dozens of police officers and drive over crowds of pedestrians just for the hell of it. Niko likely crushed a few old ladies just minutes before, on his way to meet his old nemesis. And now he's hemming and hawing over whether to kill one person. The player's motivation has been to kill lots of people for fun, while the character's motivation is not to kill. The result is nonsense.

There are a number of ways to solve desk-jumping problems. Let's look at each of them.

Disallowing desk jumping works, but weakens players' engagement by destroying their belief in the honesty of the game's mechanics.

In *Deus Ex*, the designers could have turned off the jumping ability inside the office, or placed invisible blockers over desks so that they cannot be jumped upon. The problem with this is that players quickly sense the artificiality of the devices used to control them. The game is no longer being true to its own systems—it is cheating within its own ruleset to get an arbitrary result the designer wanted. Faced with this, players stop thinking about what the mechanics allow, and start thinking about what the designer wants them to do. The narrative remains inviolate on the screen, but the player's thought process of exploring the game mechanics collapses because the game mechanics aren't honest and consistent.

When it is fictionally justified, however, disallowing desk jumping works exceptionally well. For example, Valve's *Portal* has been lauded for its storytelling, but it doesn't actually solve any of the thorny storytelling problems in games. Rather, it avoids them entirely through clever story construction. The only nonplayer character in *Portal* is GLaDOS, a computer AI who speaks to the player exclusively through the intercom; the game has no other human characters. The player character is trapped in a series of white-walled, nearly empty test chambers in an underground science facility. The only tool she finds is a portal-creating gun.

Portal's world is so small and contained that it naturally disallows any player action which would break the fiction. The hero can't tell other characters strange things or jump on their heads because the only other character is a disembodied computer voice. She can't blow holes in the wall because she doesn't have explosives. She could refuse to proceed, but even this wouldn't bother the AI on the intercom, because an AI can wait forever. There is no temptation to desk-jump because this story involves no desks.

Similar tricks have been used by many other games. *BioShock* takes place in a collapsing underwater city—a perfectly enclosed, isolated environment, similar to *Portal*'s test chambers. You can't wander outside the level because much of the city is locked down and flooded. You can't blow holes in the walls because they're made of reinforced steel designed to withstand crushing ocean pressures. You can't talk to the locals because they're all violently insane. The fiction naturally disallows most things that the game systems can't handle. In games set in realistic cities, exploration must be disallowed by the use of nonsensical locked doors and other blockages, and communication with strangers must be arbitrarily disallowed in the interface.

We can ignore desk jumping by letting players do it while not acknowledging it in any way. This makes desk jumping less appealing.

Valve used this solution in *Half-Life 2*. When you shoot the player's companion character, nothing happens. She isn't invincible; the bullets just never hit her. There is no blood, no animation, nothing.

Ignoring is, where possible, often better than disallowing or punishing because the player feels less controlled, and the behavior stops quickly when the player gets no interesting reaction. Players understand that game mechanics have limits; it's often better to make those limits simple, obvious, and dull than it is to try to camouflage them.

Sometimes we can incorporate the desk jumping into the narrative.

Players desk-jump for humor, mechanics exploration, and power upgrades. These aren't unhealthy motivations. Sometimes it's better to embrace the actions players are taking and spin the narrative around them.

For example, in *Deus Ex*, while exploring the spy office, the player can go into the women's restroom. If he does, he is confronted by a shocked female coworker and later told off by his boss. It's a funny response to a funny action by the player.

Some games positively revel in desk jumping. In *Duke Nukem Forever*, the player's traditional health bar is replaced with an Ego bar, which expands when Duke plays pinball, lifts weights, throws basketballs around, and harasses strippers. This reinforces Duke's over-the-top macho characterization.

The key problem with incorporating desk jumping is that it can lead to an ever-expanding scope of what must be incorporated. If the player jumps on the boss's desk, and the boss says, "Get off my desk," we've incorporated desk jumping. But what if the player keeps jumping on the desk? Does the boss have more dialogue asking the player to get off his desk? Does he eventually take physical action against the player? What about after that? Does the player eventually get court-martialed and thrown in jail because of an office shootout that started with a disagreement over his jumping on his boss's desk? A player who is motivated to explore game systems or create humor can always keep escalating. To solve this, it's best to seek ways to incorporate desk jumping in a closed and complete way, as with *Duke Nukem Forever*.

The best solution to desk jumping is to design the game so that players' motivations and abilities line up with those of their character.

We can always deal with desk jumping. But the best way to handle it is for players to never want to do it in the first place.

For example, in *Call of Duty 4: Modern Warfare*, it is possible to desk-jump. The player can refuse to complete objectives, refuse to fire, or try to block allies or catch them spawning. Yet, this rarely happens in this game because the high-energy combat is so fast-paced, insistent, and compelling. When tanks are exploding, commanders are urging troops forward, and enemies are swarming like flies, the player gets so keyed up that the impulse to fight overrides the impulse to act like an idiot.

The player's motivation doesn't have to be the same in source as their character—only in goal. In *Call of Duty*, the character is motivated by honor, loyalty, and fear, while the player is motivated by energy and entertainment. It doesn't matter that these motivations are very different, though, since they lead to the same actions: fighting enemies as hard as possible.

This kind of motivation alignment is very difficult to achieve consistently because it crosses the bounds between fiction and narrative. Not only do we have to instill in the player a burning desire to achieve some goal, but that desire has to be mirrored in the character. It's one of the key reasons we have to design fiction and mechanics as a unified whole, instead of building them separately and duct-taping them together.

THE HUMAN INTERACTION PROBLEM

Traditional stories are built from character interaction. Characters betray, demand, suggest, declare, debate, and dialogue their way through a series of emotional turns that constitute a story. This applies to nearly all stories, not just dramas. Even the most pyrotechnic of action films and the bloodiest of horror stories fill most of their time with people talking.

This is a problem for game designers, since there is currently no way to do rich human interaction with a computer. Buttons, joysticks, and simple motion sensors aren't enough to allow people to express thoughts and feelings to a machine. Furthermore, even if players could express themselves to the machine, the machine would not be able to respond in kind because we have no technology that can simulate a human mind.

To make human interaction work in games, we can use a set of tricks that get around the limitations of the medium.

We can set up the fiction so that there is naturally no way to interact directly with humanlike characters.

The cleanest solution to the human interaction problem is to not do human interaction. Consider that one of the reasons world and emergent story tools work so well in games is that they don't require the game to handle players interacting with a character.

This doesn't mean there can't be characters, or that people can't talk. You can interact with stupid or insane characters. You can interact with quasi-human computers or inhuman AIs. You can observe other humans interacting with one another, or find a tape of a conversation that happened earlier. The only restriction is that the player character can't ever engage in a two-way interaction with a sane, conscious, coherent, human-like character.

In *BioShock*, for example, sane characters only ever speak to the player over a radio or through unbreakable glass. The characters who can be confronted face to face are all violently insane. You can watch these madmen as they go about their broken lives and listen to their deranged muttering, but this works because you're not interacting, just watching as they follow a predefined script. As soon as you try to interact, they fly into a murderous rage that the computer can simulate without trouble.

DIALOGUE TREES can handle human interaction by predefining a list of actions players can take and matching responses from other characters.

Some games model interpersonal interaction with dialogue trees that allow the player to choose among a number of social interactions their character can perform. This works because the game designers can author every side of every interaction. There is no need to simulate anything.

The downside is that the player only has a handful of choices instead of the near-infinite variety available in real life.

We can reuse standard game verbs as options in a dialogue tree.

The actions players can take in games are usually all about moving, collecting, pushing, jumping, and shooting. It is possible to use these kinds of interactions to express human interactions.

One example is a situation in which the player is forced to choose between killing two different characters. In *Grand Theft Auto IV*, the protagonist is presented with an old enemy tied up on the ground and given an opportunity to kill him. The player can choose to either shoot the defenseless man or walk away. Both actions are expressed through controls that are used throughout the game: shooting and walking. But here, these actions are used to drive a predefined plot branch instead of a normal piece of gameplay.

Such interactions are fundamentally the same as dialogue trees since the player's options and the world's responses are all predefined. The only difference is that they express their choice with normal game actions instead of a special dialogue tree interface. This can help preserve flow because it doesn't break the player's natural control rhythm. It also avoids the interface complexity of real dialogue trees.

Multiplayer games can use real players to fill the roles of game characters.

In *Dungeons & Dragons*, the Dungeon Master plays the role of every nonplayer character in the game. He speaks for them and decides how they'll respond to any action the players take. There doesn't need to be a limit on what the players can do because, being a real person, the Dungeon Master can understand and respond to anything.

Real people can create remarkable stories together when they're motivated to do so. The trouble with this method is aligning player motivation with character motivation. It means motivating every player to properly play their role in the game narrative, which is exceptionally difficult. It works in face-to-face games played among friends because social pressure motivates people to participate in good faith. In video games, with anonymous strangers, or in competitive games, it's difficult to impossible to arrange players' motivations so that sustained, rich role playing can happen.

Case Study: Fallout 3

Let's examine a game-driven narrative experience and break down the narrative tools used to generate it. First, I'll tell you a story that happened to me when I played Bethesda Game Studios' 2008 post-apocalyptic RPG *Fallout 3*. After that, I'll break it down.

The game begins with the player character's birth in Vault 101. Built underground centuries ago, the Vault's purpose is to protect its inhabitants from nuclear holocaust. This story picks up as the player character leaves the Vault for the first time at age 19.

MY STORY

The landscape was a windblown expanse dotted with dead trees, smashed cars, and human bones. With the Vault door closed behind me, I had nowhere to go but forward.

Within minutes I encountered a tiny settlement called Megaton. While wandering through town, I encountered a store called Craterside Supply. Like every other structure in Megaton, the building was no more than tacked-together sheet metal and junkyard scrap. It was only identifiable by the name scrawled in white paint beside the front door.

The inside didn't look much better than the outside. Dust hung in the air, glowing yellow under the arc-sodium lighting, while ramshackle shelves lined the walls. A young woman in grubby blue coveralls swept the floor behind the counter, her flame-red hair pulled back into a messy ponytail. I approached her.

"Hey!" she said. "I hear you're that stray from the Vault! I haven't seen one of you for years! Good to meet you!" Her voice seemed to pitch higher and higher with every syllable. After the dour Wasteland, her enthusiasm was almost unnerving. "I'm Moira Brown. I run Craterside Supply, but what I really do is mostly tinkering and research." She paused for a moment. "Say, I'm working on a book about the Wasteland—it'd be great to have the Foreword by a Vault dweller. Help me out, would you?"

She seemed friendly, and I needed friends. "Sure," I said, "I've got plenty to say about life in the Vault."

"Great!" she replied. "Just tell me what it's like to live underground all your life, or to come outside for the first time, or whatever strikes your fancy!"

I thought she might be playing with me, so I decided to play back. "This 'Outside' place is amazing," I said. "In the main room, I can't even see the ceiling!"

"Hah!" said Moira. "Yeah, you wouldn't imagine how hard it is to replace that big lightbulb up there, too! That's great for a Foreword—open with a joke and all that. That'll be good for the book. In fact, want to help with the research? I can pay you, and it'll be fun!"

"What's this book you're working on?" I asked.

"Well, it's a dangerous place out there in the Wastes, right? People could really use a compilation of good advice. Like a Wasteland Survival Guide! For that, I need an assistant to test my theories. I wouldn't want anyone to get hurt because of a mistake. Nobody's ever happy when that happens. No. . .Then they just yell a lot. At me. With mean, mean words."

I considered this. "Sounds like a great idea!" I said. "I can't wait to help! What are you looking for?"

"Well, food and medicine. Everyone needs them once in a while, right? So they need a good place to find them! There's an old Super-Duper Mart not far from here. I need to know if a place like that still has any food or medicine left in it."

I agreed and said goodbye. An hour out of the Vault, and already I'm Moira Brown's survival guinea pig.

Once outside the town gates, I followed my compass toward the Super-Duper Mart. I soon crested a hill and found the husk of Washington, DC, laid out in front of me. Shattered buildings stretched away to the horizon, forming a jagged border against the yellow sky. I trudged toward them.

I found the Super-Duper Mart on the outskirts of town. Whoever architected it must have lacked in either creativity or money, because it was no more than a giant concrete shoebox, identifiable only by the huge block-letter sign looming over the parking lot.

As I entered the parking lot, I heard the *boom* of a big hunting gun alternating with the *pakpakpak* of an assault rifle. I rounded a corner and found a Wasteland raider battling it out with a man in an ancient leather coat. "What's wrong? Can't stand the sight of your own blood?" screamed the man in leather. They were his last words. The raider shot him down with a burst from the assault rifle and he fell, gurgling. Then she turned on me.

As with most raiders, this one had dressed to impress. She sported a tight black jumpsuit covered in spikes, a double Mohawk, and thick eyeliner that lent a demonic quality to her face.

She fired with her assault rifle. I fired back with my pistol. I must have hit her in the arm, because she dropped her weapon. I kept firing as she rushed to pick it up and take cover behind an ancient car.

Then she opened up, this time from behind the car. I was caught in the open and took several hits. It looked bad—my pistol wasn't powerful enough for me to trade blows with her assault rifle like this.

Just as I was getting desperate, I heard a boom from behind me. I turned to find a leather-clad woman firing at the raider with a huge rifle. She fired once more, and the raider fell.

I approached the dead raider and stripped her of everything she carried, including her assault rifle and ammunition. I even took her spiky clothes. They weren't my style, but I thought I might sell them later.

Just as I finished looting the corpse, an explosion went off right beside me and my vision filled with white. Coming to, I realized what had happened. The car the raider had used as cover had begun to burn when it was hit by stray shots. It had continued burning as I looted her corpse, and only exploded just now.

The explosion had crippled my right leg and left arm. I couldn't aim or move properly like this. I looked through my pack and found a Stimpak healing device. The chemicals flowed through my veins and healed my limbs enough to make them usable again. I chugged a Nuka-Cola to shore up my strength.

As I approached the Super-Duper Mart's front entrance, I noticed three corpses strung up in front of the store, twisted into grotesque poses. These weren't just casual murder victims—they were raider trophies on display. It seemed that the raider in the parking lot wasn't just passing through. The Super-Duper Mart was a raider base.

I reloaded my pistol and entered the building.

The store was dark inside. Sunlight struggled to penetrate windows caked with centuries of grime. A few of the fluorescent ceiling lights were still burning, forming yellow blobs of light in the choking dust. Shopping carts were scattered randomly over the floor, and the shelves displayed rows and rows of nothing.

I saw no one from my position at the door, but I knew they must be there. I crept into the room, using the dark to stay hidden. As I edged up to a checkout counter, I noticed a lone raider patrolling across the tops of the aisles, weapon in hand.

I snuck closer, took careful aim, and fired my pistol. The shot skimmed past the raider's head and thudded into the rear wall of the store. Return fire erupted from all around as raiders emerged from the woodwork, alerted by my attack. I retreated back to the checkout counter as bullets pinged around me. I found targets and fired, killing several raiders.

Two attackers approached from the left. One fell quickly to my pistol. The other aimed a gigantic rifle at me and fired, hitting the counter in front of me. I threw four rounds at his chest. One of them hit, but he kept coming, his rifle making great crashing sounds as it tried to tear off my head.

I retreated behind a pillar, desperate. Looking through my inventory, I found the assault rifle I stole from the spike-wearing raider in the parking lot. I readied it and waited. As the rifleman came into view, I put eight rounds into him in one long burst. He fell with a clipped scream.

The store went quiet. It seemed the fight was over, so I began scavenging. Dead raiders yielded armor and ammunition. I grabbed the hunting rifle off my last victim. Vending machines produced Nuka-Cola. Exploring the bathrooms, I found mattresses and drugs on the floors. It seemed this was where the raiders had been sleeping. A fridge yielded an assortment of food—the first thing Moira wanted me to find.

I proceeded into the back of the store to find the medicine Moira wanted. More unfortunate dead Wastelanders hung from the ceiling. The last was nailed to the wall in a vaguely Christlike pose. Like many of the others, he was headless.

As I studied him, I heard a burst of automatic weapons fire. I saw my blood and heard my cries of pain as the bullets hit me. Turning, I saw my ambusher. It was a raider with an assault rifle, wearing a motorcycle helmet with antlers nailed to the sides. He kept shooting, wounding my left arm. I stumbled back, firing blindly with my pistol. His next burst shattered my leg just as I dropped behind the cover of the pharmacy counter.

I looked through my pack and noticed a frag grenade. I stood up and tossed it. It landed at the antlered madman's feet and exploded, separating his legs at the knees and launching him into the air.

The store quieted again.

I repaired my arm with my last Stimpak and began scavenging. I picked the locks on some ammunition cases, taking bullets, grenades, and improvised mines. On various shelves I found machine parts, scraps of food, and a book called *Tales of a Junktown Jerky Vendor.*

Trying to get into the pharmacy's back room, I found myself blocked by a door that was too advanced for my rudimentary lockpicking skills. Searching around, I found a key for the pharmacy in a metal box some distance away. I returned and used it to open the door.

The pharmacy storage room was filled with rows of broken-down shelving. Most of it was covered with junk, but I did find darts, more grenades, liquor, a pressure cooker, and a miniature nuclear bomb. I also found the medical supplies Moira wanted to know about. I used one of the Stimpaks to heal my wounded leg.

As I left the pharmacy, I heard a voice over the store P.A. system. "We're back. Somebody open up the. . .Hang on, something ain't right here." Raiders were entering the store from the front door, and I was trapped at the back.

It was a hard fight, but I made it. By the time I got back to Megaton, the sky had faded to a dusty blue. Moira was cheery as always. "Huh. Did you know that the human body can survive without the stomach or spleen?" she enthused. "Oh, what's up?"

BREAKDOWN

This story is a particular experience that a player can have in *Fallout 3*. It will never happen exactly the same way to two players. Still, it can be understood as a story. It has pacing, exposition, a beginning, and an end.

Fallout 3 uses many different narrative tools. World story is everywhere, in the landscape, the architecture, and the mise-en-scène of junk, loot, and corpses. Other parts of the story, such as Moira's dialogue, are hard-scripted. Still others, such as combat encounters, are soft-scripted.

The integrated story that the player experiences arises emergently from the interaction of scripts, game systems, and the player's decisions. This emergence happens at all levels—on the micro level of individual motions and attacks, and on the macro level of quest choices and travel destinations. And because there are so many permutations, each player's experience is unique.

My story opens through world narrative. The Capital Wasteland is a desiccated husk of a landscape. The scorched buildings and cars tell the history of a world cremated by nuclear fire. The town of Megaton tells its own world story through architecture: sheet-metal shacks and hand-painted signs speak of a hardscrabble life of extreme poverty. And people are characterized appearances, too: Moira Brown's grungy coveralls and simple hairstyle mark a woman more interested in tinkering than popularity. You can tell she's a geek.

But world story isn't all that's happening here. The player experiences this world story through his choices of where to go and what to look at. So as the player wanders the space, there are two story threads running: the backstory of nuclear war, and the emergent story of the player character walking around the Wasteland after escaping the Vault. One story goes, "This town was built by desperate people." The other goes, "I walked into town and explored to my left." The player experiences both stories at once, simultaneously feeling the emotional output of each.

Once I began talking with Moira, the game switched from exploratory world narrative to a dialogue tree. All of my words were chosen from lists of speech options, and Moira's responses were all scripted.

To avoid the infinite story branching problem, *Fallout 3*'s dialogue trees loop back on themselves often. For example, every time you greet Moira, you get the same list of dialogue options, each leading to a different topic: purchasing gear, purchasing furniture for the player's home, local gossip, repairing objects, any quests in progress, and so on. After each topic resolves, the dialogue returns to the root topic list. So the dialogue tree itself is arranged in a hub-and-spokes content ordering structure.

The approach to the Super-Duper Mart created a sense of anticipation of the challenge ahead. This part of the story wasn't in any script, but it was implied by the geometry of the world.

My encounter with the raiders and leather-clad hunters outside the Super-Duper Mart was an interesting convergence of narrative tools. The raiders were scripted to be there and will always appear in the same places. The hunters, however, were not part of any script. Hunters appear randomly in the Wasteland throughout the entire game. In this case, they happened to show up just as I arrived at the Super-Duper Mart. The hunters and raiders, being mutually hostile, began fighting as soon as they saw one another, and this emergent fight was still going on as I arrived.

My introduction to this battle was hearing the hunter's bravado ("What's wrong? Can't stand the sight of your own blood?"), and seeing it get cut short by the raider's assault rifle. The madly brave hunter screaming his last threat as he dies is a poignant emotional exchange. What's interesting about this is that it is not modeled in the game mechanics. It is an interpretation constructed apophenically in a player's mind from randomized dialogue barks and straightforward combat interactions.

After the first hunter died, I was pinned down by assault rifle fire from a second raider. This short fight formed a miniature emergent story with its own emotional arc. Being pinned made me tense. After an unseen hunter saved my life, I was filled with relief and gratitude toward my savior. It almost seemed like she was saving me as an act of kindness, or killing to exact revenge for her murdered companion. Naturally, these interpretations are all pure apophenia, but they feel real and affect the player nonetheless.

The fighting inside the supermarket forms another mini-story. My stealthy entrance into the space is exposition. It gave me time to understand their situation before diving in. When raiders started coming out of the woodwork, the tension ratcheted up. It peaked as the rifle-wielding raider approached. This tension was finally resolved with the epiphany of remembering the assault rifle taken from the raider in the parking lot and the triumphal counterattack. This little arc is like a scene from an action movie, but instead of being authored by a designer, it emerged from the interaction of game systems, soft scripts, and player choices.

The final ambush from the antlered assault rifle foe was not scripted. His "ambush" was emergent and there was no real intent behind it in the artificial intelligence—he just happened to be left over after the main fight. But even though it wasn't in the mechanics, apophenically, it seemed like this last mad survivor had laid a trap.

The antlers gave that final raider a special personality by labeling him. He isn't just a raider; he's the weird raider with the goofy antlers. This label makes it easier to construct a story about him. Labeling is one area that *Fallout 3* could have improved. Most characters are just nondescript raiders. Had they had more identity—crazy doctor, bartender, master, slave—players would have been able to construct better stories about them.

THE GOOFY UNDERTONE

The world of *Fallout 3* has a strong undertone of goofiness: Moira's overwhelming enthusiasm, raiders with antlered helmets, and so on. These humorous juxtapositions are essential. Had the game been purely about surviving in a desperate, dead world, the emotional heaviness would have been too much for most players. Occasional absurdities lighten that emotional load.

Absurdity also helps justify less realistic parts of the game. For example, *Fallout 3*'s goofy vision of nuclear radiation permits it to throw all sorts of strange beasts at the player, from giant flies to 30-foot-tall humanoid behemoths. Had the radiation been modeled realistically, none of this would have been possible.

Finally, the unserious undertone reduces the impact of the inevitable logical absurdities in the game's emergent stories. For example, I once walked up behind a caravan guard and shot him three times in the back of the head. He turned, scowled, and said, "I thought I heard something!" Instead of feeling wrong, this moment just felt funny.

CONTENT ORDERING

The content is ordered by both scripting and world geometry. For example, the player must pass through the parking lot before going inside. Once inside, he must pass through the main room before experiencing the pharmacy. Finally, the raiders coming in the doorway are scripted to appear only after the player has explored the pharmacy.

The player can leave and return to the quest at any time. He might do half of it, walk away, and come back 20 hours of play later to finish it up. This creates a vast number of possible paths through the game, as the player juggles many different quests.

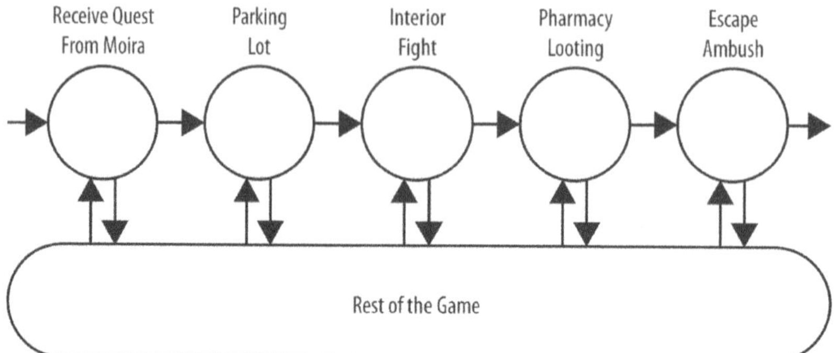

PACING

The pacing of this story is irregularly spiky. Tense moments of combat fall between longer periods of dialogue, exploration, healing, and scavenging. This mixture keeps players engaged without exhausting them.

We could argue that the pacing of this story would benefit from a greater sense of progression—more intense fighting as the quest goes on, ending with a climax. To create this, however, we would have to reconcile such a pacing curve with the fact that players can suspend and reactivate quests at any time. Our carefully crafted pacing is likely to be sliced and diced by easily distracted players. In such an unpredictable environment, the game's steady-with-spikes pacing might be the best solution because it is robust against being chopped up and reassembled.

SETTING

Fallout 3 is set in a postapocalyptic world. This setting supports the game well by justifying good and flexible game mechanics.

For example, it makes sense that starving, desperate people would often become violent. This omnipresent violence supports the game in several ways. It justifies repeated use of the game's combat systems. And it allows the game to tell emergent stories by having characters run and shoot instead of having them stand and talk, largely avoiding the human interaction problem.

The dead world justifies a very low population density. This dovetails well with the game's technical and design limitations. It saves the designers from having to create even more characters than the game's already-large cast. And it explains the absence of the large crowds which the game's technology is unable to handle.

5

Decisions

The brains sat around the dinner table, their moist neocortical folds glistening in the candlelight.

"What about you, Albert?" asked the narrow, gray brain. "What are your tastes these days?"

Albert, a wide, pink brain, quivered. "I like them big, and not too often. I want something that takes time to digest."

"Pah," said Isaac, a long, cylindrical brain. "Who wants to chew that long? I prefer a rapid series of tiny pieces. Bite-sized morsels."

The table exploded in debate—many, few, varied, consistent, big, small—as the waiters served the brains their individually preferred meals.

Seen as a whole, an interactive experience is an inscrutable tangle of interactions, thoughts, and emotions. To understand interactivity well enough to craft it, we need to examine the individual units of interactivity. Those units are decisions.

In some games, the decisions are easy to see. In a poker hand, a player must decide whether to fold or call. In *Civilization V*, the player must decide whether to invade the Babylonians now, or wait another turn. Games like this hand decisions to us, one by one, each a unique and perfectly formed puzzle.

Other games don't make it so easy. In real-time, multilayered games, decisions flow together like bubbles in a straw. They overlap, merge, and divide in a continuous dance of perception and thought. In *StarCraft II*, a professional player manages one attack while defending against another, guiding a scout, and growing his economy. In boxing, a fighter keeps track of his energy, stance, attack, and defense, deciding at each moment what to do with every part of his body. These competitors' various thought processes overlap so much that it's hard to identify the individual decisions. But even if we can't easily draw lines around the decisions, they're still there. And they're important, because decisions are powerful sources of emotion.

When we explain a decision, we use logical reasoning. We describe the why and how of the circumstances surrounding the decision, the desired goal, and how our choice gets us to that goal. But in reality, logic is only part of the process of choosing. The other part—and often this is the largest part—is driven by emotion. The purely rational human decision is a myth, no more real than Spock from *Star Trek*.

Whether you're choosing which pair of socks to put on, whether to get a divorce, or which opening move to use in chess, your decision is guided by how you feel about each option. You look at the black pair of socks and feel a twinge of boredom. You look at the orange pair and something lights up inside you. So you reach for the orange. Or you think about advancing your queen and a trained instinct injects you with a shot of unease. You look over at the pawn, and you feel better. So you move the pawn. In each case, some part of the unconscious evaluates the decision and triggers an emotion to guide your behavior. Those emotions are part of the play experience.

Understanding decisions is critical in game design because decisions are the only emotional trigger that is unique to games. Many media can provoke emotion through spectacle, character, or music; only games can do it through decision.

But crafting decision-generating systems is wickedly hard. Decisions themselves come in countless shapes and sizes. They can be important or inconsequential, difficult or easy. Some involve lots of information, others very little. They can be crystal clear, or shrouded in uncertainty. Some are rushed, while others allow long contemplation. They may be packed together, or generously spaced. Each variation and combination creates a different emotional flavor.

As an added challenge, we can't design decisions directly without breaking them. More than in any other field, in game design decisions must be emergent to work well. So instead of writing them one by one, we have to create systems that generate them on the fly.

Decision design is game design at its purest. While games can be enhanced by narrative, fiction, image, and sound, none of these is essential to the form. The heart of games is in interactivity, and the heart of interactivity is the moment of decision.

Feeling the Future

Most emotional triggers are described as working by something happening in the present. You see a scary monster, so you feel fear. You win a victory, so you feel triumphant. In each case, an event occurs, and the player's mind perceives that event and produces an emotional response a moment later. The cause and effect are obvious, and they make intuitive sense.

But decisions don't create emotion this way, because decisions aren't about the present. Decisions are about choosing among multiple possible futures. The emotions provoked by decisions aren't about something that has happened, but something that might happen.

Something doesn't have to happen to generate emotions. The player need only sense the possibility of it happening.

Imagine standing on the edge of the Empire State Building. Your toes hang over the void, and a gust of wind buffets your back. You look down and see cars crawling along like beetles 86 stories below. You're petrified. Your emotions, honed by millennia of natural selection, scream into your mind: *get the hell back!*

Now imagine standing on the edge of a friend's front porch in summer. Your toes hang over the flower bed, and a gust of wind blows through the front door and buffets your back. You look down and see a ladybug crawling along the edge of a flower petal. You feel at peace.

There is no difference in the events that took place in these two situations. In both cases, you stood on an edge and wind almost pushed you off. In neither case did you die. The only difference is in the possible futures presented by each. On the porch, your unconscious detected nothing dangerous in any nearby possible future, so there was no need for a powerful emotion to compel any decision. But on the skyscraper, your unconscious detected an immediate possibility of death. So it attempted to influence your decision-making process using the feeling of terror. You felt afraid even though *nothing happened.*

This is important. We're accustomed to thinking of the process of creating entertainment as a process of deciding what happens. Traditional storytellers think and talk about the sequence of events in a plot. Game designers talk about the situations that will rise emergently from the mechanics. The unspoken assumption is that anything which doesn't happen is irrelevant. But the human ability to feel emotions about possible futures means this is wrong.

In games, the player doesn't just experience what happens. His decision-making process mentally interacts with every possible outcome his mind can detect. His unconscious runs a constant simulation of the world stretching into the future, where he wins, loses, lives, and dies. These perceived possible outcomes affect his emotions, regardless of whether they occur or not.

So it's not enough for a game designer to think about what the player will do and how the game will respond. We also have to think about what the player will consider doing, and what he'll think the game might do in response. Because even though many of these situations never come to pass in reality, they still affect the player's experience because the player's mind senses that they *might* occur.

In high-level chess, players spend a lot of time staring silently at the board. A naïve observer might complain: "Why aren't they doing anything?" But they *are* doing something. They are deciding. Their bodies remain still, but their minds are blasting through the possibility space of chess, dancing across the surface of a thousand moves and countermoves, hunting for the one gem that solves the puzzle. Their emotions rise and fall as they sense possible attacks and then see the inevitable response. It's the quality of this internal decision process that makes chess fascinating, not the movement of pieces on the board.

The opposite is also possible. A poorly designed game can be packed with movement and color, but be utterly barren of meaningful decisions. Degenerate gameplay systems and gaps in decision pacing leave people disengaged no matter how many clashing swords and speeding cars flash onscreen. Physical action alone does not feed the mind's internal experience. For that, we need expectation, uncertainty, consequence, and decision.

For example, one large studio has two separate third-person action franchises that use much of the same technology and share many player abilities. Just from watching them, one can see that they look extremely similar. In both games, the player character climbs up walls and over obstacles and fights groups of enemies with a sword. But the experience of playing the two games is very different because of how the structure of the world feeds players' decisions.

The first game is set in an open world. The hero can run, climb, and jump anywhere to approach or escape from his enemies. Sometimes he might choose to be sneaky and strike from rooftops. At any time he may assault enemies in the street with a sword. He can run or climb in any direction in a massive world. This means that every moment is packed with a hundred possible futures. The player can look into the future and see himself swimming away in a river, hiding on a rooftop, or fighting to the death. And his mind is constantly churning on these possibilities, evaluating them, driving him toward one or another with levers of emotion. Even if he doesn't consciously consider these futures, he's feeling them—always.

The second game is very similar to the first in controls, except it is crushingly linear. Each area has one entrance, and one exit, and one particular sequence of jumps and climbing paths which allow the player to progress. There is never more than one possible future for the mind to think about, which means that there are no decisions. The player just does the one thing he can do at every point, so the game is emotionally empty. Even though the actions on the screen are the same as the first game, the thought process behind them—and the accompanying emotions—is very different.

PREDICTABILITY

It's usually an insult to call a game predictable. But it shouldn't be, because predictability is essential to meaningful decision making.

To feel a possible future, the player must sense and understand it. Standing on the edge of a skyscraper is scary because you understand how little it would take to fall to your death. If you did not understand what was going on, the possibility of death would not scare you because you would not sense it was there.

When we want a decision to be meaningful, its outcomes must be neither unknowable nor inevitable. They must be partially predictable.

Without any prediction of the future, planning and decision are impossible. There may be a million interesting futures out there, but they're meaningless if they're lost in a haze of incomprehensibility. When this happens, the decision-making thought process vanishes. The player can't look ahead, so the game degenerates into an emotionally barren exercise in reactivity, where the player just responds as fast as possible to things as they occur.

At the same time, the future cannot be totally predictable. A totally predictable future creates no meaningful decisions because there is no mental work to do in finding a way to a desirable result. We need only select the most favorable outcome.

Prediction of a possible future depends on it being driven by a consistent, comprehensible system.

Pick up a teacup, hold it out at arm's length, and drop it. What will happen?

Obviously, we all know the answer: shattered china and spilt tea. The reason we know is because we intuitively understand everyday physics. We know that gravity pulls things down over time, so things dropped from a greater height will hit the floor with more force. We know that a teacup is made of a brittle material that will shatter if struck hard enough. This is all part of a system of rules—physics—which we understand. Since we understand that system, we can predict what it will do.

The unconscious predicts possible futures by applying knowledge of the systems which drive the universe. Physics is one, but there are many others: psychological, economic, mechanical, and so on. Your kid's mind is a system. So are the politics at your workplace and the lawnmower in your garage that needs fixing. Feeling the future means first seeing the future by using our mental models of these systems to predict what will happen in response to any given action.

The same principle applies in prediction in games. The main difference is that the systems here are artificially designed arrangements of game mechanics. But to be predicted in an emotion-driving way, those mechanical systems must have certain properties.

First, they must be *consistent*. Like gravity, they must act the same way in different situations so that lessons learned in one place can be applied elsewhere. If the rules change constantly, prediction is impossible.

Second, they must be *comprehensible*. This means they must be simple enough that the player can wrap his mind around them. A consistent system isn't predictable if it can't be understood.

When game systems fulfill both of these criteria, the player can see and thus feel the future, and a universe of emotion arises from every predicted threat and opportunity. But when game systems are inconsistent or incomprehensible, those emotions vanish. Even if the threats and opportunities are there, the player won't be able to feel them since she can't detect them through the haze of inconsistent or incomprehensible systems.

For example, Mario always jumps the same way. His maximum jump height is always exactly the same. His control characteristics and falling speed never change. And these systems aren't complicated; there are only a few rules and numbers. This means that Mario's jumps are driven by a consistent, comprehensible system. So a player can, with practice, look at an obstacle course and know exactly which jumps will get him to the exit, what dangers he will face, and how he might defeat them. He can envision various paths, possibilities, and opportunities, and feel each one.

If Mario's jumping systems changed randomly, or were incomprehensibly complicated, that predictability would vanish. The player couldn't plan a jump path. Without those mental images of the future, he couldn't feel good about an opportunity or scared about a future danger. All he could do is react.

PREDICTABILITY AND PREDEFINED DECISIONS

Before we go on, I'd like to clarify something. When people talk about decision making in games, they're often referring to predefined plot branches, like those in an old *Choose Your Own Adventure* novel. In this kind of decision, the game designer explicitly defines each of the player's options and every outcome that those options lead to.

For example, a designer might script a character to approach the player and offer heroin. If the player accepts the heroin, a scripted sequence plays out where cops chase the player. If the player rejects the heroin, the criminal attacks the player. The choice, along with every possible result of the player's decision, all play out the same way every time because they're authored that way by a designer.

Such predefined decisions are different from the decisions I'm discussing in this chapter because their outcomes aren't determined by game systems the player can learn and predict. They're determined by the designer's arbitrary choice of what should happen. This means the thought process of making such decisions is completely different from that which drives mechanics decisions.

In the best predefined decisions, the player chooses for fictional reasons. He might turn down the heroin because he wants to be a good guy. Or he might accept it because he wants to be evil. In the worst cases, the player second-guesses the designer to try to get some optimal result. He'll look at the designer's habits in the past and choose to accept or reject the heroin based on his guess of which path will get him more money. Either way, the thought process isn't the same as a mechanics-driven choice like a chess move or fighting game attack. The player isn't thinking through game systems. He's thinking through sentimental values or trying to read the designer's mind.

Predefined choices do serve a purpose. They allow a player to coauthor a narrative with the designer in a way that isn't possible with systems-driven choices. We can't make a system to simulate a human mind or an entire narrative world, so if the player is going to affect these at all, they must make predefined decisions. But these predefined choices shouldn't be confused with the systems-driven decisions discussed in this chapter. They're authored differently and contribute to the experience in distinct ways.

PREDICTABILITY AND AI

There's a common assumption that smarter AI is better AI. The reasoning goes like this: A game is about simulating some fictional world with people in it. A more accurate simulation is better. Therefore, more accurate simulations of characters' minds are better. And, since real people are always smarter than game AI, smarter AI is always better, because it is more like a real person.

The problem with this is that people in games often shouldn't be simulations of real people because games aren't simulations of life. Games are mechanics wrapped in fiction, not mechanics trying to trick you into thinking they're real. The fiction wrapper enhances and communicates the mechanics, it doesn't define them.

And mechanics designs are often harmed by smarter AIs, because smarter AIs are often unpredictable. An AI driven by a few simple behaviors can be predicted. The player can plan an approach deep into the future because he knows what will happen at each step of the way. But a very smart AI with a complex, layered mind can't be predicted. The player can't plan around its actions because they're driven by an incomprehensible mind. The more the AI thinks, the less the player is able to think.

In most cases, AI is best thought of as a mechanic like any other, not as a simulation of a real mind. A character who follows straightforward, predictable, consistent rules often contributes more to a play experience than a realistically chaotic mind simulation.

For example, most soldiers in real-time strategy games act more like automata than people. Given an order, they carry it out exactly and immediately, and they do it the same way every time. This means that the same fight always ends the same way, and that the same counterstrategies always work. This consistency is what allows players to plan complex strategies. If soldiers had complex internal AI, the same battle would randomly swing from victory to defeat and back as the AI decided to go left instead of right, or lost and regained its courage. The AI soldiers would determine the outcome of fights instead of the player, which isn't what we want. Automata-like soldiers make less sense in the fiction, but their mechanistic predictability is what makes it possible for players to strategize with confidence that their strategies will play out consistently.

The exception to this rule is in designs where fiction is more important than mechanics-driven decision making. When a game's emotional triggers revolve around nuanced interaction among AI characters, it can be worth sacrificing the crystalline predictability of simple AI.

Information Balance

The character, difficulty, and complexity of a decision depend on the information that the player has while making it. The same decision can be made incomprehensible with too little information, fascinating with the right amount of information, and trivial with too much information.

This means that even without changing the decision at all, we can transform the mental process of making it by adding and subtracting information. I call optimizing decisions this way *information balancing*.

INFORMATION BALANCING is the design process of providing or denying information to a player to make a decision comprehensible without being obvious.

This is an elegant method of game design because it doesn't require changing the mechanics themselves. The game stays the same. All we're doing is hiding or revealing different parts of it, which is usually quicker and easier than reworking how the systems actually work.

The two ways information balance can go wrong are *information starvation* and *information glut*.

INFORMATION STARVATION

Inconsistent or incomprehensible systems aren't the only way to break predictability. Predictability can also break if the player doesn't have enough information about what is happening. This is called *information starvation*.

It's easy to induce information starvation in a game. Just hide a bunch of information. Put a vertical piece of cardboard in the middle of a chessboard and play without being able to see the other half of the board. Play *Magic: The Gathering* with all creature, artifact, and enchantment cards hidden from the opponent. Play tennis in the dark. In each case, the game collapses into reactive thrashing and random choices.

In rare cases, information starvation is a design goal. For example, *Battleship* and most gambling games are information-starved. This works because these games' primary emotional triggers aren't built around decision making. For them, the randomness induced by information starvation is a benefit since it makes the game more accessible and social by reducing the game's value as a lens of competition. But in games that are about the decisions of play themselves, information starvation can be deadly.

Some cases of information starvation are obvious and relatively easy to fix. We can increase the sight radius of a unit in a strategy game, or reveal more cards in a card game. But other times, information starvation can arise from the interaction of other seemingly unrelated elements in hard-to-predict ways.

For example, a common uncorrected cause of information starvation is what I call the *authored challenge preparation problem*. Many games are structured as a sequence of authored challenges. The player completes the first level, then the second, then the third, and so on. The information starvation appears when the game asks the player to prepare for future challenges before seeing them. The player has no way of deciding how to prepare since he has no in-game way of predicting what the next challenge will be.

The authored challenge preparation problem appears constantly, even in otherwise excellent games. For example, role-playing games often start by asking the player to create his character. The player must choose a race (human, elf, dwarf), class (fighter, sorcerer, thief), skills, attributes, and so on. These decisions are very important; they affect everything that happens through the rest of the 50-hour experience. Unfortunately, they're also broken. At the start of play, the player knows nothing at all about the game. He has no sense of the balance of combat, or his tool preferences. He doesn't know what foes he will face.

Given such a critical choice without the data needed to make it, players often fall back on the most familiar, safe option, missing out on the most interesting parts of the game. For example, in *Mass Effect 2*, there were six classes, the magic-using Adept to the tech-wizard Engineer. But post-release metrics revealed that 80% of players chose the Soldier—the most familiar and unoriginal class in the game. Given a set of incomprehensible options, people just went for the one they understood, and missed much of the value in the game.

Another common uncorrected cause of information starvation is the ambiguity of information delivered through a game's fiction layer. The critical decision-driving information that players want is usually purely mechanical: damage statistics, movement rates, quest structures, various mathematical tables for the game's economics. It is hard to deliver this information in the fiction because it doesn't exist in the fiction. The fiction says that the player is firing a rifle at a target, and it should do widely variable damage of many possible types based on range, hit location, random internal bullet tumbles, and many other variables. The mechanics say that a bullet is an instant trace that reduces hit points by a fixed amount. That amount cannot be communicated within the fiction, so it often isn't communicated at all. In these cases, it is frequently better to go around the fiction and deliver some of this mechanics information directly.

Sometimes the Internet solves information starvation for us. Websites like GameFAQs.com provide massive player-authored text files called FAQs (Frequently Asked Questions) which explain every ability and level in a game, often including hidden statistical data that players were never supposed to know. At first glance, reading a FAQ seems like a form of cheating that would ruin a game. But in an information-starved game, FAQs can dramatically improve the play experience. With the FAQ, players can plan, predict, and decide meaningfully and intentionally, and the experience blooms. Because they understand the implications of their choices, those choices suddenly become interesting.

A useful FAQ is a warning sign. When a text file makes a game noticeably better, that game is probably information-starved. It's full of value—the designer just needs to help players understand that value by giving them access to more information.

Information starvation is an insidious problem because designers can't see it due to their unique knowledge of the game, and because it's emotionally painful to find.

Information starvation is common because it hides itself from designers. It does this in two ways.

First, it is inherently invisible to designers. A designer knows everything about his game—far more than most players will ever discover. We can try to pretend that we don't know what we know, but there is no way to actually have the experience of an uninitiated player. Without playtesting or other safeguards to detect these problems, it's easy to think a game is working well when it is actually critically information-starved and unplayable for anyone who doesn't already know it inside and out.

But information starvation also hides itself in another, even more insidious way. It uses emotional blackmail to make us not *want* to find it.

It feels good to see a new mechanic finally work after weeks of design effort. For many designers, that sense of accomplishment is our main reason for doing the work. But hunting information starvation puts that feeling in jeopardy. It threatens to show that that feeling of success was just an illusion—that, in front of real players, the mechanic is an impenetrable mess. That's a terrible letdown for a designer, and it's emotionally difficult to take actions to seek that result.

But it must be done. Information starvation is always found eventually. It's better that it happens before release, when we can still do something about it.

INFORMATION GLUT

While too little information makes decisions confusing and random, too much information erases them entirely. A decision is about seeing the correct answer implied by the information given. If the answer is already plainly stated in the information given, there is no mental process in seeing it. The thought process vanishes; the decision is no longer a decision.

That means that sometimes we can generate a decision from nothing just by subtracting information. By not handing players the answer, we give them an interesting problem to think through.

For example, in *Modern Warfare 2* the player can attach a heartbeat sensor to the side of his rifle. The sensor displays a map with the locations of nearby enemies in front of the player, even if they're behind walls.

If this is all it did, it would be an awful design. Much of the best play in *Modern Warfare 2* derives from the challenge of figuring out where enemies are. A player given complete information on enemies' locations could blunder around corners with no care, tension, or thought, and never have to guess at enemies' movements. The game would devolve into a reactive shooting contest, and the pokerlike game of cat and mouse would collapse.

The solution is to subtract information. But how, exactly?

How would you do it? What would you change about the heartbeat sensor to make it interesting again without cutting it altogether? Take a moment to think about this before reading on.

Infinity Ward's designers fixed the sensor by adding two key limitations. First, the sensor doesn't work on enemies who have the *Ninja* character perk. This means that just because the sensor says nobody is there doesn't mean nobody is there. Someone with *Ninja* could still be there, so the player must think and decide whether someone with *Ninja* is around a corner before he turns it. This also adds another layer of strategy at high skill levels: a smart player will remember who and how many of his adversaries are using *Ninja* and calibrate his assumptions appropriately, perhaps even giving up the heartbeat sensor entirely.

Second, the sensor does not show enemies' locations continuously. Rather, they're seen as periodic blips, once every 3.5 seconds, like on an old-style radar screen. Between pulses, the sensor displays nothing. This means that even when he has someone on the sensor, the player must make a mental effort to figure out where the enemy has moved since the last blip. And in *Modern Warfare 2*, a skilled opponent can easily flank and kill you in that time. Again, this adds another layer of strategy: skilled players will realize when they're being tracked on heartbeat sensors, and deliberately start moving to avoid being where the blip says they are.

These limitations make a world of difference in how the sensor plays. And that difference was made without changing any mechanics interactions at all. Weapon damage, movement, and environments are all the same as before. But by dialing a torrent of information down to a slow drip, we create entirely new classes of decisions and strategies.

Information glut isn't so much a failure as a missed opportunity. Nothing breaks when there is too much information. Testers don't get confused and cry for help. In fact, the game hums along too smoothly because they understand everything. That's why often, the hardest part about tackling information glut is realizing that it's happening in the first place.

WAYS TO HIDE INFORMATION

We've seen how when the player knows everything, decisions disappear due to information glut. At first this seems to imply that decisions are only possible in what are known as *incomplete information games*.

In an incomplete information game, part of the game state is hidden from some players.

For example, poker is an incomplete information game because you can't see other players' cards. In contrast, chess is a complete information game since both players can see everything on the board.

But this traditional distinction doesn't cover all the ways that decision-relevant information can be hidden. Even seemingly complete information games can have decisions because they hide information in other, less obvious ways.

Information can be hidden in the future behind chains of complex cause and effect.

Complete information games reveal their present, but not their possible futures. We can see what the whole chessboard will look like after we make one potential move, but we can't see what it will look like three turns down the line. This information is hidden in the future behind a chain of interactions, and extracting it requires interesting mental effort.

Information is hidden in players' internal states.

Imagine how much easier chess would be if you could read your opponent's mind, know his planned future moves, the vulnerabilities he has perceived in your position, and the vulnerabilities he hasn't perceived in his own. This information is part of the game just as much as the positions of the pieces on the board, but it's hidden.

The most powerful multiplayer experiences are often about divining and exploiting internal information like this. Reading or controlling an adversary's mind is one of the most satisfying forms of victory.

Information can be hidden by speed.

The brain takes time to perceive, process, and use information. This means that information that has arrived within the last fraction of a second is effectively hidden from our decision-making process. We don't decide based on the information we perceive now, but based on the information we perceived a tenth of a second ago.

This is how we play rock-paper-scissors. Since both players throw at the same time, neither one has time to use the other's move in making his own decision, even if one throws a few milliseconds earlier.

INFORMATION BALANCE CASE STUDY: POKER

The history of poker is a perfect example of a design process swinging back and forth through different types of information balance.

The first version of poker was almost purely a game of chance. Four players anted up, and then each drew five cards from a 20-card deck. Each player bet once, and hands were shown. If you had a good hand, you might bet high. If not, you would either fold or try to bluff.

Old poker was information-starved. It lacked complex decisions because there wasn't enough data to think on. Each player knew only the contents of his own hand and the bets that had been made so far. With just one betting round, this isn't enough information to form coherent strategies. So the game had a low skill ceiling because it was almost totally random.

The Mississippi riverboat hustlers who played the game wanted it to support a higher skill level so that they could fleece the tourists without resorting to risky cheating methods. So they redesigned the game.

The first change was the switch to the 52-card English deck instead of the old 20-card deck. Thirty-two additional cards vastly increased the number of possible hands. That change alone, however, would have just made the game even more information-starved since it increased the number of possible hands without giving any more information to distinguish them. The more important change was the introduction of multiple draw and betting rounds. Instead of placing one nearly blind bet, play now went around the table several times. On their respective turns, each player could throw away cards he didn't want and draw new ones to replace them. Then, the player could either fold or bet whatever amount he wished.

This multiround structure added a tremendous amount of information to the game. Now, players could respond to one another's draws and bets across betting rounds. By watching how someone drew and bet, they could figure out what the other player was holding. This style of poker survives today in the form of *draw poker.*

But even draw poker is still heavily luck-based. It's not as blind as old poker, but still leads to a lot of guessing and hoping. So the game kept evolving.

During the Civil War, someone created *stud poker,* named after the horses used to pull artillery. Stud poker didn't allow drawing. Instead, players were dealt cards one at a time, with betting rounds in between, and three of each player's cards were dealt face up for everyone to see.

Stud poker has a very different information balance than draw poker. In draw poker, it's hard to tell exactly what someone has by watching him draw cards. A player who draws one card could be bluffing, trying to make a pair, three-of-a-kind, a full house, or a flush. But in stud poker, players got to watch one another's hands form card by card. A good player could guess the two hidden cards from the three visible ones and the changes in someone's betting patterns. You might see someone with four, five, and six suddenly start betting high after drawing a particular card and guess that he made a straight.

But the game's information balance had swung too far. Now there was an information glut. In many stud hands, it's patently obvious who has the best hand. Sometimes a winning hand is plainly visible in the three face-up cards. For example, there is no reason to bet against someone showing a three-of-a-kind when you're holding a pair, since you're guaranteed to lose. What might have been an interesting decision has been erased by an information glut that handed you the answer for free. So the game kept evolving.

In the mid-20th century, someone invented *community card games.* In these games, as in stud poker, cards are laid down one by one between betting rounds. The difference is that some of the face-up cards are shared among players instead of being held by individuals. Texas Hold'em is a modern example of this kind of game.

The community card mechanic finally hit a perfect point of information balance. The game rarely generates obvious or incomprehensible choices. There is only a small amount of hidden information (two hidden cards in Texas Hold'em) to keep track of, but that information is linked closely to the community cards and players' betting patterns. The face-up cards can't make winners obvious because everyone shares these cards—if there are three aces face up, everyone has a hand with three aces. The only question is who has another hidden pair, or the fourth ace, or a high card? This perfect information balance means that nearly every hand generates fascinating decisions, giving just enough information to feed on, but never so much as to make an answer obvious.

The basic mechanics of poker have mostly stayed the same over the centuries. You get your hand, and you check, bet, or fold. But the game has transformed itself several times over just by changing how it structures and reveals information. By hitting the point of perfect information balance, it extracts as much meaning and emotion from every decision as possible. And finding that point only took two centuries.

Problematic Information Sources

To analyze information balance, we have to know exactly what information players have while making a decision. But it's often not obvious what players will know or how they will know it, because information can be revealed or hidden in unexpected ways.

FICTIONAL AMBIGUITY

Fiction helps communicate with players by wrapping mechanics in familiar images and sounds. But there is a dangerous ambiguity in this process, because no game mechanic completely simulates everything about its fictional wrapper.

Information from the fiction is often ambiguous because the player can't know which aspects of the fiction are real game mechanics and which aren't.

Imagine you're playing a game and you see a roast turkey on a table. What can you do with it? Can you pick it up, put it in a backpack, and carry it around? Can you eat it, and if so, what does that mean in the game? Can you sell it? Can you freeze it? Can you throw it somewhere to attract animals, perhaps allowing you to sneak past? Can you hide a pistol inside it? In real life, you can do any of these things and more with a roast turkey. And various games have allowed each of these actions. But no game allows all of them.

The problem is that the player has no way of knowing which of these possibilities is real in a given game just by looking at the turkey. This means he can't predict any interaction involving the turkey because he doesn't understand the mechanical system it signifies. The image of the turkey is just a symbol for an unknown game mechanic underneath.

This is an endemic problem in classic adventure games. For example, one adventure game in the early 1990s had a puzzle that required sneaking past a guard. In the player's inventory were some sticks, some string, and some mud. The fiction implies a near-infinite number of ways to use these tools to sneak past someone. You could throw mud in his eyes and run past while he is blinded. You could throw a stick nearby and sneak past while he looks at the noise. You could fashion a weapon and kill him.

This game required that the player combine the sticks, string, and mud into a mask so that the guard doesn't recognize him (seriously). While this is possible in the game's fictional wrapper, there is nothing special about it among the thousands of other equally plausible ways you could use these tools to get past a guard. The result is that the player approaches the puzzle while information-starved. Since he is denied the mechanics-level understanding needed to make the decision, his only option is to exhaustively try every interaction available to him. The game collapses into a rote exercise in random flailing.

Even good games have these problems. A more recent, critically acclaimed adventure game has a puzzle that tasks the player with waking up a pilot who ejected from his plane, got his parachute hung in a tree, and fell asleep. The problem is that the pilot has headphones on, so he can't hear anything. It being winter, some solutions are immediately obvious. Make a snowball and chuck it at his face. Poke him with a long stick. Wait until he wakes up naturally. Shake the tree. These all would work in the fiction, but none of them works in the game. The real solution is to climb into his crashed plane, twiddle some dials on the airplane radio until it displays his frequency, then travel to a nearby radio station and transmit a message through his earphones to wake him up. Again, it makes fictional sense, but so do about a thousand other equally plausible solutions.

Puzzle design is the most obvious example of fiction-mechanics ambiguity, but it's not the only one. Anything communicated through fiction is vulnerable to this problem. Will that wooden plank protect me from bullets? Will a fireball spell kill a person in one shot? Can I break that glass? Can I open that door?

The solution is to take the puzzle out of the fiction. Instead, construct puzzles out of well-understood mechanics.

Good game decisions, including good puzzles, are always based around nonobvious uses of mechanics that work in obvious ways.

The player should know all the mechanics involved in a problem. The decision is in figuring out how to use them to get to a solution.

For example, the *Super Mario* games have jumping puzzles. These are arrangements of platforms and hazards over which Mario must jump to get to some goal. But to do this, the player must find a good path. Finding this path is an interesting puzzle because the player can think through the jumps without ambiguity or uncertainty since Mario's jumping is consistent and comprehensible. This creates a rich puzzle-solving thought process as the player's mind spins through possibility after possibility. And when he sees the solution, he'll know it immediately and fill with a rush of insight.

The exception to this guideline is when the decision itself only has meaning in the fiction. A game can offer a moral or character choice that is totally outside the game mechanics and only affects fictional elements. In this case, fictional information can be used alone to make the decision because the decision itself has no mechanical meaning—it works on a purely make-believe level. But the moment the choice starts feeding back into the game mechanics by changing stats or level paths or tool upgrades, it becomes a different type of decision and needs to be fed by unambiguous mechanical information.

METAGAME INFORMATION

Players have more information than what the game itself gives them. They draw this knowledge, or *metagame information*, from outside the game itself.

METAGAME INFORMATION is information the player gathers from the real world outside the game.

Players know a lot about a game even before they begin play. They can guess its length from genre convention. They know how hard it is because their friends talk about it. They can predict NPC (Non-Player Character) behavior and plot twists by watching for clichés or by knowing the habits of the studio behind the game. They know the limits of computer technology, so they know the game will never put 10,000 characters on-screen at once. They've seen the trailers and the box art, so they might know key characters, themes, and plot points. None of this is inside the game mechanics or the fiction, but players still know it, so it still affects their decision process during play.

Metagame information can twist an experience by giving players information that the designer assumes they don't have. Often this causes information glut.

For example, in many games, players collect and use resources like ammo and health. Often, the fiction implies that these resources should be very limited: the player character is trapped in a zombie-filled castle or an alien-infested spaceship. In such a place, one would expect to go long periods without finding a first-aid kit or ammunition. The fiction is claiming that it is going to starve the player. It threatens the player with unfair, arbitrary death to make him feel afraid.

But is the game really as unfair as the fiction suggests? Usually not. And the player's unconscious knows it. The player knows that there will never be an extremely long gap during which he won't find any resources, because that would break convention and feel unfair. He knows the game won't do something so mean because it was created for his entertainment.

This metagame information twists his mental process of thinking about resource management. Now, instead of thinking in the terms defined by the game fiction, he's thinking about designer habits and genre conventions. He can guess when the next resource will appear because he knows what's fair, and he knows the game will play fair because it is a game. This reduces tension and weakens immersion.

Metagame information problems are hard to see because their effects are mostly internal. Like most information glut problems, they don't break the game entirely—they weaken it by distorting players' internal thought processes.

Different players have different metagame information. A game journalist has a massive vault of metagame information. A young child has much less. Most players are somewhere in between. But even the most naïve player will still know quite a bit. He knows that the game is played with a certain interface, on a certain type of machine. It is confined to a television screen or a game board. It was made by people from a certain culture, who designed for the purposes of entertainment.

There are two basic ways to handle metagame information. One is standard. The other is a little bit crazy.

The standard solution is to accept that it's there and design systems that still create the desired experience even given metagame information. This means not trying to make the player be afraid of something he knows can't happen, or hope for something he knows is impossible. Threaten the player with justifiable, fair, gamelike threats. Give him explicitly balanced, attainable goals. Flex the fiction to work within the player's metagame information. Treat it as one more design constraint.

The crazy method is to call his bluff. Show the player that you're not a normal designer; that the rules don't apply to you. Be unfair. Be arbitrary. Break established technical limits.

The crazy method is dangerous and difficult. Game conventions exist for a reason. In most cases, it's not a good idea to break them. At the same time, there are experiences that can arise from unreasonable, unfair threats and challenges that can't be had any other way. For example, *System Shock 2* is terrifying because it doesn't lie to the player. The game is set in a massive, dead, monster-infested spacecraft. The fiction implies that resources should be extremely limited, enemies numerous, and the player shouldn't have much of a chance at survival. And all of this is the case. The game is actually unfair. A sloppy, careless player will be whittled down until death. There are no fail-safe mechanisms. In some sense, it sounds like bad game design. But it's also wonderfully immersive, because it means the mechanics mirror the fiction. The player feels starved and trapped because he really is starved and trapped.

Decisions and Flow

The purpose of flow is to pull the player's mind into the game. When we're not in flow, pieces of the real world constantly intrude on our consciousness. We feel our fingers pushing a button. We hear the clock ticking, or dogs barking outside. We pause to go to the bathroom, take a drink, or talk to a friend. All this is experiential clutter. It constantly gets in the way of the experience that the game is seeking to create.

But when we're in flow, the real world vanishes. Mind and game enter into an unencumbered dance of action, reaction, decision, and outcome.

This means that flow is a foundation for good game experiences. Problems that seem to arise in other areas of a design often come down to nothing more than breaks in flow. Without flow, players feel and complain about every annoyance. With flow, they'll accept strange fictions, chunky graphics, or unclear interactions. The most important design mistakes are the ones that break flow, because they weaken the link between the player's mind and the game, interfering with every other part of the experience.

People talk about games as forms of escapism, and they are. But we often assume that escapism is about fantasy—that we want to escape our boring life by pretending to be a sorcerer or a race car driver. But does anyone want to be a short, fat Italian plumber, or a jumping cube of meat? No—yet *Super Mario Bros.* and *Super Meat Boy* still generate powerfully escapist experiences. Because this form of escapism is about flow, not fiction. And it's not driven by the fictional wrapping, but by the mechanics.

Earlier, we looked at how flow arises from a balance between ability and challenge. But that was the basic, simplified concept of flow. It's not enough to tell a game designer just to balance skill against challenge. Real flow isn't smeared with a big brush over a whole experience by the measurement of these gross quantities. Rather, it's a delicate dance of moment-to-moment decision timing.

Imagine the player's mind is a small cup with a hole in the bottom. The game can place quantities of water into the cup. Maintaining flow means ensuring that water is always draining through the hole, without the cup ever overflowing. This means constantly putting more quantities of water in, without ever putting in too much.

Those quantities of water are decisions. As soon as they enter the mind, it starts working on them. Most last only moments. To keep the mind flowing, we have to keep feeding it decisions at just the right rate. Too little, and it drains out within seconds and boredom sets in. Too much, and it overflows, breaking flow. To do this, we have to get the size and timing of decisions just right.

DECISION SCOPE

DECISION SCOPE is the amount of thought a decision takes to make.

Decision scope is the "size" of a decision as it passes through the mind. In the water and cup metaphor, it is the amount of water that this decision puts into the cup. Complex decisions involving many variables are large in scope because they can occupy the mind for a long time. Easy decisions with just one or two variables are the opposite.

We can group decisions into five categories of scope. From smallest to largest, they are nondecisions, twitch decisions, tactical decisions, profound decisions, and impossible decisions.

Nondecisions are decisions whose answers are so obvious that they cease to be decisions at all. For example, when you make breakfast cereal, you pour milk into it. The decision to pour milk into the cereal isn't really a decision because it only engages the mind in the most cursory way. It's such an obvious thing to do that you can do it by pure habit. When you were a child, this might have been a decision. But today, the decision has shrunk to nothing, leaving only a thoughtless action. Nondecisions like this can keep the player's fingers busy, but they don't contribute to flow since they don't engage the mind.

Twitch decisions are the smallest meaningful decisions. They take less than a second to think through, and require only simple conscious reasoning. Punch or kick? Reload now, or wait one more second? Look left or look right? Jump or dodge? Twitch decisions are a common basis for flow in games because they're easy to generate. We don't have to set up interesting, elegant systems of partially predictable cause and effect and have the player think through them. We need only compress a simple choice into a small time space. That's why action games are often called *twitch games*—they are based almost entirely on twitch decisions.

Tactical decisions are the next class of decisions. They require one to five seconds of thought, and noticeably engage the player's conscious mind. Which equipment should I buy? Which units should I build? These kinds of decisions involve more information than twitch decisions. A player might consider the positions of multiple characters, and their abilities, conditions, and tools. He might even think back to the outcome of a similar situation that took place earlier.

Profound decisions are the largest decisions, taking 10 seconds or longer to make. Decisions this large use so much information that they go beyond the game itself and draw from the player's broader knowledge of emotion, culture, and humanity. They push the player to look inside himself and scrape his thoughts, memories, and emotions for every fragment of information he can find. When chess grandmaster Garry Kasparov stares at a chessboard for a quarter hour, he is making a profound decision. He is putting all his knowledge from years of study to work. His mind is swimming through knowledge of his opponent's habits, hundreds of possible future game states, recently discovered tactics and strategies, previously made plans, examinations of his own judgment in the moment. Profound decisions only arise from the most elegant, subtle, fascinating game systems. Most games never present one.

Impossible decisions are beyond a player's ability to understand. If a decision requires a subtlety or volume of knowledge that is totally beyond the player, or the potential outcomes are vastly too numerous to understand, the decision becomes noise. The player must be able to wrap his mind around the decision and choose one path for comprehensible reasons, with a coherent expectation of results. If he cannot, the decision is impossible and does not contribute to flow because the player will just choose randomly.

Games can present decisions of any scope, or any mix of scopes. This mixture characterizes the pacing and feel of play. A game packed with massive numbers of tiny twitch decisions is a frenetic action game. A plodding march of profound choices is a slow strategy game. A game with one near-impossible mind-bender is a puzzle.

Player skill changes the effective scope of decisions.

A decision that is profound for a novice is a nondecision to an expert. As a player learns, a previously impossible decision might become profound, then tactical, then twitch, before finally becoming a nondecision.

This gives us another way to think about skill ranges: a game's skill range is the range of skill levels at which it frequently presents twitch, tactical, or profound decisions. This means that its skill ceiling is defined by the scope of its largest decisions. When a player learns enough that the largest-scoped decisions in a game become nondecisions, he has passed the skill ceiling. Nothing is going into the cup, so flow becomes impossible, and the player walks away.

The two characteristic ways that flow can break are when the cup runs dry and when it runs over. Let's look at each of them.

AVOIDING FLOW GAPS

Flow is very short-lived. The most important part of maintaining flow is generating that stream of decisions so that the cup stays full but never overfills. Even the tiniest breaks in the pace of decision can degrade flow. Players can feel the boredom of a gap of even one second. If there are enough of these gaps, a smooth, flowing experience degrades into a stop-start exercise in frustration. I call these sorts of delays *flow gaps*.

A FLOW GAP is a period of time—whether a second or an hour—when the player's mind has nothing to chew on.

Flow gaps can emerge into an experience in a thousand ways.

For example, designers might decide to add a delay to a tool to balance its power level. A wizard's wand in a fantasy game might be configured to only be able to cast thunder bolts once every two seconds. But while this may balance the wand, it also introduces flow gaps if the player has nothing else to do between shots.

Other times, flow gaps can appear due to fictional or aesthetic design elements. Menu transitions, movement animations, and dialogue can all block the player's ability to act for a moment, creating a gap in the decision stream.

This is a classic mechanics-fiction conflict, because it is caused by a piece of art that looks good and enhances the game's make-believe layer, while weakening the mechanical decision-driving interaction of the game. Obviously, the best solution is to find a design that both looks good and sustains flow. But if a choice must be made, most games benefit more from sustained flow than fancy menu transitions or animations. Because while graphics look good the first time, flow feels good forever.

If a delay can't be removed, we should find some way to introduce decisions into the gap to fill it. Sometimes this is as simple as making other abilities available. The wizard's rod may be recharging, but the player can still move and attack with a knife.

Other times, we need more exotic designs to handle unusual situations. For example, many different games across genres have included some sort of stun attack. Fantasy games have stunning spells, military games have nonlethal stun grenades, Spiderman can throw a web on his enemy, and a boxer can punch his opponent in the ribs to stun him. It's a good design because it combines elegantly with other follow-up attacks, and it varies the pace of combat.

But there's a problem with stuns: the victim gets a brutal flow gap.

The most naïve version of a stun is freezing the victim. But while this makes fictional sense, and it may be fair, it's an infuriating flow breaker. The victim cannot make any decisions during the stun since he can't act. How do we solve this?

Different games have used a variety of methods to keep the essence of stun without this side effect. For example, some games stun by interfering with the victim's controls while still allowing him to act. The stun grenade in *Modern Warfare 2* slows the player's turning rate and makes his view sway. This degrades his aim and makes it easy to attack him from the side, but it still allows the stunned player to keep interacting and deciding. Old arcade fantasy games used to model stun spells by scrambling all the player's controls, so pushing up made the character move down and vice versa. Again, the victim is affected, but can still act. The flashbang grenade in *Counter-Strike* whites out the victim's screen for several seconds, but leaves his controls fully functional. This means that a blinded player can still play in a reduced capacity by remembering his positioning and listening for footsteps. In each case, the stun is meaningful, but flow is preserved.

AVOIDING OVERFLOW

An OVERFLOW is a moment where the player is overwhelmed by decisions.

Overflows are more obvious than flow gaps. Whereas flow gaps create little moments of boredom, overflow announces itself through complaining, stressed playtesters. Since it's so obvious, designers tend to correct it naturally by easing off the decision pressure. So I won't cover overflows further here. Watch for them, and reduce the decision pressure when they occur.

Overflows in finished games usually happen with players of lesser skill. The designer might have reached a good rate of flow for the players he tested with, but weaker players have a terrible time as they flail around below the skill barrier. To some degree, this is inevitable. There are almost always some players who are so unskilled that they can't play. This is why it's a good idea to deliberately choose a minimum skill level and design around that instead of trying to include everyone.

TURN-BASED DECISION PACING

Up until now, I've discussed flow in terms of a real-time system. This doesn't apply to turn-based games because turn-based games allow players to pace their own decisions. When faced with a large-scoped decision, players simply take a long turn. Given a small decision, they take a short turn.

This doesn't, however, mean that turn-based game designers can ignore decision scope—only that the consequences of doing it wrong are different. In fact, two of the classic endemic problems in turn-based game design can be described in terms of poorly scoped decisions.

Micromanagement happens where there are too many small-scoped decisions. Players are forced to endlessly shuffle around tens or hundreds of nearly meaningless tokens to optimize their performance. They end up experiencing a flow gap, because the time it takes to move the tokens is more than the time it takes to decide what to do. The game becomes about the boring physical act of moving tokens instead of the mental dance of decision making.

Analysis paralysis occurs when decisions are scoped too large. Players end up sitting and thinking for an excessively long time. Sometimes, as in chess, this isn't necessarily a problem. Other times, as in board games with many players or games that are intended to have a faster pace, it's an experience killer.

DECISION VARIATION

While a game can hold flow with a long string of the same-scoped decisions appearing at the same rate, it's a plodding, repetitive sort of flow. To keep things interesting, we should spice things up with different decision densities and scope. Don't just feed the player a tactical decision every four seconds for an hour at a time. Toss him a compressed sequence of twitch decisions, followed by a profound mind-bender that allows as much time as desired, followed by some five-second tactical decisions, and so on.

We can also vary decisions by flavor. Decisions of similar scope can have a different qualitative flavor if their subject matter is different. For example, in a strategy game, a tactical choice about how to move an army may be roughly similar in scope to a decision about where to build a new production structure. Repeating one of these decisions endlessly, however, is less interesting than alternating between the two.

The classic pacing curve that I reference in Part I is one guideline for this. Start out slow, go through several cycles of rising action interleaved with troughs of calm, before finally spiking to a climax and falling into a denouement.

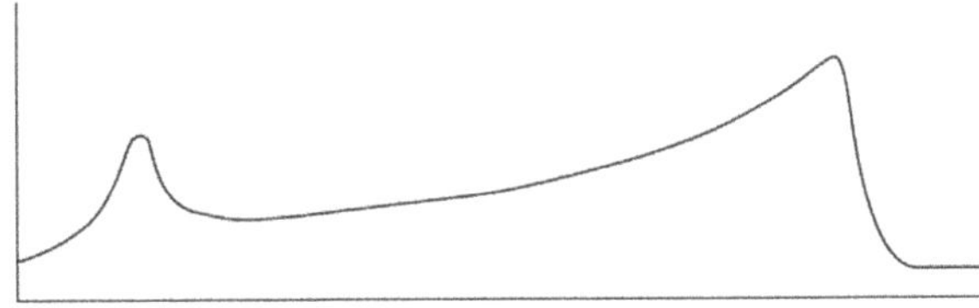

But the standard intensity curve isn't the only way to vary decision pacing. Rich game systems are often too unpredictable to follow to the standard curve all the time. Often they'll climax several times at random intervals, or have slow sections that seem too long on paper. Since we can't predefine decisions (because mechanics must generate them on the fly for them to be systems-based and thus predictable), it's hard to achieve that traditional pacing formula every time. But that's not a problem.

The only hard-and-fast rule of flow pacing is that it should vary. Neither bore the player with long, slow periods, nor exhaust him with long, fast ones.

It's possible to do a rough decision-pacing analysis on a design that has not been implemented. Just imagine playing the game as a player would. You are emulating the game systems in a very inaccurate way using your brain. Think about what's going on, what you know, what you don't know, the decisions being presented, and the thought process required to make those decisions.

But there's a trick to this. The human mind will naturally skip to the most interesting parts of any imagined or remembered story. This will hide flow gaps. To think about decision pacing in a useful way, you must go through every second of the experience in your mind in real time, without skipping anything. This isn't natural or easy. It's palpably uncomfortable to sit there and imagine every boring animation, loading screen, and pointless button press. It feels weird to spend five minutes thinking about a five-minute experience. But it's essential to preserve time if you're to gain any useful knowledge about pacing. This process isn't as good as playtesting the game, but it's better than nothing and much, much easier.

Decisions Case Study: Counter-Strike

I first played *Counter-Strike* back in 1999, when it was just a *Half-Life* modification made by two people. The gameplay was straightforward: teams of special ops soldiers would fight it out with gangs of balaclava-clad terrorists. Once one team was eliminated or completed its objective, everyone would reappear for another round. Players would gather money for killing enemies or completing objectives, which they could use to buy better weapons and armor in later rounds.

It was a good game. The standard pattern for good games is to get an explosion of popularity which slowly tails off to nothing over a few years. But that didn't happen with *Counter-Strike.*

I stopped playing by 2001, but the community kept going. Technologically advanced competitors like *Unreal Tournament 2003* came and went, but people kept playing *Counter-Strike. Half-Life 2* came out, and people kept playing *Counter-Strike.* The game got a graphical update, and the years kept passing. The mega-hit *Call of Duty 4* slammed into the market in 2007, but, as you can guess, people kept playing *Counter-Strike*. As of this writing, more than 13 years after its original release, *Counter-Strike* is still the number one most-played game on the popular Steam PC gaming service.

Why?

It's not the fiction. There are many military games out there, some successful, some not. No, the success that *Counter-Strike* enjoys is due to its mechanics. It's because of the game's balance, pace, skill, and decisions. Let's take a look at the decisions in a typical *Counter-Strike* match.

Counter-Strike generates decisions such as the following:

Should I reload now or later? What if the enemy comes around the corner while I'm reloading? But what if I run out of ammo while I'm fighting?

Should I move my position forward, backward, laterally, or not at all? What if I get shot while I'm in between cover? But what if I lose because I don't make my objective? What if I get killed because I'm too far out in front of my team? But what if the teammates covering the other entrance are killed and I get shot in the back?

Should I buy a weapon now? What if I run out of money when I need it later? But what if I die this round because I'm unarmed?

As in all skilled flow-sustaining games, these decisions appear constantly and at a rapid rate. A two-minute round might have 100 such decisions. The density is so high that we can't practically analyze even minutes of play in this game. To watch *Counter-Strike* work, we need to brake into ultra-slow motion and examine a player's thoughts second by second. In this case, I'll examine the first 20 seconds of a typical match.

Our player, Bob, joins a game. Bob doesn't start playing immediately; he must first watch the current round until it finishes. This allows him to gather some basic information: the map is de_aztec, Bob is on the terrorist team, and each team has five players. The scoreboard shows that his team is losing. Watching the round finish up, he sees that the opposing team has an expert sniper named Alice, who is dominating the Main Courtyard area from its western edge.

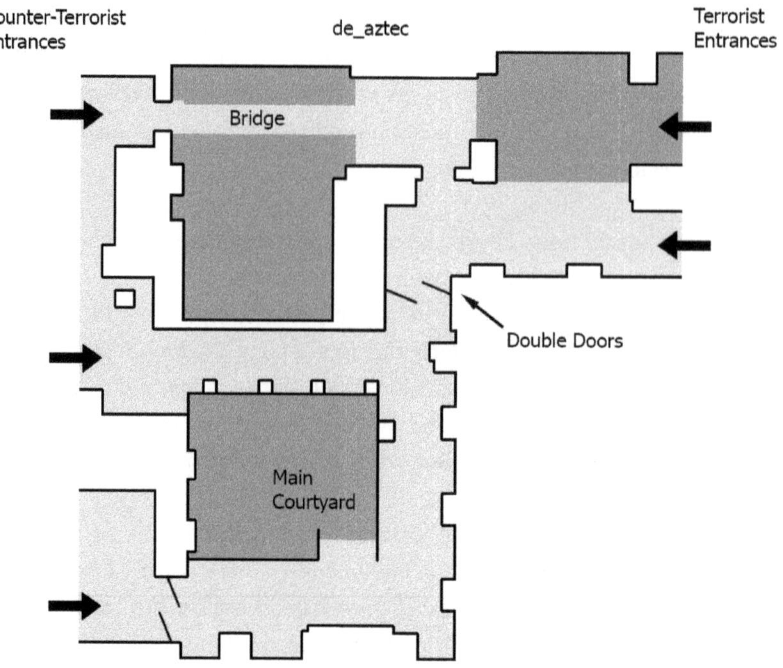

Bob can only watch the game during this phase, but that doesn't mean he isn't in flow. His hands are still, but like a chess master hunched over a board, his mind is not. He's deciding his strategy for the next round. This is a profound decision. He notes his own team's lack of countersniping ability, his inability to afford a flashbang or a powerful weapon, Alice's likely future presence covering the Main Courtyard, his own particularly high skill level at close combat, and many other factors. By the time the round begins, he has decided.

Graphed out, his decision pace so far looks like this:

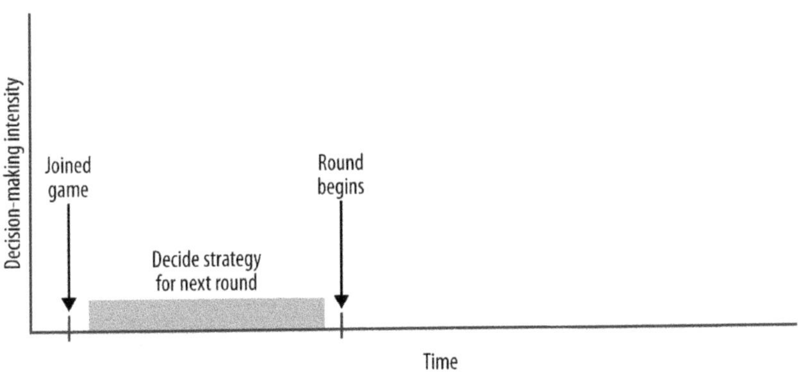

On the timeline, we can see the strategy decision is large in scope by its area. But it is stretched over a long time, so the decision pace is slow. He had a lot of time, but the decision was so large in scope that it filled the space, and there was no flow gap.

The next round begins. Bob appears with his team on the eastern side of the map. He can only afford a cheap, short-ranged MP5 submachine gun, so he knows he is at a disadvantage in open areas. As he already decided to do, he takes the northern route across the bridge, because he wants to avoid Alice, who he is guessing will attack the Main Courtyard. Bob wants to flank her and use his close-quarters fighting skills to take her down. *If I can just get across the bridge alive,* he thinks, *I can hit Alice at close range. I'm good at close-quarters combat, and her sniper rifle will be useless if I'm right in her face.*

Consider the information available to Bob at this point. He doesn't know how the other team is moving yet since they're at the other end of the level, behind walls. *I'm going to assume they've split up and are taking all their paths,* he thinks. *It's unusual for a team to all use the same route.* He also isn't sure of the intentions of his teammates. He prefers playing with buddies since they can work out plans and respond to one another's intentions. But today he is playing on a public server known for its expert players. All he knows about his teammates is that they are skilled. This metagame information allows him to assume they'll take optimal paths and make their shots—but not much else. Finally, Bob sees a few teammates with long-range rifles, which indicates to him that they'll attempt to aggressively engage over the bridge or the Main Courtyard instead of, say, hanging back and trying to ambush the enemy.

Three of Bob's allies go through the Double Doors to the Main Courtyard while one moves with Bob. Bob hears a gunshot. Looking at the death announcement ticker, Bob gains new information: Alice killed one of his teammates in the Main Courtyard. This doesn't affect Bob's plan; it's what he expected. So he continues on his flanking path.

Just as Bob is approaching the bridge, however, the death ticker tells Bob that Alice was killed. The map in Bob's head now looks like this:

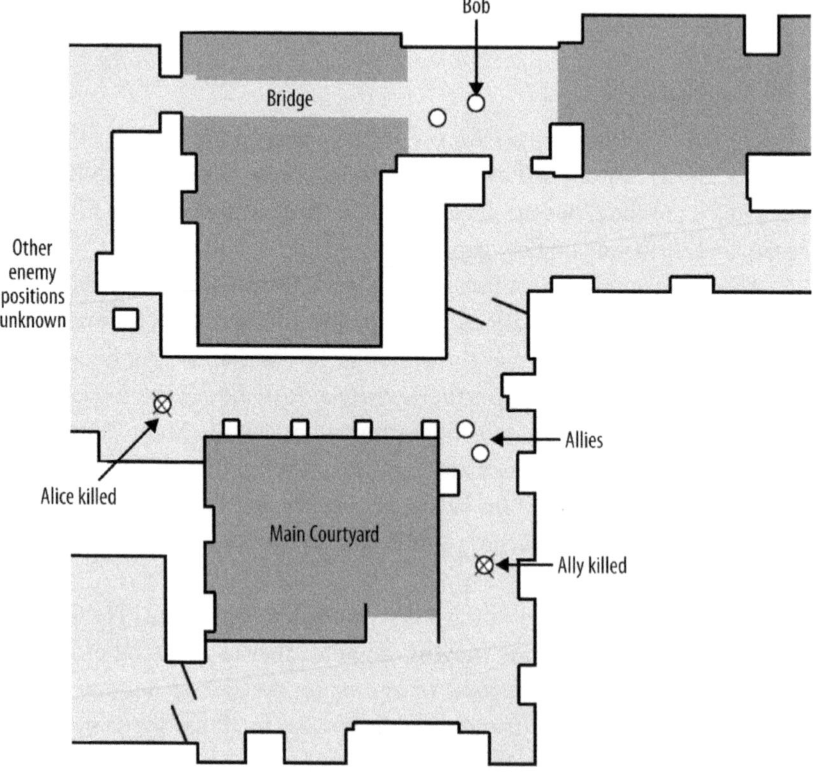

Up until Alice died, Bob wasn't deciding much. His strategy was set before the round even started, so his mind was mostly at rest as he executed his plan. He was just running the route he had planned.

Now, though, circumstances have changed, and Bob's mind springs back into action. The pace of his thoughts revs up. His cup fills, though not to overflowing. He takes in his circumstances.

Bob sees that he is accompanied by only one other team member in his flanking maneuver on the bridge—less than he hoped for, which will make it harder to make it across the bridge into his preferred close-combat territory if there is resistance. Also, Alice's sniping skills have been removed from the equation, making his risky flanking plan pointless. Bob knows that his dead teammate dropped a weapon superior to his own somewhere in the Main Courtyard. *It would be good to get that gun*, he thinks.

After a half-second of thought, Bob decides to abandon the bridge route and join his teammates in the Main Courtyard. He reverses course away from the bridge and passes through the large Double Doors. Here's what Bob's decision pacing looks like right after the decision to reverse:

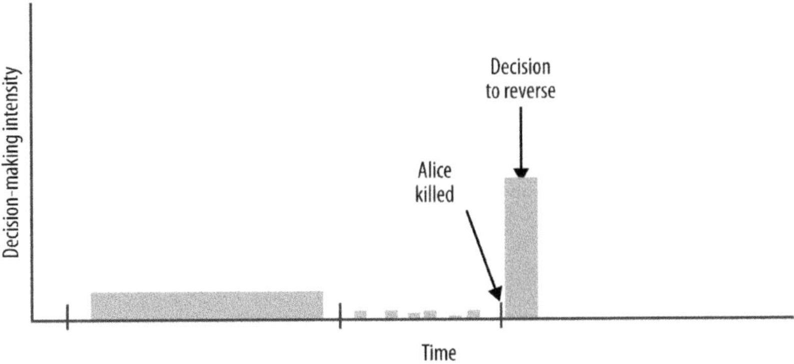

The low decision pace of his plan-following gave way to a large, compressed decision about changing plans.

As Bob enters the Main Courtyard, he surveys the scene. His two teammates are 20 meters away, in open territory, as is the dead teammate. Indeed, the dead friendly dropped an AK-47, a much better weapon than Bob's MP5. Bob wants it.

But a moment after Bob comes through the doors, his exposed teammates come under fire from remaining enemies along the western edge of the Main Courtyard.

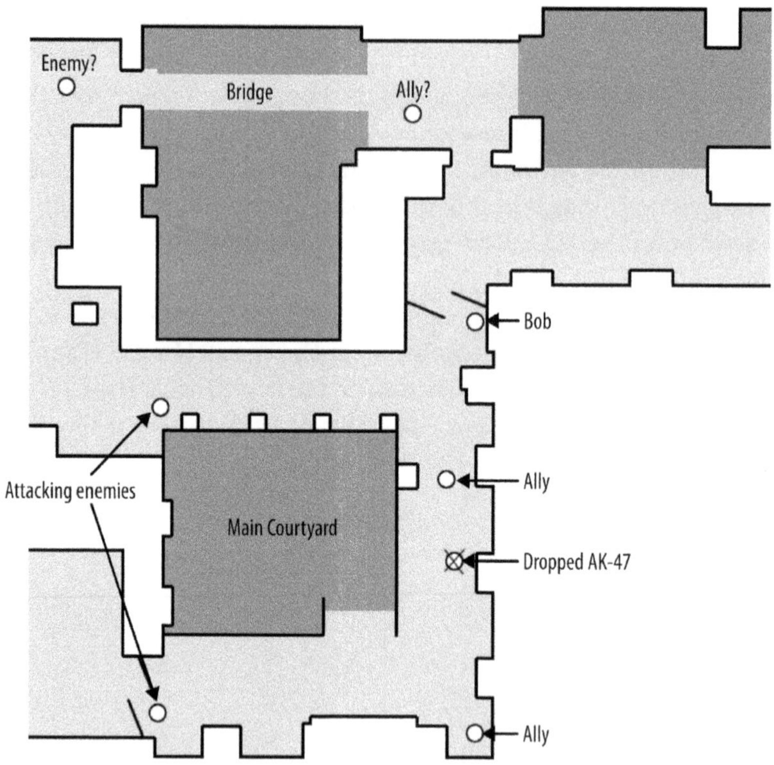

Bob's mind has been at rest for the four seconds since he reversed course at the bridge. But now, his decision pacing spikes again.

He has just a moment to decide whether he wants to attempt to retrieve the AK-47 lying out in open territory. He wishes he knew more about exactly who was shooting at him, and with what, but he doesn't have time to find out. It would take another second to observe the exact armaments, facing, and movements of his enemies and allies. And Bob doesn't have another second, even though all this information is in front of him. So this information is hidden by speed.

In an instant, Bob tries to look into the future, following each of his potential options to a predicted conclusion. The outcomes are hidden behind fuzzy cause and effect, but he can use his knowledge and skill to see them, even if only in blurry, uncertain form. He feels a sense of pleasure as his mind exercises its well-honed tactical skills.

These are the outcomes Bob sees:

He could stay put and ignore the AK-47. This would keep him in cover, but his teammates might die without his support, in which case he would end up fighting four enemies with only one teammate and a weak MP5. However, if his teammates win the engagement without him, Bob can simply grab the AK-47 in safety afterward, putting him in a strong position for the rest of the round, as well as future rounds.

Alternatively, Bob could make a run for it and try to grab the AK-47. Doing this could get him shot as he crosses the open areas of the Main Courtyard. On the other hand, his appearance might distract the enemies and give his allies time to make a kill, or Bob might get the AK-47 and be able to join the fight.

This decision isn't easy. Either choice could lead to disaster or triumph. It's not a puzzle where you work out the solution; it's a judgment call. The decision is guided by Bob's evaluation of exactly how likely and how desirable the various outcomes are. This decision process crosses the bounds of conscious and unconscious thought. Awareness and instinct merge together into a deciding machine. It's not just about what Bob thinks about his options, because he has no time to think. It's what his emotional unconscious, conditioned by hours of practice, makes him feel about those options. And one of those options feels better than the other. So Bob decides to go for the AK-47.

I won't trace a specific outcome to this situation further. Perhaps Bob will die immediately, and his decision pacing would instantly fall to a slow, strategy-deciding throb until the next round. In this case, he might experience one of the flawed outcomes of *Counter-Strike*'s design: time spent dead between rounds can sometimes go on longer than players need to decide their strategy for the next round, creating a long, dull flow gap.

Alternatively, if Bob doesn't die, he might be entering a 10-second period of frenetic battle. Decisions will come fast and furious, once or more per second, as allies and enemies shoot, fall, or flee. If this decision-saturated period went on much longer than 10 seconds, it might start to get exhausting. But *Counter-Strike*'s high-decision-paced periods are always quite short because the weapons are so deadly.

Assuming the battle continues, this is what Bob's decision pacing will look like:

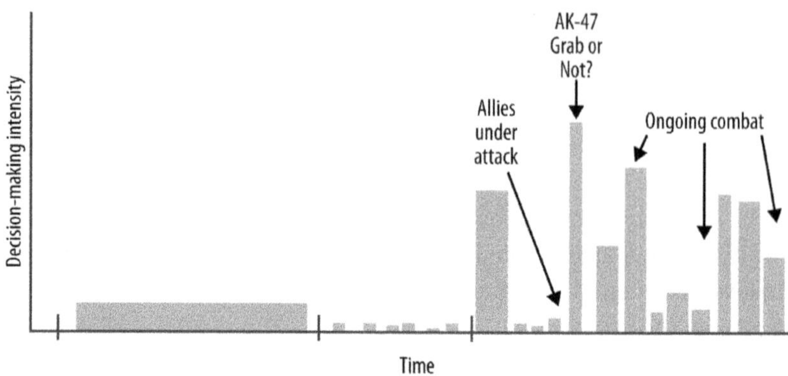

Counter-Strike's decision pacing is spiky and unpredictable. Play swings between suspenseful hunting and wild shootouts, and there are enforced rest periods between rounds. And the decisions are different in scope and flavor, because they mix twitch shooting with tactical movement and team strategy. Along with an unattainable skill ceiling, it's this strong mix of well-paced decisions which makes *Counter-Strike* such a sustainably compelling experience.

6

Balance

The small boy wanted the cookies. But they were always on the kitchen counter, just out of reach.

He tried everything to get them. He crawled up the stool, but it fell over. He attached string to toys and threw them. He faked illness, hoping to get one by pity. He tried to make a deal with his big brother. He even tried to train the dog to bring him a cookie. Nothing worked.

After each failure, his mind worked harder on new solutions. The quest for the cookies became his focus in life. Every failure became a fascinating new problem. Failure made him stronger, smarter, cleverer.

One day, someone knocked over the jar and a cookie fell to the floor. The boy ate it, went to his room, and did nothing. The cookie hadn't filled him up. It had emptied him out.

BALANCING means adjusting game mechanics to change the relative power of different tools, units, strategies, teams, or characters.

Sometimes balancing just means changing numbers. A designer might decrease the tire traction of a car to make it worse at cornering, or increase the speed of an arrow to make it more effective. Games have thousands of numbers that can be tuned like this—speed, price, mass, health, damage, energy, and so on.

But balancing can also require more fundamental changes than knob twisting. A designer might remove the sorcerer's shield ability to make him easier to attack with archers, or take the nitrous oxide boosters off a certain vehicle to compensate for its high engine power.

This chapter covers balancing—why we do it, why it's hard, and ways to do it well.

Goals of Balance

The word *balance* is one of the most abused terms in game design. People will call a game balanced when it seems fun, or imbalanced when it seems unfair. But lumping all these ideas into one word confuses the method with the goals.

Balancing is a method. It means changing the relative power of different game mechanics. This method can be used to pursue almost any goal. Fictional coherence, clarity, simplicity, and elegance can all be improved by balancing. For example, a designer might reduce the health of a beggar to emphasize his fictional frailty, or increase the speed of a jet to clarify its role.

But among all the different goals that balance can achieve, two stand above the others. They are *fairness* and *depth*.

These goals are so associated with balancing because balancing is the key method of achieving them. Other design goals are mostly achieved in other ways. We tell a story with art or writing, and we make games clear with good interface design. But to achieve fairness and depth, we must balance.

BALANCING FOR FAIRNESS

A game is FAIR when no player has an advantage at the start of play.

We pursue fairness because it lets players feel that their wins and losses are legitimate. In competitive games, players want to know that their wins mean they were really better than the other player. If the game itself is unfair, the competitive ritual is meaningless because it reveals nothing about the people involved. The loser can complain that he only lost because the game was unfair, and the winner doesn't get the satisfaction of an incontrovertible win.

Some kinds of games are automatically fair because players start in the same situation. This kind of game is called *symmetric* because each side is exactly the same. For example, hockey is symmetric because both teams start in the same positions and are subject to the same rules. Hockey is automatically fair because the only difference between the teams is inside the players themselves. When designing a symmetric game, fairness is not a concern because it is automatic.

But truly symmetric games are unusual. Most games are *asymmetric*. In these games, players can start in different situations. For example, in a fighting game, players might use different characters with different attacks. In chess, white goes first. And in *StarCraft*, players can choose to command armies of different species. Such asymmetric games are not guaranteed to be fair the way symmetric games are. To make them fair (or at least fair enough to satisfy), they must be carefully balanced.

It might seem like just making a game symmetric is an easy way to achieve balance. But often, asymmetry is an inherent part of the game. Someone has to go first in chess. Players of the game *Risk* must have different starting territories on an asymmetric world map. In a World War II game, someone has to play the Axis and someone has to play the Allies. Often, symmetry isn't an option.

There is also a third option besides symmetry and balanced asymmetry. We can create asymmetric games that are deliberately unfair. This approach loses any sense of competitive legitimacy, but it unlocks unique experiences that can't be had in a fair game.

For example, many historical war games have unfair scenarios because their players are more interested in exploring history than in competing. They want to find out whether the German army could have won from its disadvantaged position at the Battle of the Bulge, or if the Japanese could have held Iwo Jima. Such games must be unfair because historical battles were unfair.

Other times, designers use unfairness because it creates wild stories and funny interactions more often than honest competition. For example, the classic board game *Cosmic Encounter* equips every player with wacky, unfair powers because the game is designed to generate humor and, as designer Peter Olokta said, "Fair isn't funny!" So there aren't any competitive *Cosmic Encounter* tournaments—but the game is bloody hilarious.

BALANCING FOR DEPTH

I've described depth as the property of a game that makes it provide meaningful play at high skill levels. Balance is essential in depth. Because for a game to be deep, it must generate decisions that are so balanced that even experts aren't sure of the best answer.

For example, imagine that the hero in a swords-and-sorcery fantasy game encounters a murderous ogre. The hero has two options: he can attack with his sword, or he can cast a spell to set the ogre on fire. The sword would cause a lot of immediate damage, while the spell would do small, repeated amounts of damage over time as the ogre burns. Which does he choose?

If either option is obviously more powerful overall—for example, if the sword did more damage than the fire could do in 10 minutes—the answer would be obvious, and the decision would become a nondecision. For this decision to be meaningful, the player's different options must be balanced so that the best answer isn't obvious. In this case, a designer might have the sword do more damage overall if the fight lasts less than 30 seconds, while the fire does more damage if it continues to burn for more than 30 seconds. Now the player doesn't just choose the obvious answer. He has to guess whether the fight should be more or less than 30 seconds long. Guessing the future like this is an interesting and emotionally meaningful thought process.

Some people treat this sort of balancing as though it's about matching different tools against one another in some vague measure of power. They try to balance the sword, the flame, and every other tool so that they're all basically equal. But this approach doesn't work because it misconceives the goal of this kind of balancing. Our goal isn't to balance the tools. That's impossible, because every tool has different levels of usefulness in different situations and combinations with other tools. The fire might be great against the ogre, but useless against a crowd of weak goblins. The sword might be good against the goblins, but poor against the ogre. So which is better? Without context, such comparisons are meaningless.

Our real goal is to balance the *strategies* among which the player chooses in any given situation.

STRATEGIES are specific combinations of actions that players can decide to take in pursuit of a goal. A game's decisions become richer when the thought process required to find the best strategy is more nuanced.

So, in the fantasy ogre example, we're not really balancing the fire spell against the sword. We're balancing the choice between these two strategies in this particular situation against this particular ogre.

A simple strategy might mean using a single tool to solve one problem. For example, if your opponents were advancing with cavalry, a good counterstrategy would be to place your spearmen in front of your army. Since charging horses don't do well against entrenched lines of long pointy sticks, your strategy is effective. You've used one of your tools against one of their tools to achieve one goal.

But strategies can also be astonishingly complex. These kinds of strategies aren't single actions—they're nuanced sets of contingencies. They depend on synergies among multiple tools in specific circumstances, and are customized against certain combinations of opposing strategies. For example, an expert will see an enemy army with cavalry on the right side, archers on the left, and spearmen in the back. He will respond by feinting his cavalry toward the enemy archers while rushing his spearmen up the center. He's thinking through several contingencies: if the enemy's archers stand and fire at his spearmen, his cavalry can charge them. But if the enemy has his archers flee and sends cavalry in response, our expert might be able to trap them on the field with his spearmen.

When we balance strategies against each other, we make for a richer play experience because all the player's decisions involve more nuanced thinking about more variables. The game becomes deeper because these complex thought processes can't be executed perfectly, even by very skilled players.

BALANCING FOR OTHER REASONS

The core of balance is generating fair play and nuanced decisions. But even if a balance change creates wonderfully rich decisions and perfectly fair play, it's worthless if it destroys narrative coherence, flow and pacing, accessibility, or clarity.

For example, we can't balance an archer's bow by giving it a 10-foot range. This might be fair, and it might create fascinating strategic decisions, but it wouldn't make any sense in the fiction layer. We can't balance a jumping puzzle by making the player character's jump shorter in this level only, because this would defy player expectation and create frustration. We can't balance a car in a driving game by making it painfully slow and sluggish, because driving it would be a chore, even if it was a fair chore.

The work of balancing must be done within these constraints. Or, at least, the benefit of a balance change must be traded off against the cost to other parts of the experience, because balance affects everything.

Degenerate Strategies

One of the paradoxes of game design is that adding a tool can actually cause a game to lose interesting decisions instead of gaining them. This happens when the new tool produces a *degenerate strategy*.

A DEGENERATE STRATEGY is a strategy that is obviously the best choice in a given decision.

For example, imagine that the designers of a strategy game add a new unit, the Chuck Norris. Chuck, being a perfect human, is obviously the most powerful unit in the game. He can defeat a whole army of soldiers by himself.

At first, Chuck might seem like a great design, because he's awesome, and he gives players what they want. But Chuck actually destroys the game itself almost as completely as he destroys his enemies.

Adding Chuck Norris to the game has reduced its depth because there is no longer any decision process in deciding what units to use. No matter what the situation, the answer is always the same: just send Chuck. He is a degenerate strategy.

Chuck Norris is a simplified example. In real design, degenerate strategies are never this obvious. They hide in the emergent interactions among different tools and mechanics.

For example, in the fantasy RPG *The Elder Scrolls: Morrowind*, it is possible to become massively powerful by creating potions that enhance the player character's Intelligence stat, and then using the newly enhanced Intelligence to create even more powerful Intelligence-giving potions, in an exponentially rising Intelligence singularity. Once the player's Intelligence is a few hundred times that of any reasonable value, the player can mix potions that massively enhance all their other stats forever. So, within a few minutes of starting the game, the player can create a character that can leap over mountains and punch dragons to death in one hit. This trick is simple and easy to execute, and anyone who knows it can nullify many of the game's carefully crafted challenges. And it's not immediately obvious from the design of the game that this is even possible.

Even sports can have degenerate strategies. Consider basketball. It's hard to imagine people exploiting this traditional sport the way they exploit imbalances in a video game, but it has happened. In the late 1990s there was a crop of unusual players who were excellent on offense yet strangely deficient at shooting free throws. Shaquille "Shaq" O'Neal was the best-known example of this phenomenon. In response, opposing teams developed a strategy called *Hack-a-Shaq* in which they intentionally tried to foul Shaq whenever his team had the ball. In basketball, when a player physically interferes with another, the referee calls a foul, and the fouled player gets a free throw. The opposing teams thought it more likely that Shaq would miss the free throw than that the ball could be taken from his team in normal play. So the games degenerated into Shaq being chased in circles by opposing players trying to slap him while the ball was nowhere nearby.

Players are always trying to find degenerate strategies. They endlessly hunt for chinks in the armor of the game design, looking for an imbalance they can abuse for easy wins. The irony is that if they ever find one, they'll hate the designer for allowing them to destroy the game. They want to hunt for degenerate strategies, and they want to not find them.

THE VIABLE STRATEGY-COUNTING FALLACY

Clearly, for a decision to mean anything, there needs to be more than one viable strategy that might reasonably lead to a good outcome. If there is only one viable strategy, that strategy is degenerate and the decision becomes a nondecision.

For a long time, I thought this meant that the goal of balance was to maximize the number of viable strategies. The idea was that the more viable strategies there were, the richer the decisions would be, and the better balanced the game was. I wrote this whole chapter based on this assumption, and it was beautiful on paper. Then I went searching for counterexamples. And to my horror, I found two, both of which utterly destroyed what I had written.

The first was the joke game rock-paper-scissors-lizard-Spock. Traditional rock-paper-scissors has three viable strategies. But there is also a version of the game called rock-paper-scissors-lizard-Spock (my favorite outcome is "paper disproves Spock"). That version has five strategies, and all of them are viable because each has an equal chance of winning. And we can easily add more and more symbols to this game, up to an arbitrarily large number of viable strategies. But are we improving the game's balance? Of course not. The game is no deeper than before. It's just more complex. Adding more viable strategies didn't make the game better.

The second counterexample was poker. Instead of being a bad game with an arbitrarily large number of strategies, poker is an excellent game with very few strategies. Poker is endlessly fascinating, but there are only a handful of moves in each situation. In many hands, players only have two viable strategies: fold or call. If the number of viable strategies were important, how could poker be so good with so few of them?

Over time, I realized that the idea of counting viable strategies was a red herring. My faulty logic had gone like this: if two viable strategies are better than one, that must mean that three viable strategies are better than two, right?

Wrong. Once you've got two viable strategies, there is no inherent value in adding more. More viable strategies might make a decision more interesting. But they might not, or it may not be the best way to do so. We could invent a version of poker with many more useful moves, but it wouldn't necessarily be better.

The real goal of balancing for depth is to create a rich thought process inside the player's mind. We want to spark a fascinating chain of internal logic that gives players epiphanies, doubts, and dilemmas, and we want to do it even when the player is very skilled. For that to happen, there must be more than one viable strategy. But once we have two such viable strategies, adding more doesn't automatically improve the experience. Improving the experience means making the decision process more nuanced.

This idea has an important implication for designers. It means that the practice of adding more choices as a way to deepen a game is wrong. More choices might be easy to create and easy to measure, but they aren't inherently valuable. Often, they add more complexity than they're worth.

The designer's real goal is to enrich the player's internal experiences. That goal is harder to achieve, and it's damned difficult to measure. But it's the truth. And pursuing that truth makes our designs smaller, simpler, more focused, and more elegant than they could ever get by strategy counting.

Balance and Skill

Young kids enjoy tic-tac-toe. It's a real game for them, with real skill, real challenge, and real strategy. This seems hilarious to adults because the game is so simple, and the perfect strategy is so obvious. We're bored by tic-tac-toe. So how can a game that is fascinating to one group be pointless for another?

A game that is balanced for players at one skill level may be imbalanced for players at another because players at different skill levels have access to different strategies.

What is a degenerate strategy for an expert is still a fascinating mystery for a novice. The expert knows the degenerate strategy and has the skill to execute it. When he plays the game, he does the same thing every time without thought, just as an adult plays tic-tac-toe. But the novice hasn't discovered the degenerate strategy, or lacks the skill to perform it. For the novice, the game is still a mystery. Kids love tic-tac-toe because they don't yet have the ability to use the degenerate strategy. So for them, it might as well not exist.

We also find the opposite case: players disliking a game because they lack the skill to use the strategies that make it balanced. For example, *StarCraft II* is one of the best balanced games ever, but it often doesn't seem that way for new players. There is a class of opening strategies in *StarCraft II* called *rushes*. Rushes involve attacking the other player very early, before he builds any military units at all. They are relatively straightforward to execute, which makes them available to novices. But they are quite difficult to stop. A midlevel player can stop a rush, but a novice can't. To a novice getting stomped over and over by other novices using rushes, *StarCraft II* seems imbalanced.

But rushes are perfectly defensible at higher skill levels. Professional players rarely rush one another because rushes usually don't work against people who know how to stop them. At the top of the skill range, it's the defender of the rush who has the advantage. But at the bottom of the game's skill range, it's the attacker, since rushes are easy to execute and harder to stop.

This creates a strange situation where rushes are a degenerate strategy—but only at low skill levels. The strategies used to counter rushes aren't available to novices, so to them, the game seems degenerate.

WHO TO BALANCE FOR

Tic-tac-toe and *StarCraft II* are both expressing variations on the same problem:

It's nearly impossible to make a skill-driven game that's balanced for players of all skill levels. A designer must target which skill level he wishes to balance for, and allow the other skill levels to have degenerate strategies.

If we find a problem at one skill level, we can usually solve it. But once we start worrying about multiple skill levels, the number of strategies we have to consider multiplies immensely. Balancing one skill point is hard; balancing all of them at once is nearly impossible. The only response is to let the game be imbalanced at some skill levels. It sounds like accepting defeat, but nearly all games do this.

Even the balance team on the masterfully crafted *StarCraft II* is open about their willingness to sacrifice balance at low skill in exchange for balance at the top of the range. Dustin Browder, lead designer of *StarCraft II*, said, "The goal is always to get solutions that will affect everybody. . .But when you put a gun to my head and say, 'You've got to make a decision' . . .we tend to go with [the most skilled players]." Browder recognizes that balancing the game all across the skill range is impossible. Instead, his team concentrates on ensuring that the game stays balanced at the expert level, while opportunistically picking up whatever else they can along the rest of the skill range. And for *StarCraft II*, this is the right choice, since the game is intended to support long study by professional players.

Narrative-driven games usually take the opposite approach. Instead of balancing at the top of the skill range, they balance at the middle or the bottom because they're not intended to be played as intensely as a competitive game like *StarCraft II*. For example, *BioShock* includes super-powerful enemies called Big Daddies who are not aggressive unless provoked. Big Daddy battles are intended to be tough, climactic fights, but there are actually a number of degenerate ways to kill them without fighting at all. The player can attach a number of proximity bombs to an explosive barrel to create a giant super-bomb that kills a Big Daddy in one hit. Or the Big Daddy can be lured into a large pile of traps and killed instantly. *BioShock* is full of degenerate strategies like this, but it doesn't matter because the game lasts less than 10 hours, and few players will work out these strategies in such a short time. And even if they do, the game stays interesting because the game's meaning comes from narrative and role-play, not skill optimization.

That's why the degenerate strategy caused by the intelligence potions in *Morrowind* doesn't break the game. *Morrowind* isn't about winning—it's about exploring a world. A player might try the intelligence potion trick once, but he'll quickly return to the normal game because he wants to experience the game's narrative.

WHETHER TO BALANCE

For any given game, a designer must decide whether the benefit of pursuing balance at high skill levels is worth the cost. The answer depends on how much the game is about skill-driven challenge, and how much it is about other kinds of experience like art and story.

Balancing for the top of the skill range is expensive. It means that any idea that can possibly lead to a degenerate strategy at any skill level must be eliminated. This restriction disallows many ideas that are worthwhile in other ways. Furthermore, testing at high skill levels is costly because it means letting someone study the game for weeks or months, hunting for optimal strategies. Finally, players usually find degenerate strategies after the game is released, which means it must be patched—sometimes for years.

Balancing for lower skill levels is much cheaper. As long as degenerate strategies aren't completely obvious, the goal has been achieved. Mechanics that create strong narrative or social experiences can be included in a game even if they cause degenerate strategies. Testing balance is easy since it doesn't require long study or especially dedicated players. And if someone finds a new degenerate strategy after release, so what? The game still plays well since it's not about skill.

In a game of skill that attempts to support endlessly deep play, high-skill balance is nonnegotiable. If such a game can't stand up to skilled play, it is worthless. This means spending design resources on exhaustive balance testing and analysis, vetoing many fictional ideas that can't be balanced, and even allowing imbalances at lower skill levels. These are the inherent costs of designing a game of mastery. But for skill games like *StarCraft II*, *Counter-Strike*, or *Street Fighter II*, these costs must be paid.

Designers of games that aren't based on intense skill competition should balance for a low to medium skill level. These games' meaning comes from socializing, narrative, or other non-skill-dependent emotional triggers, so the expense of high-skill balance isn't worth it. Story games like *BioShock* and *Morrowind* don't benefit enough from deep balancing for it to be worth the cost. These games are better left somewhat imbalanced, so all those design resources can be redirected into enriching the game's world and story.

Balance Challenges and Solutions

Let's go back to the original example of the hero facing the ogre. The hero's two tools are the sword, which causes a lot of immediate damage, and the flame spell, which causes slow damage over time. If this were the only place these mechanics were used, the game would be easy to balance. But in a real game—especially an elegant one—those mechanics are used in thousands of other places as well. The hero could also use the sword or flame against goblins, orcs, or stingy shopkeepers. Adjusting those two tools to make the choice work well against just the ogre is easy. But any change made to fix this particular situation also affects all the other places where those tools are used.

This is the fundamental challenge of balance. We often want to solve one problem. But any change we make will have many different effects in many different places in the game.

Tuning a mechanic changes *all* the strategies it is involved in, not just the ones we intend.

A good game is a complex system in the intimidating academic sense. It exhibits nonlinear, unpredictable emergent behaviors that are far more complex than design itself. In complex systems, changes to one variable don't affect just that variable, nor do they push other variables around in simple, predictable ways. Rather, they can set off intricate chains of cause and effect which can be nearly impossible to predict. This is one of the greatest powers of games since it allows marvelous variety of experience from simple designs. But it is also one of the greatest challenges of game design—especially balancing.

Psychologist Dietrich Dörner expresses the challenge of handling complexity:

> We could liken a decision maker in a complex situation to a chess player whose set has many more than the normal number of pieces, several dozen, say. Furthermore, these chessmen are all linked to each other by rubber bands, so that the player cannot move just one figure alone. Also, his men and his opponent's men can move on their own and in accordance with rules the player does not fully understand or about which he has mistaken assumptions. And, to top things off, some of his own and his opponent's men are surrounded by a fog that obscures their identity.

This is the challenge of game balancing. Changing one mechanic changes every strategy connected to that mechanic, which changes every strategy connected to those strategies, and so on, in an exponentially expanding network of implications. You might power down the sword to fix the fight against the ogre, only to see it become too weak against the goblin. You might then make them weaker to match, and find that they're too easily defeated by the wizard's rod and the unarmed attacks. Everything is linked in a web of relationships with thousands of connections.

This is why balancing is so hard, and great balance is so rare. Approach this problem haphazardly, and the game will thrash from one imbalanced state to another, as each solution causes more problems than it solves. The only way to make real progress is with careful, structured, deliberate approaches that solve problems without causing new ones. Let's look at some of them.

BALANCING METHODS

Figure out which aspects of a tool are essential to its role and identity. Turn these knobs as far as possible and lock them in place. Then, solve balance problems by turning the other knobs.

A rocket backpack must launch the wearer far and fast, because launching people is what rocket backpacks are about. Armor must protect. An artillery cannon must lob shells over long distances; otherwise, it's not an artillery cannon. Crops must feed; otherwise, they're not crops.

These properties are essential to the role and fiction of these tools. So push them as far as possible. Make the rocket backpack launch people really, really far and fast. Make the armor incredibly strong.

When we push these dials to the furthest possible extreme, tools become distinct and their roles become crystal clear. The game's breadth of experience stretches, and a wider range of strategies appear as players explore the broader possibility space.

These key properties are so important that we must regard them as unchangeable because if we changed these key properties, we would be blurring tool roles and breaking coherence with the fiction. If each property is like a knob the designer can turn, we must push these to the max and then lock them in place.

Since those knobs are fixed, we must balance by turning other ones. Luckily, every tool has many properties which aren't essential to its identity. The rocket backpack must be fast, but we can do anything we want with its price, weight, or vulnerability. And if that's not enough to balance it, we can create new mechanics to strengthen or weaken it. If it's too powerful, we can make it explode when damaged, or leak fuel continuously, or slowly suck away the wearer's health. If it's too weak, we can let it shield the user's back like armor, or make it silent so that enemies won't hear it descending on them. But under no circumstances can we slow it down.

Similarly, armor may be made expensive, obvious, heavy, or obstructive. It might prevent the player from carrying a second weapon, or make lots of noise so that enemies can hear you easily. But it can't be made fragile.

By finding the key properties of each tool and locking them at an extreme, we ensure that the game has a set of distinct tools spanning a broad space of possibility.

Cut as deep as needed to solve problems.

Every now and then, a tool can't be balanced without changing its key properties. In these cases, it's often best to simply cut it rather than weaken it. Having no rocket backpack is often better than having an unsatisfyingly slow and strategically pointless rocket backpack.

Blizzard Entertainment, the studio behind *StarCraft II*, *Diablo*, and *World of Warcraft*, is famous for doing this. If the Blizzard designers can't perfectly balance a tool by knob twisting, they don't hesitate to cut as deep as needed to solve the problem. For example, in *StarCraft II* there is a large walking tank unit called the Thor. Early in development, the Thor unit was far more massive than anything else in the game. It was so large that it couldn't come out of the factory and had to be constructed in the field like a building. If it was destroyed, it could be resurrected like a partially collapsed structure. It moved slowly, turned slowly, and was nearly impossible to kill. Everything about it expressed its concept of an ultra-massive mech walker, and it was awesome.

But it was impossible to balance. In-field construction meant it could be mass-produced too quickly to counter since there was no slow buildup of production facilities. Resurrection made it too hard to defeat. Its slow turning speed made it annoyingly easy to kill by the use of small, fast units running circles around it (a classic degenerate strategy). These problems weren't obvious on the surface. They only became apparent after testing by skilled players.

The exotic mega-mech concept was cool. It sounds compelling and different. But if it can't be balanced, it can't be used. Blizzard's designers didn't try to paper over the problems with layers of inelegant special case rules. They sucked up the pain and cut deeper, scaling the Thor way down into a manageably sized mech walker that is built from the Factory like any other unit and cannot be resurrected. It's boring on the surface—but it works. And in the end, the game turned out better than it would have if it was full of gimmicks, imbalances, and special cases designed to prop up someone's pet idea.

As a designer, it's hard to cut this deep—intellectually, socially, and emotionally. It can seem terribly wasteful to throw out large amounts of work and such cool ideas because of one strategy interaction hidden somewhere in the game's possibility space. There's real emotional pain in doing that. But if you're seeking high-skill balance, it's not a choice. Degenerate strategies left in the game will always be found, and sometimes the only way to fix them is to cut fun ideas. As in any creative field, sometimes a game designer must murder his darlings.

Don't be reactive.

When something that seems wrong happens in a playtest, often our first instinct is to rush in and turn some knobs to make sure it doesn't happen again. And this is always easy to do. But trying to balance by solving single problems one by one is like pushing bubbles out of wallpaper. Since strategies are coupled together, every solution to one problem is the cause of another. The game lurches between balance points, running in circles but getting nowhere. In the worst cases, this can go on forever, with the game making no forward progress at all.

The mistake here is focusing on the problems that we do have and ignoring those we don't. As Dietrich Dörner puts it:

> We may believe that we have been pursuing a single goal until we reach it and then realize—with amazement, annoyance, and horror—that in ridding ourselves of one plague we have created perhaps two others in different areas. There are, in other words, "implicit" goals that we may not at first take into account at all and may not even know we are pursuing. To take a simple example, if we ask someone who is healthy about her

goals, she will not normally name "health" as one of them. It is, nevertheless, an implicit goal, for it we were to raise this point specifically, she would agree that maintaining her health is important. In general, however, health will become one of her explicit goals only if she falls ill.

It's human nature to ignore the problems we don't have. Existing problems have in-your-face emotional punch, while potential problems are abstract possibilities. It's cognitively easy to think about problems that are occurring; it's much harder to think about all the other potential problems our solutions might cause.

But we have to. Balance changes only improve a game if they create fewer problems than they solve. It's easy to find changes that solve one problem while making two more that we don't know about. It's much, much harder to find solutions that handle both the explicit and implicit goals—those that solve the problem and don't cause others.

Doing this means not being reactive. Slow down, breathe, and think broadly. Suppress that desire to rush in and change things when something goes wrong. Going slow provides the time for emotions to fade and brings perspective on the broader implications of a change. Because what seem like the easiest solutions often come with terrible hidden side effects. The real solution is usually not so obvious.

Every now and then, have a Nigel Tufnel moment. Turn it up to 11.

A balanced game does not mean that every strategy creates equally valuable outcomes. Such a game is meaningless in the same way the game of coin tossing is meaningless. It is balanced, but also flat. There is no reward for skill, and nothing useful to learn.

A game's strategic landscape should have hills and valleys. There should be peaks of incredible effectiveness alongside deep troughs of failure. The reason these varying outcomes can still be balanced is because their prices of entry vary. The skill required to execute a strategy is comparable to its effectiveness; the best outcomes require the highest skill. This arrangement motivates players to hunt around the strategic landscape, searching for the most lucrative peaks, clawing their way up the skill landscape. And when, after great struggle, they reach a summit, they are richly rewarded for it.

That's the outcome we want. But you can't get there by being too reasonable. As a designer, when you see things that seem too good or too bad, the first instinct is often to sand them down until everything is smooth and even. This makes the game balanced, but also makes it flat. It loses the spice of the unpredictable, the promise of valuable lessons, the tension of dramatic change.

The solution is to periodically temper reasoned progress with madness. I call this a Nigel Tufnel moment, after the fictional musician in the film *This Is Spinal Tap*. Nigel owned a set of amps that had knobs that went up to 11 (instead of the normal 10). When he needed an extra punch on stage, he would turn the knobs up to 11. That's how he got out of the prison of normalcy.

We can do the same thing by deliberately letting go of reason. You have to forget your craft for a moment and transform into a naïve 18-year-old hacker-designer from 1992, hopped up on Red Bull, who *just wants to make something awesome, dude!*

What if this shield ability actually makes you completely invincible instead of just absorbing some damage? What if it shields your whole team? What if this character moves 5 or 10 times faster than anyone else in the game? What if she moves infinitely fast—or can teleport? What if you can jump a hundred feet, or get infinite money? Wouldn't that be extreme, awesome, and incredible?

After the Red Bull wears off, you'll often find that your knobs need to come back down from 11. Most of these experiments don't work out, which is why professional designers generally do better work than 18-year-old hackers in the long run. But every now and then, a Nigel moment shows us an opportunity we missed, or reminds us of an emotional moment that we smoothed out. When this happens, instead of just reversing the changes, incorporate them and preserve them. Do this every now and then, and the game will have the spice of madness.

Don't use feedback to gather suggestions. Use it to gather player experiences.

To balance, one must playtest with other people. By default, most playtests will return a pile of suggestions. One player wants the horse to go faster, another wants the second level to be easier, and a third wants batteries to be cheaper.

But suggestions aren't what balance designers need the most out of playtests. We can come up with ideas for how to change the game by ourselves. What we can't do is experience the game the way another player does. We're so close to the design that we lack the perspective of other people. That's why the real purpose of playtests is not to gather suggestions—it is to understand the experiences other players have with the game.

A designer can often understand someone's experience just by watching the person play. I've run many playtests without even needing to ask any questions afterward. It's obvious from watching when players succeed and fail, how quickly they proceed, and what decisions they make. Their internal perceptions are written on their choices of where to look and what to do. You can even watch their faces to see how they're feeling.

But sometimes just watching play isn't enough. In these situations, you have to ask carefully designed questions to ferret out the knowledge you need. For example, if you want to understand what seemed important to them, ask them to tell you the story of what happened, and they'll report the parts that were most salient in their mind. If you're wondering about whether they perceived something, ask them a question that tests their knowledge: "How many men arrived in the helicopter?" If they seem confused, they didn't notice the helicopter. If you want to understand one of their decisions, ask them to walk you through their thought process.

Stay open, neutral, and professional. Ask questions in a wondering way, not an accusatory way. Try to avoid any personal interaction or emotion that might distort or hide the tester's experience. Don't encourage or reward positive or "right" answers.

If the tester starts making suggestions, try to work backward and figure out what experience motivated the suggestion. Sometimes this means asking the tester why he is making the suggestion. Other times, you can simply guess what happened. If he's asking you to remove the rifle, it's probably because he had a bad experience with the rifle—but you might want to drill in with further questions to dig out the precise bad experience he had. Did he miss a shot he thought should have hit? There might be a problem in the aiming system. Did he feel like he ran out of ammo too often? The game's economy might be imbalanced. Did he not understand a feature of the rifle? Maybe it needs a better tutorial or clearer interface.

Don't think through stories. Test enough to build a mental model of how the game works as a system. Only then do you have the mental context to make balance decisions.

Real understanding of a game's balance can never come from watching one or two tests, much less playing the game yourself. It comes from absorbing many different players' experiences and combining them into an integrated mental model of how the game is working.

After one playtest, you've got a story. After three, you've got three stories. After 10, 15, or 20 playtests, though, you'll find your understanding of the game begins to transform. You won't be thinking in stories anymore. You'll start thinking in terms of systems and relationships. Your mental model of the game will grow and evolve to include a hundred new nuances of cause and effect. You'll be able to imagine the effects of one change rippling outward, touching other parts of the game, and changing them. You'll perceive the truth of the game—that it is a system, not a story.

Once you've got the system in mind, then you can think meaningfully about balance. You won't have to consider how a change might impact the three stories you saw play out. You'll perceive how the change affects the system overall.

So test a lot. Test with as many different players as you can. Gorge yourself on the data and let your mind build its model. Only after that's done will you have the mental context to understand all the effects of a change, not just the most obvious and immediate ones. And only then should you decide what to do.

7

Multiplayer

The gunslinger, the criminal, and the sheriff faced off in the town square. A tumbleweed drifted by. They reached for their six-shooters.

The gunslinger had a split second to decide whether to shoot the criminal or the sheriff. He couldn't wait to see where each of them was aiming—by then it would be too late. He had to decide now, as he drew his weapon. But which should he choose?

He had been paid to shoot the sheriff. So that's what he should do.

But wait. The sheriff knew that the gunslinger had been paid to kill him. So the sheriff would shoot the gunslinger in self-defense, which would leave the criminal free to shoot who he pleased. And the criminal had a vendetta against the gunslinger because the gunslinger had stolen the criminal's horse six months earlier. So the criminal would probably shoot the gunslinger as well. And the gunslinger knew the criminal was a much better shot than the sheriff. So to defend himself, he'd draw on the criminal and hope the sheriff missed.

But then, the sheriff knew all this as well, so he knew the gunslinger would try to stop the criminal first. This would leave the sheriff open to shoot whomever he wished. So he would shoot the criminal, because it was his job, and because he didn't want to be caught in an even fight against the better-shooting criminal if both of them shot the gunslinger together.

But the criminal knew this. And the gunslinger knew he knew that. And the sheriff knew that they both knew something else. Around and around the logic went in the gunslinger's mind as his hand closed around the pistol grip.

Game Theory

GAME THEORY IS A field of mathematics that analyzes the interaction between moves and countermoves in multiplayer games. Despite the name, game designers often ignore game theory because it seems too abstract to apply to the real world. But while we don't need to calculate exact numbers like mathematical game theorists, the fundamentals of game theory do illuminate key concepts in multiplayer game design.

Game theory helps analyze situations where players must anticipate and respond to one another's decisions.

Think of the difference between knocking down an abandoned castle and attacking an occupied one.

Knocking down an empty castle is a physics puzzle. You might have to work out the best place to put a crane, or the best way to clear away rubble. But while these tasks may be complex, an empty castle doesn't think back at you—it just follows the laws of physics. This is like a single-player game, since it's a single player's mind facing a mechanical system.

Knocking down a castle full of defenders is very different. Now there are two intelligent minds, each trying to outthink the other. The defending general will anticipate your moves and respond. He will toss back your ladders, drop fire on your battering ram, and send assassins to kill your general. And he will anticipate your responses to his responses. He'll send false signals to lure you into a trap, or try to hide a weakness in the wall. Game theory describes the interactions between your mind and his.

Imagine that one night during the siege, you're choosing your strategy for the next day. Your choice is between attacking the gate with the battering ram and sending sappers to blow up the wall, while the defender chooses between readying a pot of flammable tar at the gate and preparing archers to shoot your sappers. You've each only got enough men to do one thing, and since you must prepare during the night, you won't know what the other general decided until the battle is joined. Game theorists would graph out this situation in a *payoff matrix* like this:

Attacker's choice \ Defender's choice	Put archers on wall	Ready flammable tar at gate
Attack gate with battering ram	Attacker Wins (breaks down gate)	Defender Wins (burns battering ram)
Attack wall with sappers	Defender Wins (shoots sappers)	Attacker Wins (blows up wall)

As you can see, there is no one best choice. You and the defender are each making a decision whose outcome depends on the decision of the other; each can win by predicting what the other will do. You don't win this by having a bigger battering ram, but by figuring out how to trick the other guy into thinking you'll attack the gate as you prepare your sappers. This game isn't about walls and arrows anymore. It's about habit, assumption, information, and deception. This is the kind of situation that game theory helps us understand.

Game theory isn't just about competition either. It covers any interaction among players who must respond to one another's actions. Zero-sum competitive games where only one player can win are one category of this, but so are cooperative games, and mixed competitive/cooperative situations where players' goals partially align. Even attacking a defended castle isn't quite a zero-sum game, because one side may surrender or sue for peace.

One classic noncompetitive game theory example involves a pair of prehistoric hunters, Thag and Blarg. Since they live in separate tribes, Thag and Blarg cannot communicate when choosing where to go to hunt that day. Each must choose to go to the hunting ground of stags or the hunting ground of hares. If both choose to hunt stags, they can cooperate to take one down and both will eat well. Hares can be caught alone, so either one who chooses the hare will get a small, guaranteed meal. But if one chooses a hare while the other tries for the stag, the stag hunter starves.

		Thag's choice	
		Hunt stag	Hunt hare
Blarg's choice	Hunt stag	Both eat well	Thag eats a little Blarg starves
	Hunt hare	Thag starves Blarg eats a little	Both eat a little

As with the castle battle, Thag's and Blarg's choices depend on the choice of the other. One caveman's decision process isn't about stags and hares as much as it is about predicting the other caveman's decision process. Each must think about not just how hungry he is, but how hungry his counterpart is, and how hungry his counterpart thinks he is, and so on.

Recall the mental layer of skill reinvention—the pokerlike psychological mind game where each player tries to predict and manipulate the mind of the others. This is game-theoretic thinking. When there is someone else actively thinking back at you, the game becomes about more than mechanics. It becomes a lens through which two minds interact, each attempting to envelop the other inside its own mental model. And for competitive players, there's no victory sweeter than that.

GAMES AND STRATEGY INTERACTIONS

Before we go on, I'd like to clarify a definition.

Game theorists use the word *game* differently than game designers. To them, a game is a specific interaction between strategies. For example, a single round of rock-paper-scissors is considered a *game* in game theory. But in game design, a *game* is an entire system of mechanics, not a single decision point.

To emphasize the difference, I'll be calling game theory games *strategy interactions* from here on. The games we design generate many strategy interactions during the course of play, each of which can be examined individually using game theory.

This simple issue of definition may be why game theory is so often ignored in game design. Game theory can't solve an entire round of *Mortal Kombat*, so many people immediately assume it's useless in analyzing the game. But it is the best way to analyze a specific, fraction-of-a-second interaction between punches, blocks, or throws. It can't cover an entire match of soccer, but it can predict where a player will aim a certain shot and where the goalie will dive. It only works when applied at the level of interactions between strategies, not entire designs.

NASH EQUILIBRIA

The core concept of game theory is the *Nash equilibrium*.

A NASH EQUILIBRIUM is a configuration of strategies where no player can improve his own result by changing his strategy alone.

Let's break this down.

The first part of the Nash equilibrium is the fact that it's a configuration of strategies. A configuration of strategies is just a set of possible choices that all players could make. Each box in a payoff matrix is a configuration of strategies. In the stag hunt example, *Blarg hunts stag/Thag hunts hare* is a configuration of strategies. So is *both hunt hare, Blarg hunts hare/Thag hunts stag*, and *both hunt stag*.

A Nash equilibrium is just a specific kind of strategy combination. Specifically, it's one where none of the players has any reason to change strategy if they assume that nobody else will change theirs. This sounds like an arbitrary distinction, but it turns out to be an extremely powerful idea.

For example, in the stag hunt, there are two Nash equilibria. The first is when both hunters choose stag. In this case, both are getting the best possible result; if either changed his strategy to hunting hare, he would reduce the amount of food he got. The second is when both hunters choose hare. This one is more interesting, because it highlights the subtle aspect of Nash equilibria, which is that it's not necessarily optimal for anyone. If both hunters are chasing hare, they could theoretically both change to stag together, thus both getting much more food. But if either one switches to stag alone, he ends up starving while the other munches on hare. So even though it's not the best possible result for either hunter, *both hunt hare* is a Nash equilibrium.

Nash equilibria are important in real multiplayer games because play tends to gravitate toward them. Nash equilibria are stable and self-reinforcing since no player has a reason to do anything different. Nonequilibrium configurations are unstable and self-modifying, since someone has a reason to change his strategy alone. The game may allow a million strategy combinations, but only the Nash equilibria will tend to actually occur. So the play experience will consist of those situations that are Nash equilibria—others might as well not exist.

This is why it's important to set up a game so that the strategy interactions have many or no pure Nash equilibria.

A strategy interaction with one pure Nash equilibrium is a broken game design because it will always settle into that same equilibrium. Each player has only one viable option, so the strategic decision vanishes.

With only one equilibrium, all players know exactly what to do, and have no reason to anticipate or even think about one another's moves. This is the definition of monotony. The mind game where each player tries to predict the decisions of the others disappears.

Situations with multiple equilibria, like the stag hunt, are better because now each player is thinking about what the other will do. But we can improve even on this.

The best outcome is to eliminate Nash equilibria entirely. For example, in the castle battle, there are no pure Nash equilibria. No matter what the configuration of strategies, one side can do better by changing his choice. This is good game design because there is always a premium on knowing what other players will do, which creates all the human fascination of anticipating, deceiving, and manipulating other people. So, if you've got a strategy interaction with Nash equilibria, redesign or rebalance it to get rid of them.

ROCK-PAPER-SCISSORS AND MATCHING PENNIES

Interactions without Nash equilibria are commonly called *rock-paper-scissors mechanics* because rock-paper-scissors is the most commonly known game without a Nash equilibrium. In rock-paper-scissors, no matter what the configuration of strategies, one player wants to change their move. In payoff matrix form, the game looks like this:

Player 2's choice \ Player 1's choice	Rock	Paper	Scissors
Rock	Tie	Player 1 wins	Player 2 wins
Paper	Player 2 wins	Tie	Player 1 wins
Scissors	Player 1 wins	Player 2 wins	Tie

But it's usually easier to think of it like this:

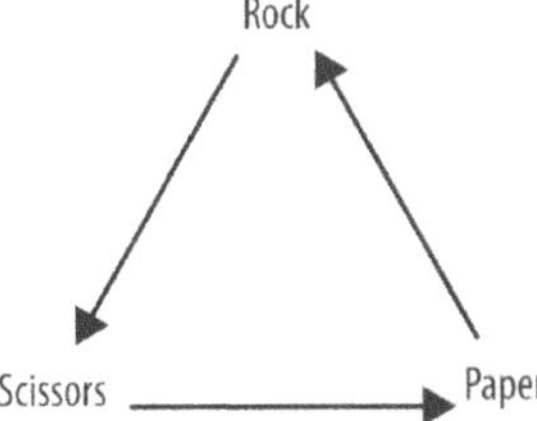

The same triangular pattern of moves and countermoves appears in many forms across countless games. In fighting games, block beats punch, throw beats block, and punch beats throw. In strategy games, spearmen beat cavalry, archers beat spearmen, and cavalry beat archers. This triangle of countermoves appears over and over because it is the simplest way to create a symmetrical game with no Nash equilibrium.

However, contrary to popular belief, the triangular rock-paper-scissors pattern is not the only basic design structure without Nash equilibria. Think of the castle battle. There are four moves, not three. And each player has two options. This isn't like rock-paper-scissors, yet it still has no Nash equilibria.

The rock-paper-scissors pattern creates no Nash equilibrium for symmetrical games where each player has the same moves. But in asymmetrical games like the castle battle, we use a different design pattern named after another old game: *matching pennies*.

In matching pennies, one player declares that he is seeking a match. Each player puts down a hidden penny, either heads-up or tails-up. They then reveal them together. If they're the same, the player who sought a match wins. Otherwise, his opponent does. It looks like this:

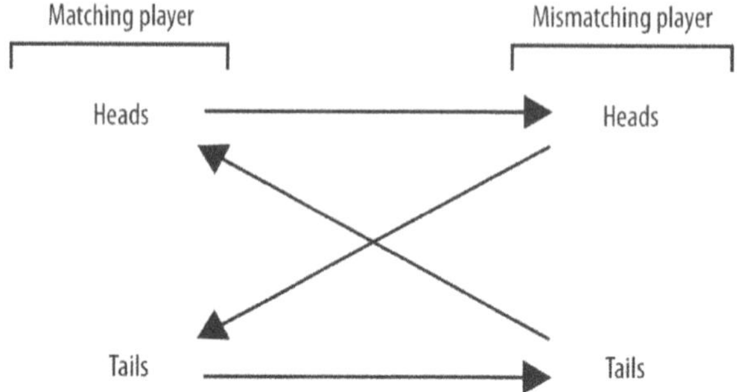

Even though it's rarely referred to by name, the matching pennies pattern appears constantly in multiplayer games. The castle battle is a matching pennies game, because the defender wants to match his defense against your attack, while you want a mismatch. In a multiplayer shooter, when you're defending an objective in a room with two doors, you're playing a matching pennies game; you want to defend the door that your opponent chooses to attack, while your opponent wants to come in the other door and shoot you in the back. In a World War II strategy game, the defender can choose whether to spend resources to lay mines, while the attacker can choose whether to spend resources to bring minesweepers. You don't want to lay mines that will just get swept up, and you don't want to sweep for mines that aren't there.

Let's look at a real example of a matching pennies design pattern. In *StarCraft II*, clashes between Zerg and Terran players often come down to four key units: the Terran Siege Tank and Marine, and the Zerg Baneling and Mutalisk. They interact like this:

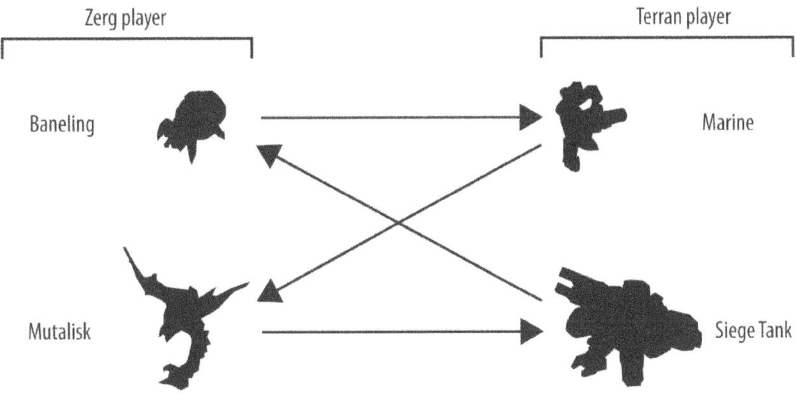

Mutalisks fly, so they automatically defeat Siege Tanks, because Tanks can't fire into the air. Marines' high damage takes down fragile Mutalisks in moments. Banelings melt tightly packed groups of Marines with their splashing acid damage. But Siege Tanks detonate fragile groups of Banelings from a safe distance. Many *StarCraft II* matches boil down to repeated interactions among these four units. Online, you can play a hundred hours in a row of variations of this pattern. But the play never becomes boring because there is no Nash equilibrium, so each player always has opportunities to gain by anticipating or deceiving his opponent. Because the game isn't really about controlling Marines and Mutalisks. It's about predicting the mind of the opponent.

Rock-paper-scissors and matching pennies are the only elegant design patterns for strategy interactions—rock-paper-scissors for symmetrical games, and matching pennies for asymmetrical games. Any alternative is no more than a pointless piling-on of more strategies. For example, in rock-paper-scissors-lizard-Spock, each symbol defeats two of the others, like this:

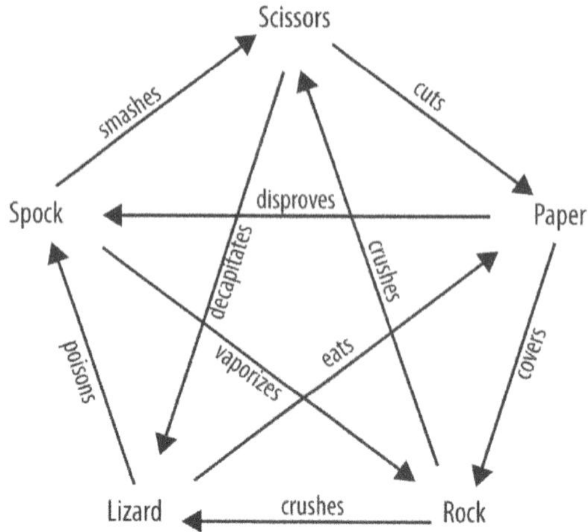

But RPSLS gains nothing in terms of decision interest over RPS. No Nash equilibrium means no Nash equilibrium. Adding more symbols does nothing to enrich the mind game of anticipation and deception. More options may add fictional interest, but it's probably not worth the extra learning burden.

MIXED STRATEGIES

So far, I've described 1games like rock-paper-scissors as having no Nash equilibrium. This wasn't entirely accurate. Rock-paper-scissors has no *pure* Nash equilibrium. It does, however, have a *mixed* Nash equilibrium.

A MIXED NASH EQUILIBRIUM is a Nash equilibrium where each player randomly chooses from a set of strategies with some given set of probabilities.

In rock-paper-scissors, for example, there is no pure Nash equilibrium, but there is one mixed Nash equilibrium. It calls for both players to throw each move 33.3% of the time. This is a Nash equilibrium since there is no way one player can gain by deviating from this configuration (since when the opponent is throwing with perfect randomness, it doesn't matter what you do; you'll always win half the games).

Other strategy mixes in rock-paper-scissors are not in equilibrium. For example, imagine you were to choose rock 35% of the time and scissors and paper 32.5% of the time. Now your opponent can beat you by changing his strategy to play paper 100% of the time. When one player can gain by changing his own strategy, the configuration is not a Nash equilibrium.

Mixed equilibria are easy to work out in simple games like rock-paper-scissors and matching pennies, where one player wins outright while the other loses. But this is an unusual case. In most real strategy interactions, different outcomes have different payoffs. For example, in a fighting game, a block beats a jab while doing no damage, a jab beats a throw while doing a little bit of damage, and a throw beats a block while doing lots of damage. This is analogous to a version of rock-paper-scissors where you get \$1 if you win with paper or scissors, but you get \$5 if you win with rock. The payoff matrix looks like this:

Player 2's choice \ Player 1's choice	Rock	Paper	Scissors
Rock	Tie	Player 1 wins \$1	Player 2 wins \$5
Paper	Player 2 wins \$1	Tie	Player 1 wins \$1
Scissors	Player 1 wins \$5	Player 2 wins \$1	Tie

A naïve strategy would be to simply play rock every game and hope for the \$5. The problem with this is that it is predictable. The opponent can counter by playing nothing but paper, and you'll walk away with nothing. To play well at this game, you need to play a mixed strategy that randomly chooses among rock, paper, and scissors. But you can't just play them evenly as in vanilla RPS, because your opponent will respond to you by playing rock more often. So how often do you play each move to maximize your earnings?

This is where the mathematical aspect of game theory comes into play. Given a strategy interaction and a set of payoffs, game theorists can calculate the precise proportions of a mixed strategy that creates a Nash equilibrium. Game designers don't need to do this numerically, but understanding how the proportions relate is important, so I'll demonstrate it with a real-life example.

In soccer, penalty kicks launch the ball at up to 125 mph. At this speed, the ball travels from foot to goal in about a fifth of a second. This is not enough time for the goalie to jump and try to block the ball after it has been kicked. His only choice is to jump before the kick. At the same time, the kicker must choose a side without knowing which way the goalkeeper is going to go.

This is a matching pennies game. The goalie wants to match kick sides with the kicker, while the kicker wants the opposite.

In this game, the kicker's payoff is the likelihood that he will score. The unequal payoffs come from the fact that every player kicks better to one side than the other. His chances of scoring when blocked correctly are better on his good side than on his bad side, and his chances of scoring unblocked are better on his good than bad side as well. (Of course, his payoff is still better on his bad side if he is not blocked than if he is blocked on his good side; otherwise, kicking on his good side would be a pure equilibrium strategy and he would thoughtlessly do that every time.)

The kicker's best strategy is to randomly choose his good and bad sides in different proportions, kicking on the good side most of the time, but mixing in an occasional off-side kick to keep the goalie honest. At the same time, the goalkeeper must mirror him, blocking his good side most of the time and occasionally going the other way.

We can calculate the exact proportions from the chances that the kicker will score with each of the four possible kick side/block side combinations. One research study gathered data from hundreds of kicks in European league games and came up with the following table of goal chance percentages (which is effectively a payoff matrix):

	Goalie jumps to good side	Goalie jumps to bad side
Kicker uses good side	63.6% chance of goal	94.4% chance of goal
Kicker uses bad side	89.3% chance of goal	43.7% chance of goal

Using these numbers, a bit of math reveals that the best strategy for the kicker is to use his good side 59.7% of the time and his bad side 40.3% of the time. This mixed strategy gives an overall success rate of 74.0% regardless of what the keeper does. Any deviation from these percentages allows the goalie to improve his results by switching to a pure strategy of always jumping to one side or the other. For example, if the kicker chose his good side 65% of the time instead of 59.7%, he would make only 72.6% of his shots against a goalie who exploited his strategy by always jumping at his good side.

The key to mixed Nash equilibria is that in equilibrium, each possible move has an equal payoff.

When playing the equilibrium strategy, on any given shot, the kicker expects a 74.0% chance of a goal regardless of which side he kicks on. If he expected a better chance on either side, the goalie would respond more often to that side, pushing down his success rate there. This equal-payoffs property is a useful intuitive way of thinking about equilibrium strategies without using math. Just look for the proportions where each option leads to the same average payoff.

Can players actually do this kind of numerical analysis? No, but averaged over many players, people are incredibly good at intuitively finding optimally mixed strategies. Studies on real-life kicking percentages reveal that kickers as a whole kick on their good side with almost exactly the correct frequency.

So is that it? We simply count the payoffs, work out the mixed strategy percentages, and let players flip their weighted coins? Thankfully, no—in real games, game theory interactions are only a foundation for a fuzzier, more psychological, more human type of interaction called *yomi*.

Yomi

YOMI is the mind game of predicting, deceiving, and outwitting an opponent to get advantages outside the game theory math.

I'm borrowing the term *yomi* from fighting game designer David Sirlin, who borrowed it from the Japanese word for *reading* (as in reading the mind of the opponent). Flipping weighted coins isn't interesting, but trying to read a person's mind is. That's why design patterns like rock-paper-scissors and matching pennies are only a skeleton of a game. The emotional value of the game grows from the yomi flesh around that skeleton—from making your opponent think you'll use one move so that you can counter with another, or letting him think he has tricked you when he hasn't, or using a move he doesn't realize you have. These are intense and intimate forms of mental conflict.

Yomi works because the real world is fuzzier than the math. In dry mathematical analyses, every payoff is countable and every strategy divides cleanly from the others. But real games aren't like this. Outcomes aren't precisely quantifiable, strategies can't be cleanly placed in boxes, and players don't have complete information or access to random number generators.

For example, in a shooter, both players have to choose whether to charge around the corner, chuck a grenade, or wait with their gun pointed at the door, but can choose to change their decision at any time or even do two things at once. Or, in a strategy game, players decide on economic strategies that smoothly mix different production goals in nuanced ways. In each case, there are fuzzy, unquantifiable edges around the core game theory interaction. The shooter player can look and move smoothly in every direction, and the strategy game player can order his production in thousands of different ways. These fuzzy edges are where yomi grows from. They are what allow players to get around the edges of the math, slightly change the payoff matrix of every decision, and learn a little more or a little less about their opponent to get ahead of them in the game.

So yomi play depends not just on creating strategy interactions without pure Nash equilibria, but also on crafting a system with interesting fuzzy edges around those core interactions. Let's look at some of the ways we can design games to generate strategy interaction that have these yomi-feeding fuzzy edges.

Yomi grows when players can smoothly blend between strategies.

Yomi play requires that a game have nuanced strategies that can be blended and combined in complex ways. For example, in *StarCraft II*, a Terran player can send a mixed force of half Siege Tanks and half Marines. Neither a pure Mutalisk nor pure Baneling force can stop this. Countering it requires a similarly mixed army of Mutalisks and Banelings. And the Terran can vary his mixture by tiny increments—one Marine more or less, one Siege Tank more or less. These two players aren't playing a lab game in which each one checks a box and then compares with the other to find an outcome. They're not just kicking left or right. They're playing in a smooth strategic space which lets them choose from a near-infinite variety of intermediate combined strategies. Each smoothly defined strategy demands a correspondingly smoothly defined response.

Smoothly defined strategies grow yomi because they allow players to outdo one another in the nuance of their strategic knowledge. Anybody can be told that the counter to Marines is Banelings and the counter to Siege Tanks is Mutalisks. But only the experts know *exactly* what they need to defeat arbitrary mixtures of Marines and Siege Tanks. What if he has 15 Marines and one Siege Tank? What if he has eight Marines and five Siege Tanks? What is the minimum you need to destroy him? A novice won't know, but an expert will. This sort of fine-grained interaction is what pushes the game's skill ceiling into the sky.

Yomi play grows from complex, difficult-to-quantify payoffs.

Different strategies have different potential payoffs. In an artificial example, we looked at a rock-paper-scissors variant in which you get $5 for winning with rock and $1 for winning with paper or scissors. Changing these numbers changes the proportions of strategies players should play. And, as you'll recall, the correct proportions are those where each individual strategy has the same average payoff.

But what if the numbers weren't handed to us? What if strategies had potential payoffs with qualitative effects, hooking into multiple goals, at various levels of certainty? These payoffs aren't known ahead of time, and they can't be described with a single number. Figuring out a good mixed strategy is no longer just a matter of equalizing the payoffs of the various strategies. First we have to figure out what the payoffs are. This evaluation process maintains flow, and heightens skill ceiling.

Uncertain payoffs also mean that we need to guess how the other player is evaluating his payoffs. If you know your opponent well, you might find a place where he overvalues or undervalues certain payoffs and exploit it to predict and defeat him. At even higher skill levels, you might predict his guess at your evaluations, and so on.

Let's go back to *StarCraft II*. Mutalisks and Siege Tanks are expensive, while Marines and Banelings are cheap. This means that for a Terran player, shooting down Mutalisks with Marines has a better payoff than shooting down Banelings with Siege Tanks, since the Mutalisks are much harder to replace and the Marines are easier to make. The same goes in reverse—the Zerg wants to kill Siege Tanks with Mutalisks more than they want to kill Marines with Banelings.

If it were as simple as that, this interaction would still be mathematically solvable by plugging in the precise value of each kind of unit. But the real payoff of the battle depends on more than the costs of the units involved. It depends on how that battle plays out through other game systems, and its context in the larger game.

Consider context. If the Terran Siege Tanks are slowly rolling toward the Zerg base, and are almost in range to begin bombarding it, the Zerg is under immense pressure to destroy the attacking force by any means necessary. The cost of not destroying it is much worse than it would be if the battle were happening in the middle of the map. Lose somewhere on the map, and your units die. Lose here, and your base dies. So the payoffs are different.

Positioning can change payoffs. A spread-out force of Marines and Siege Tanks is vulnerable to Mutalisks darting in and picking units off the edges. But a concentrated force is vulnerable to Banelings' splashing acid. A group of Marines which is normally vulnerable to Banelings might not be if it is spread across a wide area. At the same time, this spread-out group makes itself abnormally vulnerable to Mutalisks, improving their payoff against it.

Payoffs also change with the proportions of units. For example, we know that Banelings usually beat Marines. But if there are enough Marines, they can defeat small numbers of Banelings with no losses by shooting them before they get close. Similarly, even though Marines usually counter Mutalisks, a large group of Mutalisks can annihilate a small group of Marines with no losses. In these cases, lopsided numbers have reversed the relationships in the basic matching pennies game. But this reversal doesn't happen everywhere—no number of Banelings can efficiently kill a single Siege Tank.

Skill variations affect payoffs. One player may be a master at Mutalisks, increasing his payoff for this strategy. He will thus want to use Mutalisks more than Banelings, and the other player will want to counter by using Marines more than Siege Tanks, the same way the goalie jumps to the kicker's strong side more often.

Even simpler games present situationally varied payoffs, albeit at a smaller scope. For example, fighting games don't have nearly as many variables as *StarCraft II*. There are two characters, each is in a specific state, and the situation is going to resolve itself a handful of ways. Still, there are enough combinations of positions, animation status, health, energy, and other variables that evaluating payoffs is a noticeable mental challenge. The decision is smaller-scoped than in *StarCraft II*, but this is acceptable because it is compressed into a tiny fraction of a second. The complexity of the decision is proportional to the time available to make it, so flow is maintained.

At every interaction, the players must each evaluate variables and estimated probabilities to come up with a set of estimated payoffs. In *StarCraft II*, they have to account for unit counts, positioning, skill differences, economy status, economic impact, and hundreds of other quantifiable and unquantifiable variables. The problem is mind-bogglingly complex. But this is the power of human thought. Machines can't do this sort of calculation. Only a human mind running at full blast using all of its geometric, spatial, emotional, and interpersonal intuition can solve this. It's a whole-body workout for the brain.

And this evaluation process isn't just a logic puzzle. It's also an emotional challenge. Mediocre Zerg players will panic and attack prematurely as the Siege Tanks start shelling a nonessential base. Novice Terrans will foolishly leave their tanks unguarded while their Marines greedily chase Mutalisks. In each case, these players' emotions are clouding their evaluation of payoffs. The Zerg is driven by an emotional fear of loss; steelier players know that sometimes it's better to lose a base than risk an army trying to save it. The Terran is driven by a greedy desire to kill expensive Mutalisks; better players know when to let them go. Learning to evaluate well doesn't mean just knowing and thinking through logic. It means evaluating your emotions, training them, and keeping them in check.

These profound logical and emotional evaluation challenges are what keep players coming back, again and again, and stretch the skill ceiling to unfathomable heights. This depth means that no matter how good you are at these evaluations, there is always another nuance to discover.

Yomi grows from the psychology of randomness.

Did you know that there are real rock-paper-scissors tournaments? People sign up, go through qualifiers, and compete in front of spectators. Prizes can be as high as $50,000. And all this plays out in a game where the only equilibrium strategy is to be completely random.

It seems like a joke, and on some level, it is. But just past the ridiculousness, there is still a skill to playing rock-paper-scissors against a human being, because human beings cannot generate random numbers.

In game theory, mixed strategies must be perfectly randomized. But since humans can't make random numbers, we can't ever play true mixed strategies. Our minds are full of well-studied probability biases. Asked to write a random string of 1's and 0's, we consistently alternate more often than we should. Long runs of one symbol feel less probable than they are. When we've just lost with a strategy, our judgment of its value on the next play is altered. Biases like this can be exploited.

This means that there is a game in predicting faults in other players' mental random number generators. If you understand someone and you are skilled at yomi, you might be able to tell when he has a 35% chance of playing rock, even if he is trying to play 33.33%. And you can turn that knowledge into a win. Again, this pushes up skill ceiling and enriches decisions.

Yomi grows from the manipulation of information.

Making strategic decisions depends on having good and complete information about the game. Players need to know what's happening, what their opponent knows, what their opponent thinks they know, and so on. All this information can be manipulated from both sides if the game design allows it, creating opportunities for yomi.

There are three basic ways players can manipulate information.

First, players can seek information to improve their own decisions. In strategy games, players send scouts. In social interaction games, players ask their friends. In shooters, they stop and listen for footsteps. Tools like *Modern Warfare*'s heartbeat sensor or *StarCraft II*'s scan ability support this kind of action.

Second, players can deny one another information. In strategy games, they kill scouts. In social interaction games, they interfere with others' conversations. In shooters, they'll throw smoke grenades or radar scramblers. Players can even hide metagame information—tournament players in both *StarCraft* and *Street Fighter* have been known to save their best moves during early rounds, only to unleash them in the finals.

Finally, players can plant false information to deceive one another. While other kinds of yomi are about knowing the mind of the opponent, deception is about controlling it. Sometimes deception mechanics can be explicit, as in phantom units in strategy games, or lying in social interaction games. Other times, players will find ways to use normal mechanics to deceive. For example, in a shooter, a player might open a door to plant a false belief that he is passing through it, but then enter through the window. In a strategy game, a player might construct an airport, allow the enemy to scout it, and then never build an airplane while his opponent invests in useless anti-air weaponry.

These information manipulation design elements can be extended to develop layers of false information. One player can make the other player think he knows something that he doesn't. Or he can make the other player think he's ignorant of a fact that he secretly knows. This kind of multilayered deception is difficult to design directly, but it's a valuable result that can emerge from the interaction of the basic deception tools.

Yomi requires small player counts.

It's hard to mentally model the mind of one other player. Keeping track of the intentions and habits of two or three is on the edge of possibility. Scale the player count up past four, and it's impossible. So yomi breaks down beyond two or three players because there are simply too many minds to think about. With large player counts like this, a game loses its mind-game aspect and becomes about the mechanics only.

The obvious way to solve this is to keep player counts very small. But often, that's not an option. In these cases, a game can still create yomi by temporarily isolating smaller groups of players from the larger population.

For example, *World of Warcraft* has millions of players, but when they interact, it is always in small, circumscribed groups. Four players might raid a dungeon to gather loot, or two players might have a duel. Special game mechanics prevent different groups from interfering with one another. So yomi can grow within the group as long as it is isolated.

Isolation can also happen through softer, more emergent mechanisms. For example, in many shooters, players compete in large teams of 16 or more players. But not every player is fighting every other at all times. Rather, they're spread over a large map with many isolated rooms. Fights start and finish in single rooms without involving more than a handful of players. This allows players to focus on just the few people in the room with them, which makes yomi possible even with 32 players on the field.

YOMI CASE STUDY: MODERN WARFARE 2

Let's look at an example of yomi players from the multiplayer shooter *Modern Warfare 2*. This example covers a few seconds of play between Carol and Dave in a Team Deathmatch game.

Carol is inside a small shed with two entrances when she glimpses Dave approaching. She retreats farther inside so that the two players can no longer see each other.

The game-theoretic yomi-driving thought process begins. These players have entered a matching pennies game as each chooses between the two entrances to the shed. Carol can watch one entrance, and Dave wants to attack through the entrance Carol is not watching and come up behind her.

If this was all there was to it, the players could work out their mixed strategy proportions, flip their weighted coins, and get on with it. Fortunately, *Modern Warfare 2* has lots of fuzzy yomi-forming edges around its core game mechanics to add interest.

Here is Carol's thought process as she thinks through her options.

She may choose to stay in the shed or charge out of it through either door. If Carol chooses to stay:

- She may focus on watching one door. If Dave comes through this door, he will walk directly into her sights and she'll fire, instantly killing him. If Dave comes through the other door, he will shoot her in the back before she has time to turn around. But which door should she watch?
    - She may choose to watch the door through which she saw Dave. Dave might anticipate this and go in the back. She might anticipate that, and so on.
    - She might choose to watch the door closer to Dave for some time, then, having not seen him yet, switch to the other door. In this case, she is using the fact that Dave has not attacked yet as information indicating he may have chosen the other path. Again, Dave might anticipate this line of reasoning and counter it.
- She may look back and forth between both doors. This is a hedge. Looking back and forth means that she will at least see Dave soon after he enters. The downside is that Carol is disorienting herself and disturbing her aim by looking back and forth constantly. Even if a door is visible when Dave comes through it, Carol's aim is likely not perfectly settled on it as it would be if she was aiming steadily at one door.
- She may choose to move around constantly within the shed. Again, this is a hedge. Moving around makes Carol a harder target, so Dave will likely have a slightly harder time of killing her in time even if

he comes in the door Carol is not watching. The downside is that it disturbs Carol's aim, and may also create footstep sounds, which give Dave information about Carol's presence, location, and activity.

- At any time, Carol may stop waiting and charge outside.

If Carol chooses to charge out of the shed, she may or may not encounter Dave:

- If she encounters Dave, yomi play ends since both players are in sight of each other and there is no significant hidden information. The game changes into a shooting and dodging challenge. The initial advantage in this shooting challenge depends on how well Dave predicted Carol's move.
    - If Dave predicted Carol would exit the shed through the correct door, he may have simply set up in front of the door with his gun trained on it. In this case, Carol is walking right into his sights and almost certainly dies.
    - If Dave predicted Carol would exit the shed, but wasn't sure which door she would exit through, Dave may simply be in the vicinity, trying to guard both doors but not focusing on one. This hedge strategy leads to a relatively even shooting match, since neither player starts with gun trained on the other.
- If Carol does not encounter Dave after exiting the shed, she has several options depending on what she thinks Dave is doing.
    - She can go around the shed and try to come up behind Dave as Dave approaches the other door. If Dave was approaching the other door slowly, Carol may be able to come up behind him and shoot him in the back. On the other hand, if Dave was approaching the other door quickly, he may have already seen into it and discovered that Carol exited through the first door. He might now choose to turn around and wait for Carol to come around the shed, likely killing her, or he might think Carol fled through the other door, in which case he will run through the shed and out the other side.

Carol can try to flee the area entirely:

- If Dave was circling the shed quickly, he will come around the shed and shoot Carol in the back as she flees.

- If Dave predicted Carol would flee, he may have never approached the shed at all, and simply been in hiding at a distance, in which case he will shoot Carol.
- If Dave was approaching the other door slowly, Carol will be able to get away.

On the surface, *Modern Warfare 2* looks like a game about shooting people. That's why they call it a shooter. And shooting is the most meathead-friendly game verb there is. Point, pull, bang, and drop. Good mindless fun, right?

But if that was all there was to it, players would quickly tire of it. The act of shooting is just spectacle. It has no longevity—but *Modern Warfare 2* does. People play this game for hundreds or even thousands of hours. They buy sequel after sequel to do the same thing over and over. Why?

Because the game isn't really about shooting. It's about yomi—an intricate dance of mental evaluation and counterevaluation. Skilled players really do think through possibility trees like this in real time. That's what their mind is chewing on—not some repetitive shooting graphic. Far from being mindless, the game is downright cerebral.

The core reason *Modern Warfare 2* creates yomi so well is because its weapons are extremely accurate and deadly. Players die in one or two shots. If you come up behind someone, he dies before he has a chance to turn and fire back. This means that the decisions that matter are not the ones that happen as players are firing at one another—they're the ones that are made before players gain sight of one another. You want to be the one who comes up behind your opponent, not the other way around. And yomi thrives when players are out of sight, straining to hear footsteps, watching heartbeat sensors, listening for gunshots, and guessing enemies' attack paths. Without the complete information of sight, opportunities for deception blossom.

This doesn't happen in shooters with weaker weapons. The first shot isn't worth much when it takes 25 shots to kill. In these games, what players do out of sight of one another is fairly unimportant. What matters is how well they aim and dodge after the battle is joined. But while aiming and dodging are worthwhile mechanical challenges, there's no yomi in them since there's no significant hidden information.

Modern Warfare 2 actually creates much more nuanced and varied yomi than the decision tree in the previous example. In a real game, each player's options and information are more numerous, fuzzier, and subtler than described here. Players may have special tools which can help them gather or obscure information, like stun grenades, smoke grenades, silent walk abilities, heartbeat sensors, and so on. Either player may spray bullets through the wall, giving away a position but hoping for a hit. Either player may fire shots through doorways to try to give false signals. Players may be able to communicate with teammates, or simply wait and hope for help from an ally nearby. Players may have varying weapon types, so either player may have an advantage or disadvantage in any type of encounter—Carol might prefer a close-up engagement with her submachine gun, while Dave wants to fight at a distance with his rifle. In an objective-based game, one or both players may have goals beyond simply winning their encounter with the other player. If the clock is ticking, a losing player will avoid strategies that consume valuable seconds; the other player can anticipate this and drag out the encounter. Players may have varying general skill levels, and varying abilities at specific skills, like aiming, movement, or yomi itself, and each may know much or little about the other. Players may be fatigued, energized, distracted, or frustrated. Count it all up, and the complexity of these yomi-soaked decisions is breathtaking.

And that's just one choice, lasting one or two seconds. The game will keep producing these tactical puzzles by the thousands, each one flowing into the next, never repeating, never getting boring. It holds flow by sustaining a continuous contest of deception through a lens of simple, carefully crafted mechanics.

Destructive Player Behavior

Most games assign players goals: get the highest score, defeat the opponent, or survive as long as possible. Up to now we've assumed that players will actually care about these goals just because we tell them to. But sometimes they don't.

In single-player, when players pursue goals the designer didn't intend, desk jumping results. Single-player desk jumping may harm an experience, but it's usually not fatal. In multiplayer, however, player-invented goals can tear apart a game because they affect everyone, not just the person pursuing them.

Multiplayer games are usually tightly structured and finely balanced so that each player has a precise role to play. One player making strange choices throws off this balance and destroys the game for everyone, including those who wanted to play properly. For example, if a team of heroes is battling a dragon, and one of them decides to go get a snack or heal the dragon just to see what happens, the entire team is screwed.

There are two basic kinds of destructive player behavior: *divergent goals* and *skill differentials.*

DIVERGENT GOALS

DIVERGENT GOALS appear when players in a multiplayer game decide to pursue goals that break other players' experiences.

I've discussed *Modern Warfare*'s merits. Now it's time to look at one of its flaws: it has divergent player goals. The official goal of every multiplayer match is to win. Each game type sets different criteria for winning. For example, in Capture the Flag, the goal is to capture more flags than the enemy team before time runs out. The trouble is that the game also tracks how many enemies each player kills and stores this information in a persistent database. And killing is more immediately and viscerally gratifying than watching a score ticker in the corner of the screen. As a result, some players choose to ignore the official goals like capturing the flag, and instead focus solely on racking up kills. This doesn't harm their experience, but it harms the experiences of others. Their allies are forced to play with a teammate who won't capture objectives, and their opponents are denied a good, honest game.

The only reason *Modern Warfare*'s design still holds together is because killing enemies is usually still helpful in achieving team goals. A teammate who doesn't care about capturing the flag is still contributing if he's killing enemies. There is a divergent goal, but it's still aligned closely enough with the official goal that the game mostly works. So while the game is harmed, it is not destroyed.

If the divergent goal had driven players to act completely against the official goals, the game would fall apart. For example, *Left 4 Dead* is about four survivors helping one another survive a zombie outbreak. The game is designed so that the team does best when it works together. But sometimes, one player might run off and decide to see how far he can get alone, just to challenge himself. But this destroys his teammates' play experience. He gets the unwinnable but entertaining fight he wanted, but his teammates are left without his help and the carefully balanced game falls apart.

Even real-life actions like leaving a multiplayer game are a form of divergent goal. The player leaving the game has the goal of getting up and doing something else. The players left behind have the goal of continuing play.

But the worst kinds of divergent goals are the ones that are driven by the pleasure of irritating others. This is called *griefing*.

GRIEFING is deliberately destroying others' play experiences for one's own entertainment.

Shooter players wedge themselves in doorways so that their team can't leave the starting area. Strategy game players attack their allies' units or wall off their bases. Even in games with no obvious way to harm other players, finding ways to grief people becomes a game in itself. *World of Warcraft* players used to cast a water-walking ability on allies as they fell from a height into a pool. The hapless victims would splatter onto the water which was suddenly, to them, as hard as concrete. *Counter-Strike* players used to use the game's spray-tag function to place horrifyingly offensive images in high-traffic areas of the level. Other players would be forced to look at the Internet's most shocking pictures as they tried to fight their tactical battles (and that's not the kind of juxtaposition that enriches an experience).

In face-to-face games like board games, sports, or barroom billiards, people don't grief because of the threat of broken friendships or bar fights, so designers of these games don't have to worry about players moving other players' pieces or throwing the cue ball out a window. But these social enforcement mechanisms don't exist online, where everyone is anonymous and can leave at any time. In these kinds of games, the design of the game itself must handle griefing.

The first line of defense against all divergent goals is the same as with desk jumping: motivate players to have goals that make sense. Players don't assign themselves divergent goals randomly; they do it in response to the same kinds of impulses that drive them to play games in the first place. They want to conquer, explore, communicate, and affect people. If the best way to do these things is to play the game as it was intended to be played, that's what they'll do.

Unfortunately, achieving perfect goal alignment across all players at once is nearly impossible. Usually we need other measures to keep multiplayer games on track.

A large player count is a buffer against divergent goals. One person goofing off, quitting, or griefing is much more important in a team of two than a team of 12.

Sometimes specific solutions can solve specific problems. For example, *Left 4 Dead* only allows four players, and its campaigns are 45 minutes long. The chances of four strangers each playing continuously for that long are slim; there is a divergent goal when one player wants to leave while the others want to continue. But the game stays playable because as soon as a player leaves, his character is taken over by the AI, who controls it until another player joins. The AI isn't as good as a real person, but it's a workable stopgap.

Griefing problems need more extreme solutions than other divergent goals because they do much more damage when they occur.

One obvious option is to make griefing impossible. If shooter players are blocking doors, allow players to pass through one another. If MMO players are luring monsters to attack other players in town, place safe zones where monsters won't go.

These strict solutions are necessary to fix the worst cases, but unfortunately we can't disallow every possible griefing strategy. There is always some way to annoy other players, even if it amounts to deliberately losing or refusing to play. A strategy game player can simply hide their units in corners and not even attempt to win. A team shooter player could fire their weapon randomly to give away their team's location. The possibilities are endless.

But we don't have to solve every case. Griefing strategies lie along a spectrum of severity according to their entertainment value for the griefer, and their destructive effect on other players. The most severe strategies are very entertaining for the griefer and game-destroying for other players. Nonproblem strategies are those that either are not entertaining at all for the griefer, or don't harm other players. For a game to work online, designers must identify the most severe griefing strategies and solve those. Below a certain cutoff of severity, it isn't worth twisting the core game to disallow griefing. For example, strategy games remain playable because simply not fighting is not very fun for the griefer, and not very destructive for the other player who is given a free (if dull) win. And shooter players could grief their team by committing suicide, but they don't because dying isn't fun. These griefing strategies are below the level of severity to be worth worrying about. As long as we disallow the most severe griefing strategies, the game works.

Unfortunately, not all games can be griefer-proofed from the inside. These games need a final line of defense in the form of policing mechanics like voting systems or game moderators. Policing systems are messy and inelegant—voting requires players to break from gameplay to regulate their own experience, and paying moderators costs developers money. But when used as a last line of defense, they can save a game that would otherwise degenerate into a quagmire of blocked doorways, ignored objectives, and Internet shock photos.

SKILL DIFFERENTIALS

One special kind of divergent goal is the one that appears because of large skill differentials among players. When one player is an expert and another is a beginner, bad things can happen.

The unskilled player's goal is to learn the game and not be pressured too much. The skilled player's goal is to play and win a deep, skill-stretching game. The gap between these goals can cause conflicts that are unpleasant from both sides. The unskilled player gets pressured and insulted. The skilled player is either bored from playing against a terrible opponent, or annoyed at his useless teammate.

The problem is extremely common because it appears anywhere players are interdependent and success depends on skill. *Left 4 Dead*, *StarCraft II* team battles, and *Call of Duty: Black Ops*' Nazi Zombies mode are all great designs, and all suffer from skill differentials.

There are a number of ways to reduce the impact of skill differentials. The first few are all about shrinking the skill differential itself.

Obviously a simple, elegant design is the best baseline way of shrinking skill differentials. A game that is easy to pick up will get players past the skill barrier faster, making them less likely to annoy experts and get kicked from games.

Another way to shrink skill differentials is to create a matchmaking algorithm that matches players of similar skill levels. The system keeps track of each player's experience level and win rate. When a player searches for a game it puts him together with others with similar records. This solution is conceptually simple, but in practice, designing and engineering these systems to work well can be a massive challenge.

There are also structural solutions. Massively multiplayer games like *World of Warcraft* are set up so that players can play solo the first several hours without pressure from others, and then choose to group up later after they've learned the basics. This means that complete newcomers are never required to play a role in any group, which means they can't harm a group through lack of skill. Similarly, many games have both single- and multiplayer modes. Players cut their teeth on single-player mode, where their failures don't affect others, before diving into multiplayer. Again, this means that most people online won't be utter beginners, even if they're not experts.

Finally, games can reduce skill differentials with good adaptive training. For example, *Left 4 Dead* uses an adaptive training system to tell novice players exactly what to do in every critical situation. When a Hunter zombie jumps on and disables an ally, a message flashes on-screen instructing the novice to save their friend. This occurs for every critical action in the game—completing objectives, helping allies, and getting resources. So, while a newcomer might have poor aim or an unrefined strategy, they at least aren't left fumbling around in total confusion.

If we can't reduce the skill differential, we can make it less important by reducing interdependency between players. Many people treat interdependency between players as an unalloyed good—but it's not. Because while interdependency can create a feeling of shared victory, it also requires that we suffer because of the failures of others.

The best result is a system that eliminates that shared failure while permitting shared victory. For example, shooters such as *Halo: Reach* have team combat modes in which players fight on teams while mostly ignoring their teammates. But here and there, two or three players will form an impromptu alliance, defeat an enemy, and split up. This creates teamwork, but only on an optional, short-term basis, thus enabling shared victory without often enforcing shared failure.

Many naïve designs are based on the assumption that players will work together. And if we assume that, wonderful things seem easily possible. But truly cooperative, skill-matched teams are rare in the wild. A game that assumes their presence will collapse. A multiplayer design needs to be robust enough to handle the constant low-grade chaos caused by players dropping out, griefing, missing key skills, or deciding to play wrong.

8

Motivation and Fulfillment

Jude's gaming chair opened above her, automatically withdrawing the brain-computer interface from her skull. She sat up. The room was dark, but Jude could still read the clock on the wall. It was December 31, 2151.

It had been nine years since she started playing. During that time, Jude had conquered empires, grown families, and built towers to the heavens, all in the unreal realm of the computer. She would have stayed in the system, but something was wrong. Multiplayer had stopped working. There was nobody to brag to; nobody to create with. She'd searched the global gaming network and not connected with a single other player. She hated leaving the computer world, but she had to fix this.

The room was dark and dusty. Looking around the gaming café, she saw rows of other chairs stretching away from her on either side. Peering through the portholes on the nearest ones, she could see the occupants. All of them were aged, with gray hair and liver spots. All of them were dead.

Jude thought for a moment and lay back down in her chair. It folded around her in a steel embrace, gently cradling her into unconsciousness.

Dopamine Pleasure

Most of us assume that we want things because they make us feel good. At first this view doesn't even look like an opinion. Of course we want pleasure. How else could it be?

When scientists first started studying pleasure, their results seemed to confirm this. Back in the 1950s, James Olds, then a researcher at McGill University in Montreal, wanted to see how a jolt of electricity to the brain would affect behavior. To find out, he ran a thin wire into a rat's brain and connected it to a lever inside the cage. When the rat pushed the lever, it would get a pulse of electricity through the wire, straight to the cerebrum.

At first the rat wandered randomly. But once it accidentally hit the switch for the first time, its behavior changed. It started pushing the switch more and more often. Over time it became a junkie, endlessly jolting itself in a manic loop of self-stimulation.

Olds' experiments established the idea of the brain's *reward center.* When activated, the reward center spurts out a dollop of the brain chemical dopamine. Ordinarily, the reward center generates dopamine in response to everyday stimuli, like a bite of tasty food, winning money, or a look at an attractive mate. Olds' brain wire worked by forcing this natural response into overdrive.

In the 1960s, researchers started investigating this effect in humans. The first was Robert Heath, chairman of the Department of Psychiatry and Neurology at Tulane University in New Orleans. In his most infamous study, Heath attempted to "treat" a homosexual using a brain wire. The young man, known by the code name B-19, had grown up in an abusive household, had few friends, and lived on the edge of suicide. Heath wired him up, and handed him the switch. In Heath's words, "B-19 stimulated himself to a point that, both behaviorally and introspectively, he was experiencing an almost overwhelming euphoria and elation and had to be disconnected, despite his vigorous protests."

Olds' and Health's experiments cemented the dopamine theory of motivation: motivation is driven by a pursuit of pleasure, and pleasure's messenger is dopamine. And this commonsense model stood for many years.

But then the problems started to appear.

Dopamine Motivation

The first was in the timing of the dopamine flood. Researchers discovered that the dopamine does not appear at the same time as the reward is received, nor does it appear afterward. Rather, the dopamine comes *before* the reward.

If dopamine is pleasure, this doesn't make sense. When you go to the store to buy a steak, you are not having the same experience as when you are eating the steak. But your brain is still soaked in dopamine, even as you're browsing the meat aisle in the supermarket.

This strange result opened the field to later studies that tried to understand the real role of dopamine.

In 2009, 61 subjects rated their desire to vacation in various destinations around the globe. Some of them were given L-Dopa, a drug that enhances the action of dopamine, while the others were given a placebo. If dopamine was pleasure, L-Dopa would make patients feel good the same way the brain wire did. But it didn't. Instead, subjects who got the dopamine wanted to travel to more destinations and wanted to go more intensely than the control subjects. They didn't feel good—they felt motivated.

In 1989, Kent Berridge, professor of neuroscience at the University of Michigan, gave rats a neurotoxin that killed off all their dopamine-receiving cells. The rats stopped doing anything—even eating. They lost all motivation, and without help, they would have died of starvation. But when Berridge squirted a sugary liquid into their mouths, they still made little rat facial expressions that indicated pleasure. Even without dopamine, the rats could enjoy their food. They had just lost all motivation to pursue it.

It turns out that the old commonsense view is wrong. Dopamine is not the marker for pleasure. It is the marker for motivation. And the two are not always linked.

We can want something without liking it, or like something without wanting it.

It sounds strange, but when you look closer, there are examples of this everywhere. Drug addicts want their drug more and more while liking it less and less. We've all had to thank a friend for dragging us to a party we felt unmotivated to go to. And many game players have found themselves unable to stop playing long after becoming bored with a game.

Most of this book is about evoking emotional experiences that fulfill players. In this chapter, we're concerned with mechanisms that create motivation alone. We'll look at how to use them, how to pair them with fulfillment, and the ethical implications of not doing so.

Rewards Anticipation

Every game needs to use dopamine motivation because every game creates moments of displeasure. Often these moments are essential to the design. Without dopamine, players would give up the first time they failed a challenge or lost a resource. Dopamine motivates players to push through obstacles so that they can get the triumph, social connection, or artistic satisfaction on the other side.

The main way we generate dopamine motivation is by creating the anticipation of rewards.

Many kinds of rewards can elicit dopamine motivation. Food, water, sex, safety, money, possessions, power, and social status are all dopamine-driving rewards. When we anticipate getting these things, our brains release a surge of dopamine, and our motivation to pursue the goal increases.

But wait a second. Games are inconsequential almost by definition. We usually can't give players food or sex (though a few games do use pornographic content as a reward). We usually can't offer real physical security (unless the game can hurt the player, as in *PainStation*). We usually can't give real money or real social status (except if players bet on the game, or play it for an audience). Most games must work to create motivation without offering or threatening anything at all outside themselves. But how can we do this if we can't offer any real rewards?

We can do it because the human brain evolved in an environment that lacked modern games, so it has no system for distinguishing real rewards from virtual ones. Virtual rewards usually don't have the same motivational intensity as real rewards, but they retain some echo of the real reward's power. While we want to get rich in real life more than we do in a game, we still want to get rich in a game.

Some virtual rewards, like experience points, in-game money, equipment, and abilities, are about powering up the player's character. Others, like cutscenes or audio logs, use story content as a reward. Some, like points in 1980s arcade games, are no more than records of achievement—the digital equivalent of a kid scratching his name on the tallest branch of the tallest tree in his neighborhood. The fact that these rewards are all meaningless outside the game is irrelevant. They tickle the reward center all the same.

Reinforcement Schedules

In creating motivation, the reward itself often isn't the most important part of the equation. The real key to motivation is in the timing of exactly when players anticipate and receive rewards. This aspect of rewards is determined by a *reinforcement schedule*.

A REINFORCEMENT SCHEDULE is a system of rules that defines when rewards are given.

The psychologist B.F. Skinner created reinforcement schedules in the 1930s and '40s while exploring the idea of *operant conditioning*. Whereas classical conditioning is about manipulating a creature's involuntary responses (as in Pavlov's famous dog bell experiment), operant conditioning is about manipulating apparently voluntary behavior using rewards and punishments. When you give a treat to a dog after it performs a trick, you're using operant conditioning to make it perform that trick again.

To explore operant conditioning, Skinner invented the so-called "Skinner box." A Skinner box is a small enclosure in which rats or pigeons can be placed. The box might contain levers, hamster wheels, sensors, lights, loudspeakers, food dispensers, or electrical shockers, depending on the experiment. These devices are linked together by an unseen mechanism that creates a relationship between them.

For example, in one configuration, the dispenser would give out a pellet of food each time the lever was pushed. In another, it would give food every 10th push. In another, it would randomly produce pellets 10% of the time each time it was pushed. Each of these configurations is a different reinforcement schedule.

Skinner wanted to see what different reinforcement schedules would do to the rat's behavior. How would the rat respond if it got food every time it pushed the lever? What if it got a pellet randomly, or on a timer, or after it ran a certain distance on the wheel? Skinner found that the animal's behavior would change depending on when the rewards appeared—but not always in obvious ways. Even slight changes in the reinforcement schedules could cause drastic differences in behavior.

Such reinforcement schedules aren't just for Skinner boxes. Games are full of them. When you defeat an orc to get a gold piece, you're playing a reinforcement schedule created by a game designer. Just as with Skinner's rats, the details of that reinforcement schedule will affect how motivated you are to keep playing. For game designers, these schedules are tools we can use to motivate players.

There are an infinite variety of possible schedules, but the two most important ones are *fixed ratio* and *variable ratio*.

FIXED RATIO

A fixed ratio reinforcement schedule gives rewards at a fixed ratio to actions taken. For example, in a Skinner box, a rat might get a food pellet every time it pushes the lever. In a game, a player might get a gold piece every time he defeats an orc. These are both fixed ratio schedules because the ratio between action and reward is always the same.

The ratio doesn't have to be one-to-one. For example, a player might get 10 gold pieces for every 10th orc he defeats. In this case most actions are not rewarded at all. The 10th orc gives the reward that was earned over the previous nine orcs.

By themselves, fixed ratio schedules are poor motivators. They encourage long periods of low inactivity, followed by a surge of activity when the player decides he wants the next reward. Those long periods of inactivity make it easy for the player to get up and walk away.

VARIABLE RATIO

A variable ratio reinforcement schedule is like a fixed ratio schedule, except that the ratio changes every time the reward is given. Usually, a variable ratio schedule gives the reward after some randomized number of actions. For example, a player might have a 10% chance of receiving 10 gold pieces every time he defeats an orc. Depending on the roll of the dice, he could get the reward three times in a row, or plow through 50 orcs and get nothing.

Variable ratio schedules are the most powerful simple reinforcement schedule. Even when they give the same average return as a fixed ratio schedule, they motivate very differently. A player facing a variable ratio schedule always has a chance at a large reward on the next action, so activity stays high and consistent. You're always hoping the next orc will drop the big payoff.

Variable ratio schedules are everywhere in games. Any game with significant randomized elements has them to some degree, and all gambling games are based on them. Some role-playing games make them the main focus of play, with each monster and quest offering a different menu of randomized rewards at different probabilities.

And they appear in life, too. Perhaps you've dated someone like this: On some days, they are warm and welcoming. On others, they are cold and distant. They don't return every call, and randomly forget to show up when agreed. In short, they are playing hard to get. People who do this get results for the same reason that slot machines do. It's just another variable ratio reinforcement schedule.

OTHER REINFORCEMENT SCHEDULES

A *fixed interval* reinforcement schedule makes a reward available a certain amount of time after it is acquired. In a Skinner box, the rat might only get a food pellet if it pushes the lever at least 15 seconds after the last time it received a pellet. In classic deathmatch games, a health pack might not reappear until exactly 60 seconds after it is taken, at which point it can be grabbed again.

Players respond to fixed interval schedules with high motivation when the reward is available and low motivation otherwise. For example, they'll ignore the health pack until it has almost reappeared, then start checking more often until it appears, after which they grab it and ignore it for a while longer. Those gaps in motivation make fixed interval schedules poor motivators.

A *variable interval* reinforcement schedule makes the reward available a randomized amount of time after it is taken. This schedule creates continuous motivation, but at a lower intensity than the variable ratio schedule. In both cases the player could theoretically gain something with every attempt at collecting the reward. But in the variable interval schedule the chances are lower the more often the player checks, so he has less reason to quickly repeat the action.

The *differential reinforcement of low response rate* schedule is like the fixed interval schedule, except that if the player tries to collect the reward too early, the interval is restarted. This reinforces low, steady rates of activity.

With the *differential reinforcement of high response rate* schedule, the player must do a certain amount of activity within the interval to get the reward. For example, you must defeat five enemies within one minute to get the reward.

And there are countless others reinforcement schedules, each with its own characteristic pattern of motivation.

SUPERIMPOSED REINFORCEMENT SCHEDULES

Most reward schedules create dips in motivation at certain times. These points are a problem because they create a window where the player may decide to stop playing. To eliminate these motivation gaps, a game can run several reinforcement schedules at the same time.

The power of reinforcement schedules isn't in any one schedule—it is in superimposing them so that there is always at least one that is producing high motivation.

For example, a fixed ratio schedule creates a dip in motivation just after the player gets a reward. If the player can get 10 gold pieces on every 10th defeated orc, his motivation will collapse right after the 10th orc because he knows he has nothing to look forward to for the next nine orcs. This is where the player puts the game back on the shelf—a "shelf moment" in design lingo.

We can avoid such shelf moments by superimposing several fixed ratio schedules. Consider what happens when the player can get a dollar for every 10th chest, a diamond for every 10th rock mined, and an arrow for every 10th goblin killed. By the time the player opens the 10th chest, he's on the ninth rock mined, so he wants to finish that to get the next diamond. By the time he gets the diamond, he's on the ninth goblin killed. By the time he kills the 10th goblin to get the arrow, he's on the 17th chest opened, and so on. Whenever one schedule reaches a motivation gap, the others are at their motivation peak. The player shifts focus back and forth between activities, never missing a dopamine-driven beat.

So-called grinding RPGs are famous for this technique. The player is never more than a few minutes from the next major loot drop, character level, or crafting opportunity. Each time he acquires one reward, he discovers another that is just a few minutes away. The end result is that the player can't put the game down.

The same mechanism gives turn-based strategy games like *Civilization V* their addictive quality. "One more turn syndrome" appears in these games because there are so many superimposed reward schedules that the player is never more than one or two turns away from getting some reward. Next turn, that technology will finally be finished researching. One turn after that, it's a new military unit. Then, it's a new structure, then the expansion of a border, and so on. There might be 30 or more such reinforcement schedules running at once; at least one of them is always keeping motivation high.

The key to superimposing reward schedules is that the player must not be allowed to concentrate his efforts on just one reward schedule. If the player can effectively ignore all but one schedule, he can finish the schedules one by one and get into a situation where every schedule is at the maximum distance from the next reward. That's a massive shelf moment. RPGs avoid this by constructing their world so that the player is constantly presented with opportunities to kill goblins, open chests, and mine rocks even when doing something else. And in a strategy game, players cannot reasonably focus on just one research or production task to the exclusion of all others. This keeps the schedules desynchronized, and motivation constant.

EMERGENT REINFORCEMENT SCHEDULES

So far we've looked at explicitly designed reinforcement schedules. Designers build these schedules like Skinner built his boxes, deciding with mathematical precision exactly what the player will get after each action. But this kind of explicitly defined reinforcement schedule is the exception, not the rule.

Most reinforcement schedules are not designed directly. Rather, they emerge from lower-level game systems.

For example, in chess, a player will tend to capture a piece every *X* minutes. This isn't because a designer set the variable *X*. Rather, the interval *X* emerges naturally from the interaction of the lower-level mechanics of the game. In chess, the pacing of captures is very spiky—players construct interlocking defensive positions over many minutes, and then destroy them in a flurry of captures. Since that exchange could happen on any turn, chess emergently presents a variable ratio reward schedule. And if the rules changed, so would this schedule.

Players respond to emergent reward schedules the same way they respond to explicitly defined ones. Often, they're the difference between a game that grabs you and one that lets you drift away.

For example, many shooters have a multiplayer deathmatch mode. The goal of a deathmatch is to kill as many other players as possible. At the end of the match, the players are shown their kill count. This kill count is a reward, because it feels good to get a high kill count and bad to get a low one. In the language of rewards, each match is like a defeated orc, except that it spits out kills instead of money. But whereas the orc's gold drops are determined by an algorithm, the kill count emerges from the game's combat design. Different map layouts, weapon tunings, and matchmaking systems produce different patterns of kill counts.

In some deathmatch games, kill counts are very consistent. A good player always gets many kills, while a poor player always gets few kills. This produces an emergent reinforcement schedule that resembles a fixed ratio. Like all fixed ratio schedules, it creates a motivation gap right after getting the reward (i.e., right after finishing a match). After a match ends, players aren't compelled to start a new one because they know exactly what they'll get, and they know they have to finish a whole match to get it. Deathmatch modes like this don't tend to be very popular because they are monotonous. There are no great victories or crushing losses. Just match after match, each offering the same predictable reward.

Other deathmatch games are much more random. A player might come last in one match and first in the next. Skill affects the outcome, but one lucky tactical break or a few good shots can turn defeat into glorious victory or vice versa. This resembles a variable ratio reinforcement schedule, and it produces similar motivational results. Players know that any match could be the one where they get a lucky 30-kill streak, so they're always motivated to play.

Once you look, you see emergent reinforcement schedules everywhere. Many players put down the controller at the start of a level in a single-player game, just after they've finished the previous one (a fixed ratio motivation gap). Good puzzle games let players run several puzzles at once, because they might solve any at any moment (superimposed variable ratios). And players will attempt the same level of *Super Meat Boy* 300 times in a row because every try might lead to a win (a variable ratio).

Extrinsic and Intrinsic Motivation

Reinforcement schedules look so easy. It seems like all we have to do is set up a couple of superimposed reinforcement schedules, pass out gold stars, points, or some other cheap reward, and *voilà!* Instant motivation to do whatever the designer wishes.

There is some truth to this. It's why martial arts schools hand out colored belts, Boy Scouts and Girl Guides give badges, and armies give medals. These kinds of reward systems work—but they also come with a hidden cost.

Extrinsic rewards can displace and even destroy the intrinsic fulfillment of play.

Extrinsic rewards are those that are outside of the activity itself. For example, gold given for defeating an orc is an extrinsic motivator because the gold is separate from the action of fighting the orc. In contrast, *intrinsic* rewards are inseparable from the activity. If defeating an orc feels good by itself, players will be intrinsically motivated to defeat orcs even without any reward attached.

At first blush, it seems like these two kinds of motivation should just add up. If you enjoy defeating orcs, throwing in some gold only seems to sweeten the deal. But this isn't what happens. Studies have shown that extrinsic motivation can distort, displace, and even destroy intrinsic motivation. Making an orc drop gold reduces players' natural desire to fight him.

In one study, psychology researcher Edward Deci split participants into two groups. On the first day, both groups engaged in an intrinsically rewarding task, like a puzzle or a game. On the second day, one group was given a reward for the task, like money or free food, while the other group was allowed to continue playing unrewarded. On the third day, Deci removed the rewards. The group that had never been paid kept happily working away at the task. But the group that had been paid lost interest now that their reward was gone. It seemed that once they had been rewarded for the task, this group decided that the task must not be worth doing on its own. The extrinsic payment had displaced their intrinsic interest.

Many other studies have explored variations on this theme. Children create less interesting art when offered a reward to do so. Chess players solve fewer chess problems in free time when they have been paid to do so on other occasions. Student poets write less interesting poems when reminded that writers can make money.

When I was 11 years old, my parents got me a piano teacher. For five years I dutifully practiced my daily half hour and learned the pieces I was told to learn. Then, when I was 16, the teacher stopped coming. But, against my own expectations, I didn't stop practicing. I practiced much, much more. Some days I would play for three hours at a time. And the nature of my playing changed. Instead of just plodding toward whatever performance goal had been set for me, I explored the instrument freely. I played songs that were too hard or too easy, or from strange genres. I composed and improvised. I played because I wanted to, and that internal fire was much more powerful than any external push my parents or teacher could ever have given me.

The motivation-distorting effect of rewards varies depending on how interesting the task is. Extrinsic motivators work well when applied to boring tasks, because there is no intrinsic motivation to displace. Paying you to dig holes doesn't make you dislike digging, because you never liked it in the first place. It's only when the task is interesting that the effect occurs. The more interesting the task is, the greater the effect.

The damage is worst on tasks that are exploratory or creative. When rewards are offered, people stop playfully exploring a system. They switch into doing the minimum to get the goodie. That's fatal for a game based on freedom or creativity.

Many psychological mechanisms have been proposed to explain the extrinsic demotivation effect. Perhaps people use a mental heuristic that says a rewarded activity must be work, and so not worth doing on its own. Perhaps people push back against what they perceive as others attempting to control them. Or maybe rewards force us to mentally categorize a relationship as a trading negotiation instead of a free and voluntary one.

Whatever the mechanism, these findings are important for game designers. They mean that we shouldn't just toss rewards willy-nilly into every game experience, hoping for a free motivation boost. Used haphazardly, extrinsic rewards degrade, distort, and destroy the core experience of play. The player may be motivated, but the motivation is a shell of action without a core of feeling.

REWARDS ALIGNMENT

We saw how games need dopamine motivation to keep players going through hitches in an experience. But now we've also seen that extrinsic motivation destroys the intrinsic experience of play. It seems like a catch-22: you must motivate, but if you do, play becomes hollow. How do we reconcile these two?

The key to creating rewards that don't destroy the experience of play is *rewards alignment.*

REWARDS ALIGNMENT is how closely the activities encouraged by a reward system resemble those the player would have engaged in without it.

The principle of reward alignment basically says that you should only reward things that the player already wants to do. The more closely we can align the reward structure to the player's intrinsic desires, the less destructive it will be to the core experience. In the best cases, the reward system exactly matches the player's intrinsic desires, and the two kinds of motivation really do add up.

Some games are naturally amenable to reward systems because it's easy to detect when the player has achieved their goals. For example, a racing game should reward players for getting faster times, because that's the whole point of racing. Games can do this because it's easy to detect racing times accurately, and there are few other motivations in a racing game that a timer might destroy.

In other games, reward alignment is difficult or impossible. In *SimCity*, how do we reward players making a city that looks like their hometown? In a cooperative game, how do we reward players for making a new friend? What points, badges, or prizes do we give players for inventing a unique water trap in *Dwarf Fortress*? The problem with these player motivations is that the game can't detect when they have been achieved. And if we can't detect it, we can't reward it. That's why it's impossible to align a reward system with creative, exploratory, social game systems like this. In these kinds of games, the only solution is to not use reward systems, because any such system would likely destroy more motivation than it created.

But most games fall in between these two extremes. They have a place for rewards, but it's hard to design a reward system that exactly mirrors the player's intrinsic desires. In these cases, rewards design becomes a matter of craft.

The goal of rewards design is to construct a system that can detect and appropriately reward everything the player already wants to do. Since every game is different, every game needs a unique, crafted reward system.

For example, the skateboarding game *Skate 3* uses a points system to reward players for doing tricks. This isn't as simple as assigning each trick a score. *Skate 3* lets players string tricks into extremely complex sequences of jumps, flips, and grinds. This elegant design permits an uncountable variety of different combinations. The challenge is in generating scores for these moves that match how impressive they look to a human.

Skate 3's designers met this challenge head-on. They crafted a scoring system that notices every turn, flip, grind, and jump, and counts every millisecond of air time and every centimeter of grind distance. Using a series of multipliers to account for the length of a trick line, it accurately judges the impressiveness of any trick sequence.

Since it's so well balanced and fine-grained, the actions it rewards are nearly exactly the same as the actions a player would want to do if the reward system were absent. And it works beautifully. *Skate 3* is a joy to play, and high trick scores are desirable and enjoyable to pursue.

If the game's rewards alignment was worse—say, if the system rewarded players only for jumping through special floating hoops—the reward system would antagonize the creative play. Players would ignore every game system except the ones that helped them get through the hoops. The elegant trick system might remain, but the life would be sucked out of it by a poorly aligned extrinsic reward system.

But wait a moment—tricking isn't the only thing players might naturally want to do in *Skate 3*. What if they want to race? What if they want to see how badly they can injure their skater, or perfect a single, specific trick sequence? A player just exploring the game might naturally decide he wanted to do any of these things, but the scoring system alone can't detect them.

To handle these nonstandard goals, *Skate 3* includes a number of special modes that set up unusual win conditions. Some are races. In others, you're tasked with copying another skater's exact trick sequence. And in Hall of Meat challenges, you attempt to break as many of your bones as possible in one horrific accident. These modes achieve rewards alignment around these nonstandard goals.

Player's Remorse

There are games that don't even try to achieve rewards alignment. Their entire design is based around generating powerful, continuous motivation, no matter the cost to the core experience. While this can keep players playing, it can also lead to *player's remorse*.

PLAYER'S REMORSE appears after a player spends time on a game that motivates him but does not fulfill him.

When I first started making games, I never thought that I would have to face ethical questions in my work. But then, I didn't know the power of reinforcement.

The prehistoric human brain has no evolved defense against carefully tuned reinforcement schedules. Our dopamine triggers evolved to handle hunting and foraging, not slot machines. So dopamine-driving games can push people to do things that seem irrational and self-destructive.

For centuries, gambling games have ensnared people by exploiting our prehistoric dopamine triggers. Now nongambling games can, too. While we don't take money from players the same way a casino does, we do take time. And there's a real argument to be made that if we take someone's time, we should be giving something back.

Player's remorse can go beyond a few wasted hours. People have lost jobs and their spouses because they just couldn't stop playing. Is it ethically acceptable to create a game that encourages this? If it isn't, where do we draw the line? Should we just put all the responsibility of self-regulation on the player, or does some lie with the designer as well? And what if some of the players are children?

There's a spectrum of severity here. I think there's little argument to make against a well-aligned reward structure attached to a meaningful core experience. That's just good game design. The player wants to play, and he enjoys playing.

In the middle, we find games that alternate between compulsive and fulfilling play. People lose friends because they're spending hours on a game, but they also make friends through the same game. They suffer hours of boring grind, then win an exciting boss battle. Such mixed experiences are often caused by straightforward design craft mistakes. Had the game's rewards only been better-aligned, the core experience might have shone through better.

At the far end of the spectrum, we find games that don't even seriously attempt to fulfill players. These games focus every design decision around maximizing motivation. Such games are not engines of experience; they're compulsion machines. The player plays and pays, and at the end, feels nothing by remorse for wasted time and money.

Games like this are best exemplified by their parodies. For example, Ian Bogost's *Cow Clicker* is a Facebook game that displays a cow. You can click the cow, but only every six hours, unless you pay in-game "mooney" to be allowed to click sooner, or spam your friends to join you with their own cows. The game is nothing but a naked fixed interval reinforcement schedule. Bogost created it that way to highlight what he saw as abusive use of these design patterns in real games.

But people still played *Cow Clicker*—thousands of them. Bogost eventually became so disgusted with his game that he made all the cows disappear, leaving only an empty patch of ground. Even that didn't stop people. They just kept clicking the ground instead. Dopamine is a hell of a brain chemical.

B.F. Skinner believed that all organisms, including people, are no more than "repertoires of behaviors" driven purely by external forces. And he took this idea to its logical conclusion—that there is no useful concept of a self at all. In his memoirs, he wrote:

> I am sometimes asked, "Do you think of yourself as you think of the organisms you study?" The answer is yes. So far as I know, my behavior at any given moment has been nothing more than the product of my genetic endowment, my personal history, and the current setting....If I am right about human behavior, I have written the autobiography of a nonperson.

Skinner's later followers were less extreme on this point than the man himself. But his legacy lives on in some of the theories in modern game design. This view of design sees it as a task not of creating emotions or fulfillment, but of triggering behaviors. It ignores the phenomenological experience of play entirely, and treats game design as the construction of virtual Skinner boxes that extract the maximum intensity of a desired behavior from the player. And usually that behavior is giving the publisher money.

This is a book of craft, not ethics. And these questions are bigger than this quick overview. I haven't discussed the player's responsibility, compared games to other media, or looked into the mixed positive and negative outcomes of nearly all games. So I won't attempt to provide some final answer to this dilemma.

But I can offer one designer's perspective. I think that any designer who cares enough to master the craft wants to do more than build Skinner boxes. In the long run, this may be the only sustainable path. Reward-driven grinding games spread fast among naïve players because they're easy to pick up. But over time, these players learn to avoid player's remorse. And after their lust for pointless loot has been exhausted, and they have learned all our tricks, players will still want what they've always wanted from games: new ideas, new friends, and new experiences.

9

Interface

Commander Snargode picked up the strange human piece of plastic and focused all four of his eyestalks on it. "I suppose this is how they talk to the machine," he pulsed.

"Yes," replied Engineer Xyzvaz. "We've observed them manipulating that with their five-way skeletal tentacles."

"We can adapt that for our use," pulsed Snargode. "Make a version for our body shape."

"Correct," replied Xyzvaz. "The trouble isn't with that device. It's what appears on the visual rectangle when we run the algorithm. None of us can understand what's going on. Look."

Xyzvaz manipulated a control and the wall sprang to life. On it, a number of humans moved around a poorly rendered Earthly environment. They wore various kinds of dress—cloth, metal, nothing. Some sat still, others ran excitedly. A few appeared to be nonhumans, but still moved and interacted in humanlike ways. Various human technology was scattered across the image. "We've tried," pulsed Xyzvaz. "But none of us can tell what any of this means."

"Xyzvaz," pulsed Snargode, "stealing this game was supposed to help us understand the humans, not confuse us.

"Unfortunately, it seems we need to understand the humans before we can understand the game."

If a tree falls in the forest and no one is around to hear it, does it make a sound? In game design, the answer is no. Events only have emotional value if players perceive and understand them.

That which is never communicated might as well never have occurred at all.

Our tools for this are screens, speakers, and a few other output devices. But usually there is far more happening in a game than can possibly be communicated at once through such narrow channels. To transmit to players an understanding of what's happening in the game, we have to design systems that carefully structure and sequence information as it's presented.

This communication runs both ways. Players must also be able to signal their intent to the game. To get this done, we work through buttons, sticks, gamepads, touchscreens, and motion sensors. But none of these is a perfect solution. Joysticks and buttons don't naturally lend themselves to controlling a human in a 3D environment, architecting castles, or commanding armies. To make input work effortlessly, we have to design an intricate combination of restrictions, conventions, and assistance systems to help players along.

If we succeed at these challenges, the interface vanishes. The player no longer notices buttons, screens, or joysticks, and so is free to concern himself with the game itself. But if we fail, the game is buried behind its interface. No matter how internally fascinating it is, it is useless to players because it communicates nothing meaningful. And a game is no more than what it communicates.

Thankfully, game designers aren't the first to tackle such challenges. Software UI designers and filmmakers have each developed a variety of methods for communicating complex information, and we've happily appropriated them. That's why games use UI elements like mouse interfaces, hotkeys, and tool tips. And we've stolen so many film techniques that it's easy to forget that they're not ours. Slow motion, vignettes, zoom-in, establishing text, and voiceover are all filmmakers' methods.

But while these borrowed methods are useful, they can't completely solve our problems because our needs are different from theirs. UI designers are concerned with clarity and interactivity. Filmmakers are concerned with fiction, pacing, emotion, and meaning. Game designers must find solutions that satisfy all these requirements at once.

Metaphor

One of the most important reasons we wrap mechanics in fiction is to communicate faster. This is called *metaphor.*

METAPHOR is giving something new the appearance of something familiar in order to make it easier to understand.

A classic example of metaphor is computer folders. Computer hard drives are organized into a hierarchy of data structures inside other data structures. These structures could have been called anything—turtles, cars, data lumps. But we call them folders because the word instantly teaches us most of what we need to know about them. A computer folder obviously isn't a piece of creased cardboard that fits into a filing cabinet. But it has enough of a conceptual similarity to a real folder to make the comparison useful, because it organizes information in a similar way.

In a sense, the entire fiction layer of a game is a giant metaphor. We set up intricate sets of game mechanics that would be maddeningly difficult to learn from scratch. Imagine learning a complex video game if it were represented only by abstract shapes. But then we wrap them in the appearance of a growing city or an ancient war, and every relationship and system becomes clear. The fiction layer serves many emotional purposes in games, but its simplest and most basic reason for existence is to help players understand the system through metaphor.

METAPHOR SOURCES

Metaphor works by leveraging our vast reserves of preexisting common knowledge. This knowledge can come from many sources.

Metaphors can imitate real objects.

UI designers use folders and physical-looking tabs and buttons. We can use cars, people, airplanes, books, backpacks—any object that is recognizable to players.

Metaphors can imitate cultural archetypes and conventions.

There is no natural law that says that men who wear pointy goatees must be evil. But we all know that goatee-stroking masterminds are evil because the goatee is an archetypical symbol of evil in our culture.

Culture is full of symbolic associations like this. In Western societies, men with square jaws are strong and brave. Corporate overlords are rich, megalomaniacal, and evil. Black means death, blue means cold, and pink means female. All of these archetypes and conventions can be imitated through metaphor.

Metaphors can imitate game clichés and conventions.

Every experienced game player knows that food instantly heals gunshot wounds, golden armor is stronger than steel armor, and it's safe to approach lava as long as you don't touch it. These conventions don't make sense, but they have been established and reinforced by generations of games. Such nonsensical conventions are useful for communicating systems that have no clear real-life or cultural counterpart.

We can also borrow conventions from UI or film. For example, everyone knows that a small X button in the top corner of a window will close it, because most operating systems work this way. And when the game's screen slowly fades to black, we know that the scene is over, and we're about to start something new.

The trouble with these clichés is that they're indecipherable to anyone without the right cultural priming. Game clichés are especially dangerous this way. For example, I once watched a player get stuck in one room in the original *Legend of Zelda*. He ran round and round, looking for an exit. It was so painful that I eventually stepped in to tell him that he could use bombs to blow open cracked walls. If I hadn't been there, he might have just given up and walked away because of that one unclear metaphor. Because nothing about a crack in a wall necessarily means a bomb will open it—it's an arbitrary convention.

Metaphors can imitate logical systems.

Metaphor need not limit itself to physical objects or cultural symbols. We can also imitate abstract systems and relationships, if people understand them.

For example, systems like Newtonian physics, electricity, and fire are common in games. But this isn't because these systems are somehow superior to anything else we could design. We could easily make a game where gravity repels instead of attracts, or physics works through five twisted dimensions. And we might unlock interesting new kinds of play by doing that. But such games would be extremely hard to understand. Real physics is a very complex system, but everyone already knows it. Imitating it is an elegant way of creating a powerful systemic foundation for a game with almost no learning burden.

Metaphors can also imitate higher-level concepts in the modern world. We can reference systems in economics, politics, biology, or psychology, as long as players understand them. There are games with systems that imitate supply and demand (*Privateer*), the division of electoral politics into various issues (*The Political Machine*), and the way people form and break relationships (*The Sims*). In no case is the metaphor a perfect simulation of the real system. But as with folders, it's close enough that the meaning gets across.

But the most common form of system metaphor is the most abstract: the use of mathematical systems like numbers, time, and space. For example, in chess, there are 64 squares with 2,016 relationships among them. These 2,016 relationships could have been expressed in any number of ways. We might have written a long list of every relationship: a1 is left of b1; a1 is two squares left of c1, and so on. Or we might have represented each square with a Ping-Pong ball, and used 2,016 colored strings to mark the relationships. Or we could have chosen any other representation. In each case, the fundamental system of chess is intact—but the game is incomprehensible. It's only when we put the 64 squares on a 2D plane that the game becomes playable. By imitating real space itself, chess leverages the human brain's natural ability to think about complex spatial relationships. Systemic metaphor like this is nearly universal because of its incredible elegance.

METAPHOR VOCABULARY

Cars in video games usually move forward on wheels. Sometimes they need fuel. It is quite rare, however, for them to need oil changes, have registration numbers, or get parking tickets. Similarly, game people often don't go to the toilet, game dogs never get fleas, and game food rarely spoils.

Only a small subset of the functionality of the real object is actually implemented in game mechanics.

The implicit contract between player and designer says that the designer will use metaphor to help the player learn, and the player won't complain when the mechanic doesn't express every property of whatever it imitates. But this creates a problem for the player. Now he has to figure out which aspects of the game are real game mechanics, and which are just fictional dressing. It's up to designers to make this as easy as possible.

Consider my story about the bomb opening the crack in the wall in *The Legend of Zelda*. In the fiction, a bomb opening a cracked wall makes a sort of sense. A bomb might very well be able to make a doorway-sized hole in a weakened wall. The problem is that upon first seeing the cracked wall, the player has no way of knowing that this particular aspect of a real wall is expressed in game mechanics. The game is full of things that suggest uses but don't actually work. Loose bricks might be pulled out and used as weapons—but this isn't simulated. A dead monster's blood might be drunk—but this isn't simulated either. The player can't go around assuming that everything in the fiction is also in the mechanics, because he'll be wrong almost all the time. Players need some signal that this crack in the wall is actually a mechanic, not just another piece of fictional dressing.

One way to do this is to call out the interactive elements using explicit indicators. But this quickly becomes tiring. Constant screen overlays pointing out every available action obscure the fiction. A better long-term solution is to teach players how to interpret fictional cues.

A game must establish a METAPHOR VOCABULARY that indicates which elements are simulated mechanically. It must then remain consistent with this vocabulary.

Every game must set up its own metaphor vocabulary. For example, in the acrobatic game *Prince of Persia: The Forgotten Sands*, it might have been hard to tell exactly which parts of the environment can be climbed upon and which cannot. The developers solved the problem by creating a vocabulary of environmental cues that signify which actions can be performed where. Long streak marks along a wall indicate that the character can do a wall-run. A peculiar kind of protruding brick can be climbed upon. These elements are established early on in very simple puzzles. The unique-looking climbable bricks, for example, first appear in a place where there is obviously no other way to progress. The player is guaranteed to attempt to climb the bricks because he has no other option. And once the player knows what the climbable bricks look like, he can recognize them for the rest of the game because they never change. He travels through palaces, sewers, and temples. But no matter where he goes, those climbable bricks always look exactly the same.

Signal and Noise

Every piece of information the player gets is part of a signal. The signal is divided into different channels: visual information from a screen, audio information from speakers, perhaps haptic or other feedback. Players use their natural human ability to filter, prioritize, and interpret information to try to understand what the signal means. But if this process fails, parts of the signal degrade into *noise*.

NOISE is signal that fails to transmit meaningful information.

Noise isn't just meaningless signals like static in a phone line. It covers any signal that does not add meaningful information to a player's mental model of the game. It doesn't matter whether the signal is confused by layers of aesthetic beauty, requires too much skill to interpret, or is simply packed too closely together with other signals. The result is the same: the player doesn't understand game events, and thus can't think about or respond to them.

There are two main causes of noise: complex art and overcrowded signals.

NOISE AND ART COMPLEXITY

As you can probably tell by now, much of my design experience is in first-person shooters. Here's a story that I've had play out many times during the level design process.

I start designing a new level. At first, I work in graybox. *Graybox* is exactly what it sounds like: the space is constructed from flat gray boxes. A tree might be represented by a pole with a large ball on top, like a giant Styrofoam candy apple. A car is a wide, low box with a smaller box on top. Working this way lets me work very quickly. At my best, I can find a problem, fix it, and retest the game in less than 10 minutes. And graybox can express a lot—combat encounters, narrative placeholders, and level geometry can all be nearly complete without adding art. By the end of the graybox process, I have a functioning, balanced level that playtesters enjoy.

But the level has to look like something eventually. So I work with an artist to replace the giant gray candy apples with trees, and repaint the boxes in the streets to look like Volkswagens and Fords. And that's when everything goes to hell.

Puzzles that were intuitive suddenly become impenetrable. Players miss routes that they used to have no trouble finding. They can't see enemies who they used to spot easily. Just replacing gray surfaces with art has made the game become unplayable, even though the mechanics design has not changed at all. I've seen this happen over and over, on multiple games across several platforms. The problem is that art introduces visual noise.

Complex art creates noise.

In a world of gray shapes, every enemy, goal, tool, and path is easy to see. Since each shape on-screen has some mechanical meaning, the player doesn't have to do any mental work to know what's important. But when we add art, the world fills with lines and colors that have nothing to do with game mechanics. Now the brain must work to pick out which shapes actually mean something. Sometimes that work is too much to handle, and the signal degrades into noise.

This effect isn't limited to environmental visuals. All complex art creates noise. Complex sound effects are harder to interpret than simple ones. A more detailed character may be more beautiful, but all the extra shapes obscure the mechanical information he must convey: where he's facing, how he's moving, and what he's holding. Nuanced animations are harder to read than simple ones.

This is an endemic problem because it crosses boundaries between development disciplines. Left alone, an artist will rightly seek to create the most beautiful piece he can. He will pack in details that make the art look great in a high-resolution render, just like the portfolio pieces that got him his job. But as soon as that hyper-detailed character is put into a game screen alongside a hundred others, it will degrade into a blur of pixels. All those beautiful details become noise when rendered in a fast-moving game situation.

It takes close cooperation among designers and artists to craft a look for the game that is both artistically compelling and mechanically clear. Sometimes this just means balancing the amount of detail in the art, or using special cues to call out mechanics-relevant parts of the image. Other times, developers go further and create unique art styles that can be beautiful while naturally minimizing noise. For example, Valve's *Team Fortress 2* and *Portal*, and DICE's *Mirror's Edge* all use fictions that are specifically designed to create simple, comprehensible images. *Team Fortress 2*'s characters are rendered in a cartoon style, with simple textures inside exaggerated silhouettes. *Portal* is set in a scientific testing facility built exclusively from white-walled chambers (just like a graybox level). And *Mirror's Edge* is set in a city constructed chiefly of naked white concrete (again, like a graybox level). These art styles solve multiple problems at once, across several disciplines, and give each of these games their own unique look.

VISUAL HIERARCHY

In every development process, there comes a time when a playtester fails to notice some signal that the designer wanted him to notice. He doesn't notice words on the screen. He doesn't see a character. He misses a piece of dialogue.

There is an obvious solution here: make the signal louder. Add more visual indicators, louder sound effects, and more energetic animations. But, as Mark Twain said, "For every problem there is always a solution that is simple, obvious, and wrong." Often, adding visibility is the obvious and wrong solution to this problem.

The problem is that players rarely miss signals because they're not visible enough. They miss things because their perception is being overwhelmed by other signals. It's not that the signal they missed was too quiet—it's that the overall loudness of all the signals is too great, and the player is overwhelmed. Adding volume to one part of the signal just overloads the player even more.

Players can only absorb a certain number of signals at a time. Further signals added past this limit can't be processed by the player and effectively become noise.

We should try to balance the overall density signals to match the player's ability to absorb them. But this isn't a complete solution for all players, because players at different skill levels can absorb very different amounts of information. Think of how quickly you can read these words compared to a child sounding out the letters one by one. You can absorb the signal on this page many times faster than that child. In the same way, expert players can drink in a game many times quicker than an utter novice. So a signal density appropriate for newcomers will leave the expert with boring flow gaps, and a signal density appropriate for experts will overwhelm the newcomer. It seems like a catch-22.

Thankfully, there is a technique used by graphic designers that we can borrow to solve this quandary. It's called a *visual hierarchy*.

In a VISUAL HIERARCHY, everything is displayed at once, but more important pieces of information are made more visible so that people notice them first.

When presented with an overloaded signal, people unconsciously ignore the least visible parts. This isn't a skill—it's a universal capacity of the human perceptive unconscious. Things that are bigger, closer, brighter, and faster get noticed first. It's why advertisers use bright colors and credit card companies use fine print.

This is useful for designers because it means we can control the order in which players perceive information. All we have to do is assign each piece of data a different visibility—make it brighter or duller, louder or softer. The absolute visibility of each piece doesn't matter; all that matters is their relative visibilities. If each piece of information's visibility corresponds to its importance, players all across the skill range will each perceive only the information that is useful for them while automatically ignoring the rest.

For example, a novice player might not know a game, but if there is a big man hitting his character, he will automatically ignore the mini-map, health bars, inventory, music, and background characters because those elements are less visible. This is good, since he can't use any of that information anyway due to his low skill. His skill only allows him to interact with the simple big man signal; ignoring the rest is a good thing.

As his skill increases, his perception capacity goes up. He starts seeing the second-most visible element, then the third, and so on. He starts to notice his low health bar and run away from the big man when appropriate. Or he sees an ally approaching on the mini-map and stays in the fight. By arranging the relative visibilities of these elements, the designers have decided what he will perceive and when. And if they did a good job, the player will always see the next most important element as he climbs the skill curve.

Every game can have a visual hierarchy. Just look over the interface and ask: is there any part that should be learned before another part, but is less visible? If so, swap their visibility around until it aligns with the proper learning order.

Let's look at the visual hierarchy of a typical shooter.

Enemies in front of the player are very important, so they are represented by large, visible, identifiable characters in the middle of the screen.

More distant enemies are less important, and also smaller on-screen. Note that this natural relationship between distance, relevance, and visibility is one of the properties of 3D space that makes it an elegant basis for a video game.

Health is an interesting case. One of the innovations of modern shooters is that they change the visibility of health as its value changes. At critical health, they throw a red overlay over the whole screen and play pain sound effects, making the signal very visible. When the character is healthy, these effects go away and the signal quiets. It's a smart way of pushing health information into the player's consciousness only when it is necessary.

Ammo count is displayed in a corner. It can be ignored, but still found at a glance. Like health, it matters more when it is low, so some games make it more visible when the weapon is almost empty by playing a special sound or tossing text into the lower-middle part of the screen.

Each of these pieces of information has had its visibility tuned to match its importance. The end result is a visual hierarchy that makes the game comprehensible across all skill levels.

To achieve this, designers must decide the relative importance of different elements, and tune their visibilities to match. There are a thousand ways to change the visibility of a piece of feedback. For example, let's look at some ways to tune the visibility of the ammo count.

A very quiet ammo count would display it in small print in a corner of the screen. The player must deliberately look for this information to receive it. Without training, he may not even notice it.

More visible versions show a graphical UI element of individual bullets, closer to the middle of the screen. Now the player can see the ammo count out of the corner of his eye.

If we want even more visibility, we can wrap an ammo display around the crosshair in the middle of the screen. Now the player will see his ammo count without even trying to peek out of the corner of his eye. That's as far as any real game likely needs to go.

But if we wanted to increase visibility even more, we could. The ammo counter can expand to fill half the screen. The bullet icons can flash. An automated voice can state your ammo count out loud every time you fire a shot (it has been done).

We can also go quieter. The ammo count could disappear if the player does not fire or reload for 10 seconds. It could be hidden on a menu. It could be hidden deep in a series of submenus, or on the developer's website, or in a configuration file. No game displays ammo count this way, but some display other types of very low-visibility data like this.

The strength of visual hierarchies is that they automatically and instantly deliver the information needed by players across the skill range. The learning player can begin processing the next piece of data the moment his skill level allows him to do so. By never overwhelming players, a visual hierarchy avoids driving them off as they learn. By never denying them information or coddling them, it never slows down their learning.

Redundancy

Every designer has had this painful experience: we create a new graphic, sequence, or sound to communicate some critical piece of information. We get some new tech to drive it, and the art comes out great. We demo it to important people and everyone agrees that it is awesome.

Then we playtest it, and most of our players miss it completely. They are looking the wrong way, their mind is occupied on an unrelated challenge, they're answering their cellphone, or they're busy drunkenly shouting at a friend because this game is being played at a party.

In a film, everything that matters is on the screen. If you skip a minute of the film, you wouldn't blame the filmmaker when you come back and don't understand the plot. A reader who flips past 10 pages of a novel doesn't blame the author for the rest of the book being confusing. In games, though, players can be looking anywhere, doing anything, inside the game and out. They can look away from important events, or get distracted. And they'll blame us if they miss something.

The obvious solution is to force people to notice critical content. But forcing the camera to look a certain way, interrupting play with dialog boxes, and other forced-observation mechanics shatter flow and immersion. We've solved one problem by causing many others.

A better solution is to simply accept that players will miss important signals. Then, instead of forcing them to absorb the one signal we have, we send that signal several times. Redundancy means that even if the player misses half of the content in the game (a fairly reasonable ratio), he still gets enough to understand the critical parts.

The simplest form of redundancy is *homogenous redundancy*.

HOMOGENOUS REDUNDANCY is repeating the same message multiple times in the same way.

Sometimes we can do this sneakily so that players don't notice. For example, we place the same audio log in five different places, but once the player listens to one of them, we have the others silently disappear.

In other cases, we don't have a way of knowing whether the player actually got the message. For example, the player will hear a message played over loudspeakers, but there's no guarantee that he listened to it. In these cases, we might just have to repeat it. But simple repetition can be grating, so it's often better to use *diverse redundancy*.

DIVERSE REDUNDANCY is communicating the same information multiple times in different ways.

In a shooter, we might have the companion character yell at you to jump out the window (dialogue), have the character visually wave toward the window (animation), place a visually highlighted path of wooden planks leading to the window (level visuals), and place an on-screen objective marker instructing the player to jump out the window (HUD). Quadruple redundancy means that the message will probably get through, even in a high-pressure situation.

Other times, it is appropriate to only show secondary and tertiary messages when the primary message has failed. This is called *passive redundancy*.

PASSIVE REDUNDANCY is the use of secondary messages only when the primary message fails.

In the window-jumping example, if the companion character had a second or third line of dialogue that they use only if the player doesn't jump through the window fast enough, they would be using passive redundancy. The danger with this is that it is often hard to tell if the player missed the first message, or if he is deliberately ignoring it. If the player is deliberately ignoring the first message, passive redundant messages can be irritating.

Indirect Control

Sometimes we want to encourage players to take certain actions, but we don't want to tell them exactly what to do. In these cases we use methods of *indirect control.*

INDIRECT CONTROL methods can guide player behavior without the player realizing that they're being guided.

This isn't anything as exotic (or stupid) as subliminal messaging or neurolinguistic programming. Indirect control is about using straightforward methods of arranging information so that players' behavior naturally flows in the intended direction. UI and industrial designers have been doing this for decades.

There are three basic methods of indirect control: *nudging, priming,* and *social imitation.*

NUDGING

NUDGING is changing player behavior by changing how choices are presented, without changing the choices themselves.

Players tend to follow the path of least resistance in any situation. They'll choose the default option and take the most obvious route. This means that we can nudge them whichever way we want just by rearranging options and changing defaults. For example, a dialogue system could be set up so that the default selection is always the one that leads to the most interesting outcome.

We can also nudge through visual design. A lit doorway draws players in better than a dark one. A line on a floor suggests a path for the player. A blinking button demands to be pushed. In each case, players will usually make the choice that leads to the intended experience, without being forced to do so.

Nudging is useful because it is cheap. It usually costs little to implement, and it doesn't restrict options or change incentives. It simply arranges options to make the intended answers more natural than the wrong ones. There is almost no reason not to nudge at every opportunity.

PRIMING

PRIMING is activating concepts in the player's mind to influence their future behavior.

A person always has something on his mind. When you see an ad for a war movie, your mind fills with war. When you see a photo of a kitten, war is replaced with fuzziness. You remain primed with these concepts for several minutes, during which your behavior changes. Being primed with war makes you more combative and aggressive. Being primed with kittens makes you more caring and nurturing.

In one experiment, participants completed written language tests. The researchers didn't actually care about the results of the tests—only how the words in the test would affect people's behavior. One group was given tests with words related to rudeness. The other got tests with words related to politeness. Afterward, participants were told to leave the room and go down the hall to talk to the administrator. But when they got there, they found him in a conversation with someone else. What the researchers wanted to know was whether the participants would interrupt this conversation.

Sixty-three percent of subjects exposed to rudeness-related words interrupted the conversation, while only 17% of politeness-primed subjects did. Apparently, just reading words about rudeness is enough to make you act rudely, at least for a few minutes.

In another experiment, subjects were primed with words like *wrinkle*, *bingo*, and *Florida*. Afterward, researchers watched how quickly they walked down the hall on their way out of the building. The subject who had been primed with words about oldness walked slower than those primed with neutral words, because being primed with oldness also activated the related concept of slowness.

Priming happens all the time, even in accidental, self-contradictory ways. When someone instructs you not to think of pink elephants, you are primed with pink elephants. Participants instructed to avoid constructing sexist statements in a word-completion task actually produced more sexist statements than those who were given no special instructions. Just having the idea of sexism or pink elephants on the mind—in order to avoid them—makes these images and responses more available.

In games, designers can prime players to indirectly influence their future behavior.

Priming starts before play even begins. The title of the game, the picture on the cover, and others' opinions about the game are the first priming factors. And during play, players are constantly being primed with different ideas. They see a doctor, and they're primed for healing. They see people conversing, and they're primed for interaction. They see a skeleton, and they're primed for death. Every impression affects the choices players make for a few minutes afterward.

Imagine a situation in a shooter where the player is going to meet with an informant. If the game is nothing but combat up to that point, many players will shoot the informant on sight because they're primed for violence. To prevent this, the designers could give direct instructions not to shoot, or simply disallow shooting, but both of these solutions are clunky and inelegant. It's better to just prime the player with nonviolence. This can be achieved in many ways. We could have the player character lower his gun (while keeping it usable). We could let the player observe other characters in conversation. We could have a companion say, "Let me do the talking." Any combination of these will prime the player for social interaction instead of violence.

Priming is powerful, but it's not magical. It doesn't fabricate motivation from nothing. All it does is shift preferences between already-available options. As the experimenters wrote about their oldness priming study, "It is doubtful, for example, that the participants in Experiment 2 left our building to go buy condos in Florida."

SOCIAL IMITATION

SOCIAL IMITATION is when the player naturally imitates the actions of others.

The vast majority of any human's knowledge is acquired secondhand. For example, you probably didn't invent your own method for tying shoes. You probably know that black widow spiders are poisonous, even though you've never been poisoned by one. And you know lots of things about gunfights and space travel even though you probably have little to no experience with these topics. This reliance on secondhand learning isn't some human flaw—it's a necessary adaptation. Someone who had to invent all his own knowledge would die as soon as he encountered his first poisonous fruit or freezing river. So we've developed a powerful instinct to learn by imitating.

This social imitation instinct is as strong in games as it is anywhere else, and it has a strong effect on player choices. Put simply, players will do what they see others doing. In multiplayer, they'll imitate one another's strategies. And in single-player, they imitate nonplayer characters. This is how social imitation becomes a tool for indirect control. All we have to do is make the NPC do something that the player should also do, and players will tend to follow.

For example, in a racing game, if we make computer-controlled cars slow down before curves, players will learn to do the same thing. Or an economic simulation may display competitors' commodities holdings. If the player's holdings are drastically different from his competitors', he will realize that either he is making a mistake, or he (or his opponent) is intentionally pursuing an exotic strategy.

Social imitation is a major reason why so many games have companion characters. Companions serve many narrative purposes, but they're also invaluable tools for indirect control. We can make them run to the next objective, interact with puzzles, hide from danger, or use specific abilities, and the player will imitate them without even realizing it. These characters exist to guide the player from A to B as much as they exist to convey feelings or play out stories.

Input

We've discussed games' output. Now let's look at input.

The goal of input design is to achieve synchronization between a player's intent and in-game action.

A game with good input captivates players the moment they touch it. It's a pleasure just to interact with it. And that benefit is omnipresent. It lasts throughout the life of the game—for tens, even hundreds of hours.

Bad input makes even the simplest interaction into a chore. Nothing works as expected, and controls are mushy, like you're playing with your hands submerged in molasses. It wraps the entire experience in a thin caul of frustration. It's a shame when this happens, because bad input can obscure great games. Just as a great film becomes unwatchable if viewed on a fuzzy old television, a fantastic game can be destroyed by laggy, unintuitive controls.

CONTROL ARRANGEMENT

There are a huge variety of physical interfaces: buttons, joysticks, motion sensors, touch pads, and more. In each case, we have to decide which control does what. We have to determine that the A button jumps while B crouches, or a waving left arm casts a fireball while a pointing left arm casts a flame stream.

There are two key principles that should guide us in arranging controls to correspond to in-game actions: *mapping* and *control exclusivity*.

MAPPING is the relationship between physical interface elements and the actions they control.

The goal of mapping is to create a similarity between a physical control and its in-game effect. Done well, this similarity serves as a built-in mnemonic that helps players remember how to use the control. The classic example of mapping is a stovetop that looks like this:

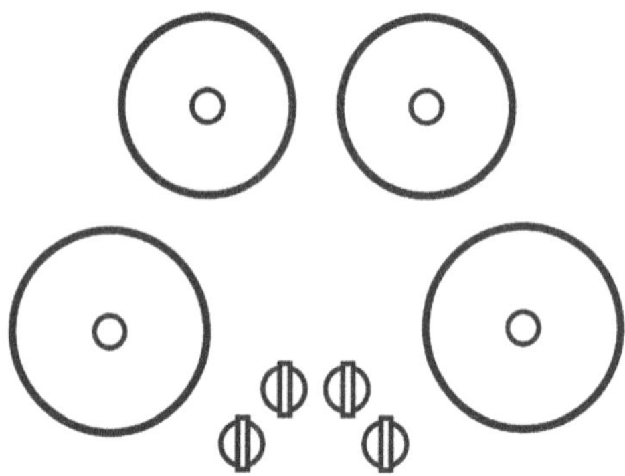

This stove doesn't need labels. The spatial mapping between the knobs and the elements means people intuitively know how they correspond with each other.

Games do the same thing. For example, in *BioShock*, the player character can fire spell-like plasmid effects from his left hand and weapons from his right hand. These are controlled with the left and right trigger, respectively. This creates a mapping between the player's physical hands and the character's hands on-screen.

Mapping isn't limited to physical position. We can map through shape, color, motion, or a hundred other kinds of signal. For example, in *BioShock* the on-screen health indicator is red, as is the button used for healing. This creates a mapping from the health indicator to the red button. Note that this is also a kind of metaphor, since there is a cultural convention that associates red with health.

Mapping reduces learning burden. It saves players from having to remember an abstract relationship between button symbols and in-game actions. This is especially important for less experienced players, so games geared toward new players sometimes go to extremes to explore new mappings. The Wii's motion controller, the Kinect body-sensing system, and *Rock Band*'s huge guitar-shaped controller are all examples of expensive physical interfaces that appeal to casual players by creating new kinds of extremely close mapping.

CONTROL EXCLUSIVITY is the physical relationships between different controls and how they can be used in combination.

Depending on the physical relationships between controls and players' bodies, some pairs of controls cannot be used at the same time. On a gamepad, there might be two buttons that are both only reachable with the left index finger. On a motion controller, the player can move their arms independently, but can't move one arm to signal two different functions at the same time.

A game must map exclusive controls to actions that are exclusive in the game. For example, the Xbox 360 controller places both a bumper and a trigger by each index finger so that it's impossible to press both at once. In *BioShock*, the bumper is used to select a weapon, while the trigger is used to fire it. This makes sense because in the fiction and mechanics, it's impossible to change weapons and fire at the same time. The physical controls are exclusive, and they're mapped to game actions that are exclusive, so there is no conflict. Even better, the exclusivity of the physical controls emphasizes and naturally teaches the exclusivity of the in-game mechanics.

When exclusive controls are mapped to nonexclusive actions, frustration and awkwardness result. Think of any game that puts a tool select on the Xbox 360 D-Pad and movement on the left stick. Both of these are controlled by the left thumb, which means that players have to stop moving to change tools. A better design will either find another control to handle tool changes, or add a restriction into the game that mirrors the restriction implied by the physical controls.

CONTROL FEEL

CONTROL FEEL is the moment-by-moment experience of projecting intent through an interface.

Way back in 1985 Shigeru Miyamoto created the progenitor of all platform games, *Super Mario Bros.* Mario is a short, mustachioed Italian plumber who saves princesses, slides through pipes, and eats mushrooms. And he jumps—a lot. He jumps constantly, over and over, thousands of times throughout the game. In fact, in his original 1981 arcade incarnation, Mario was actually named Jumpman.

On the surface, there's not much to Mario's jump. You push the A button, Mario pops into the air, and gravity pulls him back down. It seems like simple physics—but it's not.

The length of the button press matters. A quick tap makes Mario do a short hop. Hold the button down, and Mario describes a tall, lazy arc through the air. This happens because Mario doesn't just gain an instantaneous boost at the start of the jump. Rather, he is propelled upward as long as the A button is held, within the limits of his maximum and minimum jump heights.

The second half of the jump is equally unrealistic. In real life, objects tossed into the air describe a parabola because they accelerate downward at a constant rate due to gravity. But Mario doesn't do this, because his gravity is not constant. During his ascent, Mario's gravity is minimal. After the apex of his jump, it triples, and he slams back to Earth. But despite his massive gravity, he can't reach dangerous speeds because he can only fall at a certain maximum speed. Once he reaches this terminal velocity, his gravity is effectively zero.

There's more. Mario's maximum jump height isn't constant—jumping from a run allows him to reach greater heights than jumping from a standstill. He can control his horizontal movement in midair, but not as much as when he sprints on the ground. And if the player wants to jump just as Mario lands, he can press the jump button a few frames early and Mario will automatically jump the moment he touches down.

All this for a jump controlled by one button, in a game released way back in 1985. At first, this level of complexity seems almost absurd. But it's the only way to create great control feel. Miyamoto designed and tuned each rule to enrich the experience in a specific way. Some, like the extra height players can get by sprinting, raise the game's skill ceiling. Others, like the game's remembering button presses that occur right before landing, eliminate tiny moments of frustration that appear when a button press causes no result. Individually, they make little difference. But together, multiplied over the thousands of jumps that players perform in a Mario game, they lifted the experience to a level beyond its competition at the time. Mario didn't become a world-spanning mega-franchise because of his moustache or his ability to slide through pipes. Mario made billions because just controlling him is a joy.

These methods of enhancing control feel aren't limited to platform games. Variations on them apply across genres—racers, fighting games, third-person action games, shooters, and countless others all do the same thing in a thousand different ways. Controls are given tiny dead zones or smoothed over a few frames to eliminate noisy input. Inputs are remembered for a moment if they arrive early, but thrown out if another key press is sensed before they're executed. Combined controls are interpreted in subtly different ways from single controls. Push a control to the max, and it switches into a special acceleration mode where the input goes past the usual range of values. The possibilities go on and on.

At first glance, these methods look like terrible game design. In this book, I've emphasized elegance and simplicity. In school, programmers are taught to write clean, simple code. There's an intuitive sense that this sort of massive, invisible complexity is bad.

But these methods are the exception to the principle of elegance. They cost us a great amount to design, but they cost the player nothing because he never senses they're there. In fact, he senses nothing at all. Because if we do our job right, the interface vanishes.

INPUT ASSISTANCE

Mario's controls are complex, but they're still dumb. They don't try to understand what the player is doing; they just apply some simple rules that enhance the experience. In some games, this isn't enough, and we have to assist players more intelligently.

INPUT ASSISTANCE is preprocessing done on the player's raw input.

The idea of input assistance is to intelligently guess the player's intent and quietly nudge his input to match it. Ideally, the player never even realizes that he is being assisted.

Let's take aim assist as an example. In console shooters, the player aims by manipulating a tiny joystick with his thumb. This method is so fiddly, inaccurate, and frustrating that for years, people thought that console shooters would always be inferior to mouse-controlled shooters on the PC. Then, in 2001, *Halo* showed us all how to use aim assist to make shooters work on the console. Since then, they've become one of the biggest genres of console games. Without aim assist, console shooters would never have become what they are today. But how, exactly, does aim assist work?

Aim assist helps players track targets. The trick is in helping players aim without them noticing that anything is happening. Just pulling the crosshairs toward the target feels too obvious. The only way to make nonobvious, effective aim assist is to create a number of interleaved subsystems that help players in different ways. One subsystem helps players track moving targets by replacing part of their stick input with input that perfectly matches the target's motion on-screen. This doesn't force the crosshairs onto the target—it only helps compensate for a target's motion. Another subsystem helps players stop moving their crosshair when it is over a target. It detects when the stick is released, looks for nearby targets, and quietly slides the crosshair onto one of them. This sounds like it would be jarring, but the player can't feel it because it only happens during the crosshair's deceleration. A third subsystem watches for players who are about to just barely sweep the crosshair past a target, and slightly shifts the direction of the crosshair motion so that it falls onto the target. Since we're only slightly adjusting the direction of the crosshair's motion and not its speed, the player can't feel the effect. The strength of each of these effects changes depending on the target's distance to the player, its angular distance from the crosshair, the presence of other targets, the difficulty level, the weapon being used, and various other factors. And these three are just a sample—many others subsystems are used in various games.

The key to this working without players noticing is that it only influences things that players are naturally unable to detect. People notice crosshairs moving of their own accord, but they don't notice them stopping a few pixels early, or accelerating slightly faster, or adjusting their direction, because these events are masked by the motion going on around them. That's why aim assist works only in these nooks and crannies in the input stream.

Sometimes designers even use aim assist as a balancing factor. For example, *Halo*'s sniper rifle is powerful and accurate. As intended, it's effective at long range. But its power and accuracy also make it deadly in close quarters, which overlaps the roles of other weapons. One of the ways *Halo*'s designers weakened the sniper rifle at short range was by giving it zero aim assist when unzoomed. On the surface, it's still a perfectly accurate gun. But there's a hidden challenge to using it in this unintended way because of the total lack of assistance. This affects its success rate in these situations, and makes players prefer to use it as intended—all without anyone ever noticing.

Aim assist is just one type of assistance among many. Jump assist helps players aim their characters toward safe landings. Attack assistance helps players cleanly land blows. Driving assistance helps players avoid spinning out. Movement assistance helps players grab ledges and avoid obstacles. In each case, designers have developed a suite of methods for assisting players without misjudging their intent or doing anything that they'll notice.

CONTROL LATENCY

When you push a button or move a joystick, the game needs a few milliseconds to process the input and create a visible response. This delay is called *control latency*.

CONTROL LATENCY is the time delay between when a game receives input and when it displays perceptible feedback resulting from that input.

Control latency is unavoidable because it is built into the hardware. Most modern computer systems use a multistage rendering pipeline. At any given time, the system has several frames in different stages of processing. The progression is like this:

- **Frame 0 (Input received)** Input—a button press, perhaps—is received at some point during this frame. It can't be used immediately, though, since the game has already started processing the frame. Instead, it is stored until the start of the next frame.
- **Frame 1 (Game logic)** The CPU reads the input that was stored during the last frame and updates the game world based on it.

- **Frame 2 (Graphics rendering)** The graphics renderer takes the state of the game world established by the previous frame's calculations, and uses it to render a visual image.
- **Frame 3 (Frame displayed)** The rendered image is displayed.

Every stage is running all the time. Graphed out, they look like this:

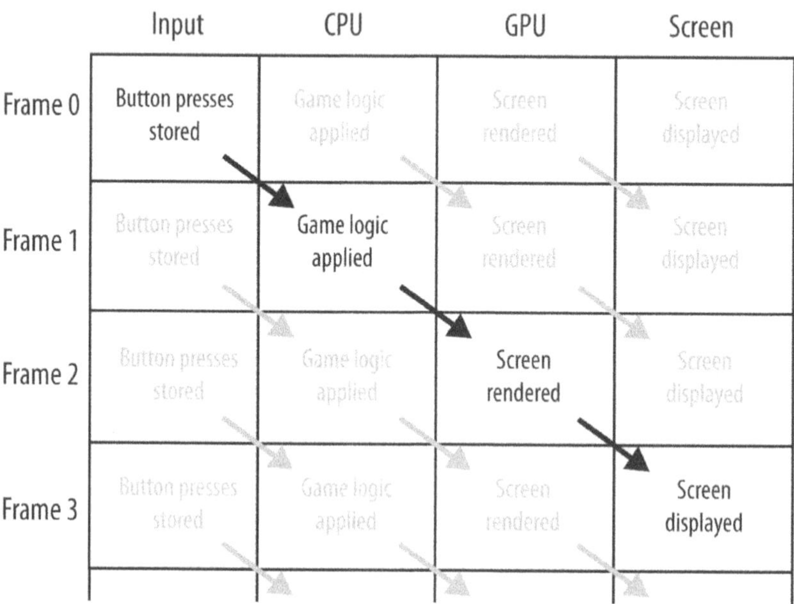

This arrangement has the advantage of very high throughput because it keeps both the CPU and GPU running at all times. Without this system, the graphics unit would have to sit idle through the first half of each frame as the CPU updated the game system.

Unfortunately, this system also introduces three to four frame lengths of lag between input and response, depending on when during the frame the input was received. (Most televisions add another frame or two to do their own signal processing before finally showing the image, but we have no control over those delays, so I'll ignore them here.)

Poorly written code can extend the delay even longer, to five, six, seven, or more frames. It is the responsibility of programmers to ensure that extra frames of latency are not creeping into the game. But once programmers have made sure they're not making mistakes and introducing extra lag, the hardware makes it impossible to get below three frames of latency.

The only choice left is to change the length of each frame by changing the overall frame rate of the game.

Which frame rate do we choose?

Some look to film or TV for guidance. Films run at 24 fps (frames per second), and television at 30 fps. These frame rates were chosen because they are the lower limits required to avoid a perceptive flicker or stutter between images. But we can't blindly apply these standards to games. The important delay in TV is between one frame and the next. The important delay in a game is between the input and the response, which, as we've seen, is three to four times longer.

Others look at human reaction times for guidance. But this doesn't work either. The question we're answering has nothing to do with the player's speed at responding to the game. It has to do with the game's speed at responding to the player, and whether that's fast enough to feel smooth and synchronized.

In fact, there's no one standard frame rate at which a game feels right. Rather, there's a smooth trade-off between graphics and responsiveness. Every millisecond of extra latency makes a game feel slightly more sluggish, while allowing more time to render complicated graphics.

Players learn to give inputs slightly early to compensate for control latency. The length of a game's control latency determines how far ahead of time players must anticipate.

For example, imagine a shooter player is moving his crosshairs toward a target at a constant rate. The player can see that the target is going to be under the crosshairs in 0.5 seconds. Imagine the game is running at 30 fps and the TV is adding 50 ms of its own lag. This means that the total input latency is 183 ms (four frames at 1/30 of a second each, plus 50 ms from the TV). If the player fires when he sees his crosshair over the target, he will miss because his input will not be fed back to the screen for nearly a fifth of a second. By that time, his crosshair will have passed the target (ignoring aim assist). So to hit the target, he'll have to learn to pull the trigger several frames early. Longer latencies mean players must anticipate farther into the future, which requires more skill and feels less synchronized.

The right frame rate depends on the needs of a design. Some old text adventure games would run at less than 1 fps, since they took time to type descriptions on the screen. Shooters like *Quake 3* can be run at 200 fps or more. Games running at 1 fps are viable if they are turn-based and controlled through key presses. The 200 fps rate is the upper level of frame rates pursued by competitive PC shooter players. These players run 10-year-old games on hardware 30 times more powerful than the best available at the game's release because they want every ounce of competitive advantage they can get.

The vast majority of games, though, run at either 30 fps or 60 fps. Few players can feel an improvement higher than 60 fps, and frame rates lower than 30 fps are so low as to be visually choppy. So usually, you'll face a choice between these two alternatives. At 30 fps, with the optimal four frames of latency, there is 100 to 133 ms of latency plus screen lag. At 60 fps, the delay drops to 50 to 67 ms plus screen lag.

In a world without limits on computing power, we'd always choose 60 fps. In real life, though, 60 fps has serious costs. John Carmack, legendary programmer of the *Doom* and *Quake* games, said that a 60 fps game has about one-third the processing power available per frame as a 30 fps game. That's a costly trade-off in graphics and processing complexity.

The choice between 30 fps and 60 fps depends on the expected skill of players, the type of control interface, and the game's specific emotional triggers. A game based on art or narrative is often best left at 30 fps because this allows for richer visuals. So is a skill-based game that doesn't depend on rapid input, like a turn-based strategy game. Where 60 fps becomes essential is when high-skill players interact with systems demanding rapid-response input. Shooters, racing games, and fighting games are the most common candidates for 60 fps.

Often, there's pressure from other development stakeholders to back down from the 60 fps standard, even when it's the right choice. This happens because the costs of 60 fps directly affect many individual stakeholders in the development process while the benefits are hard to see. Artists want to push limits of scale, detail, and beauty. Programmers want more CPU cycles to add more complexity to their AI and physics systems. Marketers and publishers want the most impressive screenshots and tech blurbs. These groups are often justifiably dubious about sacrificing two-thirds of their per-frame processing power for a seemingly invisible benefit. So there's a natural political bias against 60 fps. That's why designers always need to evangelize hard to get people on board with a 60 fps standard, even in games where it is necessary.

DESIGNING INPUT

Input is hard to design because it's hard to perceive. I've watched teams of designers reviewing a game, passing the controller around, and disagreeing about what the game is actually doing as it's doing it in front of them. It's possible, with practice, to tell good control feel from bad. But you can never know for sure exactly what's going on under the surface, because this is deliberately hidden.

And the better the input system, the harder it is to understand. Remember the old maxim: the more effortless it looks, the harder it was to achieve. Nowhere is this truer in games than in input design. To the player, Mario's jump controls and *Halo*'s aiming system are pure simplicity. But underneath their smooth exteriors lie intricate arrangements of contingencies, edge cases, and assistance systems.

Most players will never understand why a game feels the way it does. They'll credit graphics or balance for successes that were actually won in the input system. Even among game developers, it's easy to forget the importance of input. So input is often ignored. When money is short and deadlines are looming, it's hard to spend scarce resources on something nobody can see.

But input is almost always worth the investment. Because even though it's never seen and rarely noticed, the player feels it during every moment of play.

10

The Market

The Tekram was the strangest beast in the world. It was a shapeless mass the size of a house, covered by a mad patchwork of fur, scales, and chitin. Twisted limbs protruded randomly from its bulk. And if you came back the next day, it would look different.

The villagers soon learned its power: fed the right thing, it would offer forth a king's bounty of food, fine cloth, and gold. The trouble was that nobody could ever figure out what it wanted. Some days it loved bacon and would excrete diamonds for every strip tossed into the correct maw. The next day, it wanted vegetarian food only. Sometimes it liked things undercooked, overcooked, seasoned or bland, complex, simple, healthful and greasy. Sometimes it liked to eat things that weren't even food.

For centuries, merchants and wise men tried to understand the Tekram and predict its desires. They wanted to access its bounty without the trial and error of throwing random foods into its maw. All failed. After a thousand years, the villagers simply worshipped it, uncomprehending.

Design Purpose

Every game is created to serve a purpose. Some games are made to produce profit through sales, subscriptions, or in-game purchases, or by pulling quarters from people in an arcade. Other games are made for non-monetary purposes. Art games, hobby projects, academic experiments, and design tests are made for status, tenure, or self-amusement.

Every design decision is affected by the purpose the game was created to serve.

A survey of some common business models reveals how much purpose affects design.

Arcade games are designed to get players to put money into the machine. To attract players walking by, they use fast-moving, visually expressive mechanics. Long play times would reduce profits, so arcade games are designed to play out in just a few minutes. To reduce the skill barrier for passersby, controls and mechanics are extremely simple. To get players to come back and plunk in more quarters, arcade games have extremely elastic success conditions and a very high skill ceiling. Many arcade games are unwinnable; the player just chases higher and higher scores, paying all the while.

Massively multiplayer online (MMO) games typically make money by charging a monthly fee for access. Their purpose, then, is to keep players playing for as many months as possible. To this end, MMOs usually include massive amounts of content and very deep character upgrade systems. Social interaction and community-building systems get players committed to groups of peers who encourage them to stick around.

Traditional shrink-wrapped games make money by selling units, so good reviews and word of mouth are the main goals. In some sense, this business model encourages the purest game design, because the best way to generate good reviews is just to make a great experience.

Noncommercial games tend to have very different goals. Many art games are more about expressing an idea than creating an experience. They might be focused on a real-world issue, something relevant to an academic institution, or abstract concepts.

And sometimes a designer will make a game just for the hell of it. When I first started out making games as a hobby, we didn't know what we were doing, or even why we were doing it. We just did it because we wanted to.

There are countless other models, and new ones emerge regularly. In-game advertisements, shareware, advergames, edutainment, serious games, ad-supported, user-generated content, episodic content, microtransactions, premium play, and fan presell are just some pieces that can be rearranged into a thousand different business models.

Each model is a different design challenge. And in each one, there is tremendous room for craft. Making a commercially successful single-player narrative epic is hard, as is creating an original and moving art piece for a small academic audience. But in each case, the challenges, restrictions, and opportunities are different.

This is why a good game isn't necessarily a successful game. Success depends on more than applying design principles like elegance, depth, and balance. It also depends on understanding the game's purpose, where it fits into the market, and how its market positioning must affect its design.

The Tournament Market

To understand how to position a game in the market, we must first understand the structure of the market itself.

In economics, the term *rival good* refers to a product which, when it is consumed by one person, cannot be consumed by another. For example, food is a perfectly rival good because an apple eaten by one person cannot be eaten by another. Game designs, on the other hand, are *nonrival goods*, just like novels, actors' performances on film, and recorded music. Once these products are created, the cost of transferring them to additional consumers is nearly zero.

For example, plumbing is a rival good because a plumber can only work for one customer at a time. This means that a mediocre plumber has little to fear if one masterful plumber moves into town. The masterful plumber can only serve so many customers, so there will always be some left over for the mediocre plumber.

But producers of nonrival goods face no such limitations. A good game can be copied endlessly for almost no cost and distributed to any number of customers. This means that a middling narrative designer really does have to worry about one new narrative design prodigy creating one much better game, because the prodigy can steal every customer on the planet.

This nonrivalry means that the games market resembles a winner-take-all tournament. The one best game gets all the customers. The others—even if they're also very good—get none because everyone is still playing the best game.

For the tournament winner, this is fantastic. It makes it possible to have an entire market to yourself. Pull this off, and you can make an embarrassing amount of money. For example, *Call of Duty: Black Ops* took in more money than the annual GDP of Liberia (a country of 3.7 million people) because it owned the first-person shooter market.

But tournaments also have losers. In fact, they have mostly losers. It's easy to forget this because the losers are hidden. We hear about the rich winners in reviews and awards shows, while the losers die in the dark. It's only when we actively seek a more balanced view that the number of failures becomes apparent. Look at an unfiltered list of games released in any given period and you'll be struck by how numerous they are. And even this sample suffers from a survivorship bias, because it ignores games that were never released. The games tournament is harsh, and most games lose.

THE MATTHEW EFFECT

The game design tournament is made even more lopsided by the *Matthew effect,* so named by sociologist of science Robert K. Merton after the biblical verse Matthew 25:29: "For everyone who has will be given more, and he will have an abundance. Whoever does not have, even what he has will be taken from him." A game or franchise that is popular has an advantage in becoming more popular. The rich get richer.

In games, the Matthew effect appears for many reasons. First, games aren't just nonrival goods. They go even further than this. They are *antirival,* because they become better the more other people are playing them. More players mean a stronger community, more potential play partners, more user-made content and culture, and more word of mouth. Second, the developers of the successful game have advantages in money, credibility, and status, which helps them create their next game. They can pay to get the talent they want. They can get creative control from publishers. They have leverage over platform holders. Third, consumers have a strong bias in favor of the familiar, which means that the already-popular title beats the unknown in an otherwise even competition.

The Matthew effect implies a world where the haves and have-nots are permanently locked in place, like something from Orwell's *1984*. But in reality, dominant franchises are regularly overturned by upstarts. Because though it seems like the deck is stacked against them, newcomers have advantages that the big boys can't match.

THE INNOVATOR'S DILEMMA

Imagine a designer at an upstart studio. He has few shareholders, bosses, or hangers-on to tell him that a risky idea won't work. His name is not tied to any established design, and nobody expects anything from him. With nothing to lose, his ability to invent and innovate is completely unfettered. He has nothing propelling him except his own creative fire, but he also has nothing holding him back.

So he tries something wild. He takes a risk, puts his heart and soul into it. And it's a hit. He makes a huge amount of money, his studio grows, and he becomes famous. Now the dark side of success takes hold.

The forces against innovation begin to grow around and inside him. Shareholders start calling about their quarterly earnings. A growing staff builds up expectations, assumptions, and specialized skill sets. Habits form and become entrenched. Slowly, the risk-taking, ad hoc studio culture of the start-up is replaced by a ponderous paperwork machine. Worse, the successful designer stops questioning himself. Perhaps he starts thinking a little too highly of his own ideas. Perhaps he becomes afraid of change now that he has so much to lose. Perhaps he just gets too lazy to do the brow-sweating mental toil of innovation.

In the end, the successful designer and his studio lose their ability to invent. His nothing-to-lose creative fire and his willingness to try wild ideas are gone. He switches into defensive cash cow milking mode as he attempts to stretch out his initial success forever. And then he is surprised when some new kid comes along with a crazy idea and knocks him down the same way he knocked down the guy before him.

This situation is called the *innovator's dilemma.*

The INNOVATOR'S DILEMMA is a hard choice faced by incumbent leaders in a field: keep innovating by abandoning your flagship product, or don't and wait for someone else to innovate instead.

The innovator's dilemma counterbalances the Matthew effect. From the point of view of a small studio, the size and resources of an established competitor can seem overwhelming. But most of those large companies are hobbled by the innovator's dilemma. They're static targets, living off an old victory, waiting to be taken down.

Market Segments

The game design tournament is played in multiple divisions, and each division has different prizes. You can try to win a big division with a big prize, but it will take a huge investment and you will face tough competition. Alternatively, you can target a smaller division with a smaller prize. Smaller prizes mean less competition, but usually also less reward.

The divisions, of course, are market segments.

A MARKET SEGMENT is a group of players defined by their interests, preexisting skills, price range, culture, available technology, and geographical location.

There is a segment of the U.S. market that wants to play as soldiers and shoot at other soldiers in a high-skill competition. There is a segment of the Japanese market that wants to play with digital ponies and revel in their cuteness. There are segments that like racing, segments that are into steampunk, segments that have great platformer skills, and segments with deep knowledge of professional basketball.

The size of the market segments targeted by a game affects its potential payoff, because some market segments are bigger and more lucrative than others.

For example, consider *System Shock 2* and *Half-Life*. The games were released within one year of each other. Both were played from a first-person perspective, and involved playing as a lone man trapped in a huge, monster-infested installation. Both were considered masterpieces by those who played them, and received wide acclaim from reviewers. But despite the similarities, *Half-Life* outsold *System Shock 2* more than ten to one. The difference was in market targeting. *System Shock 2* is more complex and difficult, so it appealed to a small segment of hardcore, complexity-seeking players. *Half-Life* is simpler, easier, and more action-oriented, so it appealed to a much larger group. Each game won its tournament hands down—but *Half-Life* played in a much larger league, and so made more money.

The downside of targeting a larger market segment is that it will tend to have more competition because it is so lucrative.

Had Irrational Games made *System Shock 2* more similar to *Half-Life*, its sales may have actually decreased. The studio would have been targeting a bigger segment, but it would have also entered into direct competition with Valve, Epic Games, and id Software, all of which were in the action shooter market at the time. Players in this segment may have decided that they'd rather just play *Half-Life*, *Unreal*, or *Quake II*. So Irrational decided not to take the risk, and to stick with the smaller and less competitive nerdy survival horror RPG segment.

These two forces—the profitability of large market segments and the competition they attract—tend to balance out. Large, profitable market segments attract developers, which increases competition in those segments, which reduces their profitability. Over time, the game market tends to fall toward an equilibrium where no segment is more profitable than any other.

UNDERSERVED MARKET SEGMENTS

If everybody understood every market segment, then any segment that was more profitable than the others would attract developers until it wasn't the best bet anymore. The final result would be a market in perfect equilibrium, where every market segment yields the exact same profit margin, and there would be no way to get better than average results.

This is where the model breaks down. In real life, nobody perfectly understands the shape of the market. It's hard to know how many people there are in any given segment (quick, how many people like games about horses?). Market segments overlap in messy ways. Culture and technology shift constantly, so equilibrium is impossible. The result is that there are always underserved market segments offering abnormal profits to those who can find them. It's the finding them that's the trouble.

In 1993, Will Wright, designer of the 1989 hit *SimCity*, had an idea. He wanted to make a game in which players managed a family of simulated people as they built a home, got jobs, and raised children. While there had been a smattering of similar efforts over the years, like 1985's *Little Computer People*, there was no existing market for family management games.

Nobody wanted to make it. "It was a battle, the first few years, inside Maxis," Wright said in a later interview. People in the studio even called it "The Toilet Game," because the player directed the family as they cleaned their toilets. And the game's detractors had market research to back up their doubts. "We had a focus group back in 1993," Wright said, "and it tested very badly. No one liked it at all, and [it] was the worst idea out of the four we presented that night."

Who was right? Both sides had their arguments. On the one hand, the game might appeal to creative, less-combative players in the same way that Wright's hit *SimCity* did. On the other hand, who wants to clean toilets in a computer game? In an age of space marines and fantasy warriors, managing a family just seemed too prosaic. It wasn't long before the studio bosses shut down the development of The Toilet Game.

But Wright didn't give up. He kept the project alive, picking up help where he could. He found a programmer who wasn't needed and pulled him onto the project. "They were thinking of axing him," he said. "I trundled him into my Black Box—so to speak—and did a little skunkworks." Years passed. The family game—now known as *Doll House*—limped along in the background through the development of *SimCity 2000*, then *SimCopter*.

Then, finally, the winds changed and Wright got the green light to begin development with a full team. By the time *Doll House* came out, Wright had been working on it, on and off, for eight years. And it had a new name: *The Sims.*

But even then, nobody knew if the game had a market. How many people would want a family management game? The game was unlike anything that had ever come before. There was no established market segment for this kind of game, so all anyone could do was guess. Even Wright himself didn't claim to know. "I thought the game would either do a million units or. . .50," he said.

Wright was wrong. The game didn't sell 50 units, or a million units. *The Sims* spawned a franchise that has sold more than 100 million units. As of this writing, it is the top-selling PC franchise in history.

It turned out that the market segment for family management games is massive because it cuts across traditional categories. *The Sims* appeals to people who had never played a game before because it offers a creative, low-pressure experience. It also appeals to hardcore gamers looking to set wealth challenges for themselves or take a break from shooting aliens. The market segment was massive, and completely devoid of competition. So *The Sims* became massively profitable.

In hindsight, it seems obvious. Of course, a game like this would appeal to everyone from gamers to grandmas. Sure, people want a break from high-pressure competition. It's a stand-out product in a field of imitators.

But remember—none of this was obvious before the fact. Focus testers hated *Doll House.* The executives hated it. So did many of Wright's fellow developers. Even Wright himself thought it might be a dog. Luckily, it paid off. But it didn't have to.

The best market strategy is to find a segment that is underserved. But this strategy is difficult and risky because there is no good way of measuring untapped market segments.

There are huge profits awaiting anyone who is able to find underserved market segments others cannot. In the best case, a game can be alone in its own huge market segment and suck up all the profit for itself.

But finding those empty segments is difficult and risky. A designer working in an established genre knows whom he is selling to and what those customers have responded to in the past. The standards are defined for him; the basic design decisions are already made. Trying to create a new market segment is different. There are no established players. There are no references to draw from, or conventions to follow. Most importantly, it is impossible to know how many people will be interested in a radically original game.

The Sims is a wonderful example of design craft, but craft alone did not guarantee its massive success. For every *The Sims*, there have been many other equally well-crafted games that never found an audience. Because that kind of success takes more than craft. It also takes a willingness to make big bets, and it requires a lot of luck.

VALUE CURVES

The idea of market segments makes it sound like we can split the market into perfectly separate chunks, each with a little label on it. Obviously real life is not so clean. Market segments overlap in complex ways, and one game can appeal to many different market segments.

Let's look at a more precise way of thinking about how different games appeal to different people. It starts by breaking down everything a game offers into a set of *market values*.

A MARKET VALUE in game design is an aspect of a game experience that appeals to some group of people in a specific way.

For example, there are people who play *The Sims* just to build houses. They're not interested in controlling a simulated family. They just want to experiment with different room shapes, wallpapers, and furnishings. *The Sims* appeals to these people because it offers a market value that I'll call *creative home building*.

But *The Sims* also appeals to people who have no interest in building houses. Consider another player who wants to role-play a version of himself. He makes his character and proceeds to explore a dramatic alternate life full of drama, love, and tragedy in one of the premade houses that comes with the game. This player is responding to a different kind of value I'll call *life role-play*.

The Sims offers *creative home building*, *life role-play*, and many other kinds of market value in one package. It doesn't just appeal to one set of people with a single interest. It appeals to anyone who wants any of its market values. And almost all players are interested in multiple values at once. Nearly everyone who has played *The Sims* likely got at least some enjoyment from both *creative home building* and *life role-play*.

We know we want to target underserved market segments. But it's not accurate enough to just look for empty segments because every segment overlaps the others. To understand market segments more precisely, we can use *value curves*.

A VALUE CURVE is a graph that compares games by rating them on the different kinds of market value that they offer to players.

Value curves show us how to avoid competition and create uncontested market space. They do this by analyzing where two games offer the same values, and where they offer different values.

Let's look at an example. This is a value curve of the 1999 cyberpunk action-RPG *Deus Ex*:

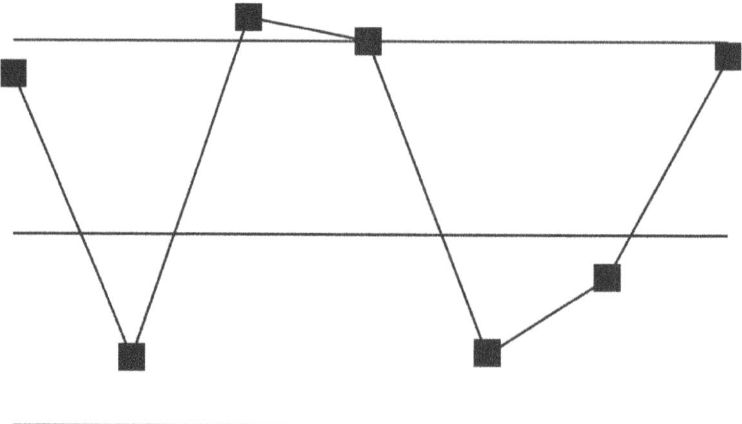

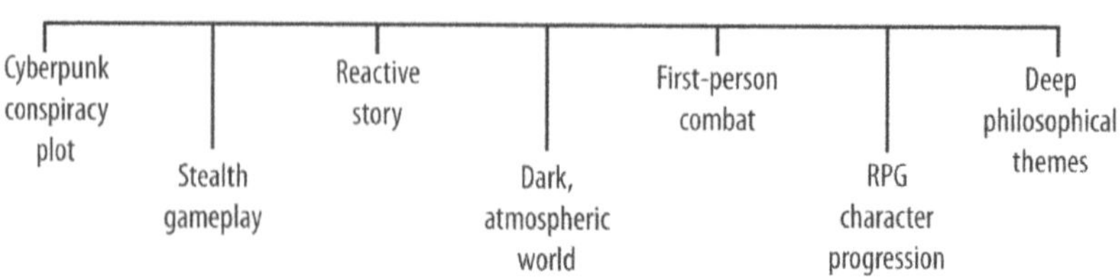

Deus Ex offers many different types of value. A player looking for a cyberpunk conspiracy plot, reactive story, dark, atmospheric world, or deep philosophical themes will be well served by this game. The game also offers stealth gameplay, first-person combat, and RPG character progression, but not to as high a level.

But a value curve of just one game isn't very useful. Value curves are tools for comparison. This means plotting several games on the same curve. Here's the graph with *BioShock* added:

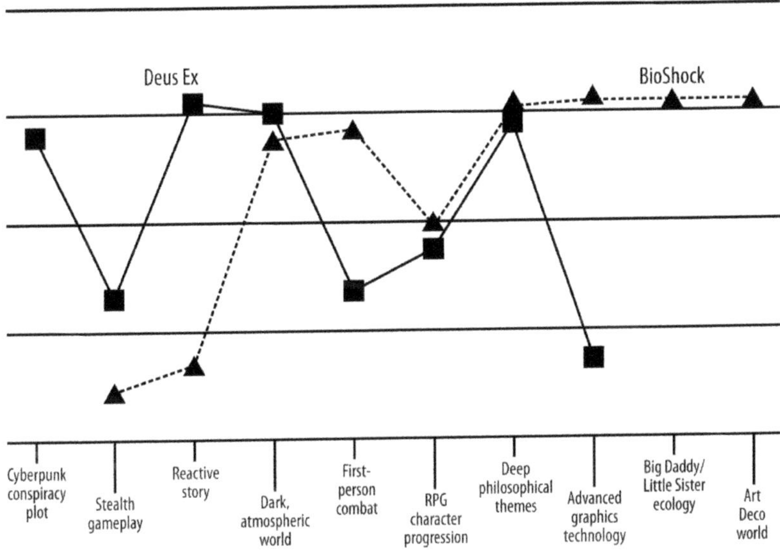

Now we can see exactly which values are unique to each game, which ones overlap, and which ones are best served by each product. Both games offer stealth gameplay, but a committed stealth fan will get more out of *Deus Ex*, since its stealth systems are deeper and better-balanced. However, *Deus Ex*'s first-person combat is weaker than that of *BioShock*, so a committed shooter player will prefer *BioShock*.

We also find some values that are completely absent in one game or the other. There is no *cyberpunk conspiracy plot* at all in *BioShock*. And the *Big Daddy/Little Sister ecology* and *art deco world* aren't part of *Deus Ex*.

To do a broader market analysis on a new game, we would conduct this exercise with every similar game on the market. The final graph might have five or six games on it, each dominating some values and missing others. Such an analysis provides clarity by showing us the values in our game that actually matter.

The important values in a game are the ones that are superior to every other offering on the market. Every other value can be fulfilled better by another product.

Values that a new game offers at a lower level than existing games aren't worth much. Players who want these values have better options elsewhere. Values that a new game offers better than all competitors are the ones that matter. People who want this value will play this game because they can't get that value better anywhere else.

But the greatest victory is in values that have no competition at all. For example, consider the unique market positioning of *BioShock*. Many games offer first-person combat, stealth gameplay, reactive story, and dark, atmospheric worlds. Competing on these values is difficult because the market is so crowded. So, instead of competing in the values that everyone else competes in, *BioShock* invented completely original values that nobody else was offering. Its art deco world and charming Big Daddy/Little Sister ecology are both fascinating and unlike anything else in the market. Players who wanted these things—and many did—had to go to *BioShock* because there was nobody else. So the game was a great success.

Value curve comparisons make it obvious which parts of a game are important and which aren't. It's the superior and unique values that really matter; the values that are better found elsewhere are not selling points. This helps designers by showing them where to focus their development efforts.

VALUE FOCUS

Every value costs resources. That's why *BioShock* didn't try to create a reactive story as deep as that of *Deus Ex*; doing so would have made the game too expensive to produce. In addition, each new value reduces the emotional purity of the experience. Too many values increase the risk of a game dissolving into a murky, overcomplicated mess. Finally, some values are simply incompatible. *BioShock* is set in an underwater city in 1960, so it couldn't possibly include a cyberpunk conspiracy plot and remain narratively coherent.

So achieving value superiority in the market isn't just about being better or working harder. It's about shifting resources and focus to where they can do the most good. Great games don't try to do everything; they do a few things very well.

The fewer resources that a designer has, the more he must focus his efforts into a smaller number of values. By competing on fewer values, he increases his chances at winning one of them. An indie game made by two people might only offer one or two values, but if it does these things better than anyone else, it can still attract players and be profitable.

For example, *Garry's Mod* is a simple first-person game that drops players into a physics sandbox with an unlimited set of wild and wacky tools. Players can make anything in *Garry's Mod*. They can spawn any object or character, stick them together with physics constraints like ropes and glue, and set up triggers so that they can activate rocket engines, balloons, or explosives. Players build wild contraptions, like flying buggies powered by dynamite, and strange make-believe worlds constructed of sheet metal and bombs. They pose characters in funny situations, take screenshots, and make comic strips to post on the Internet.

Here's our graph with *Deus Ex*, *BioShock*, and *Garry's Mod* together:

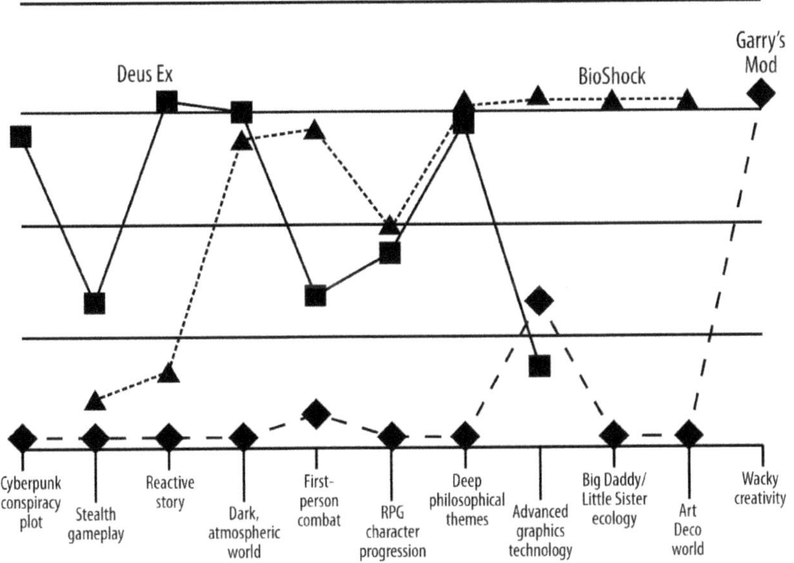

Garry's Mod is a first-person game, but it doesn't compete with *BioShock* or *Deus Ex* on any of their key values. Instead, it sidesteps them by offering something they don't: *wacky creativity*. None of what *Garry's Mod* offers is possible in *Deus Ex*, *BioShock*, or any other major game. Had it tried to compete directly against games with a hundred times its development budget, *Garry's Mod* would have certainly failed. Instead, it carved out its own small market space by pushing a single, unique value into the stratosphere. And after half a decade of owning its own market segment almost unchallenged, *Garry's Mod* had sold more than a million copies. Even at $5 to $10 apiece, that's not bad for a game made by one person.

Looking at a list of successful small games, we find that almost all of them focus relentlessly on one or two values that are underserved by bigger games. Their value curves look like tall, narrow spikes. Here's a list of some of them:

Game	Primary market value	Secondary market value
Super Meat Boy	Ultra-high-speed platforming	Charming characters and retro game references
Dwarf Fortress	Hyper-deep emergent narratives	Creative fortress construction
Counter-Strike	Hardcore tactical FPS combat	Counterterrorism fiction
Minecraft	Creative world building	Unfettered exploration
LIMBO	Brooding atmosphere	Platformer puzzle solving
Castle Crashers	Wild beat 'em up gameplay	Funny cartoon art style
Braid	Time-based puzzles	Poetic, allegorical narrative

When we look at failed games, we find the opposite: short, wide value curves resembling tree stumps, without a single value rising above the competition. These games are merely mediocre versions of a big-budget game. Such a game has no reason to exist, and players have no reason to play it, because they can get their fix better elsewhere.

Usually, stump-shaped value curves are the result of naïve overambition. A designer sees another game he likes, and decides he wants to do the same thing, but better. But without superior development resources, he is almost guaranteed to fail. He spreads himself too thin and ultimately produces no unique value at all.

I have made this mistake myself. During my hobby game design days, I created a modification called *Elemental Conflict*. My plan was to create an amped-up, futuristic version of the tremendously popular *Counter-Strike*. So I kept the same round and team structure, economy, and hardcore weapon balance as *Counter-Strike*. I tried to differentiate the game using unique futuristic combat tools like booster rocket packs and glue grenades. But I didn't remove anything. I made the classic mistake of trying to copy a successful game and placing shiny new baubles on top. The result was the most predictable market failure ever. After 14 months of work by a team of six and several released versions, we had exactly one public server, and nobody played on it. The core gameplay worked well enough, but it didn't have the years of iteration-driven polish of *Counter-Strike*. We had nothing nearly unique enough to overcome the Matthew effect.

Match your ambition to your resources. Leading a large development team, you could attempt one unique value, two superior values, and a smattering of inferior values to round out the experience. On a smaller team, you might have to focus on just one value to the exclusion of all else. Because it's better to be the best at one thing than it is to be mediocre at 10 things.

Nobody Knows Anything!

We use models like market segmentation and value curves to try to understand the market. But these models aren't reality—they're just our attempts to pack the dizzying complexity of life into something we can draw on a chart. They help us think about the market without being instantly overwhelmed, but they don't come close to capturing its true complexity. It's easy to feel too confident based on these analyses. In reality, they're paltry attempts at understanding something of magnificent and unfathomable complexity.

The market is everything. It is billions of people, all their relationships, habits, culture, and technology, and the physical world around them. It causes and is caused by natural disasters, Internet memes, fashions, political trends, business models, technologies, individual choices, and random chance.

Most of what goes on in the market is outside any model we can apply. A celebrity who plays a game and happens to like it, a news story that brings attention to a certain topic, or a politician looking for an issue can all dramatically change a game's market performance. These aren't simple, linear quantities that we can calculate. They're nonlinear causes that can be amplified by sociological snowball effects into world-changing events.

For example, take Blizzard's 1998 RTS (real-time strategy) hit *StarCraft*. *StarCraft* is a very good game, and it's been widely successful. But in South Korea, it's gone beyond simple success. In 10 years, *StarCraft* sold 5 million copies there. That is one copy sold for every 10 men, women, and children in the country—nearly half the game's worldwide total. And even that number underestimates the game's popularity in Korea, since many Asian players play in net cafés and don't own the game themselves. At the height of its popularity there, two television channels were dedicated to broadcasting professional *StarCraft* games, and top professional players became minor celebrities.

Nobody predicted it, and nobody could have. The game's narrative is about redneck-styled space-faring humans warring against the fleshy Zerg and the psionic Protoss alien races. This very American fiction doesn't seem like something that would do well in Korean culture. The developers didn't do anything to target the Korean market at all—the game didn't even have Korean language support until seven years after release.

StarCraft's Korean miracle came about because of several peculiar conditions that combined to form a popularity snowball. The first was the *PC bang* phenomenon. *Bang* means "room" in Korean; a PC bang is a high-tech gaming net café. The South Korean government pushed hard to modernize its Internet infrastructure in the mid-to-late 1990s, and progress was quick due to the country's small size and high density. At the same time, many of the old government social and pension programs were being phased out, leaving large numbers of older citizens without jobs and without quite enough income to retire on. Thousands of these 50-something retirees took the best opportunity they could find and opened PC bangs. This worked well for them, since PC bangs require relatively little effort or technical ability to run once they are set up, and they are reliable sources of income.

The PC bang business was much more appealing in Korea than in the West because of physical and cultural differences between the countries. Korea is densely populated and most people's homes are small, so young Koreans spend much more time outside the home than Westerners. Now, for less than a dollar an hour, these young people could have instant access to the games they wanted without paying for, maintaining, or finding space for a home PC setup.

This confluence of factors created the conditions for a popularity snowball to begin. More PC bangs opening meant more players at PC bangs, which made PC bang gaming more socially accepted. The fact that PC bang playing is public and social meant that the game could spread through physical, face-to-face contact and have a public presence in a way that isn't possible in the West, where everyone plays along in their own rooms. Eventually the culture crossed a tipping point where it became a typical social activity for young people to hang out for hours in PC bangs with their friends.

The PC bang snowball alone would have made the game popular, but it wouldn't have made it into a minor national sport. The final element that pushed *StarCraft* over the top was the gaming television channels that sprung up around the game. But these gaming channels didn't appear from nothing. The traditional Asian board game Go already had a huge following in Korea, and several channels were dedicated to it. The Go channels meant that it wasn't a huge leap to create a channel dedicated to video games. Had there been no Go channels, the *StarCraft* channels may never have appeared.

The snowball effect accelerated—the PC bang culture, new broadband infrastructure, a minor economic recession that made cheap entertainment attractive, and television channels all mutually reinforced one another into a sustained cultural phenomenon. None of these factors was predicted, and none could have been. All of them are outside typical market models. But they came together and made the game into a megahit.

And even this nicely packaged story is a vast and possibly misleading oversimplification. Even now, nobody is clear on the importance of these various factors in *StarCraft*'s meteoric rise in Korea. What if the country hadn't been in a recession? What if the government didn't roll out broadband in the mid-1990s? What if *StarCraft* had been a fantasy game, or a realistic game? We can only guess, even after the fact. The story tells nicely, but it's anyone's guess how well it really matches the billions of individual economic decisions that formed the Korean *StarCraft* miracle.

Had the game been released a year earlier or later, it might have been merely another popular game from Blizzard. People might have played it, loved it, and moved on. It would have made a profit and been called a great success, and nobody would have ever known how close it came to becoming more than just a game in a small Asian republic.

On these kinds of utterly unpredictable cultural phenomena, screenwriter William Goldman once shouted, "Nobody knows anything!" Goldman spent his life watching executives, writers, and directors try and fail to predict the box office performance of films. So it is with games. While we can use models to do better than nothing, we can't forget that the world is more complex than any market research study.

Confirmation Bias

Let's take a look at marketing. This is a book on craft, not sales, so I won't cover marketing in general here. There is, however, one aspect of marketing that all designers have to worry about because it deeply affects the play experience itself. That is how marketing sets expectations, and how those expectations affect the play experience.

Did you know that it's possible to make a good beer taste bad just by describing it differently? The psychologist Dan Ariely discovered this during an experiment conducted in a Boston bar. He offered pub goers two identical-looking beverages. The first was Samuel Adams beer, a well-liked but fairly typical Boston beer. The second was a secret "MIT Brew"—Sam Adams with a few drops of balsamic vinegar added. In side-by-side blind tests, MIT Brew was the clear winner. But if Ariely first told drinkers what MIT Brew was, they hated it. Vinegar in beer sounds like it would be horrible, so people expected it to be horrible, so they perceived it to be horrible, even though it was the superior beverage.

CONFIRMATION BIAS is the tendency for people to perceive things in such a way that confirms their preexisting beliefs.

Expectations are not separate from perception. Rather, we are biased to confirm our preexisting beliefs. This effect is everywhere, and countless studies have rediscovered it in various guises. Foods in expensive-looking containers are perceived to be tastier, and products with high price tags are perceived to be better. Pepsi wins the Pepsi Challenge against Coke, but only if the labels are hidden. Joshua Bell, one of the best violinists in the world, once busked in a New York subway and was almost completely ignored. Magical healing charlatans, dog whisperers, fortune tellers, and other flimflam artists all depend on expectation bias to work. The placebo effect is little more than expectation bias.

And confirmation bias is everywhere in games. It's in every review, every recommendation, and every game experience of every player. Players begin forming opinions the moment they start hearing about the game. By the time they begin play, their established opinions and expectations are already affecting their experience. When you've heard that a game is artistic, you'll look for meaningful details—and find them. When everyone says a game is scary, you will notice and remember every shiver that runs down your spine. When the reviews say a game is bad, you'll focus on every moment of frustration. Nobody plays your game by itself; people play it through the lens of what they already know about it. This means that a designer can't ignore marketing.

Confirmation bias can even reverse how we interpret an event in a game. For example, imagine a review says that a game is satisfyingly challenging. You buy the game. As you're playing, you suffer a frustrating and seemingly unfair loss. But you don't blame the game for your failure because you were already expecting it. You were primed to interpret that failure as an intentionally authored part of the experience, not as a mistake. Had the review described the game as stupidly unfair before you started playing, you would likely have interpreted your loss very differently.

SETTING EXPECTATIONS

For designers, confirmation bias means that setting expectations is critical. Expectations are set in many ways, only some of which are under our control.

The title of a game is often the first expectation setter players encounter. Consider these titles: *Doom*, *SimCity*, *Dark Souls*, *The Marriage*, *LIMBO*, *Fable*, *Condemned*, *Brain Challenge*, *Mortal Kombat*, and *Rollercoaster Tycoon*. Some sound evil and violent, others light and friendly. Some sound artistic, while others sound commercial. Every title sets off a different chain of mental associations and sets different expectations.

Next are the marketing messages. Advertisements, interviews, and articles all set expectations. Advertisements can focus on characters or action. They can be light, dark, fast, or slow. In an interview, if the developer describes how a game was inspired by his love of gardens and children, players develop different expectations than if he mentions being inspired by gore-porn horror flicks. If he says the game has a moment that will make you cry, players will watch for that moment as they play.

Finally, players develop expectations by word of mouth. This is the most powerful kind of expectation setting because it is amplified by social pressure. Humans are social animals; we naturally synchronize our opinions with those around us. When we're discussing a game with others, we don't simply state what we think. We watch for what others think—especially those of high status—and shift our own opinions to match. We're not lying when we do this. Our opinion actually changes—we adjust our memories to match the consensus. This effect occurs at a small scale among groups of friends, and at a large scale across the entire game playing community. Players take cues from reviewers, who take cues from one another. The first review of a game might bring up a talking point that's copied and recopied until it becomes part of the cultural narrative of the game—even if it was chosen arbitrarily in the first place.

We can't control word of mouth, but we can influence titling and marketing messages. So think about what expectations should be set to prepare players for the best possible game experience, and craft titles and marketing messages to match those. If you have dedicated marketing people, don't ignore them. Left alone, marketers have no way of knowing which parts of the game have to be carefully introduced a specific way, and which do not. Designers should regard marketing people as part of the core experience-crafting development team, not as extraneous add-ons—their decisions affect the experience of play the same as ours do.

PART THREE

Process

So far, we've looked at the craft of game design. We've examined mental models that help us understand how a design is working, and how to change it to make it better. But craft alone isn't enough to make a good game.

What should a game designer do, day to day, hour by hour? When should we brainstorm, program, debate, or take a break? What should we plan, how far ahead should we plan, and how should we record those plans? What do we communicate, and to whom, and how? And how do we adjust as the team grows from a single person to more than a hundred developers?

If we can't answer these questions well, all our craft will be worthless because it will be aimed at the wrong problems. We'll attack problems that don't exist, make delusional plans based on dreams, build technology we don't need, and suffer catastrophic communication breakdowns. In the end, our game will be smothered by bureaucracy, anger, and misunderstanding. We will become busy idiots, working hard in the wrong places.

It's surprisingly hard not to fall into busy idiocy. I've done it thousands of times. I've become obsessed with a programming challenge and spent days on it, even though the feature involved had almost no impact on the game experience. I've created art for something that was almost certain to be cut later. I've tested when I should have built, and built when I should have tested. And busy idiocy is also a group activity. I've asked for work without making my intent clear, leading someone else to waste their time on the wrong problem. I've called unnecessary meetings and missed essential ones. I've argued when I should have acquiesced, and acquiesced when I should have argued. I've overcommunicated, undercommunicated, and miscommunicated.

Busy idiocy is hard to avoid because it's not naturally self-correcting. When a developer fails at solving a problem, the result is obvious. Everyone can tell if code doesn't run to spec, or art is ugly, or a design is unclear. Failure of this kind produces immediate emotional feedback, so it's natural for us to improve our problem-solving skills when it happens. But busy idiocy isn't like this. In the short term, busy idiocy feels like raging genius. We feel good when we solve a problem, but our emotional unconscious doesn't signal us when the problem we solved was irrelevant. So we solve problem after problem, happily, busily, idiotically not realizing that the problems we chose were the wrong ones. The consequences of this kind of mistake only appear much later, far away from the original error, and often the connection is never noticed. This lack of feedback is why we can make the same busy idiot mistakes over and over for years or decades, and feel good about them the whole time.

Some imagine game development as a path that we follow toward our destination. I disagree with this image. I think it's more like a dark forest full of stinging monsters, waiting to inject you with anesthetic poison. Each time you bump into one, it stings you and the poison makes you feel warm and content. But under the surface, the stings are stealing your vigor, dissolving you from the inside. It's only later, as your strength runs low and the moon clouds over, that you might realize that the pleasant feeling you've enjoyed all this time wasn't progress. It was death.

This section is about finding your way through the darkness.

The Problem of Assumptions

I wish I could just lay out how things are done for you. I'd list the order of steps that every studio goes through to make a game. It would be straightforward to write, it would be well referenced, and everyone would agree on it.

But I can't do that because nobody has solved game development process yet. There is no one way things are done. Rather, there is a proliferation of methods.

Most of these methods fail regularly. Sometimes it seems like almost every game misses its deadlines and exceeds its budget. Work is trashed due to politics or misunderstanding, or retained out of fear. Money is thrown desperately at problems, only to cause more problems. The gaming industry is awash with stories of panic-driven "crunch time"—death marches of 10- or 12-hour days every day of the week lasting months or even years. People gain weight, miss watching their kids grow up, or burn out and leave the industry altogether. These repeated train wrecks erode personalities and extinguish creative energy.

And it can be a mystery why it all goes so wrong, because it seems like we do everything right. We hire smart developers. We motivate them with well-designed incentives. We get them the right resources, the right market data, the right technologies. We plan and schedule every part of the product in meticulous detail, months or years in advance. But it all falls apart, again and again. Why?

The problem is assumptions.

The failures of the game design process usually spring from deeply rooted assumptions that we don't know we're making.

Everyone pays lip service to the idea of questioning assumptions. It's much more difficult to actually do it. The real killer assumptions—the ones that will have you crunching for six months and miss your kid's first birthday—are the ones that are embedded so deeply as to be nearly untouchable. They're protected by layers of cultural momentum, habit, and vested interests. They interlock into self-reinforcing systems of thought. They let you use all your old skills and tools, and don't require you to learn anything new. If it was easy to question assumptions, everyone would do it.

Assumptions aren't necessarily wrong. Questioning assumptions doesn't mean overturning all of our beliefs—it just means identifying them and ensuring that they're based on truth instead of habit.

In games, our assumptions come from two key sources. First, every time we borrow a concept from another field, hidden assumptions come along for the ride. Second, the human mind comes biologically hardwired with assumptions. Let's look at each of these.

BORROWED ASSUMPTIONS

Why do we say a game is in *preproduction*? Why a *beta version*? Why is development led by a *director*? Why do games have *producers* instead of *logisticians* or *allocators*? Why do game teams have *junior designers* and not *research assistants, design apprentices,* or *privates*? Why *director* instead of *captain, chief editor, coach,* or *head chef*? Why don't we say that games have a *first draft*?

Each of these words signifies a process structure that was originally developed in another field. The question is whether those structures make sense in game development. Often, the answer is no.

The problem is that these structures were developed to solve problems that are different from ours. Often, there are assumptions embedded within them that hold true in their original field, but not in games.

Take the concepts of preproduction, production, and postproduction. These terms were borrowed from film. They developed in that medium because film production necessarily revolves around a short period of extremely expensive live-action shooting. It can cost thousands of dollars per minute to run a film set, so filmmakers have learned to arrange their entire process around squeezing that costly production period into a few weeks. For them, splitting their process into three parts makes sense because there is an unmistakable start and end to the production period. Everything about their process is about minimizing that middle piece, so they don't have to pay a hundred gaffers, grips, and caterers for an hour longer than necessary.

The same does not apply in games. In games, often, a studio will go from preproduction to production. . .and nothing will change. Nobody is hired or laid off, no significant resources move around, and the same old meetings keep running at the same times every week. Nothing changes because there is no massively expensive middle piece to game development. So when we say preproduction, production, and postproduction, what do we really mean? Filmmakers know what they mean. In their medium, it's unmistakable. In ours, these words means very little without further elaboration.

You might say that it's just a word. It helps people communicate—what's the problem? The problem is that these words carry assumptions hidden within them. For example, they assume that the product must be scripted or planned in some way before production starts. They assume that a script written before production can survive all the way to the end. They assume that we have to hire different people at different stages. We know that these facts are true in film. But are they true in game design? They may be—but they may not be. These embedded assumptions need to be pulled into the light and questioned. And if the word carries more wrong assumptions than right ones, maybe we should stop using it altogether.

Borrowed words and concepts proliferate because the processes commonly used in game development were never designed. They became norms by the accretion of habit over decades. The first games were authored by one person. Games today can be made by hundreds. During the transition from one to the other, games teams got bigger and bigger, and processes got more and more complex. Every time the team grew, whoever happened to be there just tweaked something to keep the system running. They looked for the easiest, most obvious fix that would be easily understood by the most people. In almost all cases, this meant borrowing a concept from film, software, or industry.

We can see evidence of this ad hoc process development in the huge diversity of processes used in different companies. Every game studio runs differently. There aren't standardized processes because nobody has codified really good ones yet. The methods in common use are folk knowledge. They are social norms that appeared more or less arbitrarily by accretion of many Band-Aid changes. And just like any social norms, they vary arbitrarily from place to place.

Thankfully, there are signs that the affliction of borrowed methods is lifting. The best studios are replacing borrowed methods with new processes natively developed to confront the unique challenges of game development. But it's a slow transition, and many borrowed assumptions remain.

INBORN ASSUMPTIONS

The human mind is optimized for solving the problems of a caveman. These optimizations work by making assumptions about the world, which help us to avoid tigers and deftly navigate tribal politics. And for a caveman, this works well.

Unfortunately, game designers face very different challenges from those of our tribal ancestors, while the assumptions in our brains have not changed. In the modern world, these assumptions show up in behavior as *cognitive biases*—places where humans make consistent, predictable errors in perception or judgment. For example:

The *halo effect* means we can't judge the different properties of a thing separately. If a man is good-looking, we find him more trustworthy. If a game character has good art, we think it controls more accurately. The human mind tends to classify things as entirely good or bad. This is deadly for game designers because our job requires that we deconstruct every game system into its aspects, understand how they fit together, and how they contribute to the final experience. Loving and hating every design element in its entirety is a lazy and misleading mental shortcut. There is always some value, and there is always some trade-off.

Loss aversion makes us fear losses more than we want gains. This leads game developers to hold onto broken ideas instead of exploring new design concepts. Over time it can cause an escalation of commitment as developers throw good money after bad for years, unable to accept the failed idea and move on.

The *availability heuristic* makes us respond only to things and possibilities that we can perceive or imagine, and ignore those we can't as though they don't even exist. The Nobel-winning psychologist Daniel Kahneman calls this WYSIATI, for *what you see is all there is*. This is why people always worry about surviving a repeat of the last terrorist attack instead of all the other dangers of life. Since that attack happened and was very memorable and dramatic, it is highly available to the mind for processing. It can be envisioned, feared, and responded to. Meanwhile, other potential dangers don't come to mind, even though they're just as likely. So they're treated as though they don't even exist.

The availability heuristic expresses itself in game design constantly, because game systems and players often do things that cannot be envisioned beforehand. We end up treating the game as though it is only what we've seen it do, instead of treating is as a system that can usually do more than we've ever seen. For example, this is why balance designers often mistakenly overcorrect for the last balance failure they saw. That last balance failure may be just one among hundreds that the game can express, but since it's mentally available and the others are not, it is treated as if it is the only one that exists. What you see is all there is.

And there are hundreds of other such biases. I won't go through any more, but look at the recommended works at the end of this book for some excellent reading on them.

To some extent, we can counteract our biases by using our rational minds to override what our emotional brains are telling us. But there's a limit to this—we can't eliminate our biases entirely because we're always human.

What we can do is choose to use processes that minimize the impact of cognitive bias. We can set up social structures with checks and balances and follow procedures that get around our individual biases. The legal system and the scientific method are examples of these kinds of antibias processes outside game design. We need similar methods in game design to get past our evolutionarily ingrained assumptions.

Our biases fill us with false confidence built from caveman assumptions. But in reality, we know far less than we feel we do. That's why the key to all the best game design processes is that they demand less from the designers—less foresight, less communication, and less mental simulation. Traditional processes require a designer to achieve such superhuman feats as planning a whole working game design on paper, or directing and understanding the precise activities of a dozen subordinates. Nobody can do these things. When our tool is the idiosyncratic human mind, and our task is as complex as crafting experience-generating machines, we must work in small steps, and with humility.

11

Planning and Iteration

> As Hans Grote, a building contractor, observes, a soccer coach will not tell one of his forwards that he can be certain of scoring if, in the sixth minute of play, he approaches the opponent's goal from the right at an angle of 22 degrees and, 17 meters in front of the goal, kicks the ball at an angle of ascent of 10 degrees, 11 minutes. . . .If the coach is going to determine the positions from which each of his players should shoot, he should keep in mind that damp earth can stick to soccer shoes. And a clump of dirt between shoe and ball can play havoc with the angle of the planned shot. It would therefore be wise to study the average size of clumps of dirt and their frequency of occurrence, as well as the places on a soccer shoe where they are most likely to cling. But then if we consider that soccer fields in the north tend to be sandy while those in the south have a more claylike consistency, we have to. . . .No one would ever go to such ridiculous lengths, you say? Oh, yes, they would!
>
> —Dietrich Dörner

The Overplanner

Here's a story that's happened many times.

A designer has an idea for a game. He wants to do it right, so he decides to not be lazy. He's going to work in the most disciplined, diligent way he knows—by writing a *Design Document*. The Document describes everything: mechanics, fiction, dialogue scripts, art style, technology, target markets. The designer rewrites it over and over, analyzing every piece, rethinking, imagining the game play out.

Months pass. Finally he finishes it. The Document is 200 pages of mechanics specs, sample playthroughs, character backstory, and interface descriptions. He might print it out now, just for the satisfaction of lifting it and feeling its weight. I know because I did this exact thing when I wrote my Document for *Elemental Conflict*.

Then he starts production. He assembles the game like a jigsaw puzzle, each piece destined for a predetermined place as defined in the Document. Months pass. Progress is slow, but the designer has faith in his Document. Eventually, he lets someone else play it for the first time. And that's when everything goes to hell.

Nothing plays out as expected. The hardest enemy falls to a simple, degenerate dodging strategy. The player misses a tear-jerking story beat because he's busy jumping on a desk. He doesn't understand the simplest mechanic, and easily masters the most complex. He misses a key passageway and ends up wandering the same room for 20 minutes. He hates the companion character, and only uses three of his 10 tools.

And good things happen, too. The player finds a new, more insightful solution to a puzzle. He falls in love with a secondary character. And now that the game is moving, the designer can see a hundred easy design opportunities. If he tweaked this character, a fascinating new strategy would appear. If he combined those story beats, the scripted story would be purer and more powerful. If he removed that resource cost, the pacing would obviously improve. It all seems so clear now.

The designer's in a bind. On the one hand, he has the Document, into which he poured so much love and time. On the other, he has the reality of the game in front of him—both the unexpected failures and the serendipitous discoveries. And these two signals point him in very different directions. There is no good way forward from here. He must either trash his Document or ignore his discoveries.

This designer's fundamental mistake is that he overplanned.

The Underplanner

Here's another story that has happened many times.

A team starts a game. They have a quick meeting to go over ideas and then they dive in. Artists start churning out character models, environments, and concept paintings. Coders start assembling artificial intelligences, world generation algorithms, and physics engines. Designers build levels, craft interfaces, and wave their hands during increasingly exciting blue-sky meetings. Progress seems rapid.

But over time, things start to sour. The game chugs along at an unplayably choppy 10 frames per second because several programmers each used the game's entire performance budget. Finding investors is hard because of the lack of a clear idea of what the game is. It turns out an artist wasted weeks working on variations of a character who only appears once.

And the design is incoherent because so many people were working separately on their own varying impressions of what the game should be. One part resembles a deep story RPG. Another is like a heavily scripted action shooter. A third is like a strategy game. The design ultimately becomes a sort of badly sewed-up Frankenstein monster of a game, the pieces never coming together into an elegant whole.

As the release date approaches, something has to give. The game doesn't work as an integrated system. The remaining work does not match the abilities of the team and cannot be measured. One subsystem is missing a huge amount of art; another has never been tested; a third is below performance requirements. Finally, there is no way to advertise the game because nobody knows what it's going to be.

In the end, the team crunches for six months, cuts large chunks of the game, tries to shore up a core of what they have, and pushes something out the door. It gets a ho-hum reception and everyone wonders what went wrong.

These developers' fundamental mistake is that they underplanned.

Underplanning and Overplanning

Without planning, a process disintegrates as different parts of the team and game work against each other. This is underplanning. But if we make a careful, detailed plan, it falls apart on contact with reality. This is overplanning. It seems like a catch-22. Either way we go, we get hurt.

Thankfully, there is a solution. But before we look at it, we must first understand the problems with underplanning and overplanning in more detail.

THE COSTS OF UNDERPLANNING

Underplanning creates several characteristic problems.

When we underplan, we almost always do work that has to be thrown out. The work turns out to be unnecessary, or is made obsolete by later progress. Plans avoid this problem. With a plan, we can determine the minimum set of steps we need to get to a goal. If we find that a piece of work isn't needed, we can remove it from the plan during the planning phase. This is more efficient than doing it and then throwing it away.

Underplanning also harms team coordination. Planning is a necessary part of coordinating a team. Even a team of two developers must talk about what they're doing in the next hour. Scale this up to a team of hundreds, and coordination becomes a massive challenge. A plan that describes what everyone should be doing for the next month or year is one way of meeting this challenge. Once developed, the plan can be distributed to everyone, and each person does his part of the project. Underplanning makes this impossible. On an underplanned project, people work without a clear idea of how their tasks fit into the whole. Incompatibilities develop between the work of different people. Some incompatibilities are technical, as in a character model that doesn't follow standards or a subsystem that uses too much memory. Others are creative, as in story details, design elements, or artistic styles that don't work together. This lack of creative unity turns the game into an unfocused Frankenstein's monster.

Finally, developers aren't the only people who need to know what a game will become. Underplanning starves these external stakeholders of information on which to base their work. For example, to get an ad on television, the ad must first be produced and scheduled into a time slot, all of which takes months. So, if we want to coordinate a December release with an ad campaign, marketers need to start producing those ads the previous summer or earlier. Similarly, investors want to know what they're putting money into and will often demand detailed descriptions of the future product. Hiring managers need to know who to hire long before those people are necessary. Retail distribution channels need advance estimates of how many copies of a game will be sold, to whom, and where, so they can plan the physical distribution of the discs. The world wants to know what the game will be and when it will appear, and underplanning makes that impossible.

THE COSTS OF OVERPLANNING

There's a common assumption that a little bit too much planning can't be a bad thing. But this is false. Overplanning destroys projects in many different ways.

It takes time to write plans. They must be invented, debated, recorded, edited, and disseminated. As plans grow into hundreds of pages, this can become a massive burden. Overplanning diverts effort from real development to planning tasks.

It also costs something to cut plans when they inevitably fail. Cutting an agreed-on idea takes discussion, debate, and political capital. And it's psychologically painful for a creative person to invest himself in an idea and then divest himself again. Overplanning creates many plans that will need to be cut later, meaning these costs of cutting must be paid over and over.

But these aren't the greatest costs of overplanning. The real price of overplanning is in how it creates a false sense of certainty about the future. Written plans are often treated as guaranteed visions of what's going to happen. But they're not—they're laden with assumptions. Work that depends on those assumptions will later collapse when they're shown to be false.

For example, imagine an initial design document says that the player character can jump 10 feet into the air. Based on that plan, a level artist builds a level bounded by 11-foot-high walls. If the plan is correct, everything should work, since the player character can't get over an 11-foot wall with a 10-foot jump. But then the designer discovers that the game feels much better if the character jumps 15 feet in the air instead of 10. Now there's a problem. Either the level needs to be reworked to handle 15-foot jumps, or the jump must stay at 10 feet where it would feel better at 15. One choice throws out good work. The other weakens the game.

And it's never as simple as this. Real game designs are networks of dependencies; changes in one place almost always imply many changes elsewhere. A simple change in jump height might affect level boundaries, enemy movement (so they can catch a high-jumping player), jumping puzzles, audiovisual effects applied to jumping, and more. And each of these changes might imply further changes—changing enemy movement might involve adjustments in the enemy art and animation. Reworking a jumping puzzle might then mean changing the plot of a level, if that puzzle was threaded together with the story. The effects of the failed plan ripple through the design, twisting art, code, mechanics, and fiction.

Game design is unusual among modern creative pursuits in the amount of uncertainty embedded in every plan.

As Soren Johnson, lead designer of *Civilization IV*, wrote, "To be a game designer is to be wrong." A designer can guess how a system or a level will play out, but he can never know. Usually, when it is constructed, the game system plays very differently than anticipated. That's why great games tend to change so much during development.

For example, *Halo* spawned one of the most popular first-person shooter franchises ever. But in its original form, *Halo* wasn't a shooter, and it wasn't first-person. It was a top-down strategy game. Instead of firing a gun through the eyes of a space marine, the player viewed the battlefield from above and used a point-and-click interface to order troops around. But during development, the designers discovered that the closer the camera got to the action, the more the game improved. They pushed this further and further, until eventually they put the camera inside the protagonist's eyes. This strange development path was not a mistake—it was essential to the game's success. *Halo* was known for innovations in large-scale multicharacter battles, vehicular combat, and open outdoor environments, all of which were carried over from the game's roots as a strategy game. Nobody could have planned that result, and nobody did.

BioShock is about exploring an underwater city built in the art deco style. The city, called Rapture, was an attempt at creating a utopia based on the principles of Ayn Rand's Objectivist philosophy. By the time the player character arrives in 1960, the utopia has failed and Rapture has descended into civil war. The game was famous for this rich and unique world narrative. But at its inception, *BioShock* didn't take place underwater and had nothing to do with Ayn Rand. It was a science-fiction game set in a spaceship. Later, it moved to an abandoned Nazi bunker infested with mutants. It was only several years into development that the game shifted into an art deco undersea city and gained its failed Objectivist utopia theme. Its designers did not plan that world on paper; they developed it through years of work on the game itself.

The Sims began development as an architecture game. Originally, Will Wright did not plan to put a family in the house. The game was about building houses and no more. The player would experiment with different house shapes, colors, and furnishings in a completely sterile environment. It was only when Wright dropped a simple character in the space that he discovered how fascinating players found it. Wright followed the opportunity he saw, and the game became more and more about the human characters until they became the focus of the game. He didn't plan this result; he discovered it.

Entire designs change, as happened to *Halo*, *BioShock*, and *The Sims*. But even the tiniest piece of a game can yield surprises. For example, when I worked on puzzle levels in the downloadable content for *BioShock*, my level had a room that had a row of rocket-launching turrets along one wall. I wanted the player to know about the turrets without being killed by them. So I used an old trick for communicating danger to the player: as the player entered the room, I spawned an enemy and had him run at the player, only to be blown to smithereens by the rocket turrets. I played it and it worked perfectly. The enemy screamed and exploded; there was no mistaking the row of turrets. The problem seemed solved. Then I watched someone else play it. He walked into the room. The enemy screamed and ran at him. Since it was a puzzle level, the player had no weapons. So he turned and ran out of the room to escape the enemy. I had to put unbreakable glass around the player to make him feel safe before he would stand his ground and watch the scene play out.

Game designs are always uncertain. Every experienced designer has numerous stories of game systems working and failing in unexpected ways. It is impossible to know whether or how a design will work by reading it on paper. It's that gap between assumed and real certainty that causes missed deadlines, broken budgets, and crunch. When you assume that plans are rock solid while they are in truth very uncertain, you'll overplan, and bad things will happen.

Iteration

We can't not plan at all, but nor can we plan every detail to the end of the project. We need a middle ground. We need to *iterate*.

ITERATION is the practice of making short-range plans, implementing them, testing them, and repeating.

The traditional creative method is linear. One plans, then builds, then tests to verify quality, and the product is finished.

Iteration is different. Instead, of running in a line, it runs in a loop.

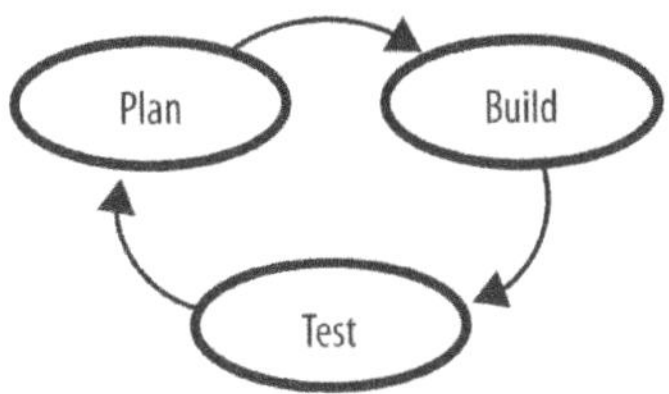

This means we don't have to predict events deep into the future. We need only plan as far as the end of the current loop. Each time we test the game, we check our assumptions against reality. That reality check provides reliable knowledge on which to base our plans for the next loop.

This loop can repeat a few times or thousands of times, depending on the project. Sometimes developers will plan the number of cycles they want before release. Other times, they'll just continue looping until the game hits a target level of quality, or until they run out of money.

We don't only iterate on an entire game. We can iterate on a level, a tool, or an interface. On larger teams, there should be many different iteration loops running at the same time.

ITERATION EXAMPLE

Since every design challenge is different, each iterative process must be tailored to the challenge at hand. Here's an example of a simple iterative process that I've used to develop combat scenarios in first-person shooters. This process wouldn't be appropriate for other challenges or developers—it's just one possible example of iteration.

I start by roughing in a basic fight as quickly as I can. I throw elements in as I think of them, not pausing to analyze. I might have an idea of where I'm going, but I don't have to. My only goal is to play the fight as soon as possible.

Within an hour, I've got the fight running—and as always, it's awful. It plays like an amateur mod by an especially unmotivated first-time designer. Gray blocks of cover are scattered haphazardly about, the world geometry is a handful of poorly scaled cubes, and enemies appear in giant clumps. And since I usually forget to give the player a weapon, he always loses.

But despite its poor quality, this first version fulfills its purpose. It has closed the iteration loop. The fight is no longer a mental movie. It's real. And playing a real fight, with hands on the controls and the real seconds ticking by, sparks thought processes that can't be replicated in any other way. This first attempt was never meant to be anything like the final product. Its only purpose is as a platform from which to jump to something less awful.

And in that, it's successful. As I play it, the ideas flow, and they're more specific, and more concrete than anything I could have thought of cold. I get excited about them, and I don't have to wait, analyze, or document. My inspiration doesn't get time to degrade. After one test, I'm back in the editor, ripping out pieces that didn't work, shuffling cover around, rearranging weapon pickups and enemies. Maybe I even remember to give the player a weapon this time.

I go through several of these cycles, changing the level and testing it again and again. Since I can iterate so quickly, I don't bother to spend time analyzing. I just drop things in the level and try them within minutes. Since everything is still rendered in simple gray blocks, the work stays fluid. This is good, since the changes I'm making are large conceptual jumps like changing a tower to a bridge or replacing the main threat with another kind of enemy. I'm not worrying about details yet.

Within a few hours, I've gone through several iteration loops, and I've probably changed the overall concept several times. Perhaps I started with enemies in a tower (actually just a tall block with snipers on top), but found that didn't work. I might try a bridge (a long, wide block over a long hole in the floor). I might have tried minefields, snipers, trenches, artillery, and any other broad strokes I could think of. Extremely rough versions of any of these can be executed in minutes.

After between three and eight loops of trying different concepts, I land on one that works. And here the process begins to change. The loop lengthens, and the changes I'm making start to shrink. Instead of testing every hour, I test every two or three. Instead of ripping and replacing entire buildings, I'm adjusting positioning on walls and pillars. As always, changes aren't made in response to imagined problems, but real ones that I observed in testing. Every test shows me new, obvious changes that need to be made.

This is where I get a level artist involved. He's probably not working on the space directly—it's still too early for that—but he is consulting on its artistic feasibility. If my overall concept is artistically nonsensical, I might restart from the beginning. More likely we discuss ways to adjust the space to make it art-friendly. For example, the level remains in gray, but a tower or a bridge might be given a specific shape that suggests a style, theme, world story, and mood. He might mock something up or make an art test level to explore artistic ideas for the space.

The iteration loops continue. The fight becomes more refined and balanced. Sometimes the space changes in response to artistic or narrative concerns, but most changes are still driven by balance, pacing, clarity, and depth concerns as I observed them in my self-tests.

Eventually, though, I hit a wall. There's a point where testing your own work no longer teaches you anything new. By this time I've made a fight that works well when I play it—but the game isn't being made for me. It has to work for all its players. And the only way to understand how well it is working with real players is to watch them play.

So I replace myself with other playtesters. Ideally, I'd get real players drawn randomly from a sample of the public representing the target market of the game. But even if this isn't possible, there are other alternatives. I usually use coworkers. I pull programmers, testers, artists, and audio engineers who haven't seen the fight, sit them down at my computer, and watch them play. I tell them nothing, stand far behind them, out of their line of sight, and wait for the design to fail.

It always does. Some players break the fight by inventing strategies I never thought of. They'll refuse to advance and snipe every enemy from a distance. Or they'll charge past enemy lines without firing a shot. Others fail in frustration because they don't know the fight the way I do, or they don't notice a key element. They'll miss a hole in the floor, and fall through to their death. They'll get shot in the back by the guy I sent to flank them. They'll step on the blinking land mine I thought was obvious. To paraphrase Bill Cosby, playtesters do the darndest things.

After one playtest, I've got a list of issues to solve. Some are simple fixes (light that enemy better so that people can see him). Others are more complex (restructure the left side flanking route so that both players and enemies can use it). I get to work. Half a day later, the changes are in, and I'm ready for the next playtest. I find someone who hasn't played the fight yet, and watch him.

The loop goes around this way 10 to 20 more times. By the end, two or three weeks have passed. The fight is well paced and well balanced, and it handles players of many skill levels and play habits. I don't have to guess how it will play out when it's handed to real players, because I already know—the playtesters showed me.

But it still doesn't look like much—flat gray cubes suggesting a theme, but not resembling a finished game. Now the artists really get involved.

Level artists do a first pass on the space, replacing gray shapes with real art assets. We test again. Even if the mechanical shape of the fight doesn't change, art changes affect how players perceive the fight, so we have to watch how it affects playtests. As we see problems, we discuss them to find solutions. Sometimes I might have to change a scripting detail, removing or adding characters or tools. Other times, the artist might have to add light to brighten a space, or simplify something to reduce art-driven noise. The iteration loop is now several days long, since making art is slow work.

If we're lucky, the art causes no major issues. Since I playtested thoroughly using gray cubes, the base level should continue working as it did before. So, within a few more loops, the level starts working both mechanically and artistically.

Now we expand the loop even more to include other development disciplines. Text boxes get replaced with real dialogue. Audio engineers do a pass on ambience and scripted sounds. We look for ways to express world narrative through the space. Writers redo dialogue. Finally, testers bang on it for a while, we fix the technical bugs, and it ships.

That's one way to develop shooter combat. Other iteration loops might look very different from this one depending on the project and the goals being pursued. This particular process was mechanics-driven, which is why it started with a combat designer working on balance and pacing. Another game might demand a narrative-driven process, where story beats are iterated first, followed by mechanics. And then there are entirely different kinds of design problems: character design, interface design, and systems design each demand a different method. Some will be tight loops done by one person. Others will have large loops lasting weeks, involving 10 different people. Some developers test alone, others over the shoulder, others with automated data metrics, others in purpose-built labs.

But no matter what kind of loop is being employed, iteration still runs on the same basic principles. It exchanges deep planning for reality checks. It tests the broad structure before investing in detail polish. And it requires that designers not get too invested in plans for the future, and instead adapt continuously to unpredictable test results.

Planning Horizon

How long should our iteration loop be? Should we test every day? Every week? Every month?

If our loop is too long, we're overplanning. Developers end up worrying about problems that don't exist, or missing problems hidden by their assumptions. Too short a loop, and we're underplanning. We lose time on unnecessary work and can't get a group of developers working together. We have to find a balance between these by choosing the correct *planning horizon.*

The PLANNING HORIZON is the length of time a designer plans into the future.

A long planning horizon would be planning and executing the next month of work before running the next test. A short planning horizon would be just throwing things into the game and testing them minute by minute to see what happens.

The basic principle in choosing a planning horizon is to consider how uncertain your plans are. When plans are very likely to work as expected, your planning horizon should be long. This is how architects design buildings down to individual nuts and bolts—they know how a building will fit together with great certainty. When the plans are uncertain, your planning horizon should be short. This is like a soccer match, where everything changes from moment to moment due to factors that are impossible to predict. Any given game development process sits at some point between these two extremes.

Let's look at some more specific situational factors that should affect planning horizon.

Unoriginal, derivative games can be planned relatively far into the future because they depend on established knowledge.

The less original a game, the deeper we can plan. *The Sims* changed entirely during development, but *The Sims 2* did not because the core of the design was already well established by the first game. Similarly, someone making a first-person shooter today can use everything that has already been learned about this genre from other games to help predict how his own game will work.

The extreme example of this is making a clone or a port of an existing game. With the entire design already established and tested against real players, it might even be possible to plan every detail ahead of time like an architect blueprinting a building.

This is why making a sequel is so different from making an original. Some game franchises go into five sequels or more with little change in basic mechanics. This makes for smooth development processes, since the design of the fifth sequel can depend on the massive amount of knowledge established in previous games.

Original games can only be planned to a short horizon because they depend on things that haven't been discovered yet.

Original games are much harder to plan because the designer has no foundation of well-tested designs to stand on. An original game composed of a collection of original mechanics controlled through an original interface set in an original world is a giant web of interlocking uncertainties. In this sort of situation, the correct planning horizon can be a day or less. Any plan made a week into the future will be invalidated by tomorrow's surprises about what does and does not work.

The appropriate planning horizon tends to lengthen over the course of a project.

At the start of the project, we stand on shifting sands of assumption. By the end, we're worrying about tiny details within an established structure. A project might start with a planning horizon of less than a day, as a small group of developers try out wild ideas. The last few months might be planned out up front in a spreadsheet listing every art asset and programming task to be completed before it ships.

When the cost of testing is low, we should plan to a shorter horizon.

At the start of my combat design process, I could build and test a combat idea very quickly. Why spend an hour analyzing an idea when I can build and test it in 15 minutes, and get a lot more information about it? It's literally not worth the cost to think hard about it. So I don't think. I just toss stuff in.

This is the benefit of good tools. It's not just that the tools let you make the game faster. It's that they change the trade-off between planning and building, and allow a more experimental development approach by reducing the cost of failure. Good tools let you take risks. This is how they let you discover designs that you could not notice if work was so slow that you had to plan and get everything right the first time.

Plan more deeply when your goal is to make conceptual leaps.

Iteration is what's known as a *hill climbing* algorithm. Imagine every possible game as points on a landscape. Points on a higher elevation are better games. Iteration makes the game act like a blind mountaineer who climbs whatever slope he is standing on. It takes short steps, tests them to see if they're improvements, and moves into them if so. The game becomes steadily better over time.

The problem with hill climbing is that since the mountaineer is blind, he can't tell if he's climbing a mountain or a hill. If we start on the slope of a low hill, we will get to the top of it, but remain unaware of the mountain not far away. We want to jump to that mountain, but if we can only take small steps, we have no way of getting there from the top of this hill. Iteration optimizes a design, but does not revolutionize it.

To make great bounds across the landscape, we have to disconnect from Earth for a while. This means making large design changes without testing. This is risky—there is no way to know where you'll land until you get there—but it's the only way to discover radically new ideas and escape design ruts. Making a deep plan lets you try to see the mountains in the distance—though you might arrive to find they're only foothills. That's the risk of deep planning.

Why We Overplan

Both overplanning and underplanning are dangerous. But in game design, overplanning tends to be the more dominant destructive force. More developers overplan than underplan, and more damage is wrought by overplanning than underplanning.

Why do people overplan in game design? There are a number of consistent biases that push us to overplan again and again. To counter these biases, we must first be aware of them.

CULTURAL HABIT

From a young age, we're indoctrinated with the planning habit. Teachers and parents instruct us over and over to plan ahead and think of the future.

And usually, this is a good idea. Careful planning built the modern world. When engineers and laborers constructed the Hoover Dam, they decided exactly what they would do before they started. They knew exactly how much concrete they needed, and exactly where it would go. They could precisely schedule their workers and materials deliveries for maximum efficiency. And the final product looked almost exactly like what was decided on during the design phase.

But game design is different from these other tasks because it is more uncertain. The Hoover Dam's architects could never discover halfway through construction that the dam had to become a skyscraper. But *Halo*'s developers discovered that their top-down strategy game had to become a first-person shooter. And as we've seen, this kind of radical design transformation isn't unusual.

INBORN OVERCONFIDENCE

Let's play a game about certainty. I'm going to give you a quiz with 10 questions, each with a numerical answer. Your task is to write a series of high and low estimates such that for each question you are 90% sure that the answer will be within the range you provide.

Keep in mind that the ranges can be as large or small as you want. You don't need to know the answers to do this. Set the range wide enough so that you're 90% sure that the correct answer is between the upper and lower bounds, and no larger. If you're very uncertain, your range will be large. If not, it will be small.

I strongly encourage you to get a pencil and write down your answers. This exercise doesn't work nearly as well just by reading.

Question	Low estimate	High estimate
Birth year of Archimedes		
Number of classified species of ant		
World population in 1900		
Diameter of the sun		
Number of named moons of Saturn		
Melting point of iron		
Total military deaths in World War I		
Land area of Antarctica		
Latitude of Santiago, Chile		
Total weight of all the gold mined in human history		

Now check your answers in the back of the book. How did you do?

Note that your performance in this test should have had nothing to do with your knowledge of geography or history. You could set your ranges as large as you wanted to achieve your own 90% confidence level. And if you did that, then you should almost certainly have gotten eight, nine, or 10 answers within your ranges.

But if you're like most people, you probably got between two and four of the answers. A small number of people get five or six answers in their confidence range. Very few go over that, even when they understand the test and have taken it before.

When I took a similar test in the book *Software Estimation: Demystifying the Black Art* by Steve McConnell (Microsoft Press), I got four correct. McConnell has given similar tests to hundreds of professional estimators. These people had years of experience estimating completion times and costs on software projects. Even among this elite group, McConnell found that less than 1% of test-takers actually get the nine answers that we should expect from an unbiased estimator. More than 90% of them got five or fewer answers correct. Why?

Humans have a natural bias toward overconfidence.

Psychologists call this the *optimism bias*. Something in human psychology makes a 90% confident estimate closer to a 30% confident estimate. This overconfidence isn't limited to estimating numbers on a quiz. People have been shown to be consistently overconfident on software development budgets, economic forecasts, business plans, and military strategies.

This bias has tremendous implications in game design planning. It suggests that without correction, a designer will have 90% confidence in a design that only has a 30% chance of actually working. This is a massive gap between expectation and reality. Such overconfidence leads us to think that we can plan things that we actually cannot. It makes us read a design document and guess that it will probably work when it really has only the slightest chance of working as expected. This biases us toward overplanning.

THERAPEUTIC PLANNING

Consider the expression *feeling unsure*. Technically, being unsure only means not having a certain piece of information. But the phrase *feeling unsure* is laden with negative emotional overtones. We judge an unsure person as incapable and ineffective. When we are unsure, we imagine ourselves feeling nervous and overwhelmed. Uncertainty is emotionally unpleasant. The response is often to hide the uncertainty by engaging in *therapeutic planning.*

THERAPUTIC PLANNING is planning done not to coordinate work, but to make us feel better about our inevitably uncertain future.

A plan can take away the anxiety of being unsure by creating a false sense of certainty about the future. But as the philosopher Nassim Taleb says, if you want to relax, have a drink, don't make a forecast—reckless forecasting is far more dangerous.

Not overplanning means accepting the cognitive stress of uncertainty. It means constantly reevaluating the situation, not socking decisions away where they can be comfortably forgotten. The desire to avoid this mental effort often leads to therapeutic overplanning.

GROUP PLANNING BIAS

Groups of people naturally reward the overconfident over the rationally uncertain.

Imagine two people, Confident Bob and Rational Alice, in a group trying to predict the weather. Rational Alice looks at the sky and accurately remembers that of all the times she has seen this combination of weather conditions, it has rained about half the time.

"I really have no idea if it is going to rain or not," she says. "We can't really know either way."

Now Confident Bob steps in. He looks up briefly, smiles as though enjoying a private joke. He turns to the group and announces, with strong eye contact and a decisive hand gesture, "It's not going to rain. Don't worry about it."

The group naturally chooses Bob. Bob gets the followers, the approval, and the social status. Alice is called weak, stupid, indecisive, or lazy, even though her answer was more accurate.

This is the group planning bias. People are naturally drawn to leaders who seem to see into the future with great certainty, even when that future sight is delusional.

The safety valve for this effect is when it does actually rain and Bob is proven wrong. Once this happens a few times, people will stop listening to him. But these kinds of consequences aren't nearly as clear in game design as they are in weather prediction. In game design, cause and effect are hard to see, results can take years to become apparent, and so much happens in the meantime that the memory of the prediction is confused, modified, or forgotten. In a simple environment with clear feedback, our instincts eventually lead us to distrust Confident Bob. But in modern design challenges, the feedback isn't there. The safety valve is broken. So the social bias in favor of the confident remains, while the safety valve of results checking does not. The biases are out of balance.

Without efforts to counter this effect, a confident leader will gain more followers than a correct one. Uncertainty gets hidden by bravado, and the overplanning begins.

HINDSIGHT BIAS

Despite all the biases covered so far, one might think that we would eventually learn from our errors. There are developers who have gone through 10 overplanned projects in a row, experiencing the same painful feature cuts, crunch time, and process chaos each time. Why don't we learn from these experiences? Because of *hindsight bias*.

HINDSIGHT BIAS is a cognitive bias that silently rearranges memories to make past events look like they were more predictable than they actually were.

In 1972, researcher Baruch Fischoff asked people what might happen during President Nixon's upcoming diplomatic trip to China. Will Nixon meet with Chairman Mao? Will there be major diplomatic progress? He asked for the likelihoods of these and 13 other outcomes.

After Nixon's trip, Fischoff again asked the same people to recall how likely they thought the various outcomes would be. The hindsight bias was clear. If someone's prediction had been correct, he said that he had been surer than he actually was. If his prediction was wrong, he said that he had been less sure. They edited their memories to make it look like they could predict the future better than they actually did.

After the fact, game development always looks smoother and more under control than it was. Our brains automatically edit the chaos of development into a clean story of linear cause and effect. When we tell the story to others, we simplify it even further. Time-wasting tangents, thoughtless mistakes, ugly misunderstandings, and uneventful days of grinding work all fall away until the story becomes a children's fairy tale of simple cause and effect. In fact, I've written stories like this in this book.

The problem is that the lessons of game design process aren't in the clean, edited story that we tell afterward. They're in the messy red herrings and false predictions that we edit out of the story. Hindsight bias prevents us from learning from our mistakes by making us think events were more predictable than they really were. Looking back, hindsight bias makes it always feel like deep planning should have been possible. So we think it will be possible in the future, and we overplan again and again, unable to learn from our mistakes.

Once you know what to look for, you'll start to see these overplanning biases in development. And you'll be able to compensate for them.

Test Protocol

The iterative process is a cycle between planning, building, and testing. Everyone focuses on planning and building, and testing is often ignored. But the testing stage is critical because it is the mechanism by which we learn lessons from the real world and secure the main benefit of iteration.

The purpose of playtesting isn't to find technical problems or gather marketing data. It is to understand how the game design works when put into action. It means getting real people to play the game and watching where the design works and where it fails. Where are players confused? Where is it too easy or too hard? Is it balanced? Are there degenerate strategies? Do players understand the narrative?

Running playtests is a skill. You don't just do it—it's just as hard as planning or building. Done well, a playtest returns the information that designers need without much cost or effort. Done poorly, it misses critical design flaws, wastes time, and can even actively mislead designers.

The key to getting good data is using the right *test protocol*.

A TEST PROTOCOL is a set of rules and procedures for carrying out a playtest.

Creating a good test protocol is hard because there is no feedback when we do it wrong. Corrupted or misleading test results often look very reasonable. Worse, bad test protocols usually make tests go more smoothly, not less. And a badly run test is worse than useless. Before the bad test, the designer knew he didn't know whether the game worked. Afterward, he thinks the game works even though it doesn't. He hasn't just failed to gain knowledge—he's gained knowledge that isn't true.

I once interviewed a senior designer on a failed multiplayer shooter. This was his test protocol: a group of players sitting in a room with food, playing the game for extended lengths of time. In this environment, the game seemed to be working well. They iterated, found problems, tested, and polished the game until it was as deep and balanced as a philosopher on a tightrope. But that success was deceptive, because their test protocol did not find any of the design failures that occur when the game is played by strangers over the Internet instead of friends in the same room. Played between well-coordinated, highly communicative teams, the game shone. But online, it collapsed. It was so dependent on intricate team tactics that it did not function when played by lazy, incompetent strangers. The designers playtested, but their faulty test protocol hid critical flaws in the design, and so the game failed in the market and with most of its players.

There are countless ways for test protocols to fail. *Unblinded tests* introduce expectation biases in the playtesters. Group tests create social competition and copycat opinions among players. Telling players to think aloud helps designers interpret players' actions, but also changes those players' actions. Tester selection introduces biases that will hide problems that only appear when people of specific ages, genders, cultures, or skill levels play the game. Small numbers of testers mean our data is skewed by surprisingly large random statistical variances.

In the end, we can never totally avoid these faults. Test protocol isn't a matter of right and wrong. It's a craft in which a designer tries to get the most useful knowledge possible with a given set of resources.

Let's look at some basic test protocols.

SELF-TESTING

The cheapest test protocol is to play alone. Even though the designer's play is biased by his knowledge of the game, just watching the game systems in motion brings a tremendous amount of understanding. It reveals many problems in flow, pacing, and balance. And, of course, technical bugs are best found in self-tests. The earliest loops of an iterative process should conclude with self-tests.

OVER-THE-SHOULDER PLAYTESTING

In over-the-shoulder playtesting, the designer watches other players. This can be as informal as grabbing a coworker and putting them in front of your computer. Or it might mean bringing outsiders into a fake living room with drinks, a game system, and hidden cameras.

Over-the-shoulder playtesting is better than self-testing because the players can vary and don't have the designer's complete knowledge of the game. You can playtest with the old, the young, men, women, aggressive people, passive people, and everyone in between. And none of them will know everything about the game the way you do, so all of them will respond to it more like real players than you will.

The greatest danger in over-the-shoulder playtesting is corrupting the test by giving players information they shouldn't have. This is why, in nearly all cases, the designer should remain completely silent through the test. Do not talk. Do not laugh. Do not groan. Do not signal your thoughts in any way. If the playtester asks you something, say in a neutral tone, "Sorry, I can't answer that."

This rule is socially awkward. When a player is confused or frustrated, it can be downright painful. Every experienced designer has watched a player get stuck for 15 minutes searching for a door or button. You desperately want to tell the player, "It's right there! Just push the blue button!" But telling the playtester what he's missing would corrupt the whole test by giving him information that real players won't have. You would no longer be testing your game, but a strange version of your game where the designer comes in the box and gives tips. The tests might go more smoothly, but only because flaws are being hidden.

Occasionally, it's necessary to give the player information to fill in for missing pieces of the game. In these cases, the extra information should be planned beforehand as part of the test protocol.

CHOOSING PLAYTESTERS

The choice of playtester affects the kind of data you'll get. The main variation among playtesters is in their knowledge of the game.

In so-called *Kleenex testing*, the designer brings in playtesters who have never played the game. This kind of testing reveals how players will react during the critical first few moments of play. But these testers can only be used once, hence the name Kleenex testers.

Other times, we want to test the high-skill balance of a game. This requires players who can play intensely for long periods of time. Usually this means having a team of dedicated playtesters who work on their skills daily.

There are variations between these extremes. For example, in my combat design process, I tested with coworkers who knew the game, but who didn't know the specific combat I was working on. So their initial knowledge approximated that of a real player encountering the combat after playing several hours into the game. They knew the game, but not the particular fight I was making.

There are also other ways to divide playtesters besides knowledge of the game. You can test with children or seniors, or people of different cultures, socioeconomic backgrounds, or interests. In general, choose a mix of testers who resemble the people you want to play the final game.

SAMPLE SIZE

It's easy to fixate on a single playtest result. Since your brain instinctively believes that what you see is all there is (WYSIATI), it'll trick you into thinking that that one experience is the entire game. But it often turns out that the first test run was just one unimportant thread through a large and diverse set of possible experiences. This is why playtesting well means playtesting a lot.

Good design decisions can only be made when a designer has built up an understanding of *all* the different experiences the game can generate. This means doing many playtests.

Without this broad mental context, designers will tend to solve the problems with the experiences they saw while causing problems with experiences they didn't see. The game might keep changing, but it won't improve because every solution causes more problems.

To make real progress, we have to solve problems with one experience without causing others elsewhere. This is impossible if we've only seen one or two of the threads players can follow through the game. We have to know everything a game tends to do across all players. Then we can pick out the design solutions that solve all their problems at once.

The process of gaining that context is straightforward: watch many playtests. Each playtester shows you a new thread through the game's possibility space. After you've absorbed enough of those, you'll develop a more complete model of all the different experiences the game can create, instead of thinking of it as a single-threaded story. You'll know all the different branch points and possibilities that can occur in every situation, and how they interrelate. You'll be able to predict all the different effects a design change will have because you'll understand the game as a system, not a story.

There's no one number of playtests that are needed for this. Different games generate different breadths of experience, so some games will need more playtesting before a designer can understand them. In a very simple, constrained game, this might happen after two or three playtests. In shooter combat development, it tends to happen with between six and 12 playtests. In unrestricted, systems-driven games, the required number of playtests could be very large.

A good rule of thumb is to stop playtesting when you start seeing testers repeating the same experiences often. Once that happens, you can be reasonably sure that you understand enough of what the game has to offer to make good design decisions about it.

QUESTIONING TECHNIQUE

We can learn most of what we need just by watching a playtest. The tester will show us where a game is too hard by failing. He will show us where it is too easy by winning instantly. He will show us where it is unclear by missing instructions or opportunities.

But sometimes watching isn't enough. Sometimes we need to understand what happened in the playtesters' mind. This means we need to ask them.

The problem is that verbal reports are unreliable. Memories are edited or invented wholesale. The report of the experience is mixed in with suggestions on the design. The tester's feelings about the designer or the studio cloud their judgment. The tester doesn't intend to do this; it's human nature. So to learn anything by talking to playtesters, we have to form our questions very carefully.

My favorite post-test question is, "Tell me the story of what just happened in the game." This question is a memory probe. It discovers what aspects of the game were perceived, retained, and considered important enough to mention. Things that aren't mentioned in the story may be dead weight in the design. Often, I've found that the story that players remember is very different from the story I intended or the story that occurred.

A designer can also tailor a question to determine whether a player perceived a specific thing. We should not ask, "Did you notice the door on the left?" because the question itself gives players information that might corrupt their answer. They'll often answer yes just to look smart or to please the interviewer. A better question might be, "Tell me about why you chose that path." The playtester will either mention the door on the left and why he didn't take it, or he will not. One indicates that it was noticed and rejected; the other indicates that it might never have been perceived at all.

Keep a professional, open tone. It's easy to become frustrated watching playtesters or listening to their feedback, especially when they don't understand the game as it was intended. But any outward sign of this emotion will make them clam up and stop giving honest answers. Playtesters are doing you a favor, so treat them with gratitude.

Grayboxing

It's wasteful to create full audio and art for a design only to discover upon playtesting that it doesn't work. To avoid this, we can iterate in *graybox*.

A GRAYBOX is a low-fidelity placeholder version of a game mechanic, system, or level.

I grayboxed extensively in my combat design process, but grayboxing isn't just for levels—almost anything can be grayboxed. Cutscenes can be replaced by still images or static text pop ups. Complex interfaces can be replaced by labeled buttons. Sounds can be rendered with cheap synthesized beeps and buzzes. Dialogue is read by a text-to-speech program or rendered as on-screen text.

When BioWare developed *Mass Effect 3*, the designers grayboxed creatures. Early in development, a giant war robot would appear as a large cube with two long rectangles underneath and two cubes attached to its sides for arms. Another enemy—this one a tall yellow block—would grab the hero with long yellow blocks attached to its sides. It looks bizarre, but it's unmistakable what is happening, so the game is perfectly playable. These graybox enemies allowed BioWare designers to test and iterate on their creatures without investing in art for unproven designs.

Grayboxing speeds iteration. A graybox can be tested like a finished game, but it might cost a hundred times less effort to build. Since most ideas don't work, it's wasteful to implement them all with full art right from the get-go. But when we build everything in graybox first, we can afford to fail a few times before getting the mechanics just right. Only after the design is proven do we invest the resources to produce it to finished audiovisual quality.

Some people worry about how grayboxing affects artists, audio engineers, and other content creators. At first glance it looks like they might get frustrated being asked to simply "art up" gray shapes. In reality, artists usually appreciate grayboxing because it means their art gets thrown out much less often. Without grayboxing, artists must work on unproven designs, so much of their work is inevitably trashed for reasons unrelated to the art itself. But when working over a well-tested graybox, the artist works with commitment because he trusts that what he creates will be used. Even better is having artists consult with designers during the graybox stage to give input on what a box could become. This way, they've already had a hand in every graybox that they're asked to beautify, so they already understand and believe in it.

WHAT NOT TO GRAYBOX

Grayboxes let us test most of a game experience, including mechanics and fictional meaning. But they aren't the whole experience. Grayboxes obviously don't generate the emotions that would have been driven by the missing art and music.

So grayboxing become less useful the more audiovisual-driven the experience is. Games like *LIMBO* and *Flower* would suffer greatly in graybox since they lean so heavily on audiovisually driven emotional triggers. However, *Counter-Strike* and *StarCraft II* would play quite well in graybox, since they were always about the mechanics.

PREMATURE PRODUCTION

There is always a temptation to break graybox and start using polished assets too early. I call this *premature production*.

PREMATURE PRODUCTION is when a designer adds art and audio to a graybox design before it is necessary to get the next round of test data.

In the short term, adding audiovisuals to an unfinished design feels great. Graphics and sound can make hearts flutter, and they bring smiles in review meetings. The problem is that this emotional benefit is short-lived, while the cost of that art must be paid again and again through the rest of the process. Every iteration loop from here on out is slowed by the process of reworking the art to match the changing mechanics. Ultimately, the art's cost is far greater than the initial effort it took to create, and it must be paid long after that initial emotional impact has faded.

Worse, premature production limits the final quality of a game. We always run out of places to add audiovisuals eventually, after which the mechanics become the limit on the game's quality. But if we hid a weak mechanical core with art, we can't fix it without tearing the art off. We end up stuck with deficient mechanics that we can't change because of the art that's been created around them.

It takes discipline to stay in graybox. After a failed playtest, it's tempting to quickly cover up design faults with art. But unless the art brings useful data in the next playtest, this is a mistake. Art should be added as late as possible to get useful test data.

GRAYBOX EVALUATION SKILL

Playing a good graybox does not feel like playing a good game. This means that evaluating grayboxes is a skill that must be learned through practice. One must have evaluated many grayboxes to have the emotional calibration to know what a good graybox feels like and what a bad one feels like. Without that skill, we're likely to reject even an excellent graybox simply because it lacks art.

This causes problems in group decision situations when some people don't have the skill of evaluating grayboxes. They'll look at the design and get a bad feeling about it just because it is ugly. This is the halo effect in action—the poor quality of visuals create an emotional impression that bleeds out to become someone's opinion of the entire design. So they'll reject the design, even if it was working well.

In real design processes, this is typically the biggest problem around grayboxes. So be careful about who makes decisions about a graybox design. Nobody without practice in evaluating grayboxes should be doing it, because they're very likely to make poor decisions due to the halo effect. If they must make such decisions, it might be necessary to engage in some premature production despite the cost.

THE SCREENPLAY METAPHOR

Many people assume that a game should start with a big design document because that's how movies are made. But that metaphor is wrong.

The closest game design equivalent of a screenplay is not a design document. It is a working graybox prototype.

A screenplay includes every event that occurs during the film. Every word of dialogue, every image, every plot twist is present. When we read it, our minds must fill in the missing audiovisual details, but this is easily done by our active visual imaginations. So just by reading the screenplay and imagining pictures in the mind, we can get a useful approximation of the filmgoers' experience.

One cannot do the same with a game design document because a design document does not specify the game events—it specifies the game mechanics. To read a design document and understand the final experience would mean not just imagining visuals, but mentally simulating all the game mechanics and players' choices to produce the events that drive that experience. This kind of mental simulation is beyond the capacity of any human being.

But in a graybox, the game handles the mechanical simulation. The player's mind need only fill in missing audiovisuals, just like when reading a screenplay. So the closest match to a screenplay is actually a working graybox prototype. A working graybox gives about as much information about the final product as a screenplay. A design document gives much less.

The Paradox of Quality

The classic workshop adage is "Measure twice, cut once." And when you're building a deck or a dam, this makes sense. Since mistakes are very expensive to reverse in this kind of work, avoiding them is a top priority. But in game design, an extreme hatred of mistakes actually leads to a poorer-quality product.

In game design, temporarily accepting poor-quality work ultimately leads to better-quality work. This is the PARADOX OF QUALITY.

Traditional advice says that if you work slowly, lovingly, attending to every detail, you end up with a quality product. If you rapidly slap pieces together, you'll end up with junk. In this view, finishing a quality product means doing quality work at every stage of the process.

Games are different because the most important single determinant of the quality of a game is the number of iteration loops it goes through. An obsession with quality at every stage slows down iteration, ultimately leading to a poorer game.

This is why it's often a mistake to reject imperfect work in early iterations. A designer who does this is like a novelist who can't get a word down because he needs it to be perfect. So every iteration loop is stretched out by overanalysis as he tries to measure twice and get the perfect cut. In the end, his fear of mistakes leads to inferior work because he only managed a few iteration cycles.

In game design, everything gets revised and rebuilt many times before it reaches its final quality. The work we do in the earliest iteration cycles isn't building the final game. It is only building the platform from which to jump to the final game.

The Fallacy of Vision

A young aerospace engineer is at his first day of work. He goes into the boss's office with a gleam in his eye, and declares, "I've got the greatest idea for a new kind of airplane."

The boss is intrigued. "Explain," he says.

The young engineer takes on a visionary expression and stares into the distance. "The passengers board hassle-free in five minutes. Then the plane takes off, silently, with barely a bump, as the passengers enjoy martinis in their private booths. As they soar over the Atlantic, a young couple enjoys the view in one of the plane's many bubble canopies, and a cute kid gets a tour of the cockpit. The captain chuckles as the kid asks why they can't fly to the moon. By the time they touch down, love has been found, lessons have been learned, and everybody is ready for whatever awaits them at their destination."

The boss leans back in his chair and takes a long drag on his cigar. "You're fired," he says.

This young aerospace engineer had a vision. But his vision was of an airplane flight, not an airplane. He described a wonderful experience, but he said nothing about the mechanical systems that created that experience. He succumbed to the *fallacy of vision.*

The FALLACY OF VISION is the idea that a mental movie of an experience is equivalent to a design for a system that generates that experience.

Humans are naturally predisposed to make decisions using mental movies. We picture a story, evaluate how the image makes us feel, and decide based on that emotional response. Psychologist Daniel Gilbert calls this technique *prefeeling.*

In many cases, prefeeling makes sense. It leverages our emotional unconscious's ability to quickly generate a nuanced opinion of a complex idea. Do you want to go to a movie? Prefeel it. Want to eat that meal? Prefeel again. It's an easy, fast, and often effective way of making decisions about the future.

We do the same thing in game design when we evaluate a potential game by imagining playing it. An especially powerful mental movie is often called a *vision*. And vision can be a wellspring of inspiration. It motivates in a way that only stories can.

But visions are also misleading. A vision defines an experience. But a game isn't an experience—it's a system for generating experiences. Just as it would be foolish to confuse a perfect flight with a perfect airplane, it's foolish to confuse a vision of a great game experience for the design of a great game.

The vision says nothing about the trade-offs and costs in the system behind that experience. It tells us nothing of all the other experiences that this game will also generate. This matters because players don't just experience the best of a game—they experience all of it. Furthermore, visions always hide flaws in a design, because we naturally envision only the best experiences in a game we create. We picture the exciting battle, not the five-minute walk from base. We picture the clutch save, but not the 10 random failures. We see the good side of trade-offs, but our minds edit out the bad. This pattern generates overconfidence in design plans and leads to overplanning. So, while designers should take motivation from a vision, we must also question its accuracy.

Try this antidote for the fallacy of vision: instead of trying to envision the best experiences generated by a game, try to envision the worst. Carefully picture every frustrating failure, boring grind, and unclear interaction. This takes more cognitive effort than picturing a wonderful movie in the mind. But it is far more informative because it shows us a balanced picture of the game instead of cherry-picking the best outcomes.

Serendipity

> There are known knowns; there are things we know we know. We also know there are known unknowns; that is to say, we know there are some things we do not know. But there are also unknown unknowns—the ones we don't know we don't know.
>
> —Donald Rumsfeld

In game design, we face many unknowns. Will the player understand this tool? Is this challenge too difficult? How long will this level take to build? These questions might be difficult to answer, but they're not the most important kind of ignorance we must deal with.

Because we also face unknown unknowns. We make mistakes without even registering the possibility. We pass by opportunities that we never even saw. We base entire designs on assumptions we don't know we're making.

Most of the really important things that happen in game development spring from unknown unknowns.

Some unknown unknowns result in disaster. A tester will find a hard-to-fix degenerate strategy that breaks an entire game system. A seemingly obvious interface will prove incomprehensible to newcomers. We'll get a wild new direction from a publisher, or a key programmer will get sick.

Unlike planned methods, iterative processes are robust against such outcomes. When we're iterating, we're not making assumptions about the distant future. This means we can quickly change direction in response to changing circumstances. Even better, the constant reality checks of iteration mean that disastrous discoveries are usually found early. This alone is a major reason to iterate.

But there's another, often more important kind of unknown unknown: serendipity. Players will fall in love with a minor character. They'll invent an interesting new tactic. They'll find emotion in a seemingly unimportant part of the game. These are positive outcomes that the designers never saw coming. And often, these serendipitous discoveries are the most valuable things that happen during the design process. Such serendipity is essential to creating revolutionary designs, because most revolutionary game designs aren't authored—they're stumbled upon.

For example, the progenitor of the video game RPG is *Dungeons & Dragons. D&D* generated most of its meaning from its role playing elements, since it allowed players to verbally play out any fantasy story they could imagine. Almost as soon as computers became capable of it, *D&D* was translated into a video game, in the form of *Rogue. Rogue* displays a dungeon from the top down in text characters. The player controls a hero who explores a sprawling, randomly generated dungeon while killing monsters, gaining experience, and looting ancient treasures. On the surface, *Rogue* is a fairly close computerized approximation of *D&D*. But it creates experiences in a very different way. Whereas *D&D* works mostly through role playing and socialization, *Rogue* is driven by emergent story and schedule-driven rewards acquisition. At the time, these were revolutionary advancements in game design. But *Rogue*'s designers didn't plan this. They stumbled upon the power of rewards scheduling and apophenia-driven emergent narrative while trying to copy the experience of *D&D*. The game worked fantastically well for reasons its creators could never have predicted.

This kind of serendipity isn't unusual. The famous Big Daddy character in *BioShock* was originally a generic mutant in a diving suit; the addition of vulnerable Little Sisters sparked the creation of a fascinating father-daughter relationship between the huge golem and the little girl. The voice of GLaDOS from *Portal*, one of the most popular game characters ever, only became robotic when Erik Wolpaw noticed that people found a temporary graybox line performed by a voice synthesizer funnier than they should. The sublime final level of *Braid* wasn't discovered until the game was mostly finished and Jon Blow realized how he could use time-shifting mechanics to reverse not just time, but character. *Tetris* emerged from a computer version of the traditional Russian puzzle game pentominoes. *The Sims* was developed from an architecture simulation when Will Wright noticed that players liked playing with the characters more than building the houses. Even Wright's original hit *SimCity* was developed when he noticed he enjoyed making maps for a helicopter combat game more than he enjoyed blowing them up.

Serendipity is one of the greatest benefits of iteration. For deep planners, capturing serendipity would means throwing out a beloved and costly plan. Often, they throw out the serendipity instead. When we iterate, we don't have to do this, because our future is open and we can fill it with new discoveries as they appear.

Serendipitous design discoveries don't only appear by luck. To capture them, we need to be observant and adaptable.

Serendipity doesn't just happen. We have to be ready for it. The key to capturing serendipity is being observant and being willing to explore new discoveries. These opportunities don't announce themselves with great fanfare and obvious explanations. They appear as strange behaviors or nonsensical results in well-understood systems. To exploit them, we must notice those hints of possibility and dig into them.

A closed-minded person can't do this because his mental model isn't flexible enough to assimilate new ideas. He'll see the hint, but ignore it or cover it up to reinforce his own worldview. To exploit serendipity, a designer must be able to reorganize his thoughts around his observations, instead of reorganizing his observations around his worldview.

Game design isn't just a process of authorship. It's also a process of observation and discovery.

As creative people, we want to project our vision into the world. But capturing serendipity requires us to loosen our authorial control. Great game designers don't have a perfect vision of a game and then simply translate it into reality. They dig around in the spaces of possibility, watching for hints of value, and seize them when they appear.

Believing in Iteration

It's hard to get past the planning habit. I try to imagine what I would have thought had I read this chapter years ago. I might have nodded in agreement, and thought I understood. But I doubt I would have, really. Intellectual understanding isn't the same as emotional belief.

Most designers I've met who understand iteration only came to believe in it after experiencing years of disasters wrought by deep planning. They had done the crunch time, broken the deadlines, and watched the plans fall apart over and over. I did the same thing. Perhaps the only way to emotionally believe in the problems with planning is to go through the pain of experiencing them firsthand.

That's not an easy experience to get. It means taking a game all the way to completion—prototypes aren't enough. The game must be significant in scope; trivial classroom games are too simple to resist planning this way. And the game must be released to real players who have no reason to be nice to the designer. Because it's only in the wild that a game reveals its true worth. And only then does the designer get the kind of incontrovertible, painful feedback that changes emotional beliefs.

12

Knowledge Creation

A GAME ISN'T AN object that we manufacture. It is a system of knowledge. It's not a chess set. It's chess.

The hard part of game design is not physically implementing the game. It is inventing and refining knowledge about the design.

Consider the work of novel writing. The hard part about the novelist's work is not typing the words—it is the arduous mental work of constructing interrelated characters, settings, themes, and plot turns.

In the same way, the major challenge faced by game designers isn't implementing the game. It is inventing mechanics, fiction, art, and technology that interconnect into a powerful engine of experience. It is the process of creating the knowledge of the design that we are going to implement. This goes much further than just coming up with ideas. It means inventing those ideas, refining them, testing them, debating them, and linking them so that they work together. Doing this means answering many questions and eliminating many uncertainties. This means we have to create knowledge.

Knowledge Creation Methods

To create that knowledge, we deploy a variety of *knowledge creation methods*. Playtesting, brainstorming, discussion, debate, and daydreaming are all knowledge creation methods.

Think of each method as a card we can play. Different cards have different effects and consume different resources. For example, brainstorming uses multiple developers to quickly spawn many unproven ideas onto paper, while high-skill playtesting uses balance testers to slowly explore the nuances of an existing design.

Mastering design process means knowing which card to play, and when. The iteration loop shows us a good basic approach, but by itself it is not enough. In reality, there is no simple algorithm for knowledge creation. To do it well, we must react continuously to the shifting conditions of the project. To do that, we have to know all of our cards very well. So let's go through the deck.

RUMINATION

Rumination means thinking about a problem for an extended period of time. Chew on an idea for hours, days, or years, and it may eventually reveal its secrets.

The mind ruminates automatically when doing easy tasks like showering, walking, or driving. Sometimes rumination can even be involuntary. Everyone's been kept up at night by thoughts they just can't stop. Unpleasant as it is, even this rumination can be productive (many of the ideas in this book were born as paper notes scrawled at 2:00 a.m.).

Rumination also happens unconsciously. Our conscious mind might forget about a problem, but the unconscious does not. It keeps working long after we give up. If you've ever spontaneously realized the solution to a hard question a day after failing to solve it, you've reaped the harvest of unconscious rumination.

There's no way to predict when unconscious rumination will spit out its results. This is why some thinkers carry around notebooks in which they randomly jot down ideas. They want to capture the fruit of their unconscious rumination whenever it arrives.

One strategy for harnessing unconscious rumination is to alternate work on different problems. While working on one task, our unconscious ruminates on the other. This is why Edison, Darwin, Leonardo da Vinci, Michelangelo, and van Gogh all worked on multiple projects at the same time.

Good rumination requires two key ingredients.

The first is knowledge. Rumination works by forming new connections between old ideas. The bigger the store of old ideas available, the more possible connections there are. Game-related knowledge is obviously essential for game designers, which is why designers should play widely. But even knowledge apparently unrelated to the problem can feed rumination. Knowledge of economics, history, Nepalese culture, or fly-fishing techniques could all form part of a creative solution to a design problem.

Humans think by analogy, so our thoughts are enriched when we have more knowledge from which to analogize.

The second ingredient of rumination is relaxation. This is why new ideas tend to come to people in showers, apple orchards, and buses. Emotions like anger, fear, and focus inhibit creativity at a neurological level. MRI imaging has shown that just before a flash of insight strikes, blood rushes to a portion of the brain's right hemisphere called the anterior Superior Temporal Gyrus, or aSTG. Fear, anger, and intense focus on a problem actually inhibit blood flow to the aSTG, which in turn suppresses free association and creativity. This makes perfect sense if you're a caveman trying to escape from a lion. You wouldn't want to waste time having ideas about lion paintings just as one leaps for your throat. But it also means that focus is a creativity killer. So, if you want to ruminate, you must first chill out.

RESEARCH

Sometimes we do research to answer specific questions. A level designer might research medieval architecture for a game set during the Crusades. A systems designer working on a strategy game might play other strategy games to find out which mechanics worked, and how. This is the kind of research we were all taught to do in school.

The second kind of research is much less targeted. This is semirandom research where we learn without necessarily knowing how our learning will be applied to the project. The goal here isn't to answer questions. It's to expand our store of knowledge to feed rumination.

We all do semirandom research every day from television, film, games, the Internet, and our daily lives. We gather ideas, memes, and cultural touchstones from everywhere. But without any direction, we tend to gain the same knowledge as other game designers. Everybody on every game team I've worked on knew *Star Wars* and *Terminator 2*. This cultural homogeneity is part of the reason so many games tend to resemble one another so much. We're locked in a world of dragon-bashing heroes and gruff space marines because we only consume one another's ideas.

To escape the cultural echo chamber, a designer must cultivate unusual interests. A strategy game designer might play *The Sims* and get a new idea for an economic system. He might read a microbiology book and think of a new biological unit production system. This kind of semirandom research is a long-term investment. It's not even project-specific—it really just means living a rich intellectual life involving many unique ideas, sources, and experiences. It's something to cultivate for personal as much as professional reasons.

In game design, having a rich intellectual life pays off in the unique work that it allows us to create. For example, *BioShock*'s designers were only able to invent the unique world of Rapture because they had previously researched art deco and objectivism. Without massive random research, *BioShock* could never have existed.

ARTISTIC METHODS

Think back to the last time you drew pictures on paper. Maybe you were in high school art class, or doodling in a business meeting. In any case, you almost certainly had this experience: you draw a shape, then notice a certain part of it reminds you of something entirely different. While expanding on the new idea, you make a mistake. To cover it up, you invent a new object to go on top of it. That new object forces you to change the surrounding shapes. The process continues like this, with one change inspiring the next. By the time you're done, you've drawn something completely different from what you originally intended. You've used the process of creating art to create a new idea.

The power of art is that it keeps the hands working while simultaneously recording our ideas. By pulling us into flow, it reduces inhibitions. By putting paper in front of us, it lets us access and record thoughts that can't be rendered in words. By introducing mistakes and physical limitations, it forces us toward new ideas.

Different kinds of artistic processes access this power in different ways. Concept art can explore characterization or mood or a space. Storyboards eliminate ambiguity in framing, coloring, and sequencing of images. Previsualizations explore different ways of communicating an idea. When Pixar was working on *The Incredibles,* it created formless color swatches for every scene to understand the visual and emotional progression of the film by color alone. Some artists even create creatures or characters in sculpture.

Orson Scott Card, the author of *Ender's Game,* described his process for inventing fantasy universes. He gets a giant piece of blank paper and starts drawing a map. He lays down cities, landmarks, and terrain features, each with names. He doesn't plan it out; he invents the world while drawing. Naming and relating each of these things forces him to think about its history, the society that created it, and its reason for being there.

Every mistake and correction forces a new approach and idea. The resulting map is a detailed description of a new fantasy world.

This method extends to nonvisual arts. Sometimes, when seeking fiction ideas, I've used short stories to get my creative juices flowing. The stories are terrible, but the process of following the story of a character living in a fictional world always creates ideas for world story. Performance-oriented people might do an improv skit to explore a character. The audio-savvy might create a soundscape. The possibilities are endless.

BRAINSTORMING

Brainstorming is a semiformalized process intended to quickly produce large numbers of diverse ideas. Different people and organizations each have quirks to their process. Some are nearly unstructured, while others use designated leaders to control the flow of conversation and record ideas. Brainstorming's pretty well-known, so I won't go into it further here.

Brainstorming is good for generating ideas in volume. It is very bad for refining ideas, and the ideas it produces will vary widely in quality.

WRITTEN ANALYSIS

Written analysis is a form of structured thought. I've slagged game design documents a little bit in this book, but they do have value and they do have their place. In writing a document, we think differently than we do in the mind alone. A document can have diagrams, references, and well-laid-out logical chains of thought. Written analysis pushes us to think about details in a way that we won't when thinking on the spot or discussing ideas with colleagues.

A deep analysis of a complex design may take weeks to complete and involve broad research and the use of formal statistical or mathematical methods. It's sometimes worth the price because it creates knowledge that can't be acquired by guessing off the cuff.

DEBATE

Debate has a specific purpose: it finds flaws in ideas. It is a large part of formal decision-making systems like the courts, democracy, and science because it is good at finding hidden assumptions and logical fallacies. But debate isn't easy. Productive debate requires a very specific combination of skills and social conditions.

Both debaters must be skilled. They must know how to attack and defend arguments quickly and effectively. A bad debater will waste time attacking strong arguments, or miss logical fallacies committed by the opponent, making the entire exercise slower and less productive.

There must be diversity of thought among debaters. This means that participants have different knowledge, opinions, experiences, and assumptions. This allows them to find weaknesses in others' ideas that they could not find in their own. Sadly, diversity of thought is rare in organizations because people tend to hire others who think like themselves. It takes specific effort to foster it.

Both debaters must be respectful. They must be able to separate their personal feelings from the logical process of debate. Otherwise, the process can destroy their relationship and become counterproductive.

Finally, the debaters must not fear one another. Debate is easily corrupted by power imbalances. The person with less power will not debate honestly for fear of retribution. This is why debate is best conducted among people who have no power over one another at all. For a boss to debate his subordinates, he must first prove his evenhandedness. Some bosses don't do this. They punish people for disagreeing, even if they do it involuntarily by sighing angrily or rolling their eyes. This makes people go soft on the boss's bad ideas, which makes the debate less useful.

TESTING

We've looked at playtesting already. It's the most important kind of testing in games, but not the only one. There are a variety of kinds of testing which each return a different kind of knowledge.

Usability testing is a method borrowed from software design which focuses on interfaces and controls. It's similar to playtesting in that it involves putting a realistic user in front of the interface to see how he tries to use it.

QA testing is done by dedicated testers and is focused on finding technical bugs. It's essential in any video game production process.

The term *focus testing* is often mistakenly used as a synonym for *playtesting*. This is incorrect. Focus testing is a form of market research in which participants discuss various product ideas in a group. It doesn't require a working game.

METRICS

In game design, the term *metrics* refers to data that is automatically collected from play sessions. The game might record objects looted, challenges failed, completion times, enemies defeated, areas explored, or a hundred other events. Metrics can be gathered from hundreds of internal testers or millions of players in a public beta. The computers can then process all these numbers into statistical reports and graphs that designers can use to make design decisions.

Metrics help designers see patterns and imbalances too small to notice in playtests. For example, in a fighting game, metrics will show that one character wins over another 55% of the time because it can sample thousands of matches. Playtesting can't reveal this kind of data with any accuracy because the sample size is too small. This is why metrics are invaluable in fine-tuning. Without the ability to see small gains, only large swings in results are visible, and progress becomes halting and erratic. By revealing even small changes in difficulty or pacing, metrics allow us to hill-climb our way to glory in tiny, measured steps.

Ken Birdwell writes about his experience using metrics to fine-tune *Half-Life*:

> Toward the middle of the project, once the major elements were in place and the game could be played most of the way through, it became mostly a matter of fine-tuning. To do this, we added basic instrumentation to the game, automatically recording the player's position, health, weapons, time, and any major activities such as saving the game, dying, being hurt, solving a puzzle, fighting a monster, and so on. We then took the results from a number of sessions and graphed them together to find any areas where there were problems. These included areas where the player spent too long without any encounters (boring), too long with too much health (too easy), too long with too little health (too hard), all of which gave us a good idea as to where they were likely to die and which positions would be best for adding goodies.

When *Half-Life* was developed in 1998, other studios depended on guesswork and self-testing for this kind of balancing. These methods are useful early in the design process, but they don't reveal the kind of fine-grained data needed for perfect difficulty balancing. Metrics brought Valve's designers a massive advantage in the quality of their design decisions. And they didn't have to be any smarter than anyone else to make a better game, because they were working in the light while everyone else labored in darkness.

In addition to fine-tuning, metrics also let designers find rare edge-case situations. Your 20 internal playtesters might not find that degenerate strategy, but if one of the million players in the public beta does, it will show up as a spike in the data.

Sometimes we can use cleverly designed metrics to gather data that seems impossible to get. For example, during the development of *Halo: Reach*, Bungie's designers wanted to learn more about the effect Internet lag has on the experience. The game was already instrumented to record a movie file including every game variable at all times, including lag. But this wasn't enough—the designers wanted to know how players *perceived* the lag, which isn't easy to see in the data. Playtesting couldn't solve this, since many lag problems are so rare that it would require massive amounts of time for designers to watch enough playtests to catch them. Worse, realistic net testing requires players to be physically spread out, which makes traditional playtest protocols nearly impossible to follow.

They solved the problem by adding a special button that reports, "I just saw lag." These button presses were recorded along with the rest of the game. Once the data started coming in, the designers could watch the movies and skip to the points where players perceived lag to see exactly what was on their screen. This ingenious method brought them a huge amount of reliable knowledge about lag perception with relatively little developer effort. They solved many subtle lag perception issues this way, and *Halo: Reach* had great online play. They had great net code, but it wasn't because they were network-coding whiz kids. Like Valve, they worked with more knowledge.

INVENTED METHODS

Some questions can't be answered by established methods. In these cases, we must go back to first principles and invent a new way to get the knowledge we need.

When making a game for the elderly, a designer might have to invent a special playtest protocol. A game with an unusual in-game economy might require new ways of analyzing and interpreting data. A design team spread across continents might have to debate and brainstorm differently from one that collocates. Inventing and refining our knowledge creation tools is an integral part of game design.

The Organic Process

Let's look at a classic example of a process of knowledge creation. This example isn't from game design. It's from invention.

As the 20th century dawned, more than one team was attempting to invent heavier-than-air flying machines.

Some acted more from bravado than ability. They strapped fins or wings to their bodies, and many died test-piloting their mad inventions off bridges or hills.

Others were more serious. These noble European inventors and famous American scientists seemed to have every advantage. One of the wealthiest was Samuel Langley, Smithsonian Institution's secretary, who used his connections to secure $70,000 in U.S. government funding.

But Langley's devices never worked, nor did those of his wealthy colleagues. Powered human flight was achieved instead by Orville and Wilbur Wright, two bicycle repairmen from Ohio. They spent less than $1,000.

How? How did two men with no particular connections beat the biggest government projects in the world on less than 2% of the budget?

They did it by mastering knowledge creation. The Wrights didn't just draw their design on paper, build it, and fly. They deployed a dizzying array of knowledge-creation methods over a period of years. They conducted hundreds of tests, many of which required them to invent new testing methods and apparatuses. They designed and built gliders, airfoils, and control surfaces, each crafted to answer a specific question. They used mathematical calculation, field testing, lab testing, rumination, argumentation and debate, research and study. At every point, they chose the best method to solve the next unknown, to get past the next hurdle. Every glider flight, redesign, and recalculation taught them a little bit more about how to fly.

They were relentless. The brothers ran 1,000 test flights on their 1902 glider, modifying it over and over, learning new things every time. Individual flights taught little, but as the data added up, the Wrights began to master the sky.

The knowledge gained was as diverse in its nature as in its source. While testing airfoils in a wind tunnel, they learned that the traditional equation for lift was wrong. While field-testing a glider, they learned that a front-mounted horizontal stabilizer lets a craft soft-land like a pancake instead of nose-diving. And they had eureka moments born of unconscious rumination: while working on the unsolved problem of how to control the roll of a winged aircraft, Wilbur idly twisted a long box in their workshop, and realized that this could be a way of changing a wing's shape to control the roll of the airplane. This observation led to wing-warping controls, in which the pilot's controls work by twisting the wings.

At the same time, Langley and others were also deploying their resources, but in the wrong ways. Most of them focused on building more powerful engines. Engine design was a well-established field at the time, so money could easily be invested in making better engines. The Wrights, however, understood that the missing piece wasn't engine power. It was accurate control. While much was known about engines, almost nothing was known of aerodynamics, and there was no aerodynamics industry. Someone who wished to purchase better aerodynamic control systems would have nobody to pay; there was literally nobody ready to do the research. So the Wrights did it themselves, using their own knowledge creation methods.

And the Wrights became masters at test design and construction. They built the world's most accurate wind tunnel and used it to test 200 different wing shapes. When trial and error with full-size gliders proved costly, they built a bicycle-like apparatus to which they could attach aerodynamic parts. Riding the bike would push a piece of wing through the air and allow measurement of their properties, achieving the same result as the glider at much lower expense. They weren't just inventing the airplane; they were inventing all the tools they needed to invent the airplane.

The brothers faced many setbacks. Gliders failed to lift, failed to turn, turned the wrong way, or plowed into the ground. Values for a coefficient of lift and wing shape test data from earlier researchers turned out to be wrong and had to be rederived. The propeller designs they hoped to borrow from shipbuilders didn't work, so they had to invent their own. No engine maker had a light enough power source, so they built one in their shop. Components broke often, delaying tests and requiring expensive replacements. Through all of this, they had no guarantee that the airplane would ever work. But they persisted.

There was no single day on which the airplane was complete. The flier's performance improved in tiny increments over many iterations. In 1899 they flew a five-foot-wide kite. In 1900 they were pulling a glider big enough to carry a man. The 1902 glider introduced new rudders and control systems that allowed a pilot to make controlled left-right turns. In 1903, they added an engine and flew under power and control, but only for a few seconds a few feet off the ground. The Wrights kept working, improving the weakest aspects of the design, learning from failures and extending successes. By 1905 Wilbur was doing 40-minute flights over distances of 20 miles. They had been working for six years.

A game designer's task has much in common with that of the Wrights. Like an airplane, a game is a system. It serves a different purpose, but the process of inventing it is fundamentally the same. Game designers are inventors of machines for generating experiences.

The Wrights' process sounds a lot like iteration. But it's clear that the three-part iterative loop is a criminal oversimplification of what they did. The Wrights tested often, but not on any fixed schedule. Their process was organic, with many different actions interacting and overlapping. Their approach changed every day in response to their needs. The same applies to game designers. Some days we must plan. Other days we must ruminate, calculate, draw, or invent a new knowledge-creation method. Invention isn't a repeatable assembly-line process. It is an ever-changing intellectual frontier.

So the diagram of iteration I showed you earlier is wrong. Real game design is more organic, like this:

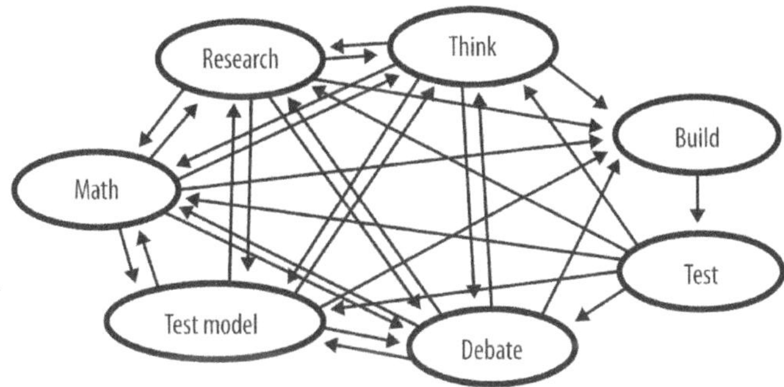

And the process becomes a thousand times more complex when teams grow beyond a handful of people. Knowledge creation is maddeningly fluid and fine-grained. It bubbles up in every developer, every second of every day. Every thought a designer has creates knowledge. Every time an artist leans back and squints at a scene to get a different view of it, he creates knowledge. Each time a programmer runs the game for five seconds to check the feel of an interface widget, he creates knowledge. An iteration loop can't direct this, and nobody could lay it out on a schedule. It's unfathomable.

That's why, as designers, we must remember that we can only direct the broad strokes of the process we're running. The reality is always more organic and complex than our conception of it.

Dependencies

After the wildlife reserve was created, the newly trained park rangers quickly decided to make some changes. There weren't enough elk, they thought, so they began a program of feeding the elk.

The elk population exploded. The huge elk herds soon began killing the aspen and willow trees. This caused the beavers to vanish, since they no longer had enough wood to make their dams. Without beaver dams to hold the water in place, the park began to dry up every summer. This denied the fish the bodies of water they needed to breed, so it wasn't long before the lakes were nearly empty of fish. With the fish gone, the grizzly bear population fell, since the grizzlies depended on fish pulled from the rivers to survive. Without grizzlies competing for their food sources, and with so many elk to prey on, the wolf population exploded. The deer population soon collapsed because there were so many wolves and because the elk were overgrazing their grasslands.

And the changes went on, rippling through the ecosystem...

A GAME DESIGN MIGHT have hundreds of mechanics, fictional elements, and subsystems. Even during the minutes after conceiving of a game idea, a designer can have 20 different ideas for challenges, systems, and interfaces to add to it. With all these ideas, how do we know what to work on first? Do we start with the most unique piece? The most basic? The easiest? The most technologically advanced? The riskiest?

They key to answering this question is in understanding *dependencies*.

A DEPENDENCY is a relationship between two parts of the design such that changes in one part would force changes in the other.

Imagine someone asks you to paint 10 houses. There are no dependencies in this task. It doesn't matter in which order you paint the houses because the way you paint one won't affect how you will paint the others.

Game design isn't like this. Different parts of a design are often interdependent. The artistic look of a level depends on the layout of that level. The layout depends on the player's tools. The player's tools depend on the basic interface. If any element changes, so must every element that depends on it.

Understanding dependencies help us reduce the risk of finished work having to change because of changes in something it depended on. For example, imagine we spent the time to fully animate a character that runs at 5 km per hour in every direction. If we later decide that he must move at 7 km per hour, all those animations must be redone. The animation art depended on the design of the movement system for the character; a change in the movement system rippled into the animation content and destroyed good work. Had we understood our dependencies better, we might have solidified the movement mechanics (in graybox) first and done the animations later.

The Dependency Stack

To understand the dependencies in a design, designers can draw a *dependency stack*.

A DEPENDENCY STACK is a simple analysis method that identifies key dependencies among design elements. It helps us know what to work on now and what to leave for later.

To build a dependency stack, we start with a game design. The design may be a paper plan at the start of development, or it may be partway implemented and tested. We break the game apart into individual elements—mechanics, controls, interfaces, and subsystems. Then we identify key dependencies among these elements. Finally, we draw out a graph illustrating all the dependency relationships. This is the dependency stack.

Let's look at an example. Pretend we're making *Fantasy Castle*, a lighthearted construction game about building a castle in a fantasy world. *Fantasy Castle* just started development, so the design team is long on ideas but short on tested, proven designs. They've written out a long design document. Each of the 22 subsystems has a fleshed-out paper design. Here are summaries of them, in no particular order:

- **Characters** Characters can exist and move around in an environment.
- **Families** Characters can have family relationships.
- **Races** The castle can be filled with an extended family of humans, elves, dwarves, and other fantasy races.
- **Interbreeding** Different species can interbreed to create hybrids with the shared characteristics of their parents.
- **Goblin raids** Periodic goblin raids will test the castle's defenses.
- **Farming** A farming and food system feeds the population.
- **Trading** They can trade with neighboring castles for special or rare goods.
- **Education** Characters can become educated.
- **Invention** Educated characters can invent new machines for the castle.
- **Religion** Characters can build religious temples and worship at them, develop relationships with specific deities, and receive characteristic benefits from these deities.
- **Deity wrath** Other deities will get angry and bring wrath upon you if you disrespect them or worship their adversaries.
- **Friends** Characters can have platonic relationships.
- **Romance** Characters can have romantic relationships, possibly starting families.
- **Construction** Characters can build things.
- **Walls** Characters can build walls to stop or channel foes.
- **Fortification** Walls can be fortified and thickened to help hold back goblins.
- **Traps** Characters can install traps or automated defenses.
- **Fighting** Characters who know how to fight can do so to defend the castle.
- **Raiding parties** You can end out raiding parties to explore nearby dungeons and bring back loot.
- **Adventurers** You can serve passing adventurers by providing inns and shopkeepers in exchange for loot stolen from ancient crypts.

- **Seasons** A full seasonal cycle affects farming, construction, and other activities.
- **Soap opera** Infidelity and other romantic dramas play out among the castle's inhabitants.

A game could include all of these elements, but how do we choose which ones to focus on first? Do we start with fundamentals of the world and build the *seasons*? Do we begin with the *characters, friends*, and *families*? Or perhaps we should start with warfare, building a *fighting* system for battles between castle inhabitants and *goblin raids*? Do we start with the game's unique elements, like *adventurers*, or build a base using the elements that have been done before in other games, like *walls* and *fighting*? The dependency stack helps us decide.

This is my dependency stack for *Fantasy Castle*:

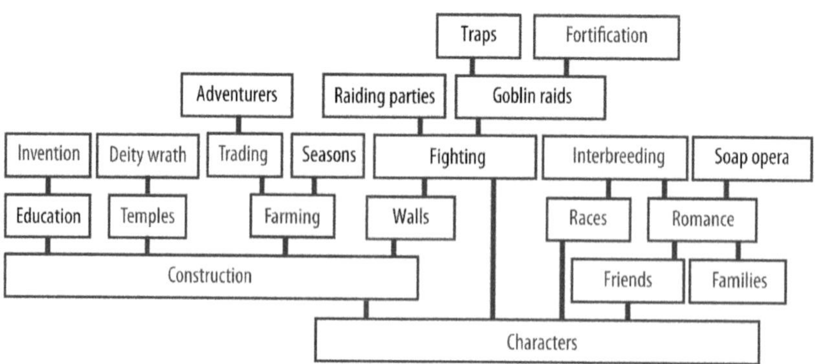

There's little point in *traps* and *fortification* systems without functioning *goblin raids. Goblin raids* don't work without *fighting. Fighting* doesn't mean much without *walls* and can't work without *characters. Walls* require a *construction* system, which requires *characters* to do the work. Each element of the design depends on the elements below it.

Before we go on, let me clarify the concept of dependency.

DEPENDENCY doesn't mean that the foundational element must fail to affect the dependent element. It only means that changes in the foundational element's design would force changes in the dependent element.

Remember that the boxes in the stack aren't just the words you see—each one represents a detailed design of several pages. The details of these designs interlock. For example, the *construction* design describes each button, highlight, and option of the interface players use to construct things. Similarly, the *farming* design describes in detail how farms are placed, managed, and removed. But the *farming* design assumes the *construction* design is true and correct. What happens if the details in the *construction* interface change—if the buttons are rearranged, or changed to a mouse gesture interface? *Construction* is still in the game, but it has changed, and now all the details of *farming* must be redesigned to match. This is why *farming* is dependent on *construction*.

There are many more dependencies of this type than are written in the stack. For example, I've placed *walls* above *construction*. But it's possible that during development, the designers may discover that they need to change the *construction* interface to make placing *walls* easier. So *walls* depends on *construction*, and *construction* depends on *walls*—a circular dependency. And these threads of dependency are all over *Fantasy Castle*. *Walls* may have to be changed to be easier to place around *farms*. The *invention* system may be affected by *friendships*, if friends can put one another in inventive or uninventive moods. In a sense, everything can affect everything else, so everything depends on everything else.

But some of these dependencies are stronger than others. Significant changes in *walls* might, in some cases, affect *construction*. But changes in *construction* will almost certainly affect *walls*. The dependency stack deliberately ignores the weakest dependencies so that we can focus on the most important and potentially dangerous ones. Finding this focus is the stack's purpose.

The dependency stack is reductive. It leaves out important parts of the reality of development. But when you're just a human, faced with a problem as complex as a hundred interdependent design elements sharing a hundred thousand relationships, intelligent reduction is the only way to make progress. We have to ignore some dependencies or we'd sink into analysis paralysis. The dependency stack isn't an academic exercise; it's a tool for making decisions. And those decisions are best guided by focusing on the strongest dependencies.

Depending on the details of the design, there may be more than one way to construct a dependency stack. One could imagine a castle building game in which there is *construction*, but no *characters*. Or one in which there are *goblin raids* without *walls*. I've constructed this stack based on imagined details of *Fantasy Castle* that I don't have space to write here. If the design documents were written differently, the stack would look different, even if all the titles were the same.

CASCADING UNCERTAINTY

We've already seen how designs don't tend to work how we think they will. The designers can write a document stating how *goblin raids* will work, but they can't be certain it will work as expected until they build it and playtest it.

This uncertainty is why we need to pay attention to dependencies. If we assumed no uncertainty, it wouldn't matter in what order we did the work. We would have our ideas, write them down, build them in any order, and on the last day of development the design would click together perfectly, like a jigsaw puzzle. And in cases of very derivative designs based on proven ideas, this can almost work, because every element of the design is so certain.

But in games with some originality, written designs often don't translate to reality. There is some probability that an element of the design will need to change during development. And it's this uncertainty that makes dependencies important.

Uncertainty multiplies through dependencies.

For example, the *goblin raids* system is described in a two-page summary somewhere in the design bible. It covers how and when the goblins are spawned, the tactics they use, the capabilities they have, and strategies for defeating them.

Like every plan, this design has some uncertainty level associated with it. This uncertainty level reflects the likelihood that the design will not work as expected. Let's assume it's a very unoriginal design, so the certainty is 80%. The designers estimate that eight out of 10 times in this situation, this system will work as written without major changes. That's pretty solid.

But does that mean that, from the start of the design process, we can be 80% sure that *goblin raids* will end up in the game as written?

Unfortunately not; that 80% figure only covers the uncertainty of the *goblin raids* design itself. But *goblin raids* is not only vulnerable to changes caused by failures in its own design. It's also vulnerable to changes caused by failures in designs it depends on.

To implement *goblin raids* as planned, we first have to implement *characters, construction, wall constructions,* and *fighting* systems. If any one of these systems shifts significantly, changes will cascade upward through the dependency stack and force changes in *goblin raids*. Even if each of those foundational elements has an extremely favorable 80% certainty tag, the chance of *goblin raids* working as expected is only 0.8 multiplied with itself five times, or 0.33 (33%), because a failure in any one of the five foundational elements will force *goblin raids* to change.

And most designs don't have nearly an 80% certainty rate. In design work on risky, potentially breakthrough games, most designs fail. Per-system certainty is often less than 30%. In these conditions, a design five layers up the dependency stack will only survive unchanged 0.2% of the time. So, basically, never.

Cascading uncertainty means that the upper elements of a dependency stack almost always need major redesign.

This means that most of the written design of *Fantasy Castle* is baloney. The foundational systems will almost certainly change when implemented or tested, and those changes will cascade through the design, forcing changes everywhere. The concepts may remain, but all the specifics will change again and again. By the end of development, most of the upper part of the stack will have been cut or redesigned several times.

It seems a simple bit of math, but there's a powerful truth here. Every working designer has seen how much games—especially original ones—transform over the course of development. But it's often hard to articulate exactly why this happens. Simple uncertainty about the individual pieces of a design isn't enough to explain it. The real problem is the way that every change creates shockwaves of further changes that ripple through the design via dependencies. This is the real culprit behind the massive to-and-fro chaos of so many design processes. It's a key reason why we have to iterate.

But not just any iteration will do. We have to iterate in a specific way, as informed by the dependencies we've identified using the stack. The general strategy is simple.

Start at the bottom of the dependency stack, and work upward through each iteration loop.

We start at the bottom, with the pieces of the design that depend on nothing. After that foundation has been iterated and playtested a few times, it becomes more certain. On paper it might have been 40% certain, but once we've redesigned it through a few playtests, it might reach 90% certainty. Next, we can build the elements that depend on that foundation and have confidence that they won't get torn apart by later changes cascading up from below. And we just work our way up the stack this way, building upward. Unexpected design results will still appear and shake the whole structure, but we reduce their frequency and impact by doing our work in the right order.

For example, in *Fantasy Castle* we might start developing the game with nothing but basic *characters, construction*, and *walls*. At first, it's just a game about people building walls. Once those have been iterated a few times and work well, we might add *farming*. Once that's been iterated a few times, we put in *trading* and *seasons*. We work our way up, building a tower of dependencies from foundations upward. And the design is likely to change partway through—we may feel after playtesting *farming* that *seasons* are unnecessary, but a new *crop diseases* element would add more interest. So the top of the stack re-forms as the bottom solidifies.

THE DESIGN BACKLOG

Just because designs at the top of the stack are very uncertain doesn't mean they're worthless. We have thoughts, ideas, and observations all the time, and that inspiration should be recorded because it is valuable. But writing them in an interlocking, detailed design requires a lot of work that is likely to be invalidated by cascading uncertainty.

The solution is to retain the ideas in a liquid, noninterlocking form, by recording them in a *design backlog*.

The DESIGN BACKLOG is an unordered, liquid reservoir of ideas, concepts, and impressions that aren't being worked on and won't be worked on soon. Most ideas should go in the design backlog.

The design backlog is named after a similar concept from the popular Scrum software development methodology, the *product backlog*. However, unlike Scrum, it isn't intended to be part of a formalized development process. It's an informal tool for retaining inspiration.

So just because most of the *Fantasy Castle* design is baloney due to cascading uncertainty doesn't mean it's worthless. Rather, it should just be reorganized. Most of it should be regarded as no more than hypothetical ideas for the future. These elements shouldn't be interconnected into a fixed plan because such an arrangement implies a certainty that we don't have. Instead, they should be liquefied and placed in an unordered pool, to be drawn from in the future. Only the pieces of the design that are going to be worked on soon should be linked together and incorporated into the official plan.

Rearranged this way, *Fantasy Castle* looks something like this:

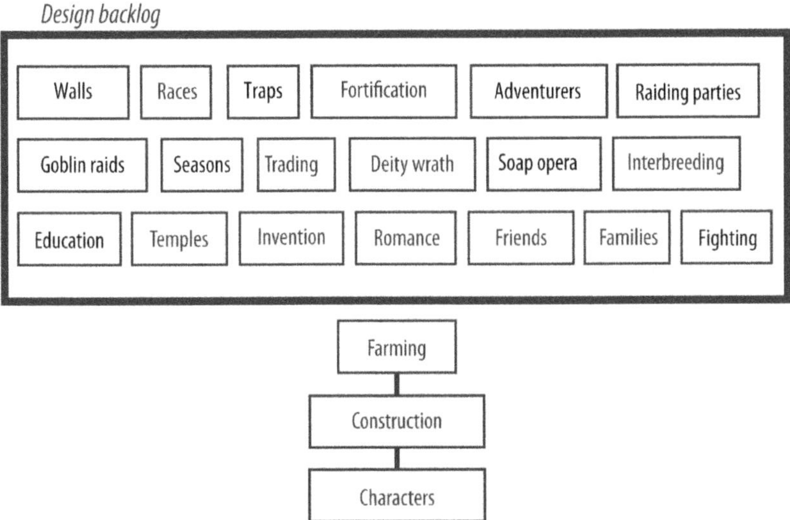

My choice here was a judgment call. I committed to the community-building elements of the design first, and moved everything else into the design backlog. Another designer might have focused on combat or religion. But whatever the choice, the point is that we're acknowledging that we have to start somewhere and iterate there before we build upward from that foundation. Otherwise, we're building on a foundation of sand.

Anything higher on the stack than those three base elements would be exposed to excessive cascading uncertainty and so wouldn't be worth implementing. At the paper design stage, that would likely push certainty below 50%. But as we implement, study, research, and test those three elements, their certainty will increase. The *farming* system, for example, will go from a design on paper with, say, 60% certainty, to a functional, playtested design with 90% certainty or better. It may change during iteration of it or its foundation, but that's not a problem since nothing depends on it yet.

Only after this foundation is solid and certain do we need to add something else to the stack. Now is the time to open the design backlog, choose something that looks right, and add it to the design, on the top of the stack. We'll be well equipped for this choice because we will know with certainty what we're basing it on.

After that, it's just a matter of repeating the process through more iteration loops. Every time the design solidifies, we rummage through the backlog, pull out another piece, and place it on top. Every time we have a new idea, we write it into the backlog and forget about it until later. Most of the backlog will never be implemented. That's fine—it means that the parts we do use are probably very good. And the design grows upward, one solidified piece at a time.

CORE GAMEPLAY

Of the 22 elements in the *Fantasy Castle* design, I chose to put all but three in the design backlog. But notice that we could still make an emotionally meaningful game with only *characters, construction*, and *farming*. Those three pieces by themselves would form a very minimal but playable game, because these three subsystems form *Fantasy Castle*'s *core gameplay*.

CORE GAMEPLAY is what emerges from the irreducible mechanics of a game at the bottom of its dependency stack. Remove everything that can be removed without making a game emotionally worthless, and what's left is core gameplay.

Try this exercise. Think of a game that you know well. Now cut something from its design. Now cut something else, and something else, and so on. Keep cutting until the game no longer creates a meaningful experience at all—until it just becomes a trivial and uninteresting piece of software. Reverse your last cut. What you've got is the game's core gameplay—the minimum set of mechanics that make the game work.

If you chose a modern video game, you could probably cut 95% of the game or more, including almost all the content, most interfaces, and most controls. If you chose a classic game or a board game, you could probably cut much less. It's hard to see how one could reduce checkers and have it remain functional. But even chess can be sliced down—remove everything but pawns and the game still works.

Some examples of core gameplay are:

- ***Civilization V*** Map, cities, settlers, warriors
- ***Unreal Tournament*** Map, players with first-person controls, a gun
- ***StarCraft II*** Map, command center, workers, Marines

Each of these complex games has at its core a simple interaction loop that creates worthwhile experiences all by itself. Even with just workers and Marines, *StarCraft II* generates interesting decisions and strategies to explore. One of the most popular ways to play *Unreal Tournament* was InstaGib mode, which removed all but one very simple instant-kill weapon. The core is the game, good or bad. Everything else is just variation and polish.

In many cases, core gameplay defines a genre. For example:

- **Tower defense** Map, a thing to defend, towers, approaching enemies
- **Dungeon crawler** Character, dungeon, hero, monsters, leveling up
- **Fighting game** Movement, punch, block, throw

Core gameplay is the proper foundation of the dependency stack, because everything else in the design depends on those basic mechanics. By identifying the core, we find the shortest path to having a testable platform for iteration. Completing the core as early as possible gets the game to a testable state as early as possible. It's only then that the benefits of test-driven iteration begin. So, as a designer, identify the core and build that first. And once that core is built, draw something from the design backlog, put it on the design, and iterate outward.

If you can't find the core, or you build it and it's terrible, consider restarting with something different. A game should have a very good reason for having no strong core. And sometimes there are good reasons for this. For example, point-and-click adventure games have no real core gameplay. Pointing and clicking aren't a working game by themselves. These games are exceptions; they work because their experience is driven by content, not mechanics.

Some games have multiple possible cores. Consider the open-world RPG *Fallout 3*. One core of *Fallout 3* could be *player character, guns, monsters*. Another could be *player character, dialogue, quests*. A third might be *player character, open world, world art*. The three cores make the game a simplistic pure shooter, a walk-and-talk dialogue story game, and a world-sized art gallery, respectively. But each one is still a functional game. The designers could have started their process with any of them and then built outward into the others.

SMALL-SCALE DEPENDENCY STACKS

So far we've used the dependency stack to analyze an entire game at once. But the dependency stack can also be used to analyze the design of individual systems. If you use it, you'll probably use it this way most of the time, since always analyzing the entire design at once can be unwieldy.

For example, consider a development of a character named Capp in a squad battle game. Capp is intended to move quickly, fall easily, and attack with acrobatic Capoeira fighting moves. As designed, these are Capp's abilities and systems:

- **Speed** Capp runs especially fast, with special physics-driven banking.
- **Spin-kick** Capp does a spinning capoeira kick that hits everyone nearby.
- **Falls down** Capp has a special vulnerability that throws him to the ground if he is damaged while attacking.
- **Wall jump** Capp jumps and bounces off walls to get to special areas, or pass over adversaries.
- **Handspring kick** Capp does a handspring kick that strikes while transitioning him into a *wall jump*.
- **Sweep dodge** To compensate for his *falls down* vulnerability, Capp has a low sweep attack that both avoids enemy attacks and strikes back in one move.

Just as most good games can be reduced to core gameplay while still working, most good game systems can be reduced while still fulfilling their role. A feature-specific dependency stack helps us do this. Here's how I've interpreted Capp's design:

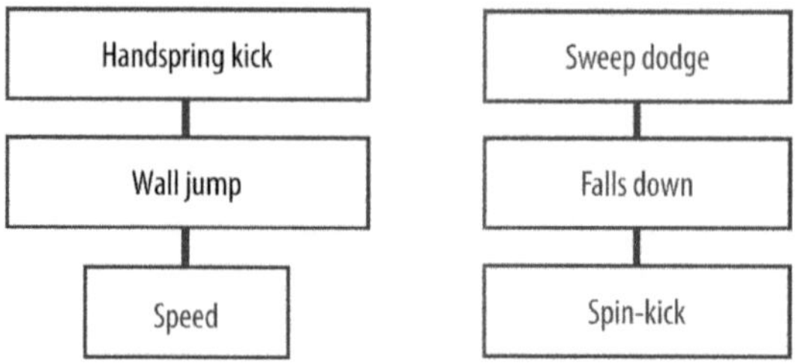

Falls down only makes sense if there is an attack to be doing when you get hit—in this case, *spin-kick*. The *sweep dodge* is an ability meant to compensate for the *falls down* weakness, so there's no point in doing it before *falls down*. Finally, *wall jump* is an extension of basic *speed*, and *handspring kick* is a special attacking version of the *wall jump*.

As always, given different design details, this stack could be different. *Speed* and *wall jump*, for example, could easily exchange places. This stack reflects my imagined paper design.

Every part of the design has some uncertainty tag:

- **Spin-kick** This has just a little uncertainty, because it is derivative of attacks we've seen in other games. The main uncertainty is in the tuning of its radius and timing. If it turns out that the spin-kick works better when it lasts a half second instead of the three seconds the designers anticipated, changes might ripple upward into other abilities.
- **Falls down** This is very uncertain. Designer's intuition says that being stunned might just be too frustrating, meaning we would have to replace this entirely.
- **Speed** There are technology-driven uncertainties here. Nonstandard, physics-driven locomotion is always difficult to implement well. AI might have trouble anticipating it or navigating with it, and players might have trouble controlling it. It might need redesign or removal.
- **Wall jump** This has similar risks as *speed*, with added problems for AI navigating along pathways that are usually inaccessible. The control system for wall jumping will also likely need a few redesigns.
- **Handspring kick** This is not so uncertain in itself, but *handspring kick* is vulnerable to a lot of cascading uncertainty from lower-level systems.
- **Sweep dodge** This is straightforward on its own, but it's vulnerable to cascading uncertainty from below.

We shouldn't just plow ahead with that entire design as though it's guaranteed to work. It probably won't. As with *Fantasy Castle*, we should find the core and liquefy everything else into the design backlog.

Capp's core gameplay is probably *spin-kick, speed*. Together, these two allow him to fulfill his unique speed demon role, which is useful and distinct from other characters. It looks like this:

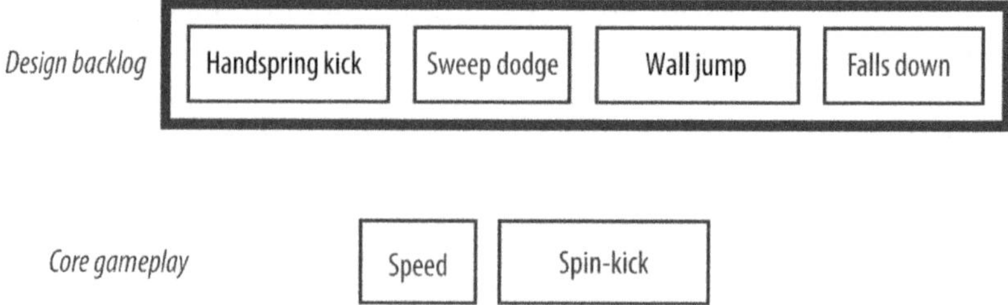

Once the core is iterated a few times, it will be certain enough to build on. Only then should we draw something from the backlog, because there's a good chance that speed and spin-kick will change before that happens, or we'll have a better idea to build on top of them.

DEPENDENCIES AND EXTERNAL DESIGN NEEDS

There's a caveat to the dependency stack. Marketing and businesspeople might need design decisions long before the game does.

In these cases, designers should negotiate to find some middle ground with the person who needs the design decision. If the decision is high in the stack and very detailed, the business or marketing benefit of providing these extremely early decisions might not outweigh the cost of making them so early. For example, it's probably not worth advertising Capp's *sweep dodge* move until it's been iterated, because it's so likely that *sweep dodge* will be twisted by cascading design changes.

Marketing and business are important. But at the same time, we shouldn't lock a game design into a prison of unchangeable design decisions. Stay fluid, don't assume the future, and pay attention to dependency-driven risk. It takes daily effort, and not everybody will understand at first. It can feel wasteful, even irresponsible. But in the end, it's the only way to do a task as hard as game design with small human minds.

14

Authority

Foreman John was tired of workers screwing up every little thing. So he bought the Puppetron—the newest wave in management technology. No longer would he have to give orders and hope to see them carried out properly. Now, he could put the Puppetron helmet on his head and control the workers' every action directly using his mind. He became like a puppeteer pulling a thousand strings, personally coordinating every action of every worker. It was miraculous.

Foreman John and his crew took a job building a bridge. Halfway through construction, the bridge collapsed and killed everyone.

Investigators discovered that the bridge was riddled with hundreds of botched weld jobs, twisted cables, misaligned spars, and missing bolts. It was as though none of the work had been done with the worker's full attention.

Making great games takes commitment. We have to explore culture and fiction, solve hard intellectual puzzles, and take scary risks. We have to push every advantage and deploy every resource. We have to care about what we're doing beyond the paycheck. We have to invest our hearts in the work.

But investing heart is a delicate process. It requires a special combination of work practices, culture, intrinsic motivation, and organizational structure. People must have the right authority in the right places, knowledge must flow smoothly to where it's needed, and we must trust one another. This chapter is about creating these conditions so that a team can run at its full creative capacity.

The Banality of Evil

The personality of an organization is not just the average of the personalities of its members. It matters how those members are structured. Structure determines how knowledge, power, and resources flow within the team. If they're made to flow the wrong way, a group of individual geniuses can collectively act like raging fools.

The most extreme examples of this are the historical genocides of the 20th century. The deadly bureaucracies of Nazi Germany, Soviet Russia, and Khmer Cambodia were staffed mostly with perfectly normal individuals who would probably be fine dinner guests in another time and place. But in a certain organization, with a certain culture, arranged in a certain hierarchy, they became cogs in a machine of death. The political theorist Hannah Arendt called this the "banality of evil." She understood that bureaucratic horrors are committed not by cackling madmen, but by legions of paper-pushers dutifully following their local incentives.

Obviously nobody dies in game development. I use these examples to show that there is no limit to how much a poorly structured organization can taint its own output, even if the people in it are good. Having good people is necessary, but they will all go completely to waste in a bad structure and a dysfunctional culture. We must get that structure right. The question, then, is how to structure good people to do good work at game development.

Taylorism

> The science which underlies each workman's act is so great and amounts to so much that the workman who is best suited to actually doing the work is incapable, either through lack of education or through insufficient mental capacity, of understanding this science.
>
> —F.W. Taylor

In the late 19th century, most workers decided their own individual working practices. A bricklayer, metal cutter, or pig-iron handler would be assigned a task by the manager, and he would complete it on his own time using the methods he had learned from his years of experience and apprenticeship.

Around 1900 a man named Frederick Taylor began studying work, and saw massive waste in the traditional methods. So he set about creating the management style that would later be known as Taylorism.

Taylor would watch a bricklayer work and use a stopwatch to determine exactly how much time each motion of his body took. He recorded the time to reach out and grab hold of a brick, to lift it to the correct spot, to pat it down, to lay cement on top of it, and to scrape off the excess. Numbers in hand, he went to the blackboard to work out the best way to lay bricks. He rearranged and removed motions to find the most efficient sequence. He cut the wasteful step many bricklayers took between their brick pile and the wall. He redesigned the tools, creating a special sled for holding the bricks at just the right position so that they could be taken quickly. Then he instructed the workers in exactly what motions to carry out until they moved like assembly-line robots. This process of "scientific management" became his stock in trade, and he applied it to fields ranging from metal cutting to pig iron handling.

Taylor didn't bother trying to make the workers understand what they were doing. To him, they were bumbling idiots, and their comprehension was unnecessary. "The workman who is best suited to actually doing the work," he wrote, "is incapable of fully understanding this science, without the guidance and help of those who are working with him or over him, either through lack of education or through insufficient mental capacity."

Taylorism is about concentrating every decision into the hands of a small group of very smart people. One thinking "mind" at the top directs the actions of many dumb "hands." By concentrating knowledge in the one best mind, Taylorism increases the quality of decisions because that mind is the best motivated, most skilled, and most capable, and can intelligently coordinate the actions of the dumb people hauling the pig iron.

Taylor's ideas became the foundation of the modern study of efficiency because they work. Over the past century, methods grown from it have provided us with better and cheaper cars, potato chips, and computers. This method of concentrating decisions within the minds of a smart few and squeezing waste out of repeated processes is so successful that it is now an assumed part of industrial culture.

But Taylorism is limited in the kinds of task it can handle. The key is the amount of knowledge a job involves. If a job involves little knowledge, Taylorism works well. A factory foreman can know everything about what each of his subordinates is doing because factory work is simple and repetitive. He can make all of the subordinates' decisions for them because there are not that many decisions being made. Every piece of knowledge in the process can be held in his head.

But what happens when the work is complex and nonrepetitive? What if there is more knowledge than one mind can handle? Now the central mind becomes overwhelmed by data. It starts ignoring details, oversimplifying, or missing important signals. Decisions become worse, and waste begins to appear.

Game development is one of those tasks where Taylorism fails, because game development involves truly massive amounts of knowledge. Imagine trying to catalog every piece of knowledge in a team development process. Each time an artist lays a brushstroke, judges, and clicks the Undo button, he creates a tiny chunk of knowledge that says that *this* idea didn't look good for *this* reason. Every 10-second self-test by a designer, every algorithmic variation invented by a programmer, every offhand conversation with colleagues or idea that pops up in the shower is potentially useful knowledge. And the volume of it grows minute by minute, second by second. No one mind or small group of controlling brains can possibly absorb and make use of all that.

And the sheer volume of knowledge isn't the only problem. Much of the knowledge in the process is difficult or impossible to communicate. This is called *tacit knowledge*. For example, skills are tacit knowledge. A trained artist can look at a flawed composition and *just know* how to fix it. A programmer can *just know* how to optimize an algorithm, and a designer can *just know* how to make an interface feel better. But none of them can explain it, because these intuitions rise from their trained unconscious minds. This knowledge can't be transferred to the leader. It is skill and took years to learn.

So Taylorism, which is our trusty default method, fails in game development. But there is a solution.

THE DISTRIBUTED MIND

To understand how to make games, we shouldn't learn from factory foremen from 1912. We should learn from ants.

Consider how ants collect food. First, a few forager ants wander randomly away from the nest. When a foraging ant finds a food source, it returns while laying a pheromone trail behind itself. Other ants then instinctively follow that trail outward to find the food source. Each one that finds the food drags its own pheromone line back, reinforcing the trail. If the trail leads to a rich food source, it is reinforced over and over, straightened and strengthened each time. As the trail gets stronger, other processes begin. Stronger worker castes of ants show up and remove obstacles on the trail. Soldiers start to patrol it, watching for threats. Some worker ants sacrifice themselves, stretching their bodies across gaps in the trail to make bridges. Together, the ants create, optimize, and defend paths to the best food sources in an extremely efficient manner. And all of this magnificent complexity happens without a central plan, by the combined behavior of stupid ants following simple, local rules. None of the ants understands the overall strategy of what is the group is doing, but all of them still somehow coordinate their actions into an integrated approach to solving the problem. It's as though the ant colony forms a collective, distributed mind of far greater power than any of its individual participants. An ant is stupid; an ant colony is smart.

Game development must work the same way because no one person can possibly understand everything happening in a development process. There is just too much happening for one human mind to contain it. So, like ants, we must instead each only play our role in the larger distributed mind, and let the greater collective intelligence emerge from our individual actions driven by local circumstances.

We can't do this with the Taylorist approach. We cannot take decisions away from the workers and put them in the hands of a few controlling brains. For distributed intelligence to work, we must spread authority over the team.

DISTRIBUTED AUTHORITY

Ants don't have bosses who tell them which way to turn on a pheromone trail. They each make their own decisions based on local conditions. This has two main advantages.

First, it uses all the brainpower of every ant. In Taylorism, the brainpower of the workers is left fallow because every decision is taken away from them. Not using such a valuable resource is a mistake—especially in game design. The entire point of working with a development team is to harness their minds, not their bodies.

Second, distributing authority makes full use of the local knowledge possessed by each ant. Every ant knows its immediate surroundings very well since it's so close by. If the queen had to tell each worker what to do all the time, she'd make poor decisions because she can only be in one place at once. She would never understand what was happening around worker #1314 the way #1314 herself would. The same applies in game design. Every developer is close to part of the work in a way that nobody else is. Every developer understands things about the level, technology, or mechanic he works on that nobody else does.

Game developers can do the same thing as ants by distributing decisions around the team. Each developer makes the choices about the work he is closest to. The programmer of a system should make internal decisions about the design of that system. The designer of a level should decide the detailed layout of the level. Each person has a sphere of *natural authority* that envelops the parts of the project that he understands best.

A developer's NATURAL AUTHORITY extends over any decision that he is better equipped to make than anyone else on the team.

This doesn't mean everyone just does his own thing. Game development is always very communication-intensive because decisions often require knowledge from many different people. For example, there's no way an artist can decide the look of a character without knowing the narrative purpose of that character. There's no way a writer can write good dialogue for a combat sequence if he has no idea how it's changed since the last playtest. To collect that knowledge together, we have to communicate.

Meetings, for example, are a way of collecting knowledge together for the purposes of making decisions. Consider the case of a meeting comprising a creative director, a programmer, a designer, and an artist as they decide which of two potential graybox designs to move forward with. They meet because each has unique knowledge relevant to the decision.

The designer has run five playtests on each graybox, so he knows where the level has balance and clarity problems. He's also been working on the level awhile, so he has a reservoir of ideas and failed experiments to draw from.

The programmer knows what size and complexity of level can work in the game engine, and various other technical limits of the system.

The artist knows best how the level fits between the previous and following levels in terms of artistic progression of the game and what art assets are available.

The creative director knows the overall structure of the game and where the level fits in, its emotional goals, its market positioning strategy, and its deeper themes, and the needs of its investors.

None of these people can make the decision alone. They meet to share their knowledge and apply it to decisions together. And this meeting is well-organized because all the people with the necessary knowledge are present, and no more. Taking any of them away would starve the decision of knowledge. Adding someone else would be pointless.

Bad decisions happen when knowledge isn't applied. For example, a level designer might decide to graybox a level that is too big for the computer to run. A programmer could have told him that before he started. But since they never talked, his decision of how to size the level suffered, and work will have to be redone. The human instinct here is to blame the level designer—but that's usually wrong. Blame the organizational structure for not getting him the necessary knowledge.

Even with great communication, though, much of the relevant knowledge is still tacit or too voluminous to be communicated. This is why it's still usually best if the person with the natural authority makes the final decision—the level designer on his level, the writer on dialogue, the director on overall structure.

ARROGATION AND TRUST

ARROGATION is claiming a decision that falls under someone else's natural authority.

The word *arrogant* comes from the French *s'arroger*, which means, "to take privileges which are not yours." People arrogate decisions when they take them away from the person with natural authority over them.

Arrogation often takes the form of *micromanagement*. Micromanagement is when leaders issue commands pertaining to low-level, specific knowledge which the subordinate understands better than they do. It usually makes for bad decisions because it discards the subordinate's special knowledge of the work.

For example, a leader might sit through an hour-long review of an evolving game system and demand a list of changes which seem, to the people in the trenches, extremely foolish. This act is lovingly known as a "swoop and poop," and it can be very destructive. But leaders don't do this because they are stupid. They do it because they don't have the hundred hours of iterating and testing on the level that the people in the trenches do. They don't know all the ins and outs of every test, every experiment, every discussion that's been had. The leader may have a great deal of experience, but general experience is rarely enough to overcome the knowledge advantage of people who have spent much more time on the work at hand.

This is a common problem because it springs from deep-seated cognitive biases. Game designs are full of hidden possibilities. One level or system might play out hundreds or thousands of different ways, so watching a game in a review isn't enough to understand a game—but it feels like it is because of the brain's deep-seated WYSIATI (what you see is all there is) assumption. The leader doesn't know how much he doesn't know, because he has never seen the things he doesn't know. Since he can't perceive his own lack of knowledge, he thinks that his understanding is complete. So he arrogates the decisions because he thinks he can make them better, and the subordinates walk away fuming.

The root cause of arrogation is leaders not trusting their subordinates. They know they're more experienced than those following them, and they don't want to give others the chance to screw up important decisions. So they take those decisions away. But it doesn't work because the leader can't know everything in the process. Ultimately the decision ends up worse.

To work together on a game, we must trust one another. This isn't a pro-teamwork rallying cry or a motivational slogan. It's a cold statement of fact, and I use the word *must* in the most literal sense. Trust is nonoptional. We can't possibly cover one another's mistakes because we can't possibly understand one another's work. So a game design leader directing a group of fools is doomed. There is no way for him to defend himself from their idiocy because there are too many decisions happening all over the studio for him to possibly understand and influence them all. Any effort he makes to defend himself from people he thinks are dumber than he is will only hobble the team. The only option is to get people you can trust, and then trust them.

COMMUNICATING INTENT

We want to distribute decisions—but this doesn't mean we can just toss a team into a room with pizza and computers and come back two years later expecting a game. Even with distributed authority, leaders still play a necessary role.

Leaders know a game's macro structure. They know the game's emotional goals, market strategy, business strategy, narrative theme, mood, design style, design foci, and overall mechanical structure better than anyone. These topics are where leaders have natural authority, and where they make decisions.

For these decisions to have effect, the leaders must still be able to direct subordinates. The key is that they should be directing them toward goals to be fulfilled, not precise actions to be taken. They shouldn't be telling people to make a character's boots a different color. They should be communicating the *intent* behind why the boots should look different, and letting the artist at work decide how to express that intent.

Leaders can't tell subordinates to do every little thing. Instead, they must communicate the higher-level INTENT of the work.

The intent is the purpose of the work. What goals is the appearance of this character supposed to serve? What is the purpose of this level? What's the role of that piece of technology in the overall design? What does the leader understand about this that the subordinate doesn't?

Intent is a concept I'm borrowing from military leadership. The captain doesn't tell the sergeant exactly where to send every soldier during his assault up a hill. He worries only about which hill should be taken and when. The sergeant doesn't worry about the details of other hills besides his own. He just worries about how to direct his soldiers to take the one hill he was told to take. And, in turn, each soldier decides independently where to point his weapon and how to move his body to get where the sergeant directs him.

By communicating intent, a leader uses his unique knowledge of the design's broader structures to equip the subordinate with information he wouldn't otherwise have. At the same time, by sticking to generalities and not arrogating low-level decisions, the leader doesn't discard the subordinate's mastery of details. The leader can't be there when inevitable problems and opportunities appear. He doesn't have the mental bandwidth to understand what's happening in detail everywhere in the design. But as long as the subordinate understands the intent, he can handle problems and seize opportunities in a way that best serves the broader purpose of his work. The subordinate might do something very different from what the leader assumes will happen, but as long as the intent is fulfilled, the game gets better.

For example, while directing a level in a horror game, an arrogant Taylorist leader might say, "The player wakes up in a bathtub full of bloody water. There's a message scratched into the mirror that reads, 'You'll never escape.' The player explores the house and finds his girlfriend's dead body. Soon after, he meets the machete enemy, and since he has no weapons, he'll have to flee the house with the enemy in pursuit." That's a list of tasks to do. And if all those orders worked as expected, there might not be a problem. But what happens when playtesters refuse to flee from the machete man, or they laugh at the cheesy message in the mirror? The subordinates can't solve these problems on their own because they don't really understand what they're doing, and they have no authority to make changes. So they have to go back to the leader. The leader will probably give them a bad solution to the problem because he lacks intimate knowledge of the level and he wasn't actually at the failed playtest. The subordinates' specific knowledge is discarded, and the process flails.

Instead, the leader should be communicating intent: "This level should teach the player all the basic controls except weapons, which should be left until the next level. It should introduce the dead girlfriend backstory so that we can play on it later. It should also introduce Machete Man. Since the next level starts outside the abandoned house, this one should end coming out the front door of the house. It's the first level, so you can start the player wherever you like. Finally, don't characterize the protagonist, because I want him to remain a mystery at this stage." Now the people in the trenches can go to work. They might start with the same design as the leader originally suggested. But during iteration, they'll likely find a better way to achieve the same goals. Playtests and brainstorming will reveal layers and layers of new problems and solutions that the leader could never have discovered alone. Being freed of a bullet-point list of things to do, the developers can seize opportunities and solve problems as they arise. The design will change, but since they understand its role in the larger structure, they can make sure it fits in well and properly sets up the following level. And the leader is freed of the burden of details.

To explain his intent, a leader must first know what it is. This means understanding the structure of the game and the purpose of every developer's work. Since this requires some difficult mental gymnastics, bad leaders often revert into micromanaging nitpicking mode. They give vague intent and then criticize the details of whatever their subordinates come back with. This kind of "judgment from on high" adds little to a game. The leader is the only one with the power to perfect the game's broad structure. He should be thinking about, analyzing, and iterating on that every day. If he's doing that job well, he won't have time to nitpick the lower-level work of others. If a leader must judge others' work to maintain quality standards, he should limit his comments to generalized statements of deficiencies and offers of help, not specific marching orders on what to do.

Once it's known, intent must be communicated clearly. Unfortunately, the phrase, "That isn't what I wanted," is heard far too often in game development. What happened was the worker didn't understand the intent, so he couldn't fulfill it. Communicating intent without micromanaging is a skill that requires attention and practice. It takes effort to understand and express the purpose behind a request instead of just telling people exactly what to do.

Subordinates must communicate SUMMARIES of newly gained knowledge upward to leaders.

Leaders iterate, too. They don't iterate on single levels or mechanics, but they do iterate on level progressions, plot structures, or market positioning. And just like everyone else, in order to iterate they need to know the results of their decisions. They don't need the details of exact moment-by-moment pacing or individual gameplay decisions. Rather, they need condensed summaries of high-level lessons that should feed back into the broader structure of the game. If one key game system just isn't working, they need to know. If playtesters are getting attached to a minor character in one level, they need to know, because these kinds of results can motivate changes in the broad structure of the game.

In a team with clear, condensed intent going downward and summaries going upward, everybody knows everything he needs to know and no more, and decisions are made by the people with the most relevant knowledge and thus the natural authority over them. The leader doesn't have to be everywhere and solve every problem, but development is still purposeful and structured. Everyone iterates on his piece—the leader on broad strokes, the workers on the details within those strokes. With everybody's knowledge being applied so efficiently, you don't need genius developers to make an outstanding game.

Motivation

Such a rush! The summit of life!
But it's not found with loving folk
It's on a peak that's much less rife
An empty room; the last brushstroke

A game designer's motivation must be both strong and carefully directed. Strong, because we need a powerful drive to overcome the great challenges of game development. Carefully directed, because it's easy for that drive to go in the wrong direction and accidentally encourage us to do things that don't help the game, or even harm it. This chapter is about motivation—where it comes from, how to grow it, and how to direct it, in ourselves and in others.

Extrinsic Rewards

It seems intuitive to say that the way to make people work better is to reward them better. Developers who work better should get more money, stock options, a parking space, health coverage, a bigger office, or a hundred other goodies. This is akin to a factory owner paying workers a dollar for each ton of pig iron they haul onto a rail car. These kinds of incentives are called *extrinsic rewards.*

EXTRINSIC REWARDS are rewards that are separate from the work itself, usually in exchange for some measurable performance on the job.

Extrinsic rewards are common in businesses ranging from finance to government to industry. But they are doomed to fail in game design. There are four key reasons for this.

First, extrinsic rewards fail in games because the work is so hard to judge from the outside. To give someone a money carrot for doing something well, we have to know when this person has done a good job and when he's done a poor job. In pig iron handling, this is easy to see—all we have to do is count the metal ingots on the train. But in games, it's very hard to see the quality of effort someone is putting out. Different developers' contributions are mixed together in complex ways, and game development is so uncertain that even good work can lead to disaster after a stroke of bad luck. Good risk-taking designers may even look worse than risk-averse slackers, as some of their attempts inevitably fail. So there's no way to reward performance, because there's no good way to measure performance.

The second reason extrinsic rewards don't work on game developers is because they displace our intrinsic love of the work. Good developers need money, but for many of them this isn't even half of their reason for working on games. The majority of their motivation is much more human. They want to create something great, to present it to the world, and perhaps be recognized for it. They want to make progress in hard problems. They want respect, authorship, and autonomy. In day-to-day work, they might not think of any higher goal than not letting down their fellows. The money is just there to keep the family fed. Making pay conditional on some measure of output can easily destroy the intrinsic motivation to do the work for its own sake. It makes people forget they're working for love and start believing they're working for money. This is similar to how in-game rewards can displace the intrinsic enjoyment of play. It's why high-priced lawyers won't offer services to needy retirees for $30 an hour, but they will offer them for free, and strangers will help you unload a sofa from a truck for free, but never for one dollar. Paul McCartney was right—you can't buy me love.

The negative effects of extrinsic rewards are most powerful in creative tasks. Harvard Business School professor Teresa Amabile ran a years-long study of creativity in real workplaces. She collected 12,000 daily journal entries from 238 creative workers in seven different companies and searched for correlations between emotions, events, and creative output. Most workers most days reported that extrinsic rewards hadn't motivated them at all, and the people who were most interested in money weren't very effective at being creative. Overwhelmingly, respondents felt most driven by challenge, community, a feeling of comradeship with coworkers, and a sense of ownership—all of which are obscured by monetary rewards.

The third problem with extrinsic rewards is that they often create perverse incentives that harm the project. When everyone is focused on maximizing his own personal rewards, game development becomes a political game. Politics and gossip lead to destructive competition among developers. Fear of punishment makes people hide work and avoid risk. Developers might form cliques and deny information to outsiders to stay safe or to gain respect. This pattern is borne out in research. Amabile found that competition hinders creativity by suppressing the movement of ideas and preventing people from helping one another. Dan Ariely found that participants in a scrambled-sentence test are much less likely to help others when unscrambling words about money. Priming the mind with dollar signs makes us risk-averse and selfish—the worst behaviors for group creativity.

The last reason extrinsic incentives harm game development is because they're distracting. They pull people's minds away from the work, filling up their valuable headspace with calculations of how to maximize rewards instead of how to help the game. Every moment thinking about how to game the extrinsic rewards system, even in innocuous ways, is a moment that wasn't devoted to solving development problems.

Even worse is when the extrinsic incentive is a threatened punishment. A boss can threaten to fire someone, cut his pay, yell at him, or even disrespect him with subtle eye rolls and guffaws. These threats might create immediate activity, but activity alone isn't enough to make a great game. Game design demands open discussion and deep thought, both of which impossible under threat. Remember how fear and anger were shown to inhibit the aSTG—the brain's center of creativity? As Frank Herbert wrote in *Dune*, fear is the mind killer—when we're afraid, we're neurologically unable to work at our creative best. That's why Amabile found that people were most likely to make a breakthrough when they were happy the day before. Happy work lets the mind relax into a powerful after-hours rumination process. Fear driven by extrinsic threats may motivate, but it also destroys our ability to do the work by consuming our ability to think.

All of these effects can hit at once. For example, consider a system I once heard of where developers got online shopping vouchers when they presented something cool in the team's show-and-tell meetings. This system is an almost unmitigated evil. People start feeling like they're working for vouchers instead of for the work, so they lose interest in what they're making. The people who happen to have visually appealing work that makes for good presentations are resented by those doing under-the-hood technical tasks that never get shown off. People spend their time perfecting their show-and-tell presentation instead of doing work that actually helps the game. They have to spend time thinking about these stupid vouchers and whether they might get one. And ultimately, they will grow to hate the system that treats them like a dog jumping for a treat.

MEANINGFUL WORK

So how do we motivate designers? We can't pay game designers per mechanic or per idea—this leads to a proliferation of worthless mechanics or ideas. Punishing failed ideas, prototypes, or tests just suppresses risk taking, which destroys innovation. Rewarding hours worked leads to lots of bodies in chairs, but deceptively little real productivity. Rewarding individuals for anything at all creates jealousy and team rivalries. Rewarding groups divides a team into slackers and unofficial slave drivers. It seems that no matter where we turn, every option creates some horrible perverse incentive.

Yet games get made, and some are very good. Though the motivation problem is structurally very hard, one special fact about developers makes it tractable.

Developers want to do meaningful work.

More than anything, creative people want to apply themselves to do work that makes a meaningful difference in the world. Developers will push themselves to find the best way to improve the game. Nobody else needs to even understand what he is doing in detail, because this motivation is entirely internal. If the developer knows he has done well, he will feel good. If not, he won't.

But it's not always easy to offer this kind of meaningful work, especially in larger organizations. There's a delicate recipe to creating meaningful work. The task must make a difference, but there are other aspects of meaningful work that are important. Ideally, it should offer a creative outlet, a balanced challenge, pride, recognition, ownership, belonging, responsibility, and freedom. The challenge of team organization is in creating an environment that consistently provides work with these qualities. John Lasseter of Pixar put it this way:

> Creative people are easily bored, moody, a bit difficult to handle. You have to make it fun for them, care for them. Creative people only produce really good work if you creatively challenge them. They have to like what they're working on. They have to be damn proud of the fact that they're a part of a particular project. That is again the task of the manager. Each time, you have to give them creative challenges. That's difficult, but nobody said it is easy to lead creative people.

Satisfying a creative developer does not require a money carrot. It requires a delicate mix of responsibility, credit, challenge, and a belief in the project. And, as Lasseter notes, the better people are, the harder they are to motivate. Uninterested, mediocre developers don't feel dissatisfied working on uninteresting tasks because disinterest is their default state. They're like pig iron handlers; they work purely for the cash. Great designers, on the other hand, live on top of an uncontrollable mental wellspring of ideas and ambitions. They must express these impulses or they grow unhappy. This aspect of their nature is both the source of their ability and the reason they are "easily bored, moody, a bit difficult to handle."

The holy grail of game development incentives is SELF-IDENTIFIED COMMITMENT.

Self-identified commitment is when the developer believes that the work is not just something he is doing, but something he is. A designer motivated to this level will ruminate on the project in the shower, in the car, and while sleeping. He'll spend every spare moment pushing concepts around in his mind, looking for opportunities and solutions. He'll do it so much that people around him will get annoyed at his absentmindedness. He will scribble down notes on cocktail napkins at random times or take to carrying a notebook. He will seek out research that helps solve the problem, come into work at random times, or get up in the middle of the night to jot down an idea that came to him in a dream. The work is no longer just a job. It is his pride and purpose.

Self-identified commitment is a force of nature. It's how upstart teams beat giant corporations, and how the Wright brothers out-innovated the rich Samuel Langley. Most organizations never see it because they strangle it in the crib with money carrots or Dilbertesque work environments. Nurture it, and it can make magic.

Climate

CLIMATE is the day-to-day emotions that people feel about work.

In productive climates, people feel energized and safe. They're secure enough to take risks and ask questions, and their brains are focused on the work. In bad climates, they're angry and afraid. Fear neurologically neuters their ability to be creative, and they spend all their energy dodging blame.

Climate grows from people's expectations of how they'll be treated. If they take a risk and it fails, do they expect to be blamed or consoled? If they question a leader, do they expect a thoughtful response or a verbal slap? If developers feel danger all around them, they will work in fear, and far below their capacity. If they feel opportunity and support everywhere, they'll push advantages and take risks.

Consider a developer with an exciting but risky idea. He is trying to decide whether to bring it up or forget about it. He wants to make the game good, but he is also concerned with his own social status and emotional well-being. So he thinks through the choice and instinctively comes up with a mental ledger of pros and cons. In a good creative climate, the ledger looks like this:

Pro	Con
▶ If idea is successful, I will be credited with its success and the game will benefit. ▶ I'll get to express myself. ▶ I'll learn more about my idea from others' intelligent responses, and thus more about how I think and how my ideas relate to others. ▶ I'll have some fun talking about a new idea with my designer friends.	▶ I'll spend at least a minute describing and talking about the idea, and it might go nowhere.

Obviously the designer will bring up the idea. This is the best outcome for the game and the studio. The idea might fail, but the decision to bring it up was a good one. And there's a chance that this idea could transform the game into a hit.

Now look at the ledger in a studio full of blame spreading, fear, and arrogation of authority:

Pro	Con
▶ If the idea is successful, I might be credited with its success (if someone doesn't steal it and if people don't forget where it came from).	▶ I'll spend at least a minute describing and talking about the idea, and it might go nowhere. ▶ I might be misunderstood or shot down before I can express my idea. This would be worse than staying silent. ▶ I may get torn apart if there's a hole in my idea I haven't thought of. This won't feel good or be good for my social position. ▶ If my idea is good and gets implemented, it might get trampled by a swoop-and-poop next time someone with power develops an interest in the subject.

In this climate, the idea stays buried. And as this pattern repeats itself thousands of times, the game fails to thrive because nobody is taking any risks. A year or two later, everyone wonders why the game is so bland, so unoriginal, so safe. Reviewers yawn at it, and it dies whimpering in the marketplace.

Usually, nobody knows what happened because bad climate is a silent killer. It doesn't cause development disasters. Rather, it causes good things *not* to occur. It makes people not bring up risky ideas and not hold necessary debates. And even though nobody notices these things not happening, their nonoccurrence harms the game every day.

Climate is one of the most powerful determinants of the quality of a game because it suffuses everything. It changes how people relate, how they think, and how they act, everywhere, every second of every day.

FEAR AND LOVE

There is a strain of leader that uses anger to motivate. These leaders like to use some combination of screaming, subtle insults, and disappointed sighs to push people. The idea is that the threat of emotional pain will keep people from getting lazy.

In other jobs, this can work well. I once watched a hidden-camera documentary about how celebrity chef Gordon Ramsay ran his kitchen in his earlier days. He inspected everything. The slightest error in a dish or a mistake in cooking would bring down his wrath. He screamed at cooks and waiters for the tiniest mistakes. He fired an employee every week. And it worked well—Ramsay received the highest honors of the chef trade at a young age. But consider the nature of the work. Ramsay's method was all about maintaining standards. His restaurant was great not because of the creativity of the team, but because of their ability to perfectly execute well-defined cooking and serving procedures. Ramsay's inspections worked because mistakes in cooking are clearly visible to a trained chef. There is no value in a kitchen staff being creative or taking risks during dinner service.

But game development is totally different from cooking. Design requires risk taking, failure, and creativity at all levels of development. Anger and fear destroy people's willingness to take risks, and their ability to be creative. Self-identified commitment becomes impossible when you're always being forced to dance while someone shoots at your feet.

Anger is seductive because it looks effective in the short term. The leader yells and sees a lazy developer scurry. What he does not perceive is the shifting risk ledgers of the 30 people watching that exchange. He does not perceive the risky but interesting idea that a subordinate will now be too afraid to bring up a day later.

The great puppeteer Jim Henson would never shout at subordinates or try to make them feel bad. Jim would say, "You're trying to get to the moon. You should be aiming for Jupiter. If you aim for Jupiter, you'll definitely get to the moon." He led by inspiration, collaboration, and appreciation. He focused on making the other person look smart, not himself. At the height of his power, when he had millions of dollars and owned houses on several continents, he remained kind and approachable. People worked for him out of love. They took risks for him because they didn't have to be afraid. They gave him their all because they didn't have to spend energy avoiding pain. Their self-identified commitment clicked, and Jim's team stayed at the top of their field for decades.

Jim didn't focus on immediate rewards. He didn't succumb to some personal need for power over others. He understood that his job is to set up others to succeed, not to use them as tools—that his team was much more important than he was.

Reaping the bounty of love requires patience. Fear is easy, quick, and obvious, but in the end it is a feeble fuel for creativity. Love is slow, indirect, and quiet, but once grown and nurtured, it is extraordinarily powerful. Only love can unlock the self-identified commitment that allows every developer to draw creative power from the core of his being.

That's why in the front room of his studio, Henson placed a giant sign with an old G.K. Chesterton quotation: "Artistic temperament is a disease that affects amateurs."

Social Motivation

We've seen how extrinsic rewards tend to harm game development motivation, and how it's the only internal drive to do meaningful work that can make us do our best work. However, there are sometimes still places for specific, targeted motivational pushes to encourage specific actions. The key here is not to use economic rewards or punishment, but instead to use subtler social signals. Let's look at some social motivations that drive game developers in specific ways.

PLAYTESTS-DRIVEN MOTIVATION

Playtests motivate well by creating natural, unlimited, trustworthy consequences to our development decisions.

We naturally want to see playtesters like our work. We love it when they ask to play again. On the other hand, it feels awful to watch a playtester slog through long periods of boredom, get shredded by difficulty spikes, or hit game-breaking bugs. The pleasure of playtest success and the pain of playtest failure are powerful motivators.

This may sound like a sort of carrot-and-stick arrangement. But there are differences between this and incentives handed out by a boss.

First, playtest results are unmediated, natural consequences. They're not a system of rewards set up by one person to manipulate another. They're real results from real life. This means they don't feel controlling the way artificial carrots and sticks do.

Second, when motivated by playtests, we don't have to limit ourselves to a boss's expectations or understanding. In pursuit of a positive judgment from a superior, one's achievement is limited to her understanding. You can't do better than an A+. You can't get a question more correct than the person judging you understands. But when you're working on reality instead of someone's judgment, there is no limit to performance, so you can unlock your entire creative potential. A playtester can always like the game even more than she already does.

Finally, playtesters are trustworthy. They don't reward us for having the same opinion or assumptions as the boss. They reward us for doing objectively good work. So developers don't doubt or rebel against the responses of playtesters the way they doubt or rebel against the manipulative opinions of a leader.

EXPECTATIONS-DRIVEN MOTIVATION

Treating people like they'll do good work drives them to do good work.

If everyone treats you like a fool, you might just start acting the part, or even believing it yourself. If everyone looks on you with admiration, you'll start digging into your ideas, speaking with confidence, and plumbing the depths of your ability to think harder and better, because you want to live up to that image.

This effect appears everywhere. For example, researchers have found that women perform worse on a hard math exam than men, unless you tell them that women and men are known to perform equally. Their expectations of themselves change their beliefs of what they can do, which changes what they do. Another study found that if teachers were told that a certain set of children were possible child geniuses, those students performed better than others, even when they were randomly selected. The teacher treated them like they were smart, so they acted smart.

Some try to do the opposite. They treat others poorly to try to get them to work better. The implicit belief behind this is that they'll push back and try to prove everyone wrong by being awesome. But this doesn't work. There's nothing more demotivating than being treated like an incompetent. It creates anger, which destroys creative capacity. Worse, it creates a feeling of helplessness. If you're treated like a fool after doing good work, why should you keep investing emotional energy into it?

That's why the best game teams tend to foster a sense of eliteness. They develop a camaraderie around some symbol or idea that separates them from others. They might just be average developers, but that belief in the specialness of the group pushes them to do more than average. This is why Walt Disney didn't just have theme park designers—he had Imagineers. It's why armies constantly emphasize the unique history of each unit. A sense of eliteness creates a precedent to live up to and an identity to inhabit. Developers who are treated as nothing special, in a gray, cubical, typical organization, have no reason to excel. Set those people apart from the world, let them create a unique identity, and they'll live up to it.

CHICKEN MOTIVATORS

Nonserious, nonexplicit, occasional social rewards and punishments can send a message without destroying creative climate.

For example, consider how to solve the problem of broken builds. In video game development, a one-line code bug, a badly configured piece of content, or a malformed script can "break the build" if submitted to the central database by making the game unplayable. This imposes a great cost on the team, since it interferes with everyone's work until the build is fixed.

There's not enough natural motivation to avoid broken builds. The costs of a broken build are mostly borne by the team, not the person who broke it. This creates a systematic motivational bias in favor of breaking the build more often than would be optimal. So how do we stop people from breaking the build?

Build breakers could face monetary penalties, but this would lead to anger and wasteful paranoia as people made too sure that their work was safe. Verbally confronting the build breaker doesn't work either—it could easily damage relationships and degrade the climate. It's better to use a rubber chicken.

The chicken motivator works like this: if you break the build, you have to fix your mistake, and you get a rubber chicken on your desk as a symbol of your (minor) shame. The chicken remains until someone else breaks the build. There is no discussion and no direct confrontation. You just return to your desk to find a chicken resting quietly on the keyboard, mocking you with its beady rubber eyes.

The person who has the chicken (as I have, many times) becomes the butt of friendly jokes, but isn't seriously despised. Everyone wants to avoid the chicken, but nobody gets angry or depressed if he receives it. It doesn't make people paranoid about breaking the build, but they're not thoughtless about it either. The chicken is ridiculous—but also a perfectly balanced, nonconfrontational motivational tool.

Napoleon once noted, "A soldier will fight long and hard for a bit of colored ribbon." The chicken is one variation on symbolic social motivational tools. Different ones can be used for other purposes. Bet someone a drink that he can't think of a way to solve a design problem (either way, you end up having drinks together). Comb the game files for cool new stuff and put it on monitors in the office for everyone to see. There are a hundred little actions we can take and systems we can set up to create and send social signals in nonobvious, nonofficious ways that still have powerful positive effects.

The Progress Principle

After Teresa Amabile did her study of 12,000 journal entries written by hundreds of creative workers, she combed through the data looking for patterns in what motivated their creative capacity. You can already guess it wasn't money or fear. But she found something surprising: it wasn't for social approval or making a good product either. Instead, Amabile found that motivation mostly comes from making daily progress in the work. She called this the *progress principle.*

The PROGRESS PRINCIPLE is the observation that the strongest contributor of good inner work life is regular, visible day-to-day progress.

Amabile found that the size of the progress isn't as important as its frequency. Motivation is best sustained by small wins—solving an algorithm, finishing an animation, or watching a playtester understand some detail he didn't the day before. Even if the game as a whole is still awful (and they always are early in development), these small wins create daily engagement.

Applying the progress principle means organizing the process so that everyone gets regular, visible small wins. All the basics of good process help with this: iteration shows constant progress from its frequent playtests, and allowing people their natural authority facilitates progress since people can enjoy their own wins instead of having them handed out by a boss. But we can also go beyond these basics by arranging and tracking work specifically to make progress frequent and visible. Even something as simple as listing tasks on a wall and crossing them off in red makes a visual indicator of progress. Every crossed-off task gives everyone a tiny emotional boost. If the tasks are small enough that two or three can go red every day, the team will feel a sense of continuous momentum.

This is similar to designing reward feedback for game players. We might ensure the player levels up every hour in a very visible way, because we know that such regular progress is compelling. The same psychology applies to the game developers themselves. The tiniest of wins can keep us going, if they're frequent and visible.

It helps to arrange work so that people can get direct feedback on their own progress without outside help. A designer might make progress on a system, but if that progress is only ever appreciated by a different person in a review or a playtest, the designer never gets to see it firsthand and so doesn't feel it. The designer should be able to see his own playtests, just as a programmer should be able to watch his code pass automated tests, and an artist should be able to decide on his own when a character finally fits in the world. This way, they create their own progress.

The progress principle applies even more to small projects than to large ones. On a large team, the momentum of the group can keep an individual going from day to day. But in a team of one or two, we need another source of motivational fuel. This is why detailed to-do lists are so beneficial for tiny teams. It's not just about keeping tasks organized. Every completed task creates a little mood boost.

In this way, small-team development is not unlike book writing. Over years of work alone with my word processor, I've learned to live and die by page counts. I don't sit down for another four hours of rewriting because I want to release a book years in the future. That's too far away to be emotionally relevant to my primate brain. But when I see the page count go up at the end of the night, I feel a moment of joy.

16

Complex Decisions

The ancient wise man left his mountaintop monastery and traveled to New York. There he made use of his enlightened wisdom. He soon became an alcoholic short-order cook and died alone.

Decision Effects

When we make design decisions, we often have to think beyond the effects of our decision on the game itself. For example, changing a protagonist's sex or ethnicity may benefit the game's story, but eliminate a marketing opportunity. Rejecting a bad design idea from another developer may reduce workload in the short term, but degrade studio climate and make it harder to retain developers. A feature might be cheap to implement, but costly to maintain over the long term. Another might be cheap all around, but create a risk of critical failure in the design later on. To make good decisions, we often have to consider these complex effects on processes, people, businesses, and markets. Let's look at some of these effects.

DESIGN EFFECTS are the effects of a decision on the game itself.

Design effects are everything about how the decision affects players. Most of the book has been about evaluating and predicting design effects.

IMPLEMENTATION COSTS are the resources required to execute a decision.

It takes time to write code, make animations, record dialog, and handle the countless other tasks that make a design work.

This category also includes the cost to fix everyday software bugs, tune systems within foreseen parameters, and other easy-to-predict tasks of this type. Since implementation costs are so straightforward, they are almost always planned for, though often underestimated.

IMMATURITY BURDEN is the cost imposed on people who have to do work that depends on incomplete parts of the game.

Most game developers don't have the luxury of working with stable, mature software and game systems. Usually the tools are buggy and poorly documented, the game mechanics are half-made, and the story shifts daily. These immature elements impose a cost on everyone working with them. Nonfatal but annoying software bugs slow down work. An unfinished story slows down level design by injecting uncertainty into level design decisions. Unbalanced game mechanics make it hard for level designers to polish and balance challenges.

The dependency stack helps us avoid depending on immature designs. But even with a clear dependency stack, it's impossible to completely eliminate immaturity burden.

CRITICAL FAILURE RISKS are the costs imposed by critical failures of immature systems.

Any immature system can reveal a fatal flaw at an inopportune time. Fatal, difficult software bugs can throw tests into chaos. Unpredicted dominant strategies can destroy months of balance work. Narrative holes can lie unnoticed for months. These problems hide in the game like time bombs, before going off and causing some critical failure.

The cost of these problems isn't so much the actual work of fixing them, but their impact on other processes. A simple mistake by a tools coder can force an artist in another building to spend two days tracking down an asset import bug. Even if the bug fix is a one-line code change, the damage has been done because the artist is now slowed, as is everyone depending on him.

The damage is worst when these critical failure time bombs go off in time-critical situations. Sometimes that one blocked artist was working on a piece of art that was critical to the next test of a new game mode, which was scheduled for the next day. The missing art forces a cancellation of the test, which starves the designers of playtest data, which inhibits decisions on the next code iteration, leaving gameplay coders without clear direction. This sort of chain reaction is not unusual in large, complex processes.

PROCESS BURDEN is the cost of tracking and scheduling work.

Every design process has some organizational layer to keep everyone coordinated. One developer might keep notes for himself. A three-person team might have daily chats to coordinate their work. As team sizes grow, the cost and complexity of coordination increase. Large teams use dedicated production staff, bug tracking systems, and design wikis. The effort spent on all of this is process burden.

A naturally low process burden is one of the greatest advantages of small teams over large ones. Back when I worked alone on *Unreal Tournament* levels for fun, four hours of work time meant ten minutes handling my notes and three hours fifty minutes in the level editor. I knew everything about the design and didn't depend on anyone else. While working on large studio projects, four hours of work time often means an hour of writing specs, another hour of discussion, and two hours in the editor. In the first case, process burden is 4% of my time. In the second, it's 50%.

POLITICAL EFFECTS affect relationships among developers.

In some sense, a group design process is always an exercise in favor trading. Everybody has some amount of influence, which he can spend and trade in the pursuit of improving the game. This affects design decisions.

For example, a studio may have a very senior veteran programmer who founded the company 15 years earlier, and doesn't care about the fiction but loves working on new graphics technology. In this studio, a design that does not push graphical limits may have great benefits, but it imposes a political cost of irritating the veteran programmer because he may push back against it.

Handling political effects often means thinking several chess moves ahead. A designer might have a feature he wants to try, but realize that he will never be able to cut it if it doesn't work because others will become too invested. If the chance of a cut is too great, the designer won't push this idea. It's an ugly outcome driven by organizational deficiencies, but from the designer's point of view it's what's best for the process and the game.

CULTURAL EFFECTS change developers' habits and the development climate.

A studio's culture is a team's shared set of expectations, assumptions, and habits. Decisions made now have long-term effects on culture, and thus on future work. Some decisions can enrich and improve culture; others can degrade and destroy it.

For example, changing story details and core design ideas too often for little reason creates an expectation of further changes. Developers don't think they can count on anything staying the same, so they start avoiding investing themselves too much into ideas. They've had to suffer the emotional pain of watching their well-loved work die due to story changes too many times. The team's personal investment and creative vibrancy slowly degrades. The studio has lost something valuable in both the social and monetary senses, but it doesn't show up on a balance sheet. They've lost their culture.

Over the long term, culture is what determines the fate of a studio. It drives every action taken by every person, all the time. It's worth sacrificing short-term gains to keep it healthy.

DECISION COST is the cost of making a good decision.

Brain time, research gathering, and written analysis aren't free. It costs something to make a good decision—and sometimes the best decision is to not spend too much effort deciding.

Unimportant decisions should be made off the cuff, by a single designer, because the decision isn't worth the effort it takes to make. It would be foolish to spend a half hour analyzing a tiny decision that will have no significant effect. In this case, what looks like laziness is actually rational indifference. You saw this in my combat design iteration process, when I avoided analysis during the early iteration phases.

Important decisions, on the other hand, need to be carefully considered. Stakeholders must be assembled, multiple rounds of discussion may be called, written reports, studies, and analyses may be completed. The benefit of getting the right decision here is worth the cost of making the highest-quality decision possible.

Decision Effects Case Study

Imagine you're a designer working on a shooter with fantasy RPG elements. Your studio, Dragon Brain Games, was founded two years earlier by a businessman and a well-known fantasy author, Allan McRae, who used his name to secure funding for your cheesily titled project, *Talmirian Gods: The Journey of an Age*.

The project is almost over. Content lock is in a month, after which only bug fixing will be allowed and you won't be able to do any meaningful design work. Since he comes from a writing background, McRae has taken an auteur approach to the game, so there haven't been any playtests until recently. You think McRae did a great job on the writing. You're not totally happy with the combat mechanics since you didn't get much iteration time, but you think you've done all right considering how narrative-focused the process was.

The game includes a key enemy called the Walrog. This giant beast is the centerpiece of a number of combat encounters. You've been sure to combine him with other enemies as often as possible to elegantly create combat variation, and you've tested the Walrog yourself to try to ensure that there isn't a degenerate strategy against him.

But you failed. Without systematic playtesting earlier in the project, you were forced to test combat encounters alone. Once you started running playtests of the whole game, though, a playtester quickly found a degenerate strategy. One of the first upgrades available in the game is the Elixir of Speed, which permanently increases a character's movement speed by a small amount. With this upgrade, it becomes possible to circle the Walrog endlessly without ever getting hit. Combats degenerate into a circus as the player runs round and round the Walrog, slowly pecking him to death. Testers laugh out loud as the fearsome Walrog gyrates helplessly. Then the testers descend into boredom as they execute the same repetitive tactic again and again.

A quarter of the playtesters choose the Elixir of Speed, and most of those naturally find the degenerate strategy. What do you do?

An obvious choice is to make the Walrog more nimble. Your best guess is that a faster turning speed would fix the problem. However, this is a risk. The game's immature monster animation code doesn't allow you to stretch and shrink the current animation set arbitrarily. To change how the Walrog turns, you would need new animations. You're not sure whether this would really solve the problem, how much adjustment is needed, or how this change would affect the balance of Walrog fights for players who don't have the Elixir. The Walrog is a key element of many combats and rebalancing them all would be a challenge. Furthermore, the animation team is overworked as it is because of some emergency corrections needed to bring the game art in line with the books the game is based on, and the art lead is on vacation for the week. Faster turning animations might solve the problem, but you're running a critical failure risk of introducing other balance problems elsewhere. And there's a chance that animation changes won't even fully solve the original degenerate strategy—but you can't know until you test.

Another option is to remove the Elixir of Speed. This simple solution is complicated by the fact that the Elixir was pitched to journalists at a trade show, so there are a decent number of fans waiting for it. It also plays a minor role in the tie-in books, and you're not sure whether McRae is willing to remove it—he hasn't always been open to making narrative changes in response to balance concerns in the past. There is also a minor gameplay sequence based on the Elixir, and it is used as a reward for a separate quest. The designer of that quest is a friend of yours and is willing to cut the sequence to help you out, but the quest would still need a new reward. The Elixir could be replaced with gold, but this might throw off the economy balance by giving players too much gold.

Another option is to do nothing. The game is a single-player action RPG, not a multiplayer competitive game, so it need not be perfectly balanced to a stratospheric skill ceiling. Even if the Walrog can be beaten degenerately, the game won't be completely destroyed. Ordinarily, doing nothing would be an attractive option. However, McRae is horrified at the test results of people laughing during his most intense scenes. Selling the do-nothing solution would be a political challenge.

You could also do nothing for now, and spend some time on analysis, trying to come up with more options. Have a brainstorming meeting, do research, write ideas on cue cards and mix them up, or just work on something else and wait for unconscious rumination to catch up.

This complex situation involves almost every process effect that a decision can have.

Various solutions have different *design effects* in how they affect various in-game balances and economies.

They have different *implementation costs*: new animations are costly; removing the Elixir is cheap.

Immaturity burdens imposed by the game's un-tunable animation system are denying you much-needed knowledge about the effects a turn speed change on the Walrog would have, which means that new potential animations pose a *critical failure risk* if they cause other problems elsewhere so close to content lock.

Replacing the Elixir with gold carries a risk of throwing off the game economy—another potential *design effect.*

Your relationships with animators, McRae, programmers, and other designers also weight each choice with different *political effects.* Removing the Elixir seems a lot more attractive since you're a friend of the designer who made a quest around it. Changing the story seems a lot less attractive since McRae is not your friend.

Finally, McRae's past behavior has created a *climate* of uncertainty around his responses to narrative changes. This added uncertainty is making your decision harder in a way that is invisible to McRae.

All of this is wrapped in layers of uncertainty. You're not sure how fans and journalists would respond to changes to the Elixir, how McRae feels about the Elixir, the exact animation changes needed to make the Walrog work right, and other design effects of each of these choices.

This situation may seem absurdly complicated. But this level of decision complexity isn't uncommon while making complicated products for a multisegmented market, together with a team of people, each with his own skills, relationships, and desires. Real designers in large studios do this every day; solving such Kafkaesque problems is a major part of the job. And there's no obvious right answer.

My answer here would be that there is too much uncertainty. The best move is to gather knowledge with a few low-risk questions. Meet with McRae and noncommittally float the idea of killing the Elixir to get a feel for the response. It's usually possible to get someone's opinion on something without actually committing to it. Talk to the animator who likes you the most about the possible need for Walrog changes and get a read on how realistic this is. It may be easier than assumed, or it may be out of the question. Either way, you gain knowledge. Finally, think hard about the problem and get rumination juices going, and email a few other designers asking for ideas. These three knowledge-gaining moves can be accomplished within a day or so, after which the situation may be approached again from a position of greater certainty. You've lost a day, but your decision is likely to be much better, so I think the trade-off was worth it.

17

Values

The sculpture was perfect—an sinusoid re-creation of the human form rendered in statuesque perfection. To show their gratitude, the townspeople offered the sculptor anything he wished. He could have herds of cattle, ornate golden weapons, or the mayor's daughter's hand in marriage.

But even with all of this bounty laid out before him, the sculptor only looked distracted. He walked past the riches and entered the village blacksmith's workshop. There he began to go through the shelves, picking out new sculpting tools.

This book has covered a lot of knowledge about being a game designer. Combine that knowledge with practice, and you'll develop skills. But I don't think knowledge and skills are all that's needed for exemplary game design. I think that to do this really well, we must also have *values*.

A VALUE is an emotionally driven choice about who we want to be. It's a human quality to aspire to. Nobody can ever fully embody their values, but we better ourselves and our work by trying.

Other professions have their own values. Soldiers have martial values like loyalty, honor, and personal courage. Scientists value rigor, impartiality, and integrity. Mainstream industrial culture values hard work, thinking ahead, and doing your part. But none of these value sets applies perfectly to game design because our task is different. Just as it would be foolish to apply military values to scientific work, it would be foolish to apply any of these to our work. We need a different set of values. But what should they be?

I don't think anyone can prescribe the best values for all designers. I do, however, think that every designer could benefit from thinking about what values they believe in. Because values keep us steady. They are immutable standards that stabilize us against the political and emotional turmoil of daily design work.

These are the designer values that I believe in. What are yours?

Openness

Openness means respectfully accepting ideas with which you disagree. Without openness, a design studio must either homogenize everyone's views, shut down debate by shutting people up, or self-destruct in a storm of bitter disagreement.

Openness doesn't just mean letting people speak—it means respecting their contribution with open body language and genuine discussion. It doesn't mean accepting every idea, but it does mean thinking about every idea in a meaningful way. This isn't always easy. As Aristotle said, "It is the mark of an educated mind to be able to entertain a thought without accepting it."

Openness grows from believing in the uncertainty of your own ideas. The best designers I've known will say, "My gut says," or "From what I've seen," or "I'm pretty sure that," or "The way I see it," at the start of almost every sentence. These aren't just verbal tics. These designers understood that being unsure is the honest truth. We're always uncertain. By constantly verbalizing uncertainty, they keep the door open for discussion. They leave room in their minds for the better ideas of others, and turn out wiser in the end.

Candor

It's seductively easy to go with the flow of opinion. It requires little thought, and doesn't risk social standing. Everyone walks away happy. But in the long run, too much agreement kills a game. Without anyone to point them out, inconsistencies creep into the design and multiply like cancer cells. The design team agrees and agrees, and the game ships full of holes. Constant agreement only looks like team cohesion on the surface. In reality, it signals either rampant mental laziness or a climate of fear.

Whereas openness is about accepting ideas, candor is about having your own ideas and being willing to present them. It means having the moral courage to voice a contrary opinion even when it would be easier to stay silent. A candid designer will point out a fault in a superior's idea, or disagree with a boardroom full of people. Candid designers are thoughtful, sincere, and direct, not weasely and lame. They put the mental effort into having ideas, and the emotional effort into expressing them.

In the end, worthwhile people respect and appreciate those who stand behind their ideas, even if they don't always agree with the ideas themselves. In our hearts, we all want to be the one who has the strength to form an independent opinion and then say it.

Humility

Game design is very, very hard. A game is a hundred game mechanics interacting on a computer with a billion transistors, running 10 different foundational technologies, each of which implements thousands of algorithms, all interfacing with human players who express all the complexity and variation of human nature and live in the world-scale madness of culture and markets. Such a system is unfathomable. Our minds did not evolve to understand this kind of complexity.

So many of the mistakes of game design spring from thinking that we understand things that we cannot. Hubris makes us overplan. It makes us judge others' work too quickly and confidently. It makes us playtest less than we need to and miss gaping design flaws. I think that one of the most important basic things we can do to become game designers is not to learn more, but to understand how little we can really understand of what we're doing. This means we have to be humble in the face of the task we're attempting.

Humility lets us accept how little we know. It helps us perceive not only our small islands of understanding, but also the ocean of ignorance beyond their shores. It helps us catch serendipity when the world is trying to teach us something. It counters our natural WYSIATI bias, and makes us more observant, more thoughtful, and maybe even a little wiser. Because there's nobody who thinks less than the one who believes he knows everything.

Hunger

Imagine you've created something excellent—a great level, a beautiful song, a perfect batch of cookies. Everyone is applauding your success. Your competition is defeated. You are the best. Now what do you do?

At this point, most people stop. Once they've outperformed every standard and defeated every competitor, they're done. Human nature is to do only what's necessary to achieve a goal. If that goal is approval or defeating a competitor or a monetary reward, there's no reason to continue once you're the best. This is how normal people act.

But there is another type of person. This type doesn't care about standards or competitors. They're not in it for external rewards or approval. They're in it for the work. They want that irreplaceable pleasure of doing something better than they did before. They're hungry.

Hunger is the belief that no matter what we've done, we can do better. It is the desire to always improve at maximum rate, regardless of outside expectations. Hunger isn't talent—a hungry designer may be no more able than his more satiable peers. But he is not chained to the standards of the world around him. No matter how good the work is, he will try to improve it.

This is difficult. It's hard to push beyond what's been done before. Often it's not even clear that it's possible to exceed past standards—but it always is. In Geoff Colvin's book *Talent Is Overrated*, he writes:

> The Olympic records of a hundred years ago—representing the best performance of any human being on the planet—today in many cases equal ho-hum performance by high schoolers. The winner of the men's 200-meter race in the 1908 Olympics ran it in 22.6 seconds; today's high school record is faster by more than 2 seconds, a huge margin. Today's best high school time in the marathon beats the 1908 Olympic gold medalist by more than twenty minutes.

In gymnastics, music, chess, and many other fields, what was extraordinary decades ago is now mediocre. This means that in 1908, any fit high schooler could have beaten an Olympian with enough effort. But they didn't because they were chained to expectation.

Hunger means never being satisfied not only with the work, but also with ourselves. There is a world of ideas out there to be learned, and a universe of knowledge to be generated. A hungry designer always has a vision of himself in the future with more skills, more knowledge, more emotional range, and more work discipline. He pushes toward that every day, always improving. In the short term, these efforts seem to lead nowhere. But over years or decades, they add up—because we're all capable of more than anyone would ever expect of us, if we can only find that insatiable hunger to improve, expectations be damned.

Endgame

This is a book of models and hypotheses, not realities and truths.

The reality of games is bigger than a book or a mind. Games stretch causal threads through players' minds and cultures, back to the history of their peoples and their species, and forward into all the lives they will affect and the future cultures that will judge them. A written model can't encapsulate this. I haven't even tried. Rather, I've attempted to create a guide to the craft that describes games in the most useful possible ways. But a guide is not the truth. It is a simple map to an astonishingly rich and diverse territory. No matter how much we learn, we shouldn't forget that the reality is much greater.

Games are mental models for pieces of life.

A game is not a chain of events like a story. It's a system. It crystallizes some part of the world into a set of mechanics and packages them up for us to play with. Instead of just showing us one thread of events the way a story does, it allows us to experience that piece of the world, again and again in a hundred variations. And that exploratory interaction teaches in ways that stories cannot.

After a failure punches my confidence in the gut, I think of poker. Poker has a message. Roughly translated into written words, the message of poker is that nobody wins every hand. But just reading that here isn't the same as playing the game. The phrase, "Nobody wins every hand," is just a piece of text to be filed away in memory. Only playing the game gets the mind running through that pattern over and over in a thousand variations. That repeated interaction doesn't just create memories. It restructures how we think. We don't just end up knowing that nobody wins every hand. We understand it, believe it, and feel it, because we've experienced it so many times.

I am the games I've played. When I take a risk, I think of chess and I remember to think about what might happen two or three moves down the line. When I feel lazy, I think of football, and how every inch you move toward a goal counts. When I'm getting tunnel vision on a problem, I think of *StarCraft*, and how one must always keep an eye on the big picture, because it's the threats you're not even considering that always get you. These thoughts aren't memories. After years with these games, they've become part of my personality.

A perfect game design is beautiful, but it can't be seen or touched. Its beauty is in the possibility space it generates. We perceive that beauty not by viewing events in a sequence, but by exploring those possibilities. As we do, the system of the game reshapes part of our mind in its own image. That's how we absorb the message of games, and their unique dialectic power. As Confucius said, "I hear and I forget. I see and I remember. I do and I understand."

All of the best games ever are still waiting to be designed.

The Sims invented its own genre and sold a hundred million copies. *Half-Life* and *Counter-Strike* revolutionized first-person storytelling and combat. *Dwarf Fortress* procedurally builds fantasy worlds with politics, economics, and history. *Braid* threads poetry into game mechanics. *Minecraft* unlocked the joyful creativity of millions. And as you read this, someone somewhere is jotting down an idea, making a prototype, or ruminating on a game that will change the world.

There's a special freedom to working on games. Their boundaries are so indefinite, I sometimes wonder if they even exist. We're not limited to ink on paper, or a reel of film. A game can be as simple as a child's blocks, or as intricate as a virtual world populated by millions. It can be explored, observed, shared, and defeated. It can last a minute or a lifetime.

In such unexplored territory, there are no beaten tracks, no guideposts, and no walls. There is no one there to help you, and no one there to hold you back. As Einstein said, "Imagination is better than knowledge." And there's so much waiting to be imagined. . .it's breathtaking.

Recommended Books

I OWE A GREAT debt to all the better thinkers from whom I borrowed ideas. Without them, this book could not exist. My borrowing was so widespread that I couldn't possibly list every source that influenced me. But I have, with difficulty, managed to pare down the list to the 10 richest seams of game design–relevant ideas I've ever found. These books expand on and clarify many of the concepts in this book.

- ***Thinking, Fast and Slow* by Daniel Kahneman** Most of game design hinges on understanding human minds—those of our players, our team, and ourselves. Kahneman's book is an owner's manual for the mind. It's the best explanation I've found of how intuitive and systematic thought interact to generate our idiosyncratic human capacities and follies.
- ***Story: Substance, Structure, Style, and the Principles of Screenwriting* by Robert McKee** Story is the best guide to basic story craft I've found. Ostensibly it's about screenwriting, but the book's lessons about story structure are broadly applicable.
- ***The Art of Game Design: A Book of Lenses* by Jesse Schell** Schell's an experienced game designer who cares about games, and it shows. He covers many topics that I don't, and his conclusions and models sometimes differ from mine. The contrast is food for thought.
- ***The Black Swan: The Impact of the Highly Improbable* by Nassim Nicholas Taleb** Taleb thinks about risk and chance differently from anyone else. In his signature pugnacious writing style, he outlines the idea of the Black Swan event—those incredibly important and completely unpredicted events that drive everything. This book will make you question your ability to predict the future.

- ***The Logic of Failure: Recognizing and Avoiding Error in Complex Situations* by Dietrich Dörner** Failure isn't a freak event like a lightning bolt from the sky. It grows slowly by its own dismal logic. Using games that simulate complex situations like African villages and ecological reserves, Dörner examines how human beings consistently mishandle complex problems, and hints at how to compensate for our ingrained bad habits. This is a good touchstone for understanding the problems of the game development process.
- ***How the Mind Works* by Steven Pinker** In this 700-page opus, Harvard's star psychologist Steven Pinker covers the mind in exacting detail from a computational, evolutionary-based view. Some of his conclusions are controversial within the academic community; all of them are thought-provoking.
- ***Getting to Yes: Negotiation Agreement Without Giving In* by Roger Fisher and William Ury** Much of real game design is about negotiation. Nobody cares how good your analysis is if you can't constructively compromise with others to get it implemented.
- ***The Art of Strategy: A Game Theorist's Guide to Success in Business and in Life* by Avinash K. Dixit and Barry J. Nalebuff** Every game designer should have a basic understanding of mathematical game theory concepts like dominant strategies and Nash equilibria. This is a readable and thorough explanation of these concepts.
- ***Talent Is Overrated: What Really Separates World-Class Performers from Everyone Else* by Geoff Colvin** Colvin's book is about learning. It doesn't matter what—golf, violin, programming, game design. Colvin shows how the key to world-class performance isn't talent or time, but deliberate practice. Deliberate practice isn't just doing the work; it's straining to get better at the work in a very specific way. For anyone wanting to improve game design skills these high-level ideas and examples are valuable.
- ***Masters of Doom: How Two Guys Created an Empire and Transformed Pop Culture* by David Kushner** Masters of Doom is about the creation of Doom in the early 1990s. But it's not a book about the mind; it's a book about heart. Kushner describes a team of designers with legendary levels of drive and hunger. In a world where we rarely meet really extraordinary people, stories like this serve as examples of what's possible.

Quiz Answers

ANSWERS TO THE 90% certainty quiz in Chapter 11:

Question	Answer
Birth year of Archimedes	287 BC
Number of classified species of ant	12,500
World population in 1900	1.6 billion
Average diameter of the sun	1,392,684 km or 865,374 miles
Number of named moons of Saturn	53
Melting point of iron	1538°C or 2800°F
Total military deaths in World War I	9,911,000
Area of Antarctica	14,000,000 km^2 or 5,400,000 sq mi
Latitude of Santiago, Chile	33°27' S
Total weight of all the gold mined in human history	165,000 metric tons or 165,000,000 kg or 363,825,000 pounds

Sources

Chapter 1: Engines of Experience

Emotional misattribution—the bridge study: Dutton, D.G., and Aron, A.P. 1974. "Some evidence for heightened sexual attraction under conditions of high anxiety." *Journal of Personality and Social Psychology* 30(4): 510–517.

Nylon stockings preferences: Nisbett, Miller, and Wilson, Timothy. 1977. "Telling More Than We Can Know: Verbal Reports on Mental Processes." *Psychological Review* 84(3): 231–259.

Savanna preference in American children: Pinker, Steven. *How the Mind Works* (New York: W.W. Norton & Company, 2009). Kindle edition, location 7785.

The two-factor theory adrenaline injection experiment: Schachter, Stanley, and Singer, Jerome. 1962. "Cognitive, Social, and Physiological Determinants of Emotional State." *Psychological Review* 69(5): 379–399.

Chapter 5: Decisions

Emotions driving decisions: Lehrer, Jonah. *How We Decide* (Boston: Mariner Books, 2010), page 47.

Counter-Strike popularity: *Steam and Game Stats. http://store.steampowered.com/stats/.* Accessed May 3, 2012.

Chapter 6: Balance

Cosmic Encounter isn't fair: Olokta, Peter. "Fair isn't Funny!" In *Tabletop and Analog Game Design*, Costikyan, Greg, and Davidson, Drew (Eds.) (Pittsburgh: ETC Press, 2011). Kindle edition, location 1856.

Dustin Browder on *StarCraft II* balance: Browder, Dustin. "The Game Design of StarCraft II: Designing an E-Sport." Speech presented at Game Developers Conference, San Francisco, 2011. Available online at *http://gdcvault.com/play/1014488/The-Game-Design-of-STARCRAFT.*

The complex chessmen: Dörner, Dietrich. *The Logic of Failure* (New York: Basic Books, 1997). Kindle edition, location 451.

Implicit goals: Ibid.

Chapter 7: Multiplayer

Professional fighting game players hide their skills: Sirlin, David. *Playing to Win*. Page 114. Available online at *http://www.sirlin.net/ptw.*

Evolutionarily stable strategies: Dawkins, Richard. *The Extended Phenotype* (Oxford, UK: Oxford University Press, 1999).

Game Theory Penalty Kicks: Chiappori, Pierre, Levitt, Steven, and Groseclose, Tim. September 2002. "Testing Mixed-Strategy Equilibria When Players Are Heterogeneous: The Case of Penalty Kicks in Soccer." *American Economic Review* 92(4): 1138–51.

Chapter 8: Motivation and Fulfillment

Rat brain wire study: Heath, R.G. 1963. "Electrical self-stimulation of the brain in man." *American Journal of Psychiatry* 120(6): 571–577.

B-19 study: Moan, C.E., and Heath, R.G. 1972. "Septal stimulation for the initiation of heterosexual activity in a homosexual male." *Journal of Behavior Therapy and Experimental Psychiatry* 3(1): 23–30.

Vacation motivation study: Sharot, Tali, Shiner, Tamara, Brown, Annemarie C., Fan, Judy, and Dolan, Raymond J. November 2009. "Dopamine enhances expectation of pleasure in humans." *Current Biology* 19(24): 2077–80.

Rewards eliminate intrinsic motivation: Deci, Edward, and Flaste, Richard. *Why We Do What We Do: Understanding Self-Motivation* (New York: Penguin, 1996).

Chess players play less when paid: Pritchard, Robert D., Campbell, Kathleen M., and Campbell, Donald J. 1977. "Effects of extrinsic financial rewards on intrinsic motivation." *Journal of Applied Psychology* 62(1): 9–15.

Students write worse poems for money: Amabile, Teresa. 1985. "Motivation and Creativity: Effects of Motivational Orientation on Creative Writers." *Journal of Personality and Social Psychology* 48(2): 393–399.

Information and quotations from B.F. Skinner: Kohn, Alfie. *Punished by Rewards: The Trouble with Gold Stars, Incentive Plans, A's, Praise, and Other Bribes* (Boston: Mariner Books, 1999).

Chapter 9: Interface

Priming: Bargh, John, Chen, Mark, and Burrows, Lara. 1996. "Automaticity of Social Behavior: Direct Effects of Trait Construct and Stereotype Activation on Action." *Journal of Personality and Social Psychology* 71(2): 230–244.

Chapter 10: The Market

Innovator's dilemma: Christiensen, Clayton M. *The Innovator's Dilemma: The Revolutionary Book That Will Change the Way You Do Business* (New York: Harper Paperbacks, 2003).

Will Wright on *The Sims*: Gillen, Kieron. "Making of: The Sims." *Rock Paper Shotgun*. January 18, 2008. *http://www.rockpapershotgun.com/2008/01/18/making-of-the-sims/*.

Value curves inspired by: Kim, W. Chan, and Mauborgne, Renee. *Blue Ocean Strategy: How to Create Uncontested Market Space and Make Competitors Irrelevant* (Boston: Harvard Business Press, 2005).

StarCraft in Korea: Anonymous. "Why is StarCraft Popular in Korea?" *Ask a Korean!* (blog). February 19, 2010. *http://askakorean.blogspot.com/2010/02/why-is-starcraft-popular-in-korea.html.*

Expectation biases: Ariely, Dan. *Predictably Irrational: The Hidden Forces That Shape Our Decisions* (Boston: HarperCollins, 2009).

AI director design: Booth, Michael. "From Counter-Strike to Left 4 Dead: Creating Replayable Cooperative Experiences." Speech presented at Game Developer's Conference, San Francisco, 2009. Available online at *http://www.gdcvault.com/play/1422/From-COUNTER-STRIKE-to-LEFT.*

Chapter 11: Planning and Iteration

Estimation performance quiz: McConnell, Steve. *Software Estimation: Demystifying the Black Art* (Redmond, WA: Microsoft Press, 2006).

The soccer coach quotation on planning: Dörner, Dietrich. *The Logic of Failure* (New York: Basic Books, 1997). Kindle edition, location 1659.

Soren Johnson quotation: Johnson, Soren. "Design success means knowing what to do with feedback." *Gamasutra.* February 6, 2012. *http://gamasutra.com/view/news/40103/Design_success_means_knowing_what_to_do_with_feedback.php.*

Half-Life was rebooted after one version: Birdwell, Ken. "The Cabal: Valve's Design Process for Creating *Half-Life*." *Gamasutra.* December 10, 1999. *http://www.gamasutra.com/view/feature/3408/the_cabal_valves_design_process_.php.*

Human overconfidence bias: Kahneman, Daniel. *Thinking, Fast and Slow* (New York: Farrar, Straus and Giroux, 2011).

Barusch Fischoff's hindsight bias study with Nixon: Ibid.

Daniel Kahneman on the illusion of a predictable past: Ibid.

Serendipity while designing *Tetris* and *Braid*: Thirion, Steph. "Game Design by Accidents." Speech presented at the Game Developer's Conference, San Francisco, 2011. Available online at *http://gdcvault.com/play/1014442/Game-Design-by.*

Chapter 12: Knowledge Creation

Darwin, Leonardo da Vinci, etc., concurrent projects: Berkun, Scott. *The Myths of Innovation* (Sebastopol, CA: O'Reilly, 2010).

MRI study on the aSTG: Rosen, William. *The Most Powerful Idea in the World: A Story of Steam, Industry, and Invention* (New York: Random House, 2010). Kindle edition, location 2232.

The Incredibles art swatches: Vaz, Mark Cotta, Bird, Brad, and Lasseter, John. *The Art of The Incredibles* (San Francisco: Chronicle Books, 2004).

Orson Scott Card's map-driven world building: Card, Orson Scott. *How to Write Science Fiction and Fantasy* (Cincinnati: Writer's Digest Books, 2001).

Half-Life data gathering methods: Birdwell, Ken. "The Cabal: Valve's Design Process for Creating *Half-Life*." *Gamasutra*. December 10, 1999. *http://www.gamasutra.com/view/feature/3408/the_cabal_valves_design_process_.php*.

Halo: Reach networking test methods: Aldridge, David. "I Shot You First! Gameplay Networking in Halo: Reach." Speech presented at Game Developers Conference, San Francisco, 2011. Available online at *http://www.gdcvault.com/play/1014345/I-Shot-You-First-Networking*.

Wright brothers' stories: Tobin, James. *To Conquer the Air: The Wright Brothers and the Great Race for Flight* (New York: Simon & Schuster, 2004).

Chapter 14: Authority

Taylorism: Taylor, Frederick W. *The Principles of Scientific Management*. First published in 1911. Free Kindle edition, location 199.

Free retiree lawyering, sofa-moving strangers, effects of money frames on helping colleagues: Ariely, Dan. *Predictably Irrational: Revised and Expanded Edition* (New York: HarperCollins, 2009), page 79.

Amabile's study on creativity: Breen, Bill. "The 6 Myths of Creativity." *Fast Company*. Fastcompany.com, December 2004. *http://www.fastcompany.com/magazine/89/creativity.html*.

On Gordon Ramsay: The documentary covering Ramsay's working methods was the 1998 Channel 4 miniseries *Boiling Point.*

On Jim Henson: Stevenson, John. "Monsters, Muppets, and Movies." Speech delivered at the DICE conference, 2011. Available online at *http://www.g4tv.com/videos/51285/dice-2011-monsters-muppets-and-movies-presentation/.*

Chapter 17: Values

Modern high school sports versus early Olympians: Colvin, Geoff. *Talent Is Overrated: What Really Separates World Class Performers From Everyone Else* (New York: Portfolio, 2008), page 8.

Index

F

G

N

Q

R

S

About the Author

Tynan Sylvester has been designing games since 2000. Since then he's worked on everything from one-man indie projects to AAA studio blockbusters. Go ahead and post a comment on his website at *tynansylvester.com* or email him at *tynan.sylvester@gmail.com*.

O'REILLY®

There's much more where this came from.

Experience books, videos, live online training courses, and more from O'Reilly and our 200+ partners—all in one place.

Learn more at oreilly.com/online-learning

©2019 O'Reilly Media, Inc. O'Reilly is a registered trademark of O'Reilly Media, Inc. | 175